"In this informative, highly readable book, Lowell Baier traces the trajectory of the federalism doctrine from its pre-founding origins to the present day. Having provided that broad context, the author ably chronicles federalism's evolution in the area wildlife management, from the 19th century public trust doctrine through landmark enactments, such as the Migratory Bird Treaty Act and the Endangered Species Act, and important Supreme Court precedents. The basic story is one of increased centralization and federal preemption, largely driven—the author shows—by an abiding and perhaps excessive faith in 'scientific management' and 'expertise.' Baier's engaged, yet judicious and commendably non-polemical discussion should be of value and interest to a broad audience."—**Michael S. Greve,** PhD, Professor of Law, Antonin Scalia School of Law, George Mason University. Author of *Real Federalism: Why It Matters, How Could It Happen*; F*ederal Preemption: States' Power, National Interests* (co-editor); and *The Demise of Environmentalism in American Law*

"American wildlife management law for over two centuries has been a crucible in which the evolution of American federalism was forged. Lowell Baier's sweeping, accessible account of that history comprehensively and insightfully assesses the conflicts and tensions leading to an ascendant *federal* presence. Looking forward, climate change presents an unprecedented challenge to conservation policy, requiring that we return to the crucible to forge a national wildlife management regime for a no-analogue future. Whether one leans towards staying with the strong federal model Baier critiques or favors returning to the more state-centric approach he advocates, this masterful history is indispensable reading for anyone engaged in the conversation about the future of our nation's wildlife and habitat conservation federalism."
—**J. B. Ruhl**, PhD, JD, David Daniels Allen Distinguished Chair in Law, Co-Director, Energy, Environment, and Land Use Law Program, Vanderbilt University School of Law

"In charting the development of federalism over the history of the United States, the book offers an instructive account of the evolving conceptions of this key structural principle. Baier illuminates two important and sometimes conflicting features of contemporary federalism—the need for concurrent federal and state regulation and the extremely powerful role of federal spending. By applying these critical insights to the field of environmental protection, the book makes a significant contribution to a crucial area of public policy."—**Robert A. Schapiro**, JD, Dean and C. Hugh Friedman Professor of Law University of San Diego School of Law

"Lowell Baier breathes life into this scholarly-but-vivid review of American federalism. The greatest tragedy of conservation law has been to sow discord among advocates who should be allies in habitat restoration and management. As someone who often sides with a more muscular federal approach, I nonetheless find common cause with Baier in understanding these origins of the internecine feud over conservation."—**Robert L. Fischman**, JD, George P. Smith, II, Distinguished Professor of Law Professor of Public and Environmental Affairs, Indiana University Maurer School of Law

"Lowell Baier provides an opening here: an opening to engage in a more serious and thoughtful debate about the future of wildlife and biodiversity in the United States. As Baier shows with a sweeping historical narrative, there is not a facet of wildlife management, or a solution to the biodiversity crisis, that doesn't implicate federalism in some fashion. Not everyone will agree on Baier's diagnosis of what went wrong in the balance of federal and state powers and what needs to be done about it. But the most viable and durable solutions will emerge only once the champions of federal and state powers over wildlife listen and learn from one another. Baier's book provides one such opportunity and his call for rediscovering a common bond, matched with responsible funding for the ESA and wildlife conservation more broadly, could not come at a better time."—**Martin Nie**, PhD, Professor, Natural Resources Policy. Director, Bolle Center for People and Forests W.A. Franke College of Forestry and Conservation, University of Montana

"Tension between the states and the federal government within the unique American enterprise of wildlife conservation and management has simmered and boiled over repeatedly since the origins of the conservation movement. Lowell Baier has produced a scholarly, thoroughly researched, clearly written history with an explanation of the roots of the current conflict, and a recipe for cooperative conservation."—**John F. Organ**, PhD, CWB, Scientist Emeritus, Cooperative Fish and Wildlife Research Units, Past President, Honorary Member, and Fellow, The Wildlife Society, 2020 Aldo Leopold Memorial Award, The Wildlife Society 2014 George Bird Grinnell Memorial Award, Wildlife Management Institute, Department of the Interior's Meritorious Service Award

"Baier correctly depicts the unwelcome drift toward federal hegemony in wildlife law, especially the Endangered Species Act. Although the ESA contemplates a federal partnership with the states, reflecting their well-established division of legal responsibility for resident and migratory species, federal programs are now preeminent. As experience in California suggests, the states are fully qualified to manage endangered species and their habitat. Baier correctly prescribes a return to shared responsibility for wildlife management, as Section 6 of the ESA intends."—**Douglas P. Wheeler**, JD, Attorney at Law, Former Secretary, California Natural Resources Agency (1991–1999)

"While the story of wildlife management in America and the evolution of its legal underpinnings from the Mayflower to the modern era might seem too grand to be told in a single volume, Lowell Baier more than meets the challenge. Pairing easy clarity with unsparing research, Mr. Baier successfully situates the development of our state and federal conservation agencies within the sweeping tapestry of our constitutional history. Laying this history before us, he leaves the reader to ponder critical questions about the relationship between state and federal authorities and how to best achieve cooperative conservation in the decades to come."—**Ronald J. Regan**, CWB, Executive Director, Association of Fish and Wildlife Agencies

"This comprehensive work provides a detailed historical accounting of the tug of war between the federal and state governments regarding the management of wildlife. A must read for those seeking to understand the historical roots of wildlife management and law in the United States. Understanding the history, as Lowell Baier sagely notes, is key to our ability to move forward in a cooperative and constructive manner – working together at the state and federal level for the betterment of our nation's wildlife and biodiversity."
—**Temple Stoellinger**, JD, College of Law, University of Wyoming

Federalism, Preemption, and the Nationalization of American Wildlife Management

OTHER BOOKS BY LOWELL E. BAIER

Inside the Equal Access to Justice Act: Environmental Litigation and the Crippling Battle over America's Lands, Endangered Species, and Critical Habitats (2016)

Saving Species on Private Lands: Unlocking Incentives to Conserve Wildlife and Their Habitats (2020)

Federalism, Preemption, and the Nationalization of American Wildlife Management

The Dynamic Balance Between State and Federal Authority

Lowell E. Baier

ROWMAN & LITTLEFIELD
Lanham • Boulder • New York • London

Published by Rowman & Littlefield
An imprint of The Rowman & Littlefield Publishing Group, Inc.
4501 Forbes Boulevard, Suite 200, Lanham, Maryland 20706
www.rowman.com

86-90 Paul Street, London EC2A 4NE

Copyright © 2022 by Lowell E. Baier

All rights reserved. No part of this book may be reproduced in any form or by any electronic or mechanical means, including information storage and retrieval systems, without written permission from the publisher, except by a reviewer who may quote passages in a review.

British Library Cataloguing in Publication Information Available

Library of Congress Cataloging-in-Publication Data

Names: Baier, Lowell E., author.
Title: Federalism, preemption, and the nationalization of American wildlife management : the dynamic balance between state and federal authority / Lowell Baier.
Description: Lanham : Rowman & Littlefield, [2022] | Includes bibliographical references and index. | Summary: "Environmental law expert Lowell E. Baier reveals how over centuries the federal government slowly preempted the states' authority over managing their resident wildlife. In doing so, he educates elected officials, wildlife students, and environmentalists in the precedents that led to the current state of wildlife management, and how a constructive environment can be fostered at all levels of government to improve our nation's wildlife and biodiversity"—Provided by publisher.
Identifiers: LCCN 2021047741 (print) | LCCN 2021047742 (ebook) | ISBN 9781538164907 (cloth) | ISBN 9781538196496 (pbk.) | ISBN 9781538164914 (ebook)
Subjects: LCSH: Wildlife conservation—Law and legislation—United States. | Federal government—United States.
Classification: LCC KF5640 .B347 2022 (print) | LCC KF5640 (ebook) | DDC 346.7304/69516—dc23/eng/20211223
LC record available at https://lccn.loc.gov/2021047741
LC ebook record available at https://lccn.loc.gov/2021047742

Contents

List of Illustrations	xi
Guide to Acronyms, Constitutional Provisions, and Terms	xiii
Foreword	xvii
Preface	xxi

1 From the Mayflower Compact to the US Constitution, 1620–1789 — 1

    The Creation of a Democratic Government — 4
    The Constitutional Convention and the US Constitution, 1787 — 5
    Fortitude and Self-Governance — 7
    Summary — 8

2 Defining the New Government and the Separation of Powers, 1789–1835 — 14

    The Marshall Court, 1801–1835 — 15
    Summary — 18

3 Westward Expansion, the First Industrial Revolution, Dual Sovereignty, and the Public Trust Doctrine, 1835–1861 — 21

    The Development of Dual Federalism and the Public Trust Doctrine: The Taney Court, 1836–1864 — 23
    Ancient Origins of the Public Trust Doctrine — 25
    Summary — 27

4	The Civil War, Reconstruction, the Advent of the Second Industrial Revolution, the Enduring Public Trust Doctrine, and State Ownership of Wildlife, 1861–1896	33
	The Enduring Public Trust Doctrine and State Ownership of Wildlife	37
	Summary	40
5	America's Changing Culture: Market Hunting, the Lacey Act, the Migratory Bird Treaty Act, and the Beginning of the Progressive Era, 1896–1910	44
	The Lacey Act and the Migratory Bird Treaty Act	48
	Summary	51
6	The Ethos of the Industrial Revolution Drives the Progressive Movement into America's Social Fabric and Laws, 1910–1919	57
	The Lochner Era: Expansion of States' Rights, Individual Liberties, and a *Laissez Faire* Economy	60
	Antitrust Legislation and Trustbusting	63
	Summary	68
7	Prohibition and Reform: The Emergence of the Administrative State, 1919–1933	75
	The Temperance Movement, the Sixteenth Amendment of 1913, the Eighteenth Amendment of 1919, and the Nineteenth Amendment of 1920	75
	The Role of the Treasury Department to Enforce Prohibition: The Greatest Expansion of Washington Bureaucracy since the Civil War	77
	The Apotheosis of the Administrative State	79
	The Ascendency of Federal Power over the States	82
	Summary	83
8	The Great Depression, FDR's New Deal, and a "New" Supreme Court Overwhelms States' Rights, 1933–1941	87
	The Great Depression Brings about a Nationalist Government	87
	The "New" Supreme Court of 1937 and a Consolidation of National Powers	90
	Summary	93

9	The Competing Ideologies that Characterized the Progressive Movement and Beyond, 1890–1940	96
	Roosevelt's Progressive Conservation Movement	96
	Ecology, Science, Education, and Federal Aid for State Wildlife Conservation Becomes the Trojan Horse of Preemption: The Leopold Years	98
	Education, Funding, and Federal Aid	103
	The Pittman-Robertson Act	104
	Summary	106
10	The Stone Court and the Development of the Presumption against Preemption in *Rice*, 1941–1946	115
	Summary	118
11	The End of the State Wildlife Ownership Doctrine following World War II, 1946–1969	120
	The Explosive Ethos of the 1960s and 1970s and the Environmental Awakening of America	125
	Summary	128
12	The Burger Court: State Ownership of Wildlife Declared a Legal Fiction and Anachronism, 1969–1986	133
	The Burger Court and the Endangered Species Act	137
	Tennessee Valley Authority v. Hill: Unintended Consequences Realized	140
	The Progeny of *Tennessee Valley Authority v. Hill*: The Slender Reed of *Geer* Overruled as a Legal Fiction	143
	Burger Continued: Congressional Intent and the Presumption against Preemption	147
	Summary	152
13	The Rehnquist Court: A Continued Swing toward Conservative Federalism and Preemption, 1986–2005	162
	Rehnquist: The Man and the Judge	162
	Rehnquist on Federalism and Preemption	164
	The State-Centered Federalism Revolution of 1995: *Lopez* and *Morrison*	166
	Real Estate Development and the Endangered Species Act	169
	A Summary of Wildlife Protection Cases in the Rehnquist Court	171

Rehnquist in Retrospect: The Digital Age Muddles the
Court's Direction   176
Can the National Political Process Protect Federalism and
State Sovereignty?   178
Rehnquist's Continued Struggle with the Preemption Doctrine:
Muddling Along!   180
Summary   182

14 The Roberts Court and the Development of Area-Specific Jurisprudence, 2005–2022   188

Roberts: The Man and the Court   188
The Information Age Balkanizes the Preemption Doctrine and
Threatens the 1947 *Rice* Presumption against Preemption   189
Roberts Continues to Muddle Along on Preemption   191
Weyerhaeuser and *Cottonwood*: Agency Overreach?   193
Summary   195

15 The Future of Federal Preemption of State Authority over Wildlife and the Presumption against Preemption Doctrine in Wildlife Cases   199

The Analysis for Determining Preemption in Wildlife Authority
and Preserving Federalism   199
Wildlife Authority and the Reach of the Commerce Clause   201
Wildlife Authority on Federal Lands and the Property Clause   203
Summary   209

16 State and Federal Cooperation and Coordination under the Endangered Species Act: Past and Present   212

The Past: Section 6, Congressional Intent, and Agency
Authority   212
Cooperative Federalism Today: Hope for the Future?   216
Summary   218

17 The Three Biggest Threats Undermining Federalism and State Wildlife Management Authority   221

The Authority of Federal Agencies, Their Regulatory Powers
and Predilection   221
Federal Grants-in-Aid and Conditional Preemption: The
Trojan Horse in Wildlife Authority and Federalism   224
Summary   228

18 Funding Endangered Species Conservation: The Achilles Heel	232
Hope for the Future: Recovering America's Wildlife Act	236
Summary	237
Conclusion	241
Acknowledgments	245
Appendix 1: Federal Environmental and Consumer-Protection Statutes and Agencies Established during the 1960's and 1970's Green Revolution	249
Appendix 2: Graphs of Preemption Statutes and US Supreme Court Cases	253
Bibliography	257
Index	283
About the Author	301

List of Illustrations

Figure 1.1: Signing of the Mayflower Compact, December 18, 1620	2
Figure 1.2: Presentation of the draft of the Declaration of Independence to Congress, June 28, 1776	6
Figure 4.1: *The Spirit of the Frontier* by John Gast (1872)	36
Figure 5.1: Advertisement for London feather sales, 1911	46
Figure 5.2: A 1912 photo of 1,600 hummingbird skins for sale	47
Figure 5.3: A market hunter at work on Marsh Island, Louisiana	50
Figure 6.1: The Gilded Age of unbridled capitalism	59
Figure 6.2: Cartoon of Theodore Roosevelt	64
Figure 7.1: Policemen in New York City executing a raid during Prohibition	77
Figure 8.1: Unemployed men outside a soup kitchen, late 1930 or early 1931	89
Figure 9.1: Aldo Leopold (1887–1948)	102
Figure 11.1: Urban sprawl defined the growth of the United States	121
Figure 12.1: The snail darter (*Percina tanasi*)	142
Figure 17.1: Thomas Jefferson (1743–1826)	225
Figure A2.1: Federal preemption and preemption-relief statutes, 1790–1991	253

Figure A2.2: US Supreme Court preemption cases by term, 1986–2012   254

Figure A2.3: Number of federal preemption statutes enacted per decade, 1790–1989   255

Guide to Acronyms, Constitutional Provisions, and Terms

GUIDE TO ACRONYMS

AFWA	Association of Fish and Wildlife Agencies
APA	Administrative Procedure Act
ATF	Bureau of Alcohol, Tobacco and Firearms
BATFE	Bureau of Alcohol, Tobacco, Firearms, and Explosives
BLM	Bureau of Land Management
CITES	Convention on International Trade in Endangered Species of Wild Fauna and Flora
EPA	Environmental Protection Agency
ESA	Endangered Species Act
FBI	Federal Bureau of Investigation
FDR	Franklin Delano Roosevelt
FERC	Federal Energy Regulatory Commission
FLPMA	Federal Land Policy and Management Act
FWS	Fish and Wildlife Service (also USFWS)
HCP	Habitat Conservation Plan
MBTA	Migratory Bird Treaty Act
NEPA	National Environmental Policy Act
NFMA	National Forest Management Act
NMFS	National Marine Fisheries Service
NPS	National Park Service
RAWA	Recovering America's Wildlife Act
TVA	Tennessee Valley Authority

GUIDE TO CONSTITUTIONAL PROVISIONS

The US Constitution is organized into articles (and amendments), sections (or paragraphs), and clauses. When courts interpret the Constitution, they discuss the relevant parts of the document, and over the years a number of commonly discussed parts have acquired their own names. The Constitutional provisions discussed in this book are reproduced below.

Commerce Clause	"The Congress shall have Power . . . to regulate Commerce with foreign Nations, and among the several States, and with the Indian Tribes." Art. I, Sec. 8, Cl. 3.
Contract Clause	"No State shall enter into any Treaty, Alliance, or Confederation; grant Letters of Marque and Reprisal; coin Money; emit Bills of Credit; make any Thing but gold and silver Coin a Tender in Payment of Debts; pass any Bill of Attainder, ex post facto Law, or Law impairing the Obligation of Contracts, or grant any Title of Nobility." Art. I, Sec. 10, Cl. 1.
Double Jeopardy Clause	"Nor shall any person be subject for the same offence to be twice put in jeopardy of life or limb." Amend. V.
Due Process Clause (Amend. XIV)	"Nor shall any State deprive any person of life, liberty, or property, without due process of law." Amend. XIV, Sec. 1.
Equal Protection Clause	"Nor [shall any State] deny to any person within its jurisdiction the equal protection of the laws." Amend. XIV, Sec. 1.
Interstate Commerce Clause	"The Congress shall have Power . . . to regulate Commerce . . . among the several States." Art. I, Sec. 8, Cl. 3.
Necessary and Proper Clause	The Congress shall have Power . . . To make all Laws which shall be necessary and proper for carrying into Execution the foregoing Powers, and all other Powers vested by this Constitution in the Government of the United States, or in any Department or Officer thereof." Art. I, Sec. 8, Cl. 18.

Privileges and Immunities Clause	"The Citizens of each State shall be entitled to all Privileges and Immunities of Citizens in the several States." Art. IV, Sec. 2, Cl. 1.
Property Clause	"The Congress shall have Power to dispose of and make all needful Rules and Regulations respecting the Territory or other Property belonging to the United States; and nothing in this Constitution shall be so construed as to Prejudice any Claims of the United States, or of any particular State." Art. IV, Sec. 3, Cl. 2.
Supremacy Clause	"This Constitution, and the Laws of the United States which shall be made in Pursuance thereof; and all Treaties made, or which shall be made, under the Authority of the United States, shall be the supreme Law of the Land; and the Judges in every State shall be bound thereby, any Thing in the Constitution or Laws of any State to the Contrary notwithstanding." Art. VI, Para. 2.
Taxing and Spending Clause (sometimes called the Tax Clause or the Spending Clause)	"The Congress shall have Power to lay and collect Taxes, Duties, Imposts and Excises, to pay the Debts and provide for the common Defence and general Welfare of the United States; but all Duties, Imposts and Excises shall be uniform throughout the United States." Art. I, Sec. 8, Cl. 1.
Tenth Amendment	"The powers not delegated to the United States by the Constitution, nor prohibited by it to the States, are reserved to the States respectively, or to the people." Amend. X.
Treaty Clause (sometimes referred to as the "Treaty Power" in combination with the Supremacy Clause)	He [the President] shall have Power, by and with the Advice and Consent of the Senate, to make Treaties, provided two thirds of the Senators present concur." Art. II, Sec. 2, Cl. 2.

GLOSSARY OF TERMS

Unless otherwise noted, all definitions are from Bryan A. Garner, ed., *Black's Law Dictionary*, 11th ed. (St. Paul: Thomson Reuters, 2019).

commandeering	Taking arbitrary or forcible possession of, as when Congress attempts to compel states to enact or administer a federal regulatory program. Adapted from *Merriam-Webster*, s.v. "commandeer," accessed September 14, 2021, https://www.merriam-webster.com/dictionary/commandeer; and from Library of Congress, "Constitution Annotated," Congress.gov, accessed June 24, 2021, searchable at https://constitution.congress.gov/.
cooperative federalism	Distribution of power between the federal government and the states whereby each recognizes the powers of the other while jointly engaging in certain governmental functions.
dormant Commerce Clause	The constitutional principle that the Commerce Clause prevents state regulation of interstate commercial activity even when Congress has not acted under its Commerce Clause power to regulate that activity. Also termed *negative Commerce Clause*.
dual federalism	A political arrangement in which power is divided between the federal and state governments in clearly defined terms, with state governments exercising those powers accorded to them without interference from the federal government.
federalism	The legal relationship and distribution of power between the national and regional governments within a federal system of government and, in the United States particularly, between the federal government and the state governments.
preemption	The principle (derived from the Supremacy Clause) that a federal law can supersede or supplant any inconsistent state law or regulation.
savings clause	A statutory provision exempting from coverage something that would otherwise be included.
sovereignty	Supreme dominion, authority, or rule.

Foreword

> This [federal] government is acknowledged by all to be one of enumerated powers. The principle, that it can exercise only the powers granted to it, [is] now universally admitted. But the question respecting the extent of the powers actually granted, is perpetually arising, and will probably continue to arise, as long as our system shall exist.
>
> —Chief Justice John Marshall, *McCulloch v. Maryland* (1819)

These prescient words of John Marshall, followed immediately by the proposition that "the government of the Union, though limited in its powers, is supreme within its sphere of action," set the stage for the wonderful, zigzagging history of federalism, preemption, and state wildlife authority told by Lowell Baier in these pages.

In addressing the extent of Congress's enumerated powers to regulate commerce among the several states in a later case, Chief Justice Marshall gave a partly functional or contextual answer rather than one based solely on the category of activity involved: it encompasses "commerce which concerns more states than one." As Lowell Baier shows, on this understanding the development of the United States from a predominantly local and rural economy to an integrated national and industrial one over the course of the nineteenth century—both generally and with respect to wildlife in particular—justified a larger federal role. He provides the vivid and poignant examples of the national and international industry in exotic bird skins and feathers, starting with the "market gunners" in local marshes and ending in fashionable urban hat shops, and the national beef industry spanning Western ranches, Midwestern stockyards, Eastern cities, and interstate railroads. These called for and forth pioneering federal legislation such as the Lacey Act of 1900, the Migratory Bird Treaty Act of 1918, the Interstate Commerce Act of 1887, the Sherman Antitrust Act of 1890, and the Pure Food and Drug Act of 1906.

Affirming Marshall's prediction, the landmark Endangered Species Act of 1973—on which the book focuses—could soon perhaps face the threat of a serious constitutional challenge. Given the Rehnquist Court's scaling back of the scope of the commerce power and the current Roberts Court's probusiness and property-rights majority, it is not inconceivable that the Endangered Species Act could be deemed, in whole or in part, insufficiently "commercial" or "economic" in nature to be within the current parameters of this power. At least one lower federal court has so found, as applied to the taking of a purely intrastate species.

This issue of the constitutionality of the Endangered Species Act is, of course, prior to the issue of its preemptive effect on state law. As the book's history shows, questions of preemption primarily arise when dealing with an area of concurrent federal and state powers, and the further back in time one goes into the era of "dual federalism," the fewer such powers were understood to exist. Accordingly, the modern centrality of preemption goes hand in hand with the general increase in the scope of federal powers and rise of "cooperative federalism" after 1937.

Curiously, but perhaps ultimately not surprisingly, the politics of preemption are not fixed and vary with time, context, and the substantive topic at issue. During the Warren Court era, to be propreemption of state law was generally perceived as a liberal stance, as with the use of federal law in landmark statutes such as the Civil Rights Act of 1964 and the Voting Rights Act of 1965 to counter the type of "states' rights" claims that were euphemisms for segregation and Jim Crow. Today, by contrast, to be propreemption generally has a conservative, deregulatory cast, preventing states from imposing their law in the face of uniform national rules that may be the result of successful corporate lobbying of federal legislators or administrators.

As a very general matter, where needed and within enumerated powers, federal laws that set a mandatory national floor but permit states to increase regulatory standards if they choose, both tend to create more optimal policy outcomes and are a better fit with the nation's overall conception of federalism. In this regard, the 1973 Endangered Species Act is reasonably well crafted.

Of course, more pressing than the general legal and political issues of federalism and preemption is an effective ESA that achieves its goal of protecting threatened and endangered species. Here Lowell Baier compellingly argues that, as originally envisaged but neglected in practice, both federal and state wildlife authorities have key and distinctive division-of-labor-driven roles to play and that cooperation and mutual trust—rather than tension and conflict—between them is essential. Accordingly, policymakers and administrators would be well advised to take the author's wise and sound counsel on the major practical weaknesses of the current regime and how to address them.

Stephen Gardbaum
Stephen Yeazell Endowed Chair in Law
UCLA School of Law

Preface

This book tells the story of how over four centuries the federal government slowly preempted much of the sole and absolute authority of the states over managing their resident wildlife. When the Pilgrims departed the *Mayflower* in December 1620, they lived off the land harvesting fish, wildlife, fruits, and herbs. That was their sole source of food and sustenance until they introduced planting vegetables. Thereafter thirteen colonies were formed by other sectarian groups, each with its own government and judicial system. Some 167 years later, the colonists formed the United States by virtue of the US Constitution in 1787. The Constitution created a centralized national government. Fearful of its sovereign power, the framers gave the federal government only specific, limited, and enumerated powers; the remainder of governmental powers were reserved to the states. One of those reserved powers was the unwritten right of authority over the resident wildlife within each state.

The division of authority between the states and federal government, and the governance thereof, was initially called *dual federalism*. The courts enforced a rigid separation between these respective sovereign powers. Under the pressures of rapid industrial and technological advancements during the Industrial Revolution after the turn of the nineteenth century, dual federalism collapsed. President Franklin Delano Roosevelt's 1937 New Deal Supreme Court established a governance of *concurrent jurisdiction* and concurrent powers shared between the states and the federal government, which scholars called *cooperative federalism*. After 1970, some scholars have termed it *coercive federalism* or *preemptive federalism*, outstripping constitutional rhetoric.

To appreciate the evolution of federalism through the country's history, one must understand the constitutional concepts of the federal government's enumerated powers and the states' reserved powers, each of which are explained.

These two concepts form the foundation of federalism. The Supremacy and Commerce Clauses, which are the foundation of preemption, are explained, as is the concept of preemption and particularly its role in sustaining federalism. The origins of discord between the states and federal government are explored in-depth to give the reader an understanding of how this problem has been exacerbated by an absolute congressional mandate to protect all of America's endangered species and their habitats from harm, whatever the cost, and thence not providing sufficient funds to carry out the mandate. Moreover, this state/federal discord continues by the Washington bureaucracy frequently evading congressional intent in legislation and usurping that intent through the regulatory process to achieve their own policy objectives by adopting binding rules, regulations, policies, and secretarial orders and by frequently attaching unreasonable conditions to funding and grants-in-aid.

This is not by conscious premeditation or design by ill intent. Rather it is congressional dereliction of duty to refuse honoring their own mandates and bureaucratic predilection to view an agency's role from a top-down perspective in managing national affairs, and prioritizing their place in a centralized federal government headquartered in Washington, D.C., populated by the President, the Supreme Court, and the Congress, with all the federal agencies headquartered all around them. Most of the key agencies are embedded inside the presidential executive departments, and the secretaries of each sit on the president's cabinet. Agency authority frequently gets confused with the lines of presidential power and congressional legislative authority—as does the judiciary—the relationships being so close, mixed, and interstitial inside the Capital Beltway.

In politics, each side has its saints and sinners, radicals, monkey wrenchers, liberals, and conservatives that together are polarized. Partisan polarization in federal/state discord derives not from the virtue or turpitude of individuals but from the polarity of the ideas they each believe in. The political battles for power are not between good guys or bad guys but between beliefs. The real villains are ignorance and the failure to comprehend our nation's history. Moreover, polarization results from the failure of our elected leaders to adhere to the constitutional principles and intellectual traditions of governance designed by our founding fathers, embodied in the US Constitution.

Throughout history, the states' historic and traditional power to manage and control their resident wildlife remained rooted as a fundamental right to the food and sustenance nature provided for the survival of their citizens. This concept was considered so inviolate that it wasn't even challenged until 1876, when the Supreme Court held that each state "owned" its wildlife. It was not until 1982 that the courts held wildlife to be no different than other natural resources; wildlife "ownership" by the states was an anachronism, a legal fiction. Wildlife was held in the public trust primarily for recreational purposes, and hunting was no longer considered an inalienable or fundamental right.

The 1900 Lacey Act prohibiting the sale of wild animals or their parts in interstate commerce, if taken in violation of state law, and the 1918 Migratory Bird Treaty Act removing migratory birds from the control of the states were the first major preemptive moves regarding wildlife by the federal government. The 1973 Endangered Species Act was Congress's second major preemptive move regarding wildlife, removing endangered species from control by the states. In between and thereafter, lack of congressional funding and the courts and the administrative agencies have slowly eroded state control and management of their resident wildlife. While this historic states' right remains somewhat intact, it is no longer the gold standard it was in the seventeenth, eighteenth, and nineteenth centuries based on its original premise that each state had sole authority over all of its resident wildlife to sustain its citizens.

The United States has moved throughout the twentieth century from a federalist government with divided authority toward a centralized government, like that of France, China, or Russia. Individual freedoms traditionally within the governance of the states have slowly moved into federal authority under the guise of the guarantee of due process and the Fourteenth Amendment. This includes health care, religious freedom, race relations, education, marriage, abortion, the environment, and biodiversity. Federal authority over wildlife is but a part of this evolution. It is a product primarily of the growth and authority of the federal agencies (the administrative state) empowered by the Congress through neglect and default and empowered by the acquiescence of the courts. How this evolution has occurred is best understood in the larger historiographic context. Accordingly, this book follows the country's historical evolution and the glacial erosion of state authority over wildlife by the federal government's congressional and administrative state and concludes with a description of its current state and a prediction of its future.

The purpose of this book is threefold: To educate the general public, the Congress, wildlife students, and, most importantly, the public servants (both career and volunteers) that administer the bureaucratic machinery of government explaining how the country got into its present state of affairs, by interpreting the historic sequence of events that got us here. From that realization, the prayer is that tensions stemming from authority over wildlife management will recede and the relationships will move from tension to a cooperative, constructive atmosphere for the betterment of our nation's wildlife and biodiversity and the temperament of our dedicated public servants. Lastly, the purpose of this book is to inspire Congress to fully fund and honor the costs of their mandate to protect the country's endangered species, whatever the cost.

Go Forth in Peace,
Lowell E. Baier
January 1, 2022

1

From the Mayflower Compact to the US Constitution, 1620–1789

The historical backdrop of our constitutional republic began with the Mayflower Compact and the colonists' right to self-governance. The special, resilient character of the American people became apparent as they fought the Revolutionary War against the King of England, and their deep practical and philosophical skepticism of centralized power and control led to the adoption of a written constitution that safeguarded their liberty. In making the case for ratification of the US Constitution, the Federalists persuasively argued that the doctrine of *enumerated powers*—the idea that the federal government could only act pursuant to one of its expressed powers in the Constitution—became fundamental to the system of separation of powers. Anti-Federalists, however, argued for a bill of rights—specifically because of their suspicion of the government's willingness to constrain itself to its *own* delegated powers. The eventual final form of the US Constitution was a compromise, which *structurally* dispelled concentrations of sovereign power both vertically and horizontally.

* * *

The history of preemption of state sovereignty over wildlife begins with the adoption of the US Constitution in 1787. "The Supremacy Clause of the Constitution [Art. IV, Cl. 2], which provides that federal law can preclude and preempt conflicting state law, is the foundation of the preemption doctrine"—its very touchstone, the fountainhead of federal supremacy.[1] Embedded within the Constitution were systemic conflicts between the enumerated, limited powers ceded to the US Congress and the residual powers reserved to states. This division of powers defined the federalist system. This balancing of powers, moreover, is what defined the great debate between the

Federalists and the Anti-Federalists as memorialized in *The Federalist Papers*, written by James Madison, John Jay, and Alexander Hamilton between 1787 and 1788; that debate continues to this day.

To understand the significance of federal preemption of the states' wildlife management authority, one first needs to understand the context in which it has occurred. That requires looking at the history and evolution of federalism from Colonial times forward, including the constitutional role of federal preemption in sustaining federalism. In England, the King and Parliament determined the public's right to hunt and fish, but the Colonists reversed that.[2] Public ownership and control of wild game as the people's food supply was a critical component of self-governance and a fundamental necessity for survival.[3] In Colonial America's beginning, each colony "owned" its wildlife and was sole trustee under a public trust for the benefit of its residents, who relied on it for their food supply. Two hundred years later, the federal government totally preempted state sovereignty over endangered species, two-thirds of which occur on private lands, as do hundreds more at risk of being listed. This book is the story of that evolution and transition from total state control over all its flora and fauna to total federal control of endangered species on private lands, within the context of the perversion of federalism and preemption.

Figure 1.1. Signing of the Mayflower Compact, December 18, 1620, Plymouth Harbor, Massachusetts, as depicted in this 1899 painting by Jean Leon Ferris. *Source*: Pictorial Press Ltd./Alamy Stock Photo.

Government in America and freedom from the Crown's oppression started on December 18, 1620, when the *Mayflower* dropped anchor in Plymouth Bay along the coast of Massachusetts.[4] On board were 102 separatist Christian Puritans from Nottinghamshire, England, fleeing persecution because they had refused to join the Church of England. The *Mayflower* had originally been bound for the Colony of Virginia but had gotten lost. In Plymouth, the colonists had no official charter to govern them.[5] Before disembarking from the *Mayflower*, they agreed that their right to self-government derived from God and natural law and needed to be memorialized. The Mayflower Compact, memorializing their agreement, created a government established by common consent to obey the laws of God and those they created, with continuing loyalty and allegiance to King James I.[6] This was followed by the 1629 Charter of Massachusetts Bay and the Pilgrim Code of Law in 1636.[7] More colonies followed, and the Mayflower Compact together with Code of Law became America's first documents creating a government. The colony was incorporated into the Massachusetts Bay Association in 1691.[8]

A total of thirteen colonies formed in America between 1620 and 1732, the last being Georgia. Each was self-governed and independent from the other. There were four different classes of colonies: In royal colonies, the governor and advisory council were appointed by the British government and bore allegiance to the Crown. In proprietary colonies, these officials were appointed by a proprietor who had received a sizable land grant; the citizens bore allegiance to him alone, and he to the Crown. Royal colonies belonged to the Crown, and the other two types of royal colonies were granted to private interests or joint-stock companies by the Crown and were virtually independent of royal authority, operating as self-governed republics. In each, the governor, the council, and a bicameral legislature were elected by the colony's property owners; the governor's advisory council served as the upper house, and the lower body was a representative assembly of propertied citizens.[9]

Royal charters were legal contracts that gave the colonists the privilege to make and enforce their laws; however, the colonists viewed the charters as constitutions of self-government.[10] The Crown had limited power over the thirteen separate colonies, which soon demanded the right to regulate their own domestic affairs as coequals with Parliament. The Crown refused these demands by enacting stamp acts, levies, and direct taxes on the colonists, as well as by suspending recalcitrant state representative assemblies.[11] The Revolutionary War over Colonial independence ensued on April 19, 1775,[12] with the "shot heard around the world" at the Battles of Lexington and Concord.[13] Military action ended October 19, 1781, with the surrender of General Cornwallis at Yorktown, Virginia.[14]

THE CREATION OF A DEMOCRATIC GOVERNMENT

During the American Revolution, in 1776 delegates from the thirteen Colonies met as the Second Continental Congress[15] in Philadelphia to form a new "national government." Their goal was to unite the Colonies on separate but equal footing, recognizing that certain functions could only be served at the national level; these included waging a war and developing a uniform currency and a postal service, establishing admiralty law for navigable waters common to all, and the regulation of interstate commerce. Their efforts yielded the Articles of Confederation (1777), replaced in 1787 by the Constitution, and reinforced by the Bill of Rights, ratified in 1791, which consisted of ten amendments to the Constitution. As in any democratic society, America's cultural values, morals, ethics, and political ideologies are what shape its laws. The best example of this principle is the US Constitution and Bill of Rights, which reflect the colonists' aspirations for personal and religious freedoms, liberty, justice, free speech, and the right to congregate—a body of laws starting with the fundamentals, such as habeas corpus (the right to be heard by a court of lawful jurisdiction) and due process (a timely legal proceeding).

The fundamental notion of self-governance of the Colonies, separate from the English Crown and later the federal government, first became embedded in the concept of statehood under the Articles of Confederation in 1777.[16] The first draft of the articles was presented to the Continental Congress on July 12, 1776, closely following the creation of the Declaration of Independence on July 4.[17] It was the Colonies' first attempt to form a national government.

Under the Articles of Confederation, a confederation of thirteen states was created. Each state remained sovereign, possessing all government powers. There was no reference to federal supremacy. In government matters, who had the final word—states or the federal government? The Congress had limited powers and no enforcement ability and was dependent on the states to carry out its directives, and the states could override a congressional directive.[18] Congress had sole authority to declare war and make treaties.[19] The closest the articles came to a Supremacy Clause was in Article XIII, which required that the document "be inviolably observed by every state."[20]

The Articles of Confederation created many issues: Not all of the thirteen states had agreed to the 1783 Treaty of Paris ending the Revolutionary War. British troops were still garrisoned in seven posts, including in Detroit, Oswego, and Sandusky, to aid in the British collection of debts.[21] Many states failed to comply with requisitions by Congress, entered into separate treaties on their own, trespassed on the rights of other states—especially in commerce—and failed to protect minorities against injustice. The lack of a supreme power to resolve conflicts, both those between states and with the federal government, was a major failure of the Articles of Confederation.[22]

THE CONSTITUTIONAL CONVENTION AND THE US CONSTITUTION, 1787

In May 1787, the Constitutional Convention convened in Philadelphia to resolve these conflicts. The delegates quickly abandoned any serious attempts to amend the dysfunctional Articles of Confederation and instead turned to creating an entirely new governmental organization. Since the original state governments had already been operating as colonies for some 167 years, the drafters of this new constitution had no reason to "constitute" them. Rather, the drafters' primary purpose was to carve out a new, stronger central government.[23] As Supreme Court chief justice John Marshall later said, "It was neither necessary nor proper to define the powers retained by the States. These powers proceed, not from the people of America, but from the people of the several States; and remain, after the adoption of the constitution, what they were before, except so far as they may be abridged by that instrument."[24] "When the revolution took place the people of each state became themselves sovereign. In that character, they held the absolute right to all their navigable waters, and the soil under them, for their own common use, subject only to the rights surrendered by the Constitution to the general government."[25] The US Constitution was unanimously approved by the convention on September 15, 1787.

An overarching goal of the constitutional delegates was to cede to the national government only those limited "enumerated or delegated" powers and retain unto the states all of the "residual or infinite" powers to operate as independent governments. This key concept was further reinforced by the Tenth Amendment to the US Constitution, ratified on December 15, 1791, at the insistence of James Madison, George Mason, and the Anti-Federalists, to further reinforce states' rights. The amendment states, "The powers not delegated to the United States by the Constitution, nor prohibited by it to the States, are reserved to the States respectively, or to the people."[26] The colonies were fiercely protective of self-governance, since they had already been operating as independent governments for 167 years. Moreover, their underlying concerns in 1787 were largely governance and economic in nature—to safeguard the emerging economic union.[27]

> The U.S. Constitution did not empower state governments. It left to the state constitutions the task of constituting state governments and delegating to them some portion of the popular sovereignty. The sovereign people were free to

Figure 1.2. The presentation of the draft of the Declaration of Independence to Congress, June 28, 1776, Independence Hall, Philadelphia, Pennsylvania, as depicted in this painting by John Trumbull. *Source*: GL Archives/Alamy Stock Photo.

delegate particular reserved powers to their state governments, or without such powers. Sovereignty remained in the people, who gave life to their system of federalism by delegating that sovereignty to their several [state] governments. The system can only be fully appreciated by viewing the whole, the equal spheres of sovereign power intended to balance and be a mutual restraint against each other's over reach.[28]

It has been an enduring paradox of federalism that one central perpetual sovereign coexists with fifty other perpetual sovereigns—which political scholars say is self-contradictory.[29] The principles and political philosophy underlying the Federalist/Anti-Federalist debate that drove the addition of the Tenth Amendment concerned states' rights advocacy versus Federalist demands for a strong central government.[30] Hence the federal system developed two powers, pulling in opposite directions: one limiting the authority of the central federal government and one checking the power of the states.[31]

The issue of supremacy and final authority in disputes between the national government and the states remained a simmering issue throughout the Constitutional Convention during the summer of 1787. A variety of proposals were presented by various delegates, including the Virginia Plan, the New Jersey Plan, and the Maryland proposal, all intensely debated. Finally a compromise committee called the Committee of Style drafted what became Article VI, paragraph 2, of the US Constitution—which became known as the "Supremacy Clause." It is the cornerstone of federalism.[32] Because treaty powers were of paramount concern to the drafters, and their potential usurpation by individual states had occurred under the earlier Articles of Confederation, the delegates specified within the Supremacy Clause that treaties are the supreme law of the land. Two legal scholars have noted that the supremacy of the federal government was the only alternative to a force of arms to maintain order among rival authorities.[33]

FORTITUDE AND SELF-GOVERNANCE

As one ponders the period from 1620, when the *Mayflower* landed, until the creation of the world's first democratic republic 167 years later in 1787, what stands out is the resolve of the human spirit to seek freedom from oppression and realize self-governance as free people. Pilgrims carved homes and farms from the raw wilderness, surviving on wild game, fish, and forage once they had exhausted the *Mayflower*'s supplies. Fifty of the 102 *Mayflower* passengers died that first winter. The security of the *Mayflower* left them when the ship sailed back to England on April 5, 1621. They were alone until November of that year when the ship *Fortune* arrived, bringing thirty-five new colonists. In 1623, one hundred more arrived.[34] As even more colonists came, they formed new colonies up and down the Atlantic seaboard. Their number reached thirteen when Georgia was established in 1732, some 112 years after the arrival of the *Mayflower*.[35]

In addition to fighting Native Americans for land, these colonists strained under the direct rule of England. British agents were designated to collect taxes, regulate domestic affairs, and maintain law and order. The colonists built villages, towns, cities, and businesses powered by the first Industrial Revolution, which began around 1760 and was driven by steam power.[36] They forged a semblance of government creating colonial legislatures to manage their growing affairs. When they rebelled against the oppression of the English Crown, and with the outbreak of the Revolutionary War on April 19, 1775, a fledgling Continental Army created only three months earlier began to fight the most powerful country in the world.

While Britain had the largest and strongest army and navy in the world, General George Washington was left to recruit, equip, and train a volunteer militia composed of farmers, merchants, and townspeople who fought for seven years, until General Charles Cornwallis surrendered at Yorktown on October 19, 1782.[37] These colonists had declared themselves a nation free from British rule and established a national government with the Articles of

Confederation in 1777; they established a democratic republic on September 17, 1787, with the creation of the US Constitution, the first of its kind in the world. The only governmental structure they'd known before this was the unitary king or monarchy in England and on the European continent. To develop a truly national republican government format with dual sovereignty was a remarkable feat of compromise and drafting by delegates from colonies, each of which had been sovereign governments for some 167 years.

To get to Philadelphia for the Continental Congress in 1777 and 1787, delegates had to ride by horseback or carriage on dirt roads. From the most remote of colonies, including Georgia and North and South Carolina, that was a seven- to ten-day journey, battling the weather, with bandits and hostile Natives a constant threat. The delegates presided using candlelight and communicated using quill pens, parchment paper, public debate in the chamber, and couriers. The postal system was rudimentary. They slept in rooming houses and ate in taverns. The maelstrom of armed conflict from the Revolution surrounded them. Ratification of the Articles of Confederation and later the US Constitution by thirteen diverse colonies spanning from Maine to Georgia was also by the same means. From this confusion, a nation was created from the sheer will and determination of these early colonists to forge their own destiny to be free, self-governing, and independent. Collectively they were resolute to build an empire on hard work, ingenuity, enterprise, and the skills of entrepreneurship and agrarian enterprise.

SUMMARY

The United States Constitution was the final political product of intense intellectual debate about the nature, scope, and limits of government power. The colonial regime under British rule, which concluded with the American Revolution, generated deep societal divisions between Anti-federalists and Federalists. However, the Federalists were ultimately successful in advancing their arguments for a constitution of limited, enumerated powers—one that properly established a framework for ordered liberty. In *Federalist No. 51* James Madison argued that, "in framing a government which is to be administered by men over men the great difficulty lies in this: you must first enable the government to control the governed; and in the next place, oblige it to control itself."[38] Since 1787, the question about the *extent* to which it controls itself has been debated, discussed, and decided by the courts.

In light of the history preceding the Constitutional Convention, the framers were especially circumspect in creating a national government. The colonies had been fiercely independent in safeguarding their right to self-governance—

as John Winthrop had famously described in 1630 the Massachusetts Bay Colony, becoming "a city upon a hill," with "the eyes of all people . . . upon us."[39] The Constitution, however, sought to create a *unified* nation—one guided by a national government "fenced-in" by enumerated powers. At the core of this political vision was a classical liberal sentiment: government exists to protect individual liberty from arbitrary government intrusion. According to the Federalists, the *structure* of the Constitution was *necessary* to achieving that aim. Indeed, because Federalists believed that the federal government could *only* exercise power pursuant to an *enumerated* power in the Constitution, the Federalists ultimately contended that a bill of rights was not necessary to safeguard liberty. The Anti-Federalists, who were ardent proponents and defenders of states' rights, however, remained deeply skeptical of the nature and scope of federal power, even under a limited Constitution. In fact, Anti-Federalists became the chief proponents of a bill of rights, and after one was ratified in 1791, the Tenth Amendment made clear that powers not delegated to the federal government would be *reserved* to the states, such as the powers to regulate the health, safety, and welfare of their citizens.

Although the concept of federalism was nascent at the time of the nation's founding, the framers understood that limiting the power of the national government while equally respecting the states' right to exist as separate, independent sovereigns would be necessary to securing the blessings of liberty. Over the next two hundred thirty odd years, the constitutional question over the vertical relationship between the federal government and state governments would be argued and reviewed by the courts.

NOTES

1. Elaine M. Martin, "The Burger Court and Preemption Doctrine: Federalism in the Balance," *Notre Dame Law Review* 60, 10, no. 5 (1985): 1233, https://scholarship.law.nd.edu/cgi/viewcontent.cgi?article=2346&context=ndlr.

Also see Jay B. Sykes and Nicole Vanatko, "Federal Preemption: A Legal Primer," Congressional Research Service, report no. R45825, July 23, 2019, https://sgp.fas.org/crs/misc/R45825.pdf; and David M. O'Brien, "The Rehnquist Court and Federal Preemption: In Search of a Theory," *Publius* 23, no. 4 (Autumn 1993): 15.

2. Gordon S. Wood, *The Creation of the American Republic, 1776–1787* (Chapel Hill: University of North Carolina Press, 1969), 354–55.

3. Michael J. Bean and Melanie J. Rowland, *The Evolution of National Wildlife Law*, 3rd ed. (Westport, CT: Praeger, 1997), 13; *Geer v. Connecticut*, 161 U.S. 519, 530–31 (1896).

4. The *Mayflower* first landed on November 11, 1620, at the very tip of Cape Cod, where Provincetown, Massachusetts, is located today. The area and terrain

was considered too difficult for the establishment of the colony, so the Pilgrims sailed across Cape Cod Bay to Plymouth on the mainland. Sarah Pruitt, "How the Mayflower Compact Laid a Foundation for American Democracy," History.com, accessed September 10, 2021, https://www.history.com/news/mayflower-compact-colonial-america-plymouth.

5. The Pilgrims expected to become part of the Virginia colony and live under that charter. But after arriving in a different location than intended, their solution was to refer to themselves as a "colony," bear strict allegiance to the Crown, and petition in a discreet manner for a charter confirming their liberties. The king never issued a royal charter granting them legal authority, but they did receive a patent permitting them to legally remain in their location. Independence Hall Association, "2a. The Colonial Experience," USHistory.org, accessed June 15, 2021, https://www.ushistory.org/gov/2a.asp; Wikipedia, "Colonial Government in the Thirteen Colonies," last modified July 24, 2021, https://en.wikipedia.org/wiki/Colonial_government_in_the_Thirteen_Colonies.

6. The creation of the Mayflower Compact resulted from a recognition that the Pilgrims had failed to arrive in Virginia as planned and were now without a royal charter that would have established their system of governance. Hence they drafted their own governance document, followed by the Code of Law, created on November 15, 1636. Historians view these documents in aggregate as "the first true American Constitution."

The Code of Law was an extension of the Mayflower Compact and resembled a constitution, prescribing a structure of government centered on a representative assembly comprised of freemen called the "General Court," which the colonists considered equivalent to Parliament in Great Britain. Their commission was to oppose any action that portended to destroy or overthrow the colony. The assembly members were required to participate in the assembly or pay a hefty fine of three shillings. The Code of Law vested in the elected governor executive powers to execute the laws and ordinances enacted by the assembly—a role similar to our president or to the state governors. Governors were empowered to adjudicate disputes as would a judge and to arrest offenders, try them like a prosecutor with convenient speed and impartiality, and imprison them, thus establishing a judicial foundation. Rights and duties of the colonists were codified in the Code of Law. The governor and his officials were bound to operate within the structure of the laws however they saw fit, but there were checks on abuses of power. The system ensured some measure of due process. This foreshadowed the right of equality under the U.S. Constitution.

These early documents from the 1600s established a constitutional-type governmental structure with a separation of powers and defined the rights and duties of government, later codified in the US Constitution. "What distinguished the Puritans in New England from other Calvinist communities in Europe and other English colonies in America was their ability to derive from their theological doctrines direct and dramatic ideas and constitutional institutions. This was, in fact, the feature that made Puritans in New England become a fertile seed for American constitutionalism." Fernando Rey Martinez, "The Religious Character of the American Constitution:

Puritanism and Constitutionalism in the United States," *Kansas Law Journal of Law and Public Policy* 12 (2002–2003): 469.

Also see General Court of the Colony of New Plymouth, Pilgrim Code of Law, promulgated November 15, 1636, archived at https://teachingamericanhistory.org/library/document/pilgrim-code-of-law; Independence Hall Association, "2a. The Colonial Experience"; Wikipedia, "Colonial Government in the Thirteen Colonies"; Julia L. Ernst, "The Mayflower Compact: Celebrating Four Hundred Years of Influence on U.S. Democracy," *North Dakota Law Review* 95, no. 1 (2020): 57–64; Donald S. Lutz, "From Covenant to Constitution in American Political Thought," *Publius* 10, no. 4 (1980): 101–33; John Witte Jr., "How to Govern a City on a Hill: The Early Puritan Contribution to American Constitutionalism," *Emory Law Journal* 39, no. 3 (1989): 41, 59; Donald S. Lutz, *The Origins of American Constitutionalism* (Baton Rouge and London: Louisiana State University Press, 1986), 27, 39–41.

7. Lutz, *Origins of American Constitutionalism*, 27, 39–41; Ernst, "Mayflower Compact," 17–20.

8. While the Mayflower and the Plymouth colonies have secured popular recognition as birthing American democracy, Jamestown was the first permanent English colony, following the first European settlement in St. Augustine in 1565 and the "Lost Colony of Roanoke" in 1585. Jamestown was established in 1607 under the Virginia Company Charters of 1606, 1609, and 1612, first under control of the English Crown, then the Virginia Company and its governor and council. In 1610 the colonists adopted a type of constitutional agreement titled the "Articles, Laws, the Orders, Divine, Politic, and Martial for the Colony." In 1619 they adopted the "Laws Enacted by the First General Assembly of Virginia—August 2–4, 1619." Ernst, "Mayflower Compact," 17–20.

9. George C. Herring, *From Colony to Superpower: U.S. Foreign Relations since 1776* (Oxford: Oxford University Press, 2008); Bernard Bailyn, *The Origins of American Politics* (New York: Alfred A. Knopf, 1968); Donald Ratcliffe, "The Right to Vote and the Rise of Democracy, 1787–1828," *Journal of the Early Republic* 33, no. 2 (Summer 2013): 219.

10. Peter Charles Hoffer, Williamjames Hoffer, and N. E. H. Hull, *The Supreme Court: An Essential History* (Lawrence: University Press of Kansas, 2007), 15.

11. Jeff Wallenfeldt, "Timeline of the American Revolution," Britannica.com, accessed April 14, 2020, https://www.britannica.com/list/timeline-of-the-american-revolution.

12. Concord Museum, "The Shot Heard Round the World: April 19, 1775," Concord Museum.org, accessed May 10, 2020, https://concordmuseum.org/online-exhibition/the-shot-heard-round-the-world-april-19-1775; Editors of the Encyclopedia Britannica, "Battles of Lexington and Concord," Britannica.com, accessed May 10, 2020, https://www.britannica.com/event/Battles-of-Lexington-and-Concord.

13. Paul Revere's famous ride to warn that the British were coming preceded the Battles of Lexington and Concord; this resulted in 272 British troops killed and ninety American militia lost. This engagement—considered the start of the Revolutionary War—was preceded by the Boston Massacre on March 5, 1770, when five unarmed

civilians had been killed by a British detachment, and by the Boston Tea Party on December 16, 1773, when £10,000 worth of tea had been thrown into Boston Harbor.

14. The Revolutionary War officially ended on September 3, 1783, with the Treaty of Paris, wherein the United States was officially recognized as an independent nation. The treaty included a significant land grant, extending all the way to the Mississippi River. Robert Middlekauff, *The Glorious Cause* (New York: Oxford University Press, 1982), 559–70, 586–90.

15. The First Continental Congress convened in Philadelphia on September 15, 1774, solely to issue a declaration of rights due every citizen—including entitlement to life, liberty, property, assembly, and trial by jury and the prohibition of maintenance of the British troops without the colony's consent. The delegates petitioned the king, pleading for redress and repeal of the Intolerable Act, which had dissolved the existing colonial governments and imposed additional taxes and levies on the colonies. The Congress moreover agreed to an economic boycott on British goods, effective December 1774.

In the Second Continental Congress, which convened on May 10, 1775, the delegates voted to form a Continental Army and elected George Washington as its commander in chief. James MacDonald, "Appointment as Commander in Chief," MountVernon.org, accessed February 3, 2021, https://www.mountvernon.org/library/digitalhistory/digital-encyclopedia/article/appointment-as-commander-in-chief/; Middlekauff, *Glorious Cause*, 234–49; see generally Edmund C. Burnett, *The Continental Congress* (Westport, CT: Greenwood Publishing Group, 1975); "First Continental Congress," Wikipedia, last modified July 28, 2021, https://en.wikipedia.org/wiki/First_Continental_Congress; "Second Continental Congress," Wikipedia, last modified July 3, 2021, https://en.wikipedia.org/wiki/Second_Continental_Congress.

16. Wood, *Creation of the American Republic*, 354–55.

17. Christopher R. Drahozal, *The Supremacy Clause: A Reference Guide to the United States Constitution* (Westwood, CT: Praeger, 2004), 5.

18. Drahozal, *Supremacy Clause*, 21–24.

19. Drahozal, *Supremacy Clause*, 21–24.

20. US Continental Congress, Articles of Confederation and Perpetual Union between the states of New-Hampshire, Massachusetts-Bay, Rhode-Island and Providence Plantations, Connecticut, New-York, New-Jersey, Pennsylvania, Delaware, Maryland, Virginia, North-Carolina, South-Carolina and Georgia, article XIII, printed Lancaster, Pennsylvania, 1777, reproduced at https://www.loc.gov/resource/bdsdcc.n001001/?sp=9&st=text.

21. Drahozal, *Supremacy Clause*, 8.

22. Drahozal, *Supremacy Clause*, 11–21.

23. Ernest A. Young, "Making Federalism Doctrine: Fidelity, Institutional Competence, and Compensating Adjustments," *William and Mary Law Review* 46, no. 5 (2005): 1733, 1775, https://scholarship.law.wm.edu/cgi/viewcontent.cgi?article=1296&context=wmlr.

24. Young, "Making Federalism Doctrine," 1775–76.

25. *Martin v. Waddell's Lessee*, 41 U.S. 367, 368 (1842).

26. US Constitution, amend. 10, archived online at https://www.senate.gov/civics/constitution_item/constitution.htm.

27. Kenneth W. Starr, "Preface," in *Federal Preemption: States' Powers, National Interests*, ed. Richard A. Epstein and Michael S. Greve (Washington, DC: AEI Press, 2007), xv.

28. Young, "Making Federalism Doctrine," 1733, 1776, 1778.

29. Starr, "Preface," xii.

30. James Madison and George Mason, *The Bill of Rights: With Writings that Formed Its Foundation* (Bedford, MA: Applewood Books, 2008); Jeff Broadwater, *George Mason: Forgotten Founder* (Chapel Hill: The University of North Carolina Press, 2006); James Madison, "The Same Subject Continued: The Union as a Safeguard against Domestic Faction and Insurrection," *The Federalist Papers*, no. 10, November 23, 1787, archived at https://guides.loc.gov/federalist-papers/text-1-10#s-lg-box-wrapper-25493273; Charles A. Beard, *An Economic Interpretation of the Constitution of the United States* (New York: The MacMillian Company, 1913).

31. Ernest A. Young, "Federal Preemption and State Autonomy," in *Federal Preemption: States' Powers, National Interests*, ed. Richard A. Epstein and Michael S. Greve (Washington, DC: AEI Press, 2007), 249.

32. Beard, *Economic Interpretation of the Constitution*, 16, 25.

33. Richard A. Epstein and Michael S. Greve, "Introduction: Preemption in Context," in *Federal Preemption: States' Powers, National Interests*, ed. Richard A. Epstein and Michael S. Greve (Washington, DC: AEI Press, 2007), 5.

34. Pruitt, "How the Mayflower Compact Laid a Foundation."

35. "Colonial America," *Land of the Brave*, accessed February 3, 2021, https://www.landofthebrave.info/; "13 Colonies," *Revolutionary War*, last modified March 4, 2020, https://www.revolutionary-war.net/13-colonies/.

36. "Industrial Revolution in the United States," Wikipedia, last modified May 30, 2021, https://en.wikipedia.org/wiki/Industrial_Revolution_in_the_United_States. And see "Second Industrial Revolution," Wikipedia, last modified August 28, 2021, https://en.wikipedia.org/wiki/Second_Industrial_Revolution; and Salesforce, "Learn about the Fourth Industrial Revolution," accessed July 26, 2020, https://trailhead.salesforce.com/en/content/learn/trails/4th-industrial-revolution.

37. The war officially spanned seven years, as the Treaty of Paris was not ratified until the following spring. "American Revolutionary War," Wikipedia, last modified September 22, 2021, https://en.wikipedia.org/wiki/American_Revolutionary_War. And see Middlekauff, *Glorious Cause*, 570–71.

38. James Madison, "The Structure of the Government Must Furnish the Proper Checks and Balances Between the Different Departments," *The Federalist Papers*, no. 51, February 8, 1788, archived at https://guides.loc.gov/federalist-papers/text-51-60#s-lg-box-wrapper-25493427.

39. John Winthrop, sermon, New England, 1630, as transcribed by the *American Yawp Reader* in "John Winthrop Dreams of a City on a Hill, 1630," text at https://www.americanyawp.com/reader/colliding-cultures/john-winthrop-dreams-of-a-city-on-a-hill-1630/.

2

Defining the New Government and the Separation of Powers, 1789–1835

The broad constitutional principles the framers had articulated (see chapter 1) inevitably began to shift as they were applied. Particularly significant was the influence of Chief Justice John Marshall—one of the most prominent figures to sit on the Supreme Court—who guided the early nation's jurisprudence from 1801 to 1835. Notably, the canonical case *Marbury v. Madison* (1803) and the principle of *judicial review* have become the cornerstone of constitutional law.[1] After *Marbury*, the Court became the *final* arbiter of the Constitution. With the advent of judicial review, the Court assumed a paradigmatic role in setting the foundation for modern federalism and preemption.

* * *

When New Hampshire became the ninth state to ratify the Constitution on June 21, 1788, the US Constitution became the governing document of the new nation. It was time for the country to heal its wounds from the Revolutionary War and its four million people—90 percent of them agrarian—to get on with the business of nation building. Congress began its first official session on March 4, 1789.[2] George Washington was elected the first US president, taking office on April 30, 1789.

Other than the provision in the US Constitution for the establishment of a Supreme Court (Article III), the concept of a separation of powers between branches of government at the national level was nascent in young America, with a Supreme Court being the ultimate arbiter of the law and legal disputes.[3] With the members of the Continental Congress barely grasping the idea of Article III of the Constitution, the separation-of-powers concept had only been explained to the public in speeches during the ratification process and in *The Federalist Papers* written to support ratification. The nation watched with great anticipation to see how these distinct branches would work, especially the Supreme Court, the one branch that had never existed before.[4] The inaugural Supreme Court's first chief justice, John Jay, a Federalist, was appointed on September 26, 1789, governing a six-member court until 1795. Following Jay, Federalists John Rutledge and Oliver Ellsworth became successive chief justices, followed by Marshall, also a Federalist, in 1801.[5]

In the 1790s, the Supreme Court's docket consisted of foundational cases that clarified and defined the language of the US Constitution. The justices began establishing the principles of the new democracy and the rights and limitations on the respective sovereignty of both the federal government and the states. These cases are critical to an understanding of future decisions addressing federal preemption and state sovereignty. For example, the struggle involving the citizens of one state challenging state authority by suing another state was decided in *Chisholm v. Georgia* (1793).[6] The young Court, deciding the case against Georgia, set up a dilemma for itself, its credibility not yet established. Their decision provoked Congress into action: It reacted with the Eleventh Amendment to the Constitution, adopted in February 1795, which removed such disputes from the Court's jurisdiction, further establishing the constitutional doctrine of a state's sovereign immunity and enhancing the principle of states' rights.[7] In *Chisholm* the Court declared that the "United States are sovereign as to all the powers of government actually surrendered: each state in the Union is sovereign as to all the powers reserved."[8]

In the 1796 case of *Ware v. Hylton*, the Court held that "treaties were not to be flouted by state courts in invalidating a state law contrary to the Constitution," thus establishing for the first time the power of judicial review of state laws.[9] Most importantly, the *Ware* decision hinted at the Supreme Court's duty to determine the constitutionality of federal legislation and the key to understanding *Marbury v. Madison*, a case that followed in 1803.[10] "In the early Republic, the new national government struggled to stake out a role in a political environment dominated by preexisting state governments. In that circumstance, it made some sense to construe federal enactments broadly and subordinate concerns about preempting too much of the preexisting state legal background. But the world is very different now [in the twenty-first century]."[11]

THE MARSHALL COURT, 1801–1835

Appointed in 1801 as Chief Justice at the beginning of John Adams's presidency, John Marshall was "a Federalist and nationalist, [but] he was also a student of older republican ideas of disinterested public virtue."[12] Born to the gentry in rural Virginia, Marshall had little attachment to the pretentiousness of the aristocracy. He'd seen combat as an officer in the Revolution, maintained a major law practice in Richmond, was a diplomat, and had served as Secretary of State (1800–1801). He was a deep thinker and strongly believed in the prospects of the new nation.[13] Every member added to the Marshall Court was a states' rights advocate, notwithstanding their Federalist backgrounds and affiliations. Two new members were open Federalists.[14] Collectively they were a strong force for a centralized national government but leaned strongly into upholding states' rights. The Marshall Court sat from 1801 to 1835 and endured the War of 1812, when the British invaded and burned the capital city of Washington, D.C.[15] Of the 1,426 opinions they issued, Marshall himself wrote 632.[16]

The Marshall Court's signature case was the landmark *Marbury v. Madison*.[17] This case held that the Supreme Court was the final arbiter in interpreting the Constitution. The decision implied that the Court had the power to declare acts of Congress unconstitutional, and it established the doctrine of judicial review by the Supreme Court, which underpinned the Supremacy Clause of the Constitution—the very foundation of preemption.[18] This ruling defined and further clarified the original jurisdiction given the Supreme Court in Article III of the Constitution and was the original pronouncement of judicial supremacy.[19] "Thus the principle of supremacy in the Constitution and federal law came to mean 'supremacy' interpreted according to the unlimited discretion of the Supreme Court."[20]

Marshall's decision in *Marbury* enlarged the jurisdiction of the Court and changed the meaning of Article III. The Constitution had not expressly given the Court the authority to review federal or state laws or to strike down acts of Congress or state legislatures, but Marshall's opinion did so, speaking for a unanimous Court. The Court's decision infuriated President Thomas Jefferson, who decried "judicial tyranny" and revealed a deep distrust of the Court. "The germ of dissolution of our federal government is in the constitution of the federal Judiciary," Jefferson wrote, ". . . working like gravity by night and by day, gaining a little to-day & a little tomorrow, and advancing its noiseless step like a thief, over the field of jurisdiction, until all shall be usurped."[21] But the Court's ruling held, and its powers of interpreting the law of the land at the federal and state level remained unlimited.[22]

In the 1819 case *McCulloch v. Maryland*,[23] the Court further held that the national government's supremacy power is not unlimited, that Congress is limited to its enumerated powers and can only exercise the powers granted to it by the Constitution.[24] In the 1824 case of *Gibbons v. Ogden*,[25] the Court further defined and enforced the supremacy powers vested in the federal government.[26] Wherever a state law interferes with, or is contrary to, federal law, "the act of Congress, or the treaty . . . is supreme . . . and the law of the state, though enacted in the exercise of powers not controverted, must yield to it."[27] The central holding was that Congress has exclusive power to regulate interstate commerce and that this power extends to every type of commercial intercourse among the several states, the United States, and foreign nations. This congressional power is not restricted to buying and selling or interchanging commodities but includes intercourse as well as traffic and navigation. *Gibbons* and the nineteen subsequent cases became the precursor to the emergence of the modern preemption doctrine in their three strands of analysis: first, discerning the scope of Congress's constitutional authority, second, articulating whether Congress's powers were plenary and exclusive over specific topics and issues, and third, determining how to protect the states' reserved police powers when an actual conflict between state and federal law existed.[28]

The Supreme Court's *Gibbons* decision, moreover, enlarged the foundation for the preemption doctrine and again reinforced treaty powers over state laws.[29] Treaty power will become significant in this history when we explore the constitutionality of the 1918 Migratory Bird Treaty Act and the 1973 Endangered Species Act. The legitimacy of both acts was initially based on treaties with foreign governments—without which they would not have survived legal challenge.

The 1823 case *Corfield v. Coryell*,[30] decided by Justice Washington, sitting as a judge for the US Circuit Court in Pennsylvania, has been cited by the modern Court[31] as a foundational case that recognizes a state's authority to manage its own oyster harvest—an authority later extended to all of its natural resources. In *Corfield*, the Court upheld a New Jersey law prohibiting the take of oysters by nonresidents, meant to protect the state's oyster beds as a food supply for their own citizens. Such a right, the Court found, falls exclusively within the state's internal police power and is not surrendered to the United States by the grant of admiralty and maritime jurisdiction. *Corfield* became the first foundation stone upon which state wildlife authority was built, with the public trust doctrine fully developed later in the 1842 case of *Martin v. Waddell's Lessee*, examined in the following chapter.[32]

Corfield is frequently cited for its recitation of the privileges and immunities of all citizens guaranteed by the US Constitution, which, as of the time of the case's ruling, had been ratified only thirty-two years earlier. The *Corfield* decision enumerated the rights of the citizens of the several states under their new federal government. These include the right to protection by the government, subject to such restraints as the government may prescribe for the general good or the whole; the right to the enjoyment of life and liberty and the pursuit of safety and happiness; the right to acquire and possess property of every kind, either real or personal; the right to pass through or reside in any state for trade, agriculture, professional pursuits, or other reasons; the right to claim the benefit of the writ of *habeas corpus*; the right to maintain any actions in the courts; exemption from higher taxes or impositions paid by other citizens of the state—and all these rights to better secure and perpetuate mutual friendship and intercourse among all the people of the many states of the Union.

What is important to recognize in Justice Washington's lengthy opinion is that the country was struggling to recognize the principles of democracy and the rules that defined their privileges and immunities under a new national, central government that was only thirty-two years old. The national government was sovereign and separate from each of the state governments that had existed, at that point in time, as many as 203 years prior, with the signing of the Mayflower Compact, and continuing to exist thereafter as sovereign governments.

SUMMARY

The US Constitution established the general rules of the new nation, based on and articulating timeless *principles* that formed a legitimate governing authority. These principles, however, did not specifically define the nature of the relationship between the federal government and state governments. Indeed, the philosophical concept of a *separation of powers* had been sufficiently explained in the 1748 publication of Montesquieu's *Spirit of the Laws*,[33] which had a palpable and enduring influence on the nation's framers. And the horizontal relationship between Articles I, II, and III dislodged power and assigned explicit duties and functions to each branch to execute in its operations. However, the notion of federalism was altogether new to the founding generation. And the question of *which* branch would regulate that balance also remained unresolved.

In 1803, however, the political stage was set to answer those fundamental questions of constitutional law when Chief Justice Marshall broadly pronounced—for the first time in Supreme Court history—the principle of judicial review in *Marbury v. Madison*: "It is emphatically the province and duty of the judicial department to say what the law is."[34] At its core, *Marbury* was a landmark decision: The Supreme Court became the *final* arbiter of the Constitution and its operative meaning. When deciding individual cases or controversies, federal courts now were implicitly authorized under *Marbury* to declare acts of Congress unconstitutional. Although the Constitution did not contain a judicial-review clause, *Marbury* laid the foundation for the Court to build its jurisprudence about the *vertical* relationship between the federal government and state governments, as well as other areas of constitutional law, such as separation of powers and individual rights.

Specifically, after *Marbury*, the Supreme Court began to play a paradigmatic role in shaping and defining the precise contours of the federalism doctrine. From *McCulloch v. Maryland* (1819) to *Gibbons v. Ogden* (1824), the nation's early Supreme Court—operating largely under the deeply pervasive federalist influence of Chief Justice John Marshall—recognized the doctrine of enumerated powers imposed on the federal government, as well as the space for regulatory authority over health, safety, and welfare reserved for the states. Most fundamentally, these early cases established the *constitutional floor* for the subsequent development of the modern preemption doctrine: In fact, the Supreme Court's decision in *Corfield v. Coryell* (1823) became the first foundational case upon which state wildlife authority was built, with the public trust doctrine developing later. Overall, because of the principle of judicial review announced in *Marbury*—"to say what the law is"—the Supreme Court became the *most* important voice on the meaning of federalism.

NOTES

1. *Marbury v. Madison*, 5 U.S. 137 (1803).
2. Gordon S. Wood, *Empire of Liberty: A History of the Early Republic, 1789–1815* (Oxford: Oxford University Press, 2009), 64–65; US House of Representatives, "1st to 9th Congresses (1789–1807)," House.gov, accessed February 3, 2021, https://history.house.gov/Institution/Session-Dates/1-9/.
3. Drahozal, *Supremacy Clause*, 4–11.
4. Hoffer, Hoffer, and Hull, *Supreme Court*, 18.
5. Hoffer, Hoffer, and Hull, *Supreme Court*, 34–41.
6. 2 U.S. 419 (1793).
7. Hoffer, Hoffer, and Hull, *Supreme Court*, 42–43.
8. Chisholm, 2 U.S at 435.
9. *Ware v. Hylton*, 3 U.S. 199 (1796); Hoffer, Hoffer, and Hull, *Supreme Court*, 42, 43, 49; Drahozal, *Supremacy Clause*, 35; Hoffer, Hoffer, and Hull, *Supreme Court*, 49.
10. Hoffer, Hoffer, and Hull, *Supreme Court*, 49; Drahozal, *Supremacy Clause*, 36–38. *Hylton v. United States* also bolstered this opinion (3 U.S. 171 [1796]).
11. Michael Greve, Jonathan Klick, Michael Petrino, and J. P. Sevilla, "Preemption in the Rehnquist and Roberts Courts: An Empirical Analysis," *Supreme Court Economic Review* 23 (2015): 353, https://www.journals.uchicago.edu/doi/pdf/10.1086/686541.
12. Hoffer, Hoffer, and Hull, *Supreme Court*, 51–52.

13. Hoffer, Hoffer, and Hull, *Supreme Court*, 51–52.
14. Hoffer, Hoffer, and Hull, *Supreme Court*, 58.
15. Wood, *Empire of Liberty*, 690–91.
16. Hoffer, Hoffer, and Hull, *Supreme Court*, 81.
17. 5 U.S. 137 (1803).
18. Hoffer, Hoffer, and Hull, *Supreme Court*, 81 From 1791 to 2000, the Court found unconstitutional and overturned 156 acts (or portions thereof) of Congress, and only one before 1866.
19. Hoffer, Hoffer, and Hull, *Supreme Court*, 54–55.
20. Edward S. Corwin, "The Passing of Dual Federalism," *Virginia Law Review* 36, no. 1 (1950): 16.
21. "From Thomas Jefferson to C. Hammond, 18 August 1821," US National Archives, *Founders Online*, Archives.gov, accessed September 10, 2021, https://founders.archives.gov/documents/Jefferson/98-01-02-2260.
22. Hoffer, Hoffer, and Hull, *Supreme*, 52–57; Drahozal, *Supremacy Clause*, 38–40.
23. 17 U.S. 316 (1819).
24. Corwin, "Passing of Dual Federalism," 14; Hoffer, Hoffer, and Hull, *Supreme Court*, 67–70; Drahozal, *Supremacy Clause*, 40–44.
25. 22 U.S. 1 (1824).
26. Hoffer, Hoffer, and Hull, *Supreme Court*, 70–71; Drahozal, *Supremacy Clause*, 44–46.
27. Gibbons, 22 U.S. at 82; Corwin, "Passing of Dual Federalism," 14; Drahozal, *Supremacy Clause*, 44–46.
28. Viet D. Dinh, "Federal Displacement of State Law: The Nineteenth-Century View," in *Federal Preemption: States' Powers, National Interests*, ed. Richard A. Epstein and Michael S. Greve (Washington, DC: AEI Press, 2007), 27–28.
29. Hoffer, Hoffer, and Hull, *Supreme*, 45–46; Gibbons, 22 U.S. 1, 75.
30. 6 Fed. Cas. 546, No. 3230 (C.C.E.D. Pa. 1823).
31. *Tangier Sound Waterman's Association v. Douglas*, 541 F. Supp. 1287 (E.D. Va. 1982).
32. 41 U.S. 367 (1842).
33. Charles Louis de Secondat, Baron of Montesquieu, *The Spirit of the Law* (*De l'esprit des loix*), trans. Thomas Nugent (London: Printed for J. Nourse and P. Vaillant, the Strand, 1750).
34. *Marbury*, 5 U.S. at 177.

3

Westward Expansion, the First Industrial Revolution, Dual Sovereignty, and the Public Trust Doctrine, 1835–1861

The Taney Court between 1836 and 1865 established both the doctrine of *dual federalism* and the *public trust doctrine*. This was the period of Westward expansion and the First Industrial Revolution. Because of the intensifying economic and industrial pressure placed on the young nation's natural resources and public lands, the Supreme Court was required to adopt an approach to federalism. Accordingly, the Taney Court advanced the federalist notion of *dual sovereignty*: while the federal government had been created under the US Constitution, states had an unqualified right to exist as *independent*, sovereign authorities. Consistent with this vision of states retaining broad, respective police powers over their citizens were the philosophical underpinnings of the public trust doctrine, as well as the landmark 1842 case that firmly secured its place and set the stage for the development of wildlife doctrine: *Martin v. Waddell's Lessee*.[1]

* * *

The Marshall Court's thirty-four-year term ended in 1835, paralleling the last five years of Andrew Jackson's eight-year term as president. By the time Roger B. Taney became chief justice following Marshall in 1836, the country was already rapidly expanding Westward, emboldened by free land and the biblical admonition of "Manifest destiny." The discovery of gold in California brought on the Gold Rush of 1849, populating the state at a dizzying rate. By midway through Taney's term, five additional states had joined the Union, for a total of thirty-five. The Erie Canal opened in 1825, creating a shipping route from the Great Lakes to the Atlantic Ocean, thus stimulating the economy of the East Coast—especially New York City. As Western cities sprang up along the nation's new railroad routes, major navigable rivers, and lakes, industry followed.

The development of blast furnaces fueled by cheap coal led to the production of iron products such as steam-powered railroad engines, iron rails, machine tools, and interchangeable machine parts. The development of manufactured iron became the dominant medium of the transportation infrastructure; it was later surpassed by steel. The first oil well was drilled in 1859 in Pennsylvania. Vulcanization of rubber by Charles Goodyear in the 1840s initiated the rubber industry, paving the way for rubber tires. Congress chartered the Bank of the United States in 1791, but Jefferson saw this as an unconstitutional expansion of federal power and let its charter expire in 1811, thus opening the door to state-chartered banks. By 1816, 246 state banks existed, providing capital for industry and commerce to expand.[2]

By the late 1820s, steam-powered freight railroads began operating, and the Baltimore and Ohio Railroad started offering passenger service in 1830.[3] The telegraph was invented in 1844, and telegraph lines followed the rail tracks with relay offices in the train stations along the way to keep the trains coordinated. The telegraph moreover transformed how the nation received its news and information within minutes. Agitation began for developing a transcontinental railroad and telegraph line to connect a growing population in California with the East Coast. It took eight to twelve months to go from the East Coast to California, either by boat around Cape Horn, across the Isthmus of Panama, or by land over the Rocky Mountains and Sierras; all options were fraught with perilous dangers.[4]

Robert Fulton developed the first commercial steamboat, operating on the Hudson River between New York City and Albany in 1807, and his boats in the Ohio and Mississippi Rivers followed in 1811. Newspapers evolved as the technique of extracting fiber from wood led to the early business of papermaking, refined much later in the 1800s. The first transatlantic cable became operational in 1866, two years after the Taney Court's term ended when the chief justice died at age eighty-eight.[5] The invention of the sewing machine in 1846 revolutionized the manufacture of clothing. The invention of the mechanical cotton gin by Eli Whitney in 1793 led to the epoch of King Cotton, and before the Civil War broke out in the mid-1800s, Southern plantations supplied 75 percent of the world's cotton. Textile mills fostered the development of production lines and factory workers, and the early Industrial Revolution revolved around the textile industry and the development of railroads. When the mills of E. I. du Pont in Delaware were created by the mid-1800s, they became the largest supplier of gunpowder to the US military. Steam power dominated the early 1800s, alleviating the need for factories and mills to locate adjacent rivers for water-driven power.[6]

THE DEVELOPMENT OF DUAL FEDERALISM AND THE PUBLIC TRUST DOCTRINE: THE TANEY COURT, 1836–1864

The great issue left unresolved by the Continental Congress and the US Constitution was slavery, which finally led to the Civil War (1861–1865), fought during Taney's last years, ending one year after his death.[7] The Thirteenth Amendment to the Constitution abolished slavery in 1865.

Roger Taney came from the Maryland planter elite, was a Roman Catholic, and a Democrat who staunchly advocated for states' rights. He was appointed chief justice in 1836 by Andrew Jackson near the end of his presidency.[8] The politically motivated Judiciary Act of 1837 increased the size of the Supreme Court from its initial six justices to nine.[9] Jackson and his successor, President Martin Van Buren, made sure the Court was dominated by Democratic states' rights advocates, most of whom supported the institution of slavery.[10] With early developments in transportation, industry and commerce, and interstate issues, divisive state regulations and private-property interests dominated the Taney Court's docket. The Jacksonian Democrats were pushing for Westward expansion, while the Federalist Republicans—now called the Whigs—wanted to limit expansion.[11]

While the explosive *Dred Scott* slavery case overshadows the historical character of the Taney Court,[12] the era of "dual federalism" began during this Court, the product of an effort to address the integration of state and federal affairs where they necessarily overlapped, while working to keep them in totally separate spheres, respecting the sovereignty of each. Taney's Court augmented state authority and maintained a philosophical, almost academic view of state versus national power.[13] The Commerce Clause was construed narrowly. Initially, the Taney Court saw mining, manufacturing, agriculture, and labor relations as *intrastate*—without a direct bearing on *interstate* commerce.[14] Tenth Amendment powers reserved to the states were considered sovereign powers, exclusive under the concept of "police powers"—which concept also emerged during this period[15]—and were thought to be unreachable by the federal government, not being among Congress's enumerated powers.[16] A classic description of the police power is found in the Vermont Supreme Court's opinion in *Thorpe v. Rutland and Burlington R.R.* (1854): "This police power of the state extends to the protection of the lives, limbs, health, comfort, and quiet of all persons, and the protection of all property within the state. According to the maxim, *Sic utere tuo ut alienum non laedas—Use your own property so as not to injure that of another*—which being of universal application, it must of course, be within the range of legislative action to define the mode and manner in which every one may so use his own as not to injure others."[17]

Early in the Taney Court, there was a clear separation of state and federal powers, each providing their own sources of revenue to support their separate governmental functions.[18] "Dual federalism was marked . . . [by] maintenance of the independent integrity of federal powers and state powers through separations of national and state spheres of action."[19] In *Abelman v. Booth*, the Court declared that "the powers of the general government, and the State, although both exist and are exercised within the same territorial limits, are yet separate and distinct sovereignties acting separately and independently of each other, within their respective spheres."[20] A recognition of the concept of dual federalism eventually appeared in the Court's thinking as national events prevailed. In 1950, legal scholar Edwin S. Corwin explicated "What I mean by Dual Federalism." "These postulates," he wrote, "are the following: 1. The national government is one of enumerated powers only; 2. Also the purposes which it may constitutionally promote are few; 3. Within their respective spheres the two centers of government are 'sovereign' and hence 'equal'; 4. The relation of the two centers with each other is one of tension rather than collaboration."[21]

This recognition of dual federalism resulted from the tremendous expansion of industrial enterprise and the Westward population growth that were forcing both the state and federal governments to cooperate and collaboratively address complex, overlapping issues facing them.[22] Concurrently, the growing pressure on the country's natural resources and its public lands forced the courts to adopt a public trust doctrine that could clearly define and protect the public estate. That doctrine was the foundation of the first environmental laws of the United States and is reflected in *Martin v. Waddell's Lessee*, decided by the Taney Court in 1842, addressing state authority over, and ownership of, natural resources,[23] and building on the 1823 *Corfield v. Coryell* case.[24] Chief Justice Taney's majority opinion was based on nebulous principles and ancient doctrines from the Institutes of Justinian (A.D. 529), the Magna Carta (1215), and the Charter of the Forest (1217, reissued 1225), which Taney described in detail. These declared the sovereign to be the trustee of the people's natural resources, which were to be held in trust for the benefit of the public.[25] This ancient concept became known in the United States as the *public trust doctrine*. While the *Waddell* public-trust holding applied only to the original thirteen states, three years later it was extended to all states in the Union.[26]

Besides holding that the sovereign is trustee of every natural resource for the benefit of the public, who are the beneficiaries,[27] the public trust doctrine creates a servitude or public easement running with the land (both publicly and privately owned), giving the public certain rights and a wide variety of uses and enjoyment of public resources. These public resources were originally defined in terms of maritime commerce, navigation, and fisheries and included the air, running water, the sea and its shores, tidelands, navigable waters, boating, and fishing. Since then, public perceptions of the values of nature have expanded in the United States. They have come to encompass recreational uses—such as bathing, swimming, sunbathing, hiking, bird-watching, fishing, hunting, and the pleasure of viewing nature's beauty and scenic wonders.[28] Moreover, a public trust in the tidelands (in addition to the seashore) has been recognized in light of their use as ecological units for scientific study, open space, and a source of food and habitat for birds and marine life.[29]

ANCIENT ORIGINS OF THE PUBLIC TRUST DOCTRINE

Earlier scholarship best shows the origins of the public trust doctrine,[30] its roots extending back to the Roman era. In the sixth century A.D., Roman emperor Justinian directed ten Roman jurists to aggregate Roman imperial law as accumulated since the second-century rule of Emperor Hadrian.[31] The jurists concentrated this law into a single overarching legal code—later known as the *Corpus Juris Civilis*[32]—comprised of four component parts: the Code, the *Digest (Pandects)*, the *Novels (New Laws)*, and the *Institutes of Justinian*.[33] The *Institutes* established the foundation of the Public Trust Doctrine[34] by providing that "things common to mankind by the law of nature, are the air, running water, the sea, and consequently the shores of the sea."[35] The purpose of this law was stated in the five accompanying sections of the *Institutes*.[36] Specifically, its express purpose was to protect the public's right to use certain public resources (the sea and the seashore) to fish and freely navigate.[37] The public rights (unencumbered access and use) were thus defined by the public's needs (fishing and navigation) of the public-trust resources (the sea and seashore).

Prior to the drafting of the Magna Carta, English citizens had little to no public-trust protections.[38] In a revolutionary moment in the thirteenth century, the Magna Carta—and Henry III's implementation of the Charter of the Forest in 1217—enshrined important legal protections for English citizens against state power, and included within this set of public interest protections was the Public Trust Doctrine.[39] Where the Roman doctrine had been adapted to the context of the Roman era, so was the English doctrine adapted to life in medieval England. The Magna Carta had established that certain public interests were paramount, such that certain rights (navigation, fishing, and commerce) were inherent to the public concerning certain public trust resources (water, navigable water bottoms, and tidelands), and it had further established that any title granted was subject to the inalienable rights of the public (*jus publicum*).[40] The public's interest in public resources was to be protected because "their natural and primary uses are public in their nature, for highways of navigation and commerce, domestic and foreign, and for the purpose of fishing by all the King's subjects."[41] Thus, as it had been in Roman law, the English version of the public trust doctrine was similarly defined by the needs of the public in the context of the place and time.[42]

Similarly, each of the original thirteen American colonies had developed its own common-law rules from English common law, to which they had originally remained subject, pursuant to their royal charters, which explicitly addressed the duty to conform Colonial law to English law and its sovereign Crown. After the Revolution, the people of each state became themselves sovereign, subject only to the enumerated rights surrendered under the US Constitution to the federal government. Hence the Roman and English concepts of the public trust doctrine were firmly embedded in America during the colonial era.

The US Supreme Court's 1824 *Gibbons v. Ogden* ruling held that state wildlife laws were immune from the national government's use of the Commerce Clause—just as the US Circuit Court for the Eastern District of Pennsylvania had determined in the 1823 *Corfield v. Coryell* case.[43] The Supreme Court held in 1842's *Martin v. Waddell's Lessee* that the tidelands, including the oyster beds, between the low water and high water marks were subject to the public trust doctrine that existed in England and through the original grants by the king that had become the law of the colonies: "When the revolution took place, the people of each state became themselves sovereign; and in that character hold the absolute right to all their navigable waters, and the soils under them, for their own common use, subject only to the rights since surrendered by the constitution to the general government."[44]

Chief Justice Taney, a states' rights advocate, wrote the forty-eight-page majority opinion in *Waddell*. His exhaustive review of the historical facts and law clearly answered the question of the states' sovereign rights and obligations relating to natural resources. Thirteen years later, in *Smith v. Maryland* the Court held that "the state's ownership of the soil [beneath navigable waters] conferred upon it the authority to regulate the taking of oysters from that soil."[45] In *Smith*, however, the Court found that because a ship owner was licensed by the United States to engage in coastal trade, he was protected from state regulation by the Interstate Commerce Clause.

For the first half of the nineteenth century, in repeated opinions issued under both Chief Justices Marshall and Taney, the Supreme Court expounded on the transfer of powers from the Crown to the new sovereign states following the American Revolution and the ratification of the US Constitution.

Their opinions were an extensively documented inventory of the royal charters granted to each of the Thirteen Colonies. All of the lands, the easements, the hereditaments, and the appurtenances attached, they found, were to be held in public trust for the Crown and were transferred after the Revolution to each of the sovereign states, to be held in trust for the benefit of the people.

SUMMARY

Federalism experienced its doctrinal iteration of of *dual federalism* during the US period of Westward expansion, complemented by the robust economic advancements generated and empowered by the first Industrial Revolution, which presented new, unanticipated challenges for the nation. Because of the innovative production of iron, steam-powered railroad engines, oil extraction, rubber, the telegraph, newspapers, the sewing machine, the cotton gin, gun powder, and the subsequent emergence of state banks to finance these economic enterprises, the Jeffersonian vision of an "agrarian" society—which would of necessity be cultivated in small communities—was fundamentally upended. Thus Alexander Hamilton had won the long-running debate about the future economic trajectory of the nation, and the United States quickly emerged as an industrial powerhouse. However, because of these developments, a new *political* movement surfaced in the nation—one that placed a premium on democratizing power, vesting more responsibility with states. President Andrew Jackson became the leading spokesperson for this new vision.

The nation's economic and industrial dynamism required the Supreme Court to adopt a vision of federalism that would account for these changes. The end of the Marshall Court in 1835 marked the end of a political era—one that had been defined by the pervasive influence of the Federalists and an emphasis placed on stabilizing a strong, central *national* government "fenced-in" by the doctrine of enumerated powers. Chief Justice Roger Taney had paradigmatically shifted the Court's view of federalism; crucially he guided the Court's jurisprudence away from a focus on national powers and more toward a *dual federalism* horizon, which safeguarded broad, reserved regulatory space secured under the Tenth Amendment for *states*. Under this framework, the Court continued to draw a bright line between federal and state powers. While the Court narrowly construed provisions of federal power—such as the Commerce Clause—the primary focus was preserving state power. In limiting the reach of federal power, the Court took seriously the assumed space for reserved "police powers" that had been guaranteed by the Tenth Amendment. Accordingly, one of the most important jurisprudential concepts that Chief

Justice Taney adopted during this time was the notion of the *mutual exclusivity* of federal and state powers. Because the federal government was assumed to be *more* limited, the Taney Court adopted the expansive view that states are *less* restricted by the Constitution.

While the lines had been drawn for the distribution of federal and state power under the Supreme Court's dual-federalism framework, the increasing economic and industrial pressures on the nation's natural resources and its public lands required the Taney Court to sufficiently develop and articulate a *public trust doctrine* that would safeguard the nation's precious resources in a manner that respected the allocation of power between the federal and state governments. Notably, the Court's landmark decision in *Martin v. Waddell's Lessee* (1842) reflected a foundational dual-federalism principle at play for the first time in US jurisprudence: the Court's recognition that *states* have *authority* over, and *ownership* of, natural resources. Indeed, *Waddell* represents the Court's vigorous attempt to protect states' reserved power to regulate activities within their own borders. Overall, because of the dual-federalism framework, the Supreme Court created the *space* for the public trust doctrine to grow under the provision of state governments.

NOTES

1. 41 U.S. 367 (1842).
2. Wikipedia, "Industrial Revolution in the United States."
3. Stephen E. Ambrose, *Nothing Like It in the World: The Men Who Built the Transcontinental Railroad, 1860–1897* (New York: Simon and Schuster, 2000), 25, 26.
4. Ambrose, *Nothing Like It in the World*, 42–57; see also Richard White, *Railroaded: The Transcontinentals and the Making of Modern America* (New York: W. W. Norton and Company, 2011).
5. Hoffer, Hoffer, and Hull, *Supreme Court*, 106.
6. See generally Independence Hall Association, "American History: From Pre-Columbian to the New Millennium," USHistory.org, accessed June 16, 2021, https://www.ushistory.org/us/index.asp; "Second Industrial Revolution," Wikipedia; B. G. DuPont, *E. I. DuPont De Nemours and Company: A History 1802–1902* (Boston and New York: Houghton Mifflin Company, 1920); Robert W. Fogel, *Railroads and American Economic Growth in Econometric History* (Baltimore and London: The Johns Hopkins University Press, 1964); George R. Taylor, *The Transportation Revolution, 1815–1860*, Economic History of the United States (Milton Park, Abingdon, Oxfordshire: Routledge, 1960); David A. Hounshell, *From the American System to Mass Production, 1800–1932: The Development of Manufacturing Technology in the United States* (Baltimore: The Johns Hopkins University Press, 1984); and Ian McNeill, *An Encyclopedia of the History of Technology* (London: Routledge, 1990).

7. Hoffer, Hoffer, and Hull, *Supreme Court*, 106.
8. Hoffer, Hoffer, and Hull, *Supreme Court*, 83–85.
9. Hoffer, Hoffer, and Hull, *Supreme Court*, 31, 84.
10. Hoffer, Hoffer, and Hull, *Supreme Court*, 84.
11. Hoffer, Hoffer, and Hull, *Supreme Court*, 88, 91.
12. Hoffer, Hoffer, and Hull, *Supreme Court*, 107; *Dred Scott v. Sandford*, 60 U.S. 393 (1856).
13. Louise Byer Miller, "The Burger Court's View of Federalism," *Policy Studies Journal* 13, no. 3 (1985): 576, 580.
14. Corwin, "Passing of Dual Federalism," 15–17.
15. Miller, "Burger Court's View," 576, 577–79.
16. Corwin, "Passing of Dual Federalism," 15–16.
17. Drahozal, *Supremacy Clause*, 113; and quotation from *Thorpe v. Rutland and Burlington R.R.*, 27 Vt. 140, (1854) (emphasis original).
18. Corwin, "Passing of Dual Federalism," 18.
19. John Kincaid, "From Dual to Coercive Federalism in American Intergovernmental Relations," in *Globalization and Decentralization: Institutional Contexts, Policy Issues, and Intergovernmental Relations in Japan and the United States*, ed. Jong S. Jun and Deil S. Wright (Washington, DC: Georgetown University Press, 1996), 29.
20. 62 U.S. 506, 516 (1858).
21. Corwin, "Passing of Dual Federalism," 4. For a discussion of the ideological thought, see also Richard A. Epstein and Michael S. Greve, "Conclusion: Preemption Doctrine and Its Limits," in *Federal Preemption: States' Powers, National Interests*, ed. Richard A. Epstein and Michael S. Greve (Washington, DC: AEI Press, 2007), 309.
22. This trend led to the slow absorption of state authority by the federal government. See Stephen Gardbaum, "The Breadth versus the Depth of Congress's Commerce Power: The Curious History of Preemption During the Lochner Era," in *Federal Preemption: States' Powers, National Interests*, ed. Richard A. Epstein and Michael S. Greve (Washington, DC: AEI Press, 2007), 72.
23. 41 U.S. 367, 411 (1842): "The grant to an individual of an exclusive fishery in any portion of [the state's dominion] is so much taken from the common fund entrusted to [the State's] care for the common benefit."

On the other hand, legal scholar George Cameron Coggins argues, that "The origins of modern federal wildlife law may be traced back to the MBTA [Migratory Bird Treaty Act]." George Cameron Coggins, "Federal Wildlife Law Achieves Adolescence: Developments in the 1970s," *Duke Law Journal* 27, no. 3 (1978): 753, 764, https://scholarship.law.duke.edu/cgi/viewcontent.cgi?article=2668&context=dlj.

24. 6 Fed. Cas. 546, No. 3, 230 (C.C.E.D. Pa. 1823).

The *Corfield* decision was reflective of an 1805 case that had solidified the common ownership of wildlife until possession. See *Pierson v. Post*, 3 Cai. R. 175 (N.Y. Sup. Ct. 1805).

25. In 1821, New Jersey's highest court was the first in the country to proclaim that "the sea, the fish, and the wild beasts" lay "in the hands of the sovereign power, to be held, protected and regulated for the common use and benefit." See *Arnold v. Mundy*, 6 N.J.L.1, 71 (N.J. 1821).

26. In *Pollard's Lessee v. Hagen*, 44 U.S. 212, 233 (1845).

27. Government "ownership" of land can be considered either proprietary or sovereign. *Proprietary ownership* provides for exclusion of trespassers, conveyance of interests, and other functions inherent to personal ownership of real property. *Sovereign ownership* entails "regulati[on], tax[ation], confer[ral of] citizenship and . . . other sovereign functions." Joseph Blocher, "Selling State Borders," *University of Pennsylvania Law Review* 162, no. 2 (2014): 241, 249–50, https://scholarship.law.upenn.edu/cgi/viewcontent.cgi?article=1544&context=penn_law_review.

28. See *Fairchild v. Kraemer*, 11 App. Div. 2d 232, 204 N.Y.S. 2d 823 (1960); and *Wilbour v. Gallagher*, 77 Wash. 2d 306, 462 P.2d 232 (1969).

29. *Marks v. Whitney*, 6 Cal.3d 251 (1971); *Forestier v. Johnson*, 164 Cal. 24127, 156 (1912); *National Audubon Society v. Superior Court of Alpine County*, 33 Cal. 3d 419, 658 P. 2d 709 (1983).

30. For the very best article probably ever written on the subject, see Joseph L. Sax, "The Public Trust Doctrine in Natural Resource Law: Effective Judicial Intervention," *Michigan Law Review* 68, no. 3 (1970): 471–566, https://repository.law.umich.edu/cgi/viewcontent.cgi?article=4782&context=mlr. For a more recent article expounding on the public trust doctrine, see Susan M. Horner, "Embryo, Not Fossil: Breathing Life into Public Trust in Wildlife," *Land & Water Law Review* 35, no. 1 (2000): 23–53, https://scholarship.law.uwyo.edu/cgi/viewcontent.cgi?article=2127&context=land_water.

31. Charles Donahue Jr., "On Translating the 'Digest,'" Review of *The Digest of Justinian*, trans. and ed. Theodore Mommsen, Paul Krueger, and Alan Watson, *Stanford Law Review* 39, no. 4 (1987): 1057.

The public trust doctrinal component of Justinian's Institutes could have come from Roman jurist Marcian. See Richard A. Hughes, "Pro-justice Ethics, Water Scarcity, Human Rights," *Journal of Law & Religion* 25, no. 2 (2009–2010): 521, 529 (which cites Patrick Deveney, "Title, Jus Publicum, and the Public Trust: An Historical Analysis," *Sea Grant Law Journal* 1 [1976]: 13, 23, suggesting that Roman law's notion of "things common to all" is traceable to the works of the Roman jurist Marcian).

Further, much of Justinian's Institutes were drawn from second-century Roman jurist Gaius. See "Justinian Code," in Bryan A. Gardner, ed., *Black's Law Dictionary*, 11th ed. (St. Paul, MN: Thomson Reuters, 2019).

32. The Corpus Juris Civilis is occasionally called the Code of Justinian, but this is confusing, as the Code of Justinian is one of the four components of the overarching Corpus Juris Civilis. See "Justinian Code" in Garner, *Black's Law Dictionary*, 11th ed.

33. Donahue, "On Translating the 'Digest,'" 1058; "Corpus Juris Civilis," in Garner, *Black's Law Dictionary*, 11th ed.

34. US Courts consistently point to the Justinian Institutes as the original seed of the modern public trust doctrine. See, for example, *PPL Montana, LLC v. Montana*, 565 U.S. 576, 603 (2012); Gowanus Indus. *Park, Inc. v. Amerada Hess Corp.*, No. 01-CV-0902 (ILG), 2003 WL 22076651, at *14 (S.D.N.Y. Sept. 5, 2003); *Matthews v. Bay Head Improvement Ass'n*, 471 A.2d 355, 360 (N.J. 1984) (citation omitted);

National Audubon Society v. Superior Court of Alpine County, 658 P.2d 709, 718 (Cal. 1983) (citation omitted); *State v. Sorensen*, 436 N.W.2d 358, 361 (Iowa 1989) (citation omitted); *Lawrence v. Clark County*, 254 P.3d 606, 608 (Nev. 2011); *Glass v. Goeckel*, 703 N.W.2d 58, 63–64 (Mich. 2005) (citation omitted); *City of Montpelier v. Barnett*, 2012 VT 32, 17, 191 Vt. 441, 450, 49 A.3d 120, 127 (2012) (citation omitted); and *Rettkowski v. Dep't of Ecology*, 858 P.2d 232, 243 (Wash. 1993) (citation omitted).

35. While there are slight variances in translations of the Institutes of Justinian, the version quoted here is the one quoted by the Louisiana Supreme Court in 1887, in *Morgan v. Negodich et al.* (40 La. Ann. 246, 251 [La. 1887]).

In full, sections 1 through 5 of the *Morgan* decision provide that

> (1) Things common to mankind by the law of nature, are the air, running water, the sea, and consequently the shores of the sea; no man therefore is prohibited from approaching any part of the sea-shore, whilst he abstains from damaging farms, monuments, edifices, & c. which are not in common as the sea is. (2) Rivers and ports are public; hence the right of fishing in a port, or in rivers are in common. (3) All that tract of land, over which the greatest winter flood extends itself, is the sea-shore. (4) By the law of nations, the use of the banks is as public as the rivers; therefore, all persons are at equal liberty to land their vessels, unload them, and to fasten ropes to trees upon the banks, as to navigate upon the river itself; still, the banks of a river are the property of those who possess the land adjoining; and therefore, the trees which grow upon them, are also the property of the same persons. (5) The use of the seashore, as well as of the sea, is also public by the law of nations; and therefore, any person may erect a cottage upon it, to which he may resort to dry his nets, and haul them from the water; for the shores are not understood to be property in any man, but are compared to the sea itself, and to the sand or ground which is under the sea.

See also Justinian I, *The Institutes of Justinian*, 3rd ed., notes Thomas Cooper, trans. George Harris (New York: J. S. Voorhies, 1852), tit. I, §§ 1–5, at 67.

36. Morgan v. Negodich *et al.*, 40 La. Ann. 246, 251 (La. 1887).

37. Morgan v. Negodich *et al.*, 40 La. Ann. 246, 251 (La. 1887).

38. Kelly Lowry, "Zoning the Water: Using the Public Trust Doctrine as a Basis for a Comprehensive Water-Use Plan in Coastal South Carolina," *South Carolina Environmental Law Journal* 5 (1996): 79, 97.

39. The US Supreme Court, however, placed the public trust doctrine in seventeenth-century England, where, "from the time of Lord Hale, it has been treated as settled that the title in the soil of the sea, or of arms of the sea, below ordinary high water mark, is in the King . . . and that this title, *jus privatum* . . . is held subject to the public right, *jus publicum*, of navigation and fishing." *Shively v. Bowlby et al.* 152 U.S. 1, 13 (1894) (emphasis original).

40. Helen Ingram and Cy R. Oggins, "The Public Trust Doctrine and Community Values in Water," *Natural Resources Journal* 32, no. 3 (1992): 517, 518, https://digital repository.unm.edu/cgi/viewcontent.cgi?article=1966&context=nrj (citing Charles Wilkinson, "The Headwaters of the Public Trust: Some Thoughts on the Source and Scope of the Traditional Doctrine," Environmental Law 19, no. 3 (1989): 425, 430).

41. Shiveley, 152 U.S. at 11.

42. Donahue, "On Translating the 'Digest,'" 1057.

43. *Gibbons v. Ogden,* 22 U.S. 1 (1824); and *Corfield v. Coryell,* 6 Fed. Cas. 546, No. 3230 (C.C.E.D. Pa. 1823).

44. *Martin v. Waddell's Lessee,* 41 U.S. 367, 410 (1842).

See also *Pollard's Lessee v. Hagen,* 44 U.S. 212, 233 (1845); *Ward v. Race Horse,* 163 U.S. 504 (1896); and *Arnold v. Mundy,* 6 N.J.L. 1, 71 (N.J. 1821).

45. 59 U.S. 71, (1855).

4

The Civil War, Reconstruction, the Advent of the Second Industrial Revolution, the Enduring Public Trust Doctrine, and State Ownership of Wildlife, 1861–1896

The notion of dual federalism continued to develop through the Civil War, Reconstruction, and the advent of the Second Industrial Revolution, throughout the second half of the nineteenth century. An important application was wildlife, continuing dual federalism's development from *Waddell* and decisions that followed. A key example was *McCready v. Virginia* (1876), in which the Supreme Court held that states have "ownership" over wildlife.[1] Indeed, *McCready* recognized that *states* have authority to regulate wildlife affairs. Thus the public trust doctrine, as construed by the Court in *Geer v. Connecticut* (1896) and in *Illinois Central Railroad Co. v. Illinois* (1892), further clarified that states had ultimate control, but only insofar as that they *protected* the public trust.[2]

* * *

Early in the evolution of the law of preemption and states' rights, the Civil War created an economic, political, and legal crisis. The Thirteenth Amendment ending slavery in the United States presented a dramatic loss of wealth of landowners as slaves became free and left Southern plantations. During the end of the Civil War and throughout the beginning of Reconstruction, national power was considerably augmented at the expense of state sovereignty following the adoption of the Thirteenth (1865), Fourteenth (1868), and Fifteenth (1870) Amendments. These amendments had to do with forcing eleven states to accept the abolishment of slavery, guaranteeing men the right to vote regardless of race, and defining the elements of citizenship, including due process, equal rights, and individual privileges and immunities. The amendments' implementation required federal enforcement and administration in each state as well as acts of Congress—including the Civil Rights Acts of 1866 and 1871 and the Reconstruction Act of 1867. Moreover, under the power of the Supremacy Clause, the federal government forced recalcitrant state sheriffs, prosecutors, and courts into facilitating federal enforcement measures,[3] curtailing part of state sovereignty. However, constitutional repercussions from the Civil War were just part of a larger story of the United States in the mid-1800s.

During one period straddling the Civil War and Reconstruction, 1842 and 1876, two significant cases, *Waddell* and *McCready*, developed the state public trust doctrine based on ownership of state wildlife and natural resources. This period also marked the earliest days of the Second Industrial Revolution, the dawning on a reliance on science and mass production. Historian James McPherson characterizes this period as the most productive in US history, with the government promoting socioeconomic development. The thirty-seventh Congress alone (1860–1862) drafted "the blueprint for modern America," enacting laws revolutionizing the country's tax and monetary structures, with an internal revenue tax on virtually every commodity and product, and a progressive income tax just at the time the US Treasury was virtually insolvent. The income tax was later repealed in 1872. A national currency of legal tender was created, allowing the government to issue paper money redeemable in gold, along with a US bond market whereby the government could raise money, and a national banking system was established.[4]

The disruption of the Civil War did not stop the aggressive development of the railroad system throughout the United States.[5] The Pacific Railroad Act of 1862 granted the railroads 6,400 acres of free public land per mile—later doubled and eventually totaling 120 million acres. It also granted a subsidy of $16,000 per mile on tracks laid on the plains and $48,000 per mile in the mountains to support rail construction spanning from Omaha to San Francisco.[6] The transcontinental railroad was completed when the east and west extensions were joined at Promontory Point in Utah on May 10, 1869, completing continuous connecting rail lines from New York to San Francisco, a trip that took seven days.[7] By then, forty-five thousand miles of rails had been laid in the United States, and by 1900 the total was 215,000 miles.[8] This necessitated the creation of the Interstate Commerce Commission in 1887 to regulate railroads and shipping rates and interstate commerce.[9]

Few mentally connect the West to the industrial growth of the Midwest and Northeast, and the concentration of capital and enormous wealth. However, the development of the West immediately following the Civil War played a critical role in the transformation of the United States, and by the 1880s US beef production had become a prime example of how corporate America operated. Railroads and the telegraph enabled ranchers to ship cattle from all over the West to the slaughterhouses and meat-processing plants in Kansas City, Chicago, and Cincinnati. The butchered beef parts were then shipped by rail to regional markets through the East, Mid-Atlantic, and South. All of it was coordinated and tied together by the telegraph on a national scale. Organized in 1883, the Swan Land and Cattle Company in Wyoming was the state's largest ranch, at six hundred thousand acres. Controlled by Scottish investors, the ranch was initially capitalized at $3.75 million and later increased to $50 million. Scottish capitalists also developed the Matador Land and Cattle Company in Texas and expanded it into Colorado, Wyoming, and the Dakotas.[10] In fact, "by 1886, four states and territories—Montana, Wyoming, Colorado, and New Mexico—alone hosted 439 corporate ranches capitalized at nearly $170 million."[11] Ranching had become as much a part of the industrial United States as were iron, steel, petroleum, timber, and the railroads. The closest precursor would have been the Hudson Bay Company's fur and mercantile business, which spanned all of Canada. At this point in US history, "ranching was an industry, a nationalized arrangement of regional specialization, modern transport, and noisome factories. A ranch in the Dakotas or Wyoming was one part of a far larger system that in turn was part of the very economic order."[12]

The 425-mile Erie Canal, completed in 1825, intensified industrial development in the East and Midwest. Connecting the Great Lakes and the Atlantic Ocean via the Hudson River, the canal became a major shipping route. Tributary canals into the Erie Canal followed.[13] These new transportation routes in turn spurred industry to expand along this new national distribution system of freight trains and barges. King Cotton's exports now spanned the globe, in turn fostering the development of textile mills and associated industry along the Atlantic seaboard. In this atmosphere of change and expansion, the applied and the natural sciences flourished with new discoveries. It was during this period, in 1866, that the term "ecology" began to be used and was developed into a field of study, later transforming into a discipline of multifaceted scientific dimensions and professions.[14] The early United States' naturalist and science academicians, scholars, writers, and theorists were emerging during this period, including George Perkins Marsh and O. C. Marsh, in the shadow of Charles Darwin and others.

Undoubtedly, the biggest elements of US expansion of the time were population growth and Westward settlement. In 1800, the US population had been 5,308,483. In 1850 it was already 23,191,876, and by 1875 it had grown to 43,991,069.[15]

On May 20, 1862, the Homestead Act gave 160 acres of free public land to any settler upon five years' residence and after improvements had been made to the land, including the building of houses, barns, and fences and clearing

Figure 4.1. *The Spirit of the Frontier*, an oil painting by John Gast (1872), depicts the notion of Manifest Destiny, with American settlers moving Westward, guided and protected by Columbia, who represents American and classical republicanism. The settlers are aided by the technological innovations of the railroad and telegraph—driving Native Americans and bison into obscurity. Columbia is bringing the "light" (signifying enlightenment) from the eastern side of the painting toward the darkened west. *Source*: Library of Congress.

the land. A half million families settled eighty million acres of homestead land west of the Mississippi River. The creation of the Department of Agriculture followed that same year. The Morrill Act of 1862 gave every state thirty thousand acres of public land for each of its members of Congress on which to build schools of higher education in agriculture and the mechanical arts. From that evolved the land grant colleges and universities, many of which would go on to become first-class, world-famous institutions. These land-grant colleges became the foundation for scientific wildlife management research and education some seventy years later.

All totaled, 225 million acres of public lands were given away for railroads, homesteads, and educational institutions out of the country's two billion acres of public lands. "This new America of big business, heavy industry, and capital-intensive agriculture . . . surpassed England to become the foremost industrial nation by 1880 and the world's bread basket for much of the twentieth century."[16] Historians Charles Beard and Mary Beard label this era the Second American Revolution.[17]

THE ENDURING PUBLIC TRUST DOCTRINE AND STATE OWNERSHIP OF WILDLIFE

During the nineteenth century, US courts generally favored state control of wildlife based on the original doctrine of state "ownership" of all natural resources, and on states' rights to protect their resources and food supplies by regulating the harvest of fish, wildlife, and natural resources. These principles were thought immune from any federal claims to resources that might have been based in interpretations of the Commerce Clause.[18] The first case following *Martin v. Waddell's Lessee* (1842) relating to state sovereignty over wildlife and the public trust doctrine was 1876's *McCready v. Virginia*. The Supreme Court went so far as to declare that states actually "owned" the fish and wildlife resources of their public trust lands and waters.[19] States control their natural resources so as to protect their citizens' food supply, the Court found, was immune from the reach of the federal government under the Commerce Clause. The *McCready* case affirmed *Waddell* together with twenty other cases cited as authority for the decision.[20]

In a later case, distinguished legal scholar and Supreme Court Justice Felix Frankfurter put the *McCready* holding in its historical perspective:

> When the Constitution was adopted, such, no doubt, was the common understanding regarding the power of States over its fisheries, and it is this common understanding that was reflected in *McCready v. Virginia*. The *McCready* case is not an isolated decision to be looked at askance. It is the symbol of one of the weightiest doctrines in our law. It expressed the momentum of legal history that preceded it, and around it in turn has clustered a voluminous body of rulings. Not only has a host of State cases applied the *McCready* doctrine as to the power of States to control their game and fisheries for the benefit of their own citizens, but in our own day this Court formulated the amplitude of the *McCready* doctrine by referring to "the regulation or the distribution of the public domain, or of the common property or resources of the people of the state, the enjoyment of which may be limited to its citizens as against both aliens and the citizens of other states (*Truax v. Raich*)."[21]

The fundamental legal principle of state sovereignty over wildlife was then considered so impregnable that it wasn't even litigated until 1896, over one hundred years after the Tenth Amendment to the US Constitution had been ratified.[22] In the landmark 1896 case *Geer v. Connecticut*,[23] which addressed market hunting, Supreme Court Justice Edward Douglass White Jr. went historically deep by first examining the laws of nature as they relate to a person's right to hunt and possess wild game (*animals ferae naturae*). Justice White then, in the context of the public good, discussed sovereign powers under Athenian law, Salic law, Charlemagne, the sixth-century Institutes of Justinian classified by the Roman law, the Magna Carta, the Napoleonic Code, and then Sir William Blackstone's *Commentaries on the Laws of England*. Justice White's examination of ancient precedents outlines an unbroken, centuries-old line of sovereign rights over the public trust and the states' ownership of wildlife; hence their authority over the right to hunt and possess wild game and regulate the use of wildlife following possession.

In *Geer* the Court held that the state could lawfully prohibit the export of game lawfully killed within the state.[24] *Geer* reinforced the states' ownership of game, from the 1876 *McCready* precedent, until wild game was reduced to possession by a hunter. *Geer* was one of the most important cases in the evolution of the public trust doctrine in wildlife law. The question before the *Geer* Court was whether the state had the authority to prosecute the defendant for possession of lawfully killed game birds with the intent to transport and sell them across the state's border in violation of state law and whether their statute violated the Commerce Clause of the US Constitution.

"The solution to the question," the Court said, "involves a consideration of the nature of the property in game and the authority, which the State had a right lawfully to exercise in relation thereto."[25] The Court's initial analysis addressed the question of what kind of property right attaches to wild animals in their natural state. They concluded that both state's right to control and ownership of the killing of game under their police power had been vested in colonial governments by the English Crown, and therefore could be exercised by the states provided they didn't govern in a manner that would conflict with the Commerce Clause.[26]

The Court then concluded with a statement that embodies the heart of the modern-day public trust doctrine in wildlife. "Whilst the fundamental principles upon which the common property in game rests have undergone no change," it stated, "the development of free institutions has led to the recognition of the fact that the power or control lodged in the State, resulting from the common ownership, is to be exercised, like all other powers of government, as a trust for the benefit of all people, and not as a prerogative for the advantage of the government, as distinct from the people, or for the benefit of private individuals as distinguished from the public."[27]

As the US population continued to explode throughout the twentieth century, putting more and more pressure on the country's natural resources and public lands, the accompanying industrialization brought greed, corruption, and collusion, especially as railroads expanded. In this era of monopolies, industrial empires, and robber barons, railroads were particularly egregious in shirking their public responsibilities. Unrestrained industrial progress during the Gilded Age of the late nineteenth and early twentieth centuries induced the Court to stringently protect the public estate and sharpen the public trust doctrine, together with the expansion of the definition of what constitutes interstate commerce.

An 1892 landmark case demonstrating a heinous violation of the public trust between politicians and a railroad enabled the Supreme Court to further define and expand the reach of the public trust doctrine necessary to protecting the public estate. In 1970, legal scholar Joseph Sax called the 1892 case of *Illinois Central Railroad Company v. Illinois* the "Lodestar in American Trust Law."[28] He thus characterized the decision because of Justice Stephen J. Field's erudite analysis defining sovereignty and the public trust doctrine, and the limits thereof, in the face of outrageous abuse by the Illinois legislature. The state legislature had been co-opted by the Illinois Central Railroad to grant them title to submerged lands one mile from the shoreline and extending one mile in length and one thousand to four thousand feet in width along the entire frontage of Lake Michigan adjacent to the central business district of Chicago, Illinois (1,000 acres). The railroad company planned to build tracks, depots, warehouses, docks, wharves, piers, and related structures, thus creating a harbor for the city of Chicago. The Supreme Court overruled this Illinois legislative action and declared the transaction null and void. The grant was a total corruption of the states' public trust responsibilities and police powers, the Court found, and an abdication to a private party of its legislative authority over navigation of the entire waterfront of a major city.[29] The extent of the *Geer* and *Illinois Central* opinions just four years apart indicate the Fuller Supreme Court's resolve at the end of the nineteenth century and the first decade of the twentieth to clearly define and protect the concept of public trust, just years after the Taney Court.

Given the explosive expansion of industrial and technological development in the United States that touched all levels of the nation's socioeconomic development, one can readily understand why Professor Edward S. Corwin characterized this period as "dual federalism" beginning under the Taney Court.[30] The crosscurrents of state and federal laws and regulations overlapping and conflicting in so many areas of human endeavor provided fertile ground for legislation and regulations governing the same issues and affairs of the day, which forced a cooperative working relationship between state and federal governments.

SUMMARY

The nation's understanding of dual federalism reached a new level of sophistication during the last half of the nineteenth century. Given the arrival of the Second Industrial Revolution, which produced exponential economic growth as well as advancements in science and technology, the Supreme Court had to confront the new *exogenous* forces threatening the public trust. Under both the Homestead Act (1862) and the Morill Act (1862), Congress had already incentivized the acquisition of public land for *private* use. Therefore, the most important questions remained unanswered: *Who* would protect the nation's precious natural resources, and what would be the *extent* of that legal protection provided?

During this period, state sovereignty over wildlife endured: The principle had become entrenched in the rule of law, and the Supreme Court upheld its meaning. Most fundamentally, the canonical *Waddell* and following decisions were later affirmed in *McCready v. Virginia* (1876), where the Court held that states have direct "ownership" over wildlife. Indeed, as Justice Frankfurter memorably wrote of *McCready* in 1948, the decision had become a "symbol of one of the weightiest doctrines in our law," further "express[ing] the momentum of legal history that preceded it."[31] At the core of *McCready* was—again—a doctrinal recognition that *states*—not the federal government—have the authority to regulate wildlife under their police powers. In short, dual federalism had become the default method for resolving these issues.

While the question of who had the authority to regulate wildlife had been made clear by the Court, the question of the *scope* of the public trust doctrine remained indeterminate. However, the Court had the institutional resolve to provide clarification in the midst of economic pressure and technological change. In both *Geer v. Connecticut* (1896) and *Illinois Central Railroad Company v. Illinois* (1892), the Supreme Court further defined the reach of the doctrine to clarify a broad, organizing principle: states have the sovereign governing authority to regulate lands within their borders, but only insofar as that authority *protects*—and does not diminish—the public trust. Thus, the principle announced in *Waddell* had withstood the test of time under the Supreme Court's dual-federalism jurisprudence, which protected state sovereignty.

However, with the economic and technological advancements on the horizon with the Progressive Movement, the overlap between federal and state authorities would pose *new* legal challenges.

NOTES

1. 94 U.S. 391 (1876).
2. *Geer v. Connecticut*, 161 U.S. 519 (1896); and *Illinois Central Railroad Co. v. Illinois*, 146 U.S. 387 (1892).
3. Hoffer, Hoffer, and Hull, *Supreme Court*, 122–23, 114–24.
4. James M. McPherson, *Battle Cry for Freedom: The Civil War Era* (New York and Oxford: Oxford University Press, 1988), 450, 452, and 442–50.
5. Ambrose, *Nothing Like It*, 63–167; White, *Railroaded*, 17, 50, 466–67, 477.
6. McPherson, *Battle Cry for Freedom*, 451.

One historian figures the federal government gave the railroads 180 million acres to subsidize their expansion. See White, *Railroaded*, 3, 17, 50, 466–67, 477. Also see Elliott West, *Theodore Roosevelt: Naturalist in the Arena*, ed. Char Miller and Clay S. Jenkinson (Lincoln: University of Nebraska Press, 2020), 170.

7. "Second Industrial Revolution," Wikipedia; and Ambrose, *Nothing Like It*, 369.
8. "History of Rail Transportation in the United States," Wikipedia, last modified June 18, 2021, https://en.wikipedia.org/wiki/History_of_rail_transportation_in_the_United_States.
9. US Congress, *Interstate Commerce Act of 1887*, Pub. L. No. 49–104, 24 Stat. 379 (1887), https://www.ourdocuments.gov/print_friendly.php?flash=true&page=transcript&doc=49.
10. Harmon Ross Mothershead, *The Swan Land and Cattle Company, Ltd.* (Norman: University of Oklahoma Press, 1971); and William Martin Pearce, *The Matador Land and Cattle Company* (Norman: University of Oklahoma Press, 1964).
11. West, *Theodore Roosevelt*, 170.
12. West, *Theodore Roosevelt*, 169.
13. Daniel Walker Howe, *What Hath God Wrought: The Transformation of America, 1815–1848* (New York: Oxford University Press, 2009), 116–20, 138, 221–22, 563, 565.
14. See generally R. P. McIntosh, *The Background of Ecology: Concept and Theory* (New York: Cambridge University Press, 1986).
15. US Census Bureau, "Pop Culture: 1800," History, last modified December 17, 2020, https://www.census.gov/history/www/through_the_decades/fast_facts/1800_fast_facts.html; US Census Bureau, "Pop Culture: 1850," History, last modified December 17, 2020, https://www.census.gov/history/www/through_the_decades/fast_facts/1850_fast_facts.html; US Census Bureau, *Statistical Abstract of the United States: 1900* (Washington, DC: US Government Printing Office, 1901), downloadable at https://www.census.gov/library/publications/1901/compendia/statab/23ed.html.
16. McPherson, *Battle Cry for Freedom*, 450–52, and quotation at 452.
17. McPherson, *Battle Cry for Freedom*, 450–52.
18. These decisions include *Gibbons v. Ogden*, 22 U.S. 1 (1824); *Smith v. Maryland*, 59 U.S. 71 (1855); and *Manchester v. Commonwealth of Massachusetts*, 139 U.S. 240 (1891).

Shortly after *Manchester*, the same Fuller Court again resolutely protected public use of navigable waters and their tidelands as part of the *jus publicum* held in trust by the state. See *Shively v. Bowlby et al.* 152 U.S. 1 (1894). In this decision, the Court goes back as far as 1807 in its citations of authority referencing the earliest recorded judicial statement then prevailing and does a complete inventory of all the states' laws and cases relative to the issue. *Shively* at 30–32 (citing *Carson v. Blazer*, 2 Binn. 475, 477–78 [Penn. 1807]).

19. *McCready v. Virginia*, 94 U.S. 391, 395 (1876).

20. *McCready* 94 U.S., at 394–95.

21. *Toomer v. Witsell*, 334 U.S. 385, 408-09 (1948) (Frankfurter, J., concurring; internal citation omitted).

22. Throughout the 1700s and 1800s, US wildlife populations that had once been considered inexhaustible were being slowly diminished by individual and market hunting to feed and clothe the growing population. Further, wildlife was decimated by the loss of habitat and connective migration corridors from fragmentation of the land as settlers cleared land for their farms and as lumberjacks leveled forests for lumber to build towns and cities; both miners and factories polluted streams and rivers with industrial-grade poisons, and railroads bifurcated the national landscape. During this period, certain events tangentially border on preemption in the wildlife arena, to be sure. Thorough analyses of the primary and secondary preemptive actions into state wildlife authority by the federal government, especially in the 1800s (and thereafter), are detailed in several sources.

An exhaustive retrospective analysis was done in 1912 by the US Biological Survey, in *Chronology and Index of the More Important Events in American Game Protection, 1776–1911*, written by T. S. Palmer, assistant chief of the Biological Survey (Washington, DC: Government Printing Office). This sixty-two-page monograph contains a detailed and narrative history of the evolution of the depletion of wildlife stocks, all game laws and regulations enacted by every state to control hunting from 1776 to 1911, and a chronological index of species, states, laws, and so on.

Also see John F. Reiger, *American Sportsmen and the Origins of Conservation* (Corvallis: Oregon State University Press, 2001), 5–104; John B. Trefethen, *An American Crusade for Wildlife* (New York: Winchester Press, 1975); Shannon Petersen, "Congress and Charismatic Megafauna: A Legislative History of the Endangered Species Act," *Environmental Law* 29, no. 2 (1999): 467–69; Shannon Petersen, "The Modern Ark: A History of the Endangered Species Act," PhD diss., University of Wisconsin–Madison, 2000, pp. 13–24; and Shannon Petersen, *Acting for Endangered Species* (Lawrence: University of Kansas Press, 2002). Also see Bean and Rowland, *Evolution of National Wildlife Law*, 19; and US Statutes at Large, vol. 27, proclamation no. 39, 27, stat. 1052 (1892), https://memory.loc.gov/cgi-bin/ampage?collId=amrvl&fileName=vl153//amrvlvl153.db&recNum=0&itemLink=r?ammem/AMALL:@field(NUMBER+@band(amrvl+vl153))&linkText=0.

Petersen references earlier actions by the federal government that touched on state jurisdiction. He starts by examining hunting laws that had been established in 1694 by the Massachusetts Bay Colony and by several New York counties in 1708. Thereafter, he reviews wildlife laws promulgated by several states based on the public trust doctrine and the case law that followed. He follows with the story of the buffalo and Congress's attempts to suspend all killing thereof in 1874 by the Lacey Act of 1864, which was foiled when President Grant pocket vetoed the bill. In 1876 a similar bill was passed in the House but failed in the Senate. Thereafter, the 1868 congressional act prohibiting the killing of certain fur-bearing animals in the territory of Alaska was enacted. In 1871 the Office of the US Commissioner of Fish and Fisheries was established to conserve fisheries along the coasts and navigable waterways.

The Forest Reserve Act of 1891 authorized the creation of national forests on unceded public lands to protect and ensure a continuing source of timber for an expanding nation and to protect water and wildlife from overexploitation. Hunting in Yellowstone National Park was prohibited by the Lacey Act of 1894, and in 1906 all hunting of birds on lands set aside for their breeding grounds was prohibited. President Harrison in 1892 reserved Alaska's Afognak Island to protect salmon fisheries in the island's waters and to protect other sea animals, fish, and birds. See Petersen, "Modern Ark," 13–24; Bean and Rowland, *Evolution of National Wildlife Law*, 19; and US Statutes at Large, vol. 27, proclamation no. 39, stat. 1052 (1892).

This history and result of diminishing wildlife populations, while far beyond the central theme of this chapter, is the story that underlies state authority over its resident wildlife and the ensuing federal preemption thereof. It moreover forced the United States and its courts to develop a clearer recognition and definition of the public trust doctrine and underscored the national need to protect the public estate.

23. 161 U.S. 519 (1896).

24. Justice White's opinion, while expansive and historically educational, was narrow in the decision, as justices a century later would so characterize it. A later 1928 Supreme Court case, *Foster-Fountain Packing Company v. Haydel*, held that "a state terminates its absolute control over the use of wildlife once it permits part or all of the wildlife to enter the stream of commerce." Bean and Rowland, *Evolution of National Wildlife Law*, 23 (citing *Foster-Fountain Packing Company v. Haydel*, 278 U.S. 1, 5 [1928]).

25. *Geer*, 161 U.S., at 522.

26. Horner, "Embryo, Not Fossil," 6–8.

27. *Geer*, 161 U.S., at 539.

28. Sax, "Public Trust Doctrine," 489, and see generally 471–566; also see *Illinois Central Railroad Co. v. Illinois*, 146 U.S. 387 (1892).

29. Sax, "Public Trust Doctrine," 489.

30. Corwin, "Passing of Dual Federalism," 15–19, 22.

31. *McCready v. Virginia*, 94 U.S. 391, (1876).

5

America's Changing Culture: Market Hunting, the Lacey Act, the Migratory Bird Treaty Act, and the Beginning of the Progressive Era, 1896–1910

The Progressive Era developed between 1896 and 1910. The growing commercial market for hunting for food and apparel from wildlife prompted swift national legislative responses that resulted in passage of the Lacey Act of 1900, which outlawed interstate trade in animal parts, and the Migratory Bird Treaty Act of 1918, both of which became a foundation for environmental preemption. The latter act eliminated—for the first time—*sole* state control of migratory birds, creating a regulatory floor for federal involvement in the supervision of wildlife. This development featured the arrival of a competing ideological vision for federalism. Indeed, while dual federalism remained the dominant model for federalism, the arrival of progressivism posed a new, formidable challenge to assumptions about the nature of dual power between federal and state governments.

* * *

The near demise of the buffalo and the massive commercial slaughter of game by market hunters, who had become the purveyors of fresh meat to urban areas, prompted the first major change in the United States' use of wildlife as the national food supply. It also forced changes in the law. Commercial market hunting and vanishing wildlife forced the courts to address the issue of federal preemption of state control over wildlife. The changing societal demands in the late 1800s underlying *Geer v. Connecticut* (1896) reflected America's growth and urbanization. Cities and urban areas had become populated, with inhabitants now living far removed from agrarian areas where food was abundant, especially fresh wild meat, fowl, and seafood.

The commercial slaughter of wildlife for food was made practical by industrial-made repeating rifles with telescopic lenses that could kill a deer or buffalo at over three hundred yards. New shotguns designed with modified barrels—some double-barreled—were deadly accurate, killing field and woodland birds, pheasants, quail, woodcock, ruffed grouse, and pigeons. At night, waterfowl hunters mounted gigantic punt guns (shotguns) resembling small cannons on the front of sneak or punt boats (skiffs) that silhouetted almost at the waterline and used spotlights illuminating and blinding sleeping waterfowl. A punt gun could scatter lead shot over a field of fire eight to twelve feet wide, killing up to twenty-five birds at once.

These market hunters harvested migratory waterfowl, insectivorous and neotropical birds, seafood, deer, elk, moose, bear and buffalo (primarily for their tongues and hides), squirrel, rabbits, ermine, sable, marten, and beaver (for men's top hats). Colorful feathers from tropical birds were used to decorate fine ladies' hats by the millinery trade.[1] At the height of the "plume boom," the US fashion industry purchased five million wild bird skins annually, representing fifty different species, with American egret plumes (called aigrettes) and roseate spoonbill skins most favored.

There are no records of how many birds were killed to decorate ladies' hats and related apparel at the turn of the twentieth century, but one market hunter was reported to have killed thirty thousand birds in one year alone and sold them for ten cents apiece to a dealer who in turn sold them in Paris or London for forty cents apiece.[2] In London alone, one and a half tons of two hundred thousand egret plumes were reportedly sold in one year. London, the international hub of the unprocessed feather market, imported nearly 7,000 bird of paradise skins from New Guinea and more than 7.6 million birds from India and Brazil in the first quarter of 1884 alone. Trade in just the London plume market was valued over £20 million annually (£1.5 billion in 2021 currency). The Paris fashion industry used three hundred million birds per year.[3] A London flyer shows that in February and May 1911, four London dealers auctioned off bird skins and plumage of 129,168 egrets, 13,598 herons, 20,698 birds of paradise, 41,090 hummingbirds, and 9,464 eagles and condors, plus 9,472 others, a total of 223,490 birds.[4]

Market hunters were rapacious, uncontrollable, and rampant; there were neither seasons nor bag limits to control their hauls.[5] They overharvested wildlife, sometimes to the edge of extinction and beyond. They extirpated the passenger pigeon (achieved by 1914), the heath hen, the Carolina parakeet, the great auk, the Labrador duck, and the ivory-billed woodpecker. Pseudo sportsmen were equally responsible for the virtual extinction of the buffalo. Aside from collecting the trophy of the head and horns, some would slaughter as many in one day as they could manage for no better reason than to brag

LONDON FEATHER SALE OF FEBRUARY, 1911

Sold by Hale & Sons		Sold by Dalton & Young	
Aigrettes	3,069 ounces	Aigrettes	1,606 ounces
Herons	960 "	Herons	250 "
Birds of Paradise	1,920 skins	Paradise	4,330 bodies

Sold by Figgis & Co.		Sold by Lewis & Peat	
Aigrettes	421 ounces	Aigrettes	1,250 ounces
Herons	103 "	Paradise	362 skins
Paradise	414 skins	Eagles	384 "
Eagles	2,600 "	Trogons	206 "
Condors	1,580 "	Hummingbirds	24,800 "
Bustards	2,400 "		

LONDON FEATHER SALE OF MAY, 1911

Sold by Hale & Sons		Sold by Dalton & Young	
Aigrettes	1,390 ounces	Aigrettes	2,921 ounces
Herons	178 "	Herons	254 "
Paradise	1,686 skins	Paradise	5,303 skins
Red Ibis	868 "	Golden Pheasants	1,000 "
Junglecocks	1,550 "		
Parrots	1,700 "		
Herons	500 "		

Sold by Figgis & Co.		Sold by Lewis & Peat	
Aigrettes	201 ounces	Aigrettes	590 ounces
Herons	248 "	Herons	190 "
Paradise	546 skins	Paradise	60 skins
Falcons, Hawks	1,500 "	Trogons	348 "
		Hummingbirds	6,250 "

LONDON FEATHER SALE OF OCTOBER, 1911

Sold by Hale & Sons		Sold by Dalton & Young	
Aigrettes	1,020 ounces	Aigrettes	5,879 ounces
Paradise	2,209 skins	Heron	1,608 "
Hummingbirds	10,040 "	Paradise	2,850 skins
Bustard	28,000 quills	Condors	1,500 "
		Eagles	1,900 "

Sold by Figgis & Co.		Sold by Lewis & Peat	
Aigrettes	1,501 ounces	Aigrettes	1,680 ounces
Herons	140 "	Herons	400 "
Paradise	318 skins	Birds of Paradise	700 skins

Figure 5.1. Advertisement for London feather sales, 1911, offering a total of 223,490 bird skins for sale. Trade in the London plume market was valued at over £20 million GBP annually in the 1880s (£1.5 billion in 2021 currency). *Source*: William T. Hornaday, *Our Vanishing Wildlife: Its Extermination and Preservation* (New York: New York Zoological Society, 1913).

of having done so.[6] In the early 1800s, buffalo herds were reduced from an estimated forty million across the West to a mere twenty-five to fifty head, all in Yellowstone National Park.[7] The beasts were slaughtered by the millions for their hides and tongues, which were considered a delicacy, their carcasses left to rot on the Western plains.

The leading naturalists of the day—including Theodore Roosevelt, George Bird Grinnell, Gifford Pinchot, Madison Grant, Fairfield Osborn, and William T. Hornaday—had been documenting the declining trends of various species and began raising public concern regarding the specter and public impact of vanishing species. As early as the 1870s, naturalists were lobbying Congress to enact a bill outlawing the killing of buffalo. The bill passed but was pocket vetoed by President Ulysses S. Grant in 1874. An identical bill in 1876 died in committee, opposed because buffalo hunting sustained the lifestyle and food source of the nomadic Plains Indians. Thus failed the first national attempt to protect a charismatic species of megafauna, a symbol of the nation's heritage.[8]

Figure 5.2. A 1912 photo of 1,600 hummingbird skins for sale at 2¢ each. Part of a lot purchased by the Zoological Society at the quarterly London millinery feather sale. August, 1912. *Source*: Hornaday, *Our Vanishing Wild Life*, 116.

THE LACEY ACT AND THE MIGRATORY BIRD TREATY ACT

The Supreme Court's 1896 decision in *Geer v. Connecticut*[9] recognized the consequences of market hunting's decimation of wildlife and is conceivably one of the most important cases in the public trust doctrine in US wildlife law to this day.

The *Geer* decision also reflected the Court's preoccupation under Chief Justice Melville W. Fuller (1888–1910) with destructive industrial monopolies—as impacted by the Sherman Antitrust Act of 1890—that were imposing unfair and unhealthy labor practices on the poor working classes and immigrants. Commercial market hunting with its rapacious destruction of wildlife and related habitats resembled the specter of evil practices that the robber barons embodied, with all their destructive practices impacting commerce, small businesses, and the poor working classes. The state of affairs raised the ire of Chief Justice Fuller and his Supreme Court.

The public political influence of a few nationally recognized naturalists prevailed upon Congress to enact the Lacey Act of 1900, which outlawed interstate trade in animal parts taken in violation of state law, and the 1913 Weeks-McLean Act, which ended the plume trade.[10] The Migratory Bird Treaty Act of 1918 followed.[11] This legislation marked an important milestone in the history of federal preemption in the environmental arena, eliminating for the first time state ownership and sole control of migratory birds, which many considered guaranteed by the Tenth Amendment.[12] Representative John Lacey (R-IA), considered the fountainhead of important game legislation,[13] believed that because states alone could not prevent species extinction, national action was required.[14] While such federal intervention deprived the states of their sole authority, the Lacey Act did not prevent states from enacting stronger wildlife regulations under their police powers. Moreover, the act authorized the federal government, pursuant to its constitutional powers over interstate commerce, to aid state enforcement of their game laws. "Whereas *Geer* had upheld a state's authority to prohibit the export of game lawfully killed within the state, the Lacey Act sanctioned a state's prohibition of the import of game lawfully killed in other states."[15]

Under the Lacey Act and the Migratory Bird Treaty Act, the federal government adopted penalties for interstate or foreign commerce in illegally taken wildlife (or parts thereof). Congress established regulations for hunting seasons of migratory waterfowl and insectivorous birds. The Migratory Bird Treaty Act ratified a federal treaty between the United States and Canada, which Mexico later joined in 1936.[16] That treaty made it illegal to ship birds taken in violation of international rules from one country to another, or within the United States from any state, territory, or district to another. Seasons and bag limits on migratory waterfowl were negotiated through these international treaties. These two congressional acts recognized the national significance of species protection and marked the beginning of federal intervention and preemption in matters of species protection, preservation, and management.[17] Just as had happened with big game and fish, by the turn of the century "the preservation of migratory birds [was recognized] as essential to the production of a due supply of food in America."[18] Federal intervention in wildlife control was expanded in 1903 when President Theodore Roosevelt created the first national bird refuge explicitly to protect Florida's birdlife on Pelican Island. Thereafter by executive order he also expanded the US forest reserves and national parks as sanctuaries for wildlife.[19]

The Lacey Act of 1900 and the 1918 Migratory Bird Treaty Act were without question the first serious encroachments into state jurisdiction over wildlife.[20] Yet these federal interventions were absolutely essential if migratory waterfowl were to have a future. Birds seasonally crisscrossed the country and international borders. Harvest rules varied by state where there were rules at all, and species were threatened with extinction. Unless all the states, Canada, and Mexico cooperated to save the birds, no effort could be effective. Hence, because only federal intervention could protect migratory wildlife, Congress terminated sole state sovereignty over migratory birds.[21]

The State of Missouri challenged the constitutionality of the 1918 Migratory Bird Treaty Act, but the Supreme Court rejected the challenge. Writing for the seven-member majority of the Court in 1920, Chief Justice White and Justices Louis Brandeis and Oliver Wendell Holmes established the supremacy of the federal treaty-making power as a source of authority for federal wildlife regulation.[22] The Commerce Clause became a supporting authority later in the century. The Court also bluntly rejected the argument that the doctrine of state ownership of wildlife barred federal wildlife regulation:

> No doubt it is true that as between a State and its inhabitants the State may regulate the killing and sale of such birds, but it does not follow that its authority is exclusive of paramount powers. To put the claim of the State upon title is to lean upon a slender reed. Wild birds are not in the possession of anyone; and possession is the beginning of ownership. The whole foundation of the State's rights is the presence within their jurisdiction of birds that yesterday had not arrived, tomorrow may be in another State and in a week a thousand miles away.
>
> Here a national interest of very nearly the first magnitude is involved. It can be protected only by national action in concert with that of another power. The subject matter is only transitorily within the State and has no permanent habitat therein. But for the treaty and the statute there soon might be no birds for any powers to deal with. We see nothing in the Constitution that compels the Government to sit by while a food supply is cut off and the protectors of our

forests and our crops are destroyed. It is not sufficient to rely upon the States. The reliance is vain.[23]

By 1900, the United States was no longer a mere confederation of thirteen separate colonies isolated along the Atlantic seaboard, each populated by colonists living off the land. It was now a union of forty-five states, one nation composed of burgeoning cities, towns, and hamlets, centers of heavy industry, farms, plantations, and ranches spread from the Atlantic to the Pacific.[24] The census report of 1900 repeated historian Frederick Jackson Turner's 1890 declaration that the American frontier was closed.[25] The 1893 World's Columbian Exposition in Chicago (also called the World's Fair and the City of Lights) celebrated the zenith of the Second Industrial Revolution, which had begun in the mid-1800s and would come to a close with the outbreak of World War I in 1914.[26] The fair confirmed beyond peradventure that the United States was the industrial, commercial, and agricultural leader of the world.

Figure 5.3. A market hunter at work on Marsh Island, Louisiana, killing migratory ducks for the New Orleans market. *Source*: Hornaday, *Our Vanishing Wild Life*, 64. Marsh Island consists of 75,000 acres and a coastline 65 miles long just off the coast of Louisiana. Approximately 70 market hunters annually harvested 100,000 birds on the island. In 1913 Mrs. Russell Sage bought the island for $150,000, and dedicated it as a bird refuge. She followed the example of Edward A. McIlhenny who earlier had established a bird refuge on his Avery Island, Louisiana estate where he manufactured Tabasco sauce. *Source*: *Brooklyn Daily Eagle*, page 25, January 26, 1913.

The Progressive movement began during this era and hasn't stopped since, with its philosophy and political policies dominating the twentieth century and the early twenty-first century. This includes the progressive philosophy of federal preemption of state sovereignty over wildlife. The federal government, moreover, struggled to regulate the evils of industrialization that defined the Progressive Era.

Legal hegemony of the national government had slowly occurred and inexorably grown as the nation expanded to the Pacific. The exercise of national authority was now required to regulate a complex, highly integrated economy dominated by corporate giants and financial trusts and monopolies. These forces wrought congressional responses and Supreme Court acceptance of a broad expansion and reach of the Constitution's Commerce Clause and treaty powers, along with increased federal power of taxation, borrowing, and spending—powers that became unlimited and that were ultimately to all but destroy state control and sovereignty over wildlife and its habitats.

As the federal government took control of wildlife, this tectonic shift in authority brought changes in the control of other natural resources. As the United States moved from an agrarian to an industrial society beginning in the late nineteenth and early twentieth centuries, concern for vanishing species of wildlife and other natural resources caused many of the unceded public lands (some within existing states) to be set aside. These became national parks and forests, game refuges and wildlife sanctuaries, and national monuments to protect natural scenic wonders, all for the benefit of wildlife, protection of natural resources, and enjoyment of the public.[27] With these changes came laws creating federal agencies to manage these resources.[28] This created a need for trained professionals to oversee and carry out the new federal powers, including the hiring of rangers, foresters, silviculturists, biologists, zoologists, botanists, geologists, hydrologists, and ichthyologists. These professionals initially came from the ranks of naturalists. However, the nation's universities soon created programs to educate armies of experts and scientists in these disciplines.

SUMMARY

The dawn of the Progressive Era marked a subtle but important philosophical departure from the early days of the constitutional republic. Up until this moment in the nation's history, the US system of government had been operating under a set of classical liberal assumptions about human nature and the role of limited government in the protection of individual rights. Indeed, the framers of the US Constitution had been acutely aware of fixed, unchanging human nature and its natural propensities for self-interest—and the subsequent abuses that would follow from a government left unchecked by enumerated powers. However, with the respective rise of the integrated national market and cultural disruption, Progressives saw a new opportunity to change the central operation of the US government: their new conception of federalism would be to *solve* national problems.

Specifically, the market hunting industry presented Progressives in Washington a clear legislative lane from which to attempt to combat the growing problems commensurate with rapacious commercial hunting for food and apparel. With leading naturalists such as Theodore Roosevelt and George Bird Grinnell raising the alarm about dwindling wildlife communities, Congress passed two landmark laws that changed the overall composition of the federal and state relationship: The Lacey Act of 1900 outlawing interstate trade in animal parts and the Migratory Bird Treaty Act of 1918, which became a milestone for environmental preemption. Under the latter enacted bill, Congress directly eliminated—for the first time—*sole* state sovereign control of migratory birds. However, under this new, particular version of federalism, Congress did not prevent states from enacting more robust wildlife regulations; the act merely created a *regulatory floor* that would be dictated, controlled, and conditioned by the federal government.

The Migratory Bird Treaty Act of 1918 signaled two core historical events: First, the dual-federalism era, especially in the environmental regulatory context—which was encapsulated by *Waddell*—was slowly but surely coming to an end. Second, the congressional preemption of wildlife pursuant to the congressional treaty power under the US Constitution represented the future of constitutional law—a more *expansive* interpretation of federal power. In rejecting Missouri's constitutional challenge to the act, Justice Holmes, writing for the Court, established the supremacy of federal treaty-making powers as a source of authority for federal wildlife regulation—a decision that hinted at future interpretation of the Commerce Clause, which would expand federal reach. Overall, while the Supreme Court's dual-federalism framework had focused on maintaining clear distributions of *power* among vertical layers of authority, cooperative federalism emerged to directly *solve* national challenges. Federal agencies and the rise of "experts" from universities would become central to achieving this new vision of a US federal government.

NOTES

1. Reiger, *American Sportsmen*, 91–96. The extermination of the snowy heron and American egret was blamed by the *New York Times* on the use of their feathers in ladies' hats. See Petersen, "Modern Ark," 26; and see "Tragedy of the White Heron,

Victim of Woman's Vanity," a subsection in "Alfred Henry Lewis on Literary Critics and Henry James," *New York Times*, August 13, 1905, p. 4, https://timesmachine.nytimes.com/timesmachine/1905/08/13/issue.html.

2. G. B. Grinnell, "Founding Audubon Society, February 1886," archived as microfilm in reel 40, box 39, folder 145, of the George Bird Grinnell Papers, Sterling Memorial Library, Yale University Library, https://archives.yale.edu/repositories/12/archival_objects/1248835.

3. Kimberly Chrisman-Campbell, "Fowl Intentions: Fashion, Activism, Conservation," *Ornament Magazine* 40, no. 4 (2018): 46–51, available online at https://lsc-pagepro.mydigitalpublication.com/publication/?m=60607&i=598875&p=48&ver=html5; Marc Bekoff, "Hats: The Deadly History of Who We Put On Our Heads," *Psychology Today*, January 11, 2020, https://www.psychologytoday.com/us/blog/animal-emotions/202001/hats-the-deadly-history-who-we-put-our-heads; Angela Serratore, "Keeping Feathers Off Hats—and on Birds," *Smithsonian Magazine*, May 15, 2018, https://www.smithsonianmag.com/history/migratory-bird-act-anniversary-keeping-feathers-off-hats-180969077/; and William Souder, "How Two Women Ended the Deadly Feather Trade," *Smithsonian Magazine*, March 1, 2013, https://www.smithsonianmag.com/science-nature/how-two-women-ended-the-deadly-feather-trade-23187277/.

4. Hornaday, *Our Vanishing Wildlife*, 36.

5. For a first-person account of the devastation of wildlife in this period, read the book of an informed advocate for the regulation of hunting who was a prominent commentator on vanishing species at the turn of the century, in Hornaday, *Our Vanishing Wildlife*. Moreover, the weekly editorials penned by anthropologist and naturalist George Bird Grinnell in *Forest and Stream* between 1880 and 1911 chronologically details the decimation of wildlife over this thirty-one-year period.

6. Charles Hallock, *The Sportsman's Gazetteer and General Guide* (New York: Forest and Stream Publishing Company, 1872), 33–35.

7. In a letter dated August 23, 1900, George Bird Grinnell wrote there were only twenty-five to fifty total buffalo left in Yellowstone National Park; he later opined that there were as few antelope on the prairies as buffalo. G. B. Grinnell to Mark Sullivan, August 23, 1900, archived as microfilm, reel 7, box 6, folder 11, of the George Bird Grinnell Papers, Sterling Memorial Library, Yale University Library, https://archives.yale.edu/repositories/12/top_containers/207138; and G. B. Grinnell to Luther North, December 23, 1903, archived as microfilm in reel 9U, box 8, folder 13, of the George Bird Grinnell Papers, Sterling Memorial Library, Yale University Library https://archives.yale.edu/repositories/12/top_containers/141869.

8. Petersen, "Modern Ark," 18–22.

The National Bison Legacy Act, signed on May 9, 2016, made the buffalo the official national mammal of the United States. US Congress, *National Bison Legacy Act*, Pub. L. No. 114–152, 130 Stat. 373 (2016), https://www.govinfo.gov/content/pkg/PLAW-114publ152/pdf/PLAW-114publ152.pdf.

9. 161 U.S. 519 (1896).

10. US Congress, *Lacey Act*, 31 Stat. 187, 16 U.S.C. §§ 3371–78 (1900) (and see *Rupert v. United States*, 181 F. 87 [8th Cir. 1910], upholding the constitutionality of

the Lacey Act on its interstate-commerce footings of regulating commerce between states, per US Constitution, Article I, Section 8, https://www.senate.gov/civics/constitution_item/constitution.htm#a1_sec8). US Congress, *Weeks-McLean Act*, Pub. L. No. 62–430, Chap. 145, 37 Stat. 828, 847–48 (1913).

11. US Congress, *Migratory Bird Treaty Act*, Pub. L. No. 65–186, 40 Stat. 755 (1918), https://www.fws.gov/laws/lawsdigest/migtrea.html.

This law was a ratification of a treaty the United States had entered into with Canada to manage and protect migratory birds. The law had been challenged by the State of Missouri on constitutional grounds under the Tenth Amendment. In 1920 the Supreme Court upheld the act, based on federal treaty-making powers authorized by the US Constitution in Article VI (see https://www.senate.gov/civics/constitution_item/constitution.htm#a6). See *State of Missouri v. Holland*, 252 U.S. 416 (1920). In 1929 the Migratory Bird Conservation Act extended the protection of birds even further.

See Dian Olson Belanger and Adrian Kinnane, *Managing American Wildlife: A History of the International Association of Fish and Wildlife Agencies* (Rockville, MD: Montrose Press, 2002), 20–25; Petersen, "Congress and Charismatic Megafauna," 463, 469–70; and Petersen, "Modern Ark," 29–30 (see also footnote 158 herein).

12. It should be noted that twelve years after the Lacey Act of 1900 the Supreme Court decided that the state's sovereign jurisdiction over wildlife based on the possession and ownership doctrine within the boundaries of a state precluded federal regulatory authority; this was the court's last affirmative statement on the matter. This decision has never been overruled and has been given quiet interment. See *The Abby Dodge v. United States*, 223 U.S. 166 (1912); and see Bean and Rowland, *Evolution of National Wildlife Law*, 16–17, 25.

13. G. B. Grinnell to John F. Lacey, February 25, 1903, archived as microfilm in box 7, folder 12, of the George Bird Grinnell Papers, Sterling Memorial Library, Yale University Library, https://archives.yale.edu/repositories/12/top_containers/141868.

14. See the statement of Rep. John F. Lacey, 56th Congress, 1st sess., Congressional Record H.4871–72, vol. 33, pt. 9 (1900).

15. Bean and Rowland, *Evolution of National Wildlife Law*, 15–16.

16. The Migratory Bird Act was first enacted in 1913 as the Weeks-McLean Act and later replaced in 1918 following a treaty with Great Britain on behalf of Canada. Two federal district cases questioned the constitutionality of the 1913 act based on the Property Clause of the US Constitution. See *United States v. Shauver*, 214 F. 154 (E.D. Ark 1914), appeal dismissed 248 U.S. 594 (1919); and *United States v. McCullagh*, 221 F. 288 (D. Kan. 1915).

In dismissing the appeal in the *Shauver* case, the Supreme Court never decided the constitutionality of the 1918 Migratory Bird Treaty Act—not until it was later upheld in 1920, based on a federal treaty with Canada. See US Constitution, Art. I, Sec. 8, Necessary and Proper Clause, https://www.senate.gov/civics/constitution_item/constitution.htm#a1_sec8; and see Art. II, Treaty Making Power) in *State of Missouri v. Holland*, 252 U.S. 416 (1920). The act was then reaffirmed in *United States v. Bramble*, 103 F.3d 1475, 1480 (9th Cir. 1996).

See also Bean and Rowland, *Evolution of National Wildlife Law*, 18.

17. Petersen, "Congress and Charismatic Megafauna," 469.

18. Resolution of the Game Preservation Committee of the Boone and Crockett Club, January 10, 1918, Annual Meeting 1918, documents, box 85, folder 4, Boone and Crockett Archives, Mansfield Library Special Collections, University of Montana, Missoula.

B & C member George Shiras III was directly responsible for the MBTA's being worked through Congress.

19. Steven Lewis Yaffee, *Prohibitive Policy: Implementing the Federal Endangered Species Act* (Cambridge: MIT Press, 1982), 37–38.

20. According to George Cameron Coggins, "The origins of modern federal wildlife law may be traced back to the MBTA." Coggins, "Federal Wildlife Law," 753, 764. See also Kimberly K. Smith, *The Conservation Constitution: The Conservation Movement and Constitutional Change, 1870–1930* (Lawrence: University Press of Kansas, 2019), 40–71.

21. The idea of managing migratory birds nationally and internationally from Washington failed to prove effective. By 1952 a National Flyway Council was created with four regional councils for the Atlantic, Mississippi, Central, and Pacific Flyways. These councils were composed of officials from each of the respective state agencies and a US Fish and Wildlife Service (USFWS) technical coordinator, who served as the state-federal liaison in census taking, surveying, banding, and establishing seasons and harvest limits. One might say this was the first solid example of shared federal/state responsibility in wildlife-conservation governance.

Then in 1989 the North American Wetlands Conservation Act established the North American Waterfowl Management Plan and the Tripartite Agreement, which amended the 1918 Migratory Bird Treaty Act. These identify and implement wetland habitat–restoration projects in Canada, Mexico, and the United States, conserving wetlands for migratory birds to ensure their survival as a species. The program requires federal grant dollars to be equally matched by the private sector, which Ducks Unlimited and others heroically support. Market hunters purveying wildlife for commercial sale to urbanites was what triggered this historical evolution of managing migratory birds, the most practical and pragmatic approach conceivable, but it set the stage for a slowly evolving, continuing shared state/federal responsibility in wildlife management.

See US Congress, *North American Wetlands Conservation Act*, Pub. L. No. 101–233, 103 Stat. 1968 (1989), https://www.govinfo.gov/content/pkg/STATUTE-103/pdf/STATUTE-103-Pg1968.pdf.

22. Bean and Rowland, *Evolution of National Wildlife Law*, 18–19.

23. *State of Missouri v. Holland*, 252 U.S. 416, 434–35 (1920).

24. Historian Frederick Jackson Turner declared the frontier closed in 1890, and the US Census Bureau repeated his declaration in its 1900 report. The frontier line is a point beyond which the population density was less than two persons per square mile. Frederick Jackson Turner, *The Frontier in American History* (New York: Henry Holt and Company, 1920); and US Census Bureau, "Following the Frontier Line, 1790 to 1890," Census.gov, September 6, 2012, https://www.census.gov/dataviz/visualizations/001/.

25. Richard White, *The Republic for Which It Stands: The United States During Reconstruction and the Gilded Age, 1865–1896* (New York: Oxford University Press, 2019), 762–63.

26. White, *Republic for Which It Stands* 756, 764, 773, 777, 786–87.

27. For a detailed account of the development of the refuge movement and wildlife refuges up to World War II, read the 1943 book of then-director of US Fish and Wildlife Service, Ira N. Gabrielson, *Wildlife Refuges* (New York: The MacMillian Company, 1943). And also see Belanger and Kinnane, *Managing American Wildlife*, 40–44; and Reiger, *American Sportsman*, 105–45.

28. The US Fish and Wildlife Service in 1940 evolved out of the Bureau of Biological Survey, so named in 1905, the origin of which dates back to the Division of Economic Ornithology and Mammalogy, created as a separate unit in 1886 out of the Division of Entomology, started in 1862 by the newly created Department of Agriculture. The reason the Biological Survey became the USFWS and moved from the Department of Agriculture to Interior is because the survey's focus changed from just a scientific agency to a scientific and management agency conserving the nation's fish and wildlife resources. US Fish and Wildlife Service, "About the U.S. Fish and Wildlife Service," FWS.gov. last modified February 12, 2021, https://www.fws.gov/help/about_us.html.

The US Forest Service was started by the Department of Agriculture in 1905 and the US Park Service in 1916 by the Department of the Interior. The first wildlife refuge, Pelican Island, was created in 1903 by Theodore Roosevelt. US Department of Agriculture, Forest Service, "Our History," FS.USDA.gov, accessed September 16, 2021, https://www.fs.usda.gov/learn/our-history; National Park Service, "Quick History of the National Park Service," NPS.gov, last modified May 14, 2018, https://www.nps.gov/articles/quick-nps-history.htm; and US Fish and Wildlife Service, "Pelican Island: History," FWS.gov, last modified October 14, 2015, https://www.fws.gov/refuge/pelican_island/about/history.html.

6

The Ethos of the Industrial Revolution Drives the Progressive Movement into America's Social Fabric and Laws, 1910–1919

A self-interested, market-driven ethos drove the Industrial Revolution, which consequently led to the Progressive Movement and national attempts to regulate and dispel concentrations of market power. Indeed, antitrust legislation and trustbusting efforts reflected these efforts. Specifically, during the *Lochner* era, the Supreme Court had constitutionalized an integrated market economy while placing limits on the application of federal regulatory power.[1] However, the Court was unable to develop a coherent preemption doctrine that would account for these new changes in the nation's governance. Thus, because the Court wrestled with how federalism should work in this new, developing age of industry, markets, and social unrest, the preemption doctrine became vague and uncertain—until 1933, with *Mintz v. Baldwin*, which furnished the *implicit* presumption against preemption.[2] Overall, the Progressive Movement displayed an impulse toward greater *national* control, which would eventually breach the dual-federalism gates, replacing it with a new iteration—*cooperative federalism.*

* * *

The images of robber barons awash in the Gilded Age of money, political and economic power, and greed, and the development of assembly and production line industries and the railroads, monopolies, and financial trusts are what most recall of the Progressive Era. Beneath the historical glimpse of greed and money, however, lies the social problems that were created by industrialization and the massive expansion of the federal government's bureaucratic machinery to support the many federal programs enacted to rein in and control the growth of the industrial United States and its demanding population.

The pace of US industrial development had quickened substantially following the Civil War, spurred by technological developments in England resulting from the advent of the first Industrial Revolution in the mid-seventeenth and early eighteenth centuries, well ahead of American enterprise. English inventors were the first to develop the spinning jenny and large-scale textile manufacturing and the mechanical reaper or swather, the first to discover vulcanization and its application to rubber, and to develop steam power and engines and iron and steel production from blast furnaces and for industry,[3] along with the Bessemer process, electrification and the incandescent lamp and the light bulb, paper making, and petroleum refining. In the United States, the development of the railroad system before and following the Civil War led to rapid industrialization, and to the American Industrial Revolution during the Progressive Era, which caused social and political unrest from 1890 to 1920 and far beyond.[4]

The Progressive Era represents a time of unbridled economic growth driven by the massive expansion of the railroad system and industrialization as epitomized by production and assembly lines utilizing cheap, unskilled labor doing simple, repetitive tasks. This caused massive concentrations of workers into manufacturing cities where they suffered poor living conditions in tenement and slum housing, unsanitary conditions, no health care, and exploitation with low wages and long working hours, all of which led to political unrest. This in turn led Progressives to propose economic and social reforms for the disenfranchised working class, including an expanded role of government to regulate industry, protect the public interests, and promote the rights of organized labor to exert power over corporate employers.[5] This was called the Gilded Age, as a class of robber barons emerged, controlling and consolidating massive industries without government interference. Government to this point had promoted a free market with a *laissez faire* policy of avoiding the regulation of business and its practices. However, unregulated capitalism's excesses led to drastic government regulations and oversight.

During the early part of the Progressive Era, enormous wealth was generated by a few. Cornelius Vanderbilt developed steamship and railroad lines; Andrew Carnegie manufactured steel; John D. Rockefeller founded Standard Oil; Thomas Edison developed the electrical system; J. P. Morgan was the major financier and banker of the era; Jim Fisk and Jay Gould were Wall Street investment bankers managing the issuance of stocks and bonds.[6] Their image as robber barons came from their lavish spending on mansions, private yachts, and lavishly customized railcars, and from their unscrupulous business practices, political corruption and influence, and outright and brazen bribery, all while the working classes suffered in squalor and poverty. As the disparity widened between the rich and poor, economic and social unrest

Figure 6.1. During America's Gilded Age, unbridled capitalism ran the nation's industrial empire through trusts and monopolies controlled by America's wealthiest and robber barons labeled in this cartoon "The Bosses of the Senate." *Source*: Granger Historical Picture Archive.

followed, and government intervention was demanded. These forces were led by William Jennings Bryan,[7] who became the voice of the common man. Traditional federal deference to local authority to solve social problems was failing because the problems were national in scale and required remedies only the federal government could deliver.[8]

As the industrial economy became more integrated, the federal government was forced to intervene in the marketplace with uniform national regulations that excluded the states. The established norm of dual federalism was increasingly inadequate to strike the balance between federal and state authority, given the conflicts created by marketplace integration, yet the Supreme Court held its ground: "The power of a State to protect the lives, health, and property of its citizens, and to preserve good order and the public morals . . . is a power originally and always belonging to the States . . . and essentially exclusive. . . . On the other hand, the power of Congress to regulate commerce among the several States is also exclusive."[9]

As the Industrial Revolution intensified and pressure continued to mount from the intellectually "enlightened" of the Progressive Era, the judicial system was hard pressed to maintain the traditional line between state and federal issues and authorities, so the development of a coherent doctrine of preemption evolved but took years to coalesce.[10]

THE LOCHNER ERA: EXPANSION OF STATES' RIGHTS, INDIVIDUAL LIBERTIES, AND A *LAISSEZ FAIRE* ECONOMY

The period spanning 1887 and 1936, which encompassed both the Progressive Era and the early part of the New Deal era—prior to the "new" Supreme Court makeup in 1937—has been characterized as the "Lochner Era" in *Federal Preemption: State Powers, National Interests*, a powerful edited collection by scholars Richard Epstein and Michael Greve, including essays by Ernest A. Young, Stephen Gardbaum, Viet Dinh, Thomas Merrill, and other scholars.[11] In the 1905 *Lochner v. New York* decision,[12] the Supreme Court had addressed the rights and liberties a worker enjoys under the Contract Clause in the Constitution and the Fourteenth Amendment's Due Process Clause versus the valid exercise of states' police powers. The case adjudicated the validity of a New York law that interfered with the right of contract between an employee and employer concerning the number of hours an employee could work in a bakery. Justice Peckham, writing the Court's opinion, characterized the issue as follows: "It is a question of which of two powers or rights shall prevail—the power of the state to legislate or the [constitutional] right of the individual to liberty of person and freedom of contract."[13] In other words, can the Supreme Court invalidate a New York statute limiting the hours a person can work in a bakery if the Court deems that the statute violates a constitutional right of freedom to contract? Isn't that purely a domestic issue for the state legislature?

Justices Holmes and Harlan dissented, arguing that, "upon this point there is no room for dispute; for the rule is universal that a legislative enactment is never to be disregarded or held invalid unless it be, beyond question, plainly and palpably in excess of legislative power."[14] In *Lochner* the Court so held and voided the New York law. The case set off a variety of similar cases nationwide that upheld the natural law's tradition of protecting property and property rights and the Fourteenth Amendment right to due process, opening up the question of federal preemption.[15]

The *Lochner* era stood for two constitutional doctrines: First, the Supreme Court constitutionalized a national, free-market economy across state lines (one country, one economic system) and developed a general hostility toward government regulation of the economy. Second, they placed limits on the scope of national power in the name of reserved power of the states.[16] The *Lochner* era was further defined by pro–states' rights, and a *laissez faire* economic policy with the Commerce Clause having unlimited latitude for federal authority.[17]

Exemplifying the development of these emerging doctrines were two landmark companion cases in 1912: *Savage v. Jones* and *Southern Railway v. Reid*,[18] the latter a railroad case, thus involving the Commerce Clause.

Savage v. Jones involved the Pure Food and Drug Act of 1906 and an Indiana law requiring that all ingredients of commercial animal food be disclosed on the label. The Court found no conflict between the law nor any impact on interstate commerce. Congress's law did not cover the entire ground on labeling, and neither could it be inferred that concurrent laws were invalid or superseded. These cases clearly established the concept and principle of preemption.[19] They invalidated state law specifically on preemption grounds, even though the state and federal regulations did not conflict with each other. Preemption was discretionary. Once Congress exercises its plenary authority over the entire field of interstate commerce, preemption was automatic, emanating from the supremacy principle of federal laws. The irrelevance of conflict was succinctly put by Justice Oliver Wendell Holmes: "That the [alleged absence of conflict] is immaterial."[20] The Court even began to explore a theory of "latent exclusivity" including the Commerce Clause.[21] These early preemption cases displayed shallow reasoning, leaving a more meaningful jurisprudence on preemption to develop later.

Finally, amid the confusion, a critical early milestone in preemption law was reached in 1913, bringing some clarity to the conflict between state and federal law. In *Chicago, Rock Island & Pacific Railway Co. v. Hardwick Farmers Elevator Co.*,[22] the Supreme Court, citing the *Southern Railroad* case as precedent, held "that the federal Hepburn Act preempted state regulations on the delivery of interstate railroad cars."[23] Interstate commerce had long been the exclusive domain of the Congress. Chief Justice Edward Douglass White said in the *Hardwick* opinion that "the elementary and long settled doctrine is that there can be no divided authority over interstate commerce and that regulations of Congress on that subject are supreme."[24] This was echoed by Justice Butler in 1925, who used almost the same wording.[25] The high court was finally beginning to address the growing problem of conflicting authority, albeit only on matters of interstate commerce.[26]

The legal usage of the term *preemption* made its first appearance in 1917 in *New York Central Railroad Company v. Winfield* in Justice Louis Brandeis's dissenting opinion, in discussion of overlap between state and federal law.[27] In the nineteenth century it was framed merely as a constitutional division of authority under the Supremacy Clause. In these foundational cases were the developing elements of a modern, more restrained preemption doctrine.[28] The Court to this point had not focused on congressional intent, which developed later, during the New Deal era.

Following World War I, with the prohibition on the sale of liquor, the emergence of Great Depression, and with FDR's New Deal programs, the Court's doctrine of dual federalism was incrementally ended and ultimately abandoned for a regime of concurrent jurisdiction. Distinguished constitutional scholar Ernest A. Young characterizes this new paradigm, writing that the Supreme Court "never again sought to draw such restrictive boundaries on national power, and it also significantly dialed back the rigor of its 'dormant' Commerce Clause restrictions on state regulation . . . to a more modest antidiscrimination principle. This meant that both state and national authorities have power to address most subjects of regulatory concern."[29]

This was later reflected in 1933's *Mintz v. Baldwin*,[30] which held that state regulations on contagious animal diseases were not preempted by the Federal Cattle Contagious Diseases Act. The Court ruled that animal health had historically been a traditional area of state dominion and control under their police powers and should remain with the states. This principle originated in *Reid v. Colorado*. The real importance of the *Mintz* case was its focus on congressional intent and the presumption that state powers survived and ran concurrently unless clearly and expressly terminated by Congress or by actual conflict between state and federal law, which became an institutionalized doctrine a decade later.[31]

"From 1933 onward, the Court bolstered the anti-preemption implications of *Reid/Savage* by expressly acknowledging for the first time a presumption against preemption in areas of traditional state regulation."[32] Between 1933 and 1937, all major Supreme Court preemption cases upheld state authority. Moreover, between 1933 and 1937 not a single federal statute contained an express preemption provision. In fact, quite the reverse was the case, as four major laws contained nonpreemption clauses, including the Securities Act of 1933; the Securities Exchange Act; and the Fair Labor Standards Act of 1938. The Social Security Act of 1935 actually required cooperative federalism, with its substantive provisions containing federal standards states must meet if they wanted to receive federal grant money.[33]

Professor Gardbaum succinctly summarizes what the *Mintz* case ushered in, charactering a new era of preemption laws as follows: "First states have real concurrent authority over subjects that Congress may regulate under its commerce power. Second, terminating states' concurrent authority by Congress is totally discretionary, not automatic because of their action. Third, Congress is presumed not to have exercised their power. Fourthly, rebutting this presumption requires a clear, express manifestation of congressional attempt to preempt."[34]

The concept of preemption grew into a distinct doctrine during the *Lochner* Era (1887–1937), starting with supremacy that voided state laws in conflict with federal law, which then evolved into concurrent federal law preempting state law even if conflict did not exist. Thence that position evolved further into state concurrent law being permitted to exist with a similar federal law unless Congress expressly and clearly manifested its intent to preempt it. "To preserve the federal 'balance' exclusive jurisdictional force of federal regulations was watered down into implied preemption and further checked by a presumption against preemption."[35] Throughout this evolution, the federal Commerce Clause remained dominate, especially in railroad cases; but in limited areas of traditional state authority, the evolving construct of preemption left room for concurrent state power. A presumption against preemption finally developed late in the *Lochner* era with the *Mintz* case in areas of traditional state authority. That holding remains in place today.[36] The prevailing theme that runs through the post–New Deal period following *Lochner* is a concern over federal excess and overreach and a loss of state autonomy.[37]

The New Deal Court reconstituted both its membership and its ideological orientation after 1937. It scaled back the reach of the Commerce Clause, rejecting the nationalist view from the *Lochner* era,[38] to invalidate only discrimination against out-of-state goods, an enhancement of state authority allowing more space for evenhanded regulatory schemes.[39] Automatic preemption was abandoned for the express-intent standard, thus allowing concurrent and diverse regulations on precisely the same subject to continue provided Congress had not expressly preempted it.[40] Later, in 1945, the modern balancing test was introduced. Additionally, in the 1940s two landmark cases further refined the preemption standard: *Hines v. Davidowitz* (1941) and *Rice v. Santa Fe Elevator Corp.* (1947).[41] The 1946 Administrative Procedure Act was a further reflection of the post–New Deal era changing the architecture of federalism.[42]

Discussion of continued evolution of the preemption doctrine starting with the "new" New Deal Court in 1937 continues in chapter 8. However, during the latter part of the *Lochner* era, the events of the 1920s and '30s that led to the development of the federal administrative state provided the underpinnings of the Supreme Court's interpretation of the evolving preemption doctrine, which is discussed in chapter 8.

ANTITRUST LEGISLATION AND TRUSTBUSTING

The massive expansion of the industrial state during the Progressive Era brought the federal government into a reckoning with the wealthiest men in America and the robber barons that controlled the industrial enterprise of the country through monopolies and trusts. This tested and challenged the power of the federal government and their constitutional authority and the reach of the US Constitution, and it threatened the balance of federalism. Preemption of private-property rights and enterprise was at the heart of the federal antitrust initiative.

To bring big business trusts and monopolies that controlled the country's industrial empire under federal control, national laws would be required. The Sherman Antitrust Act of 1890, followed by the Mann-Elkins Act of 1910 and the Clayton Antitrust Act of 1914, meant to strengthen the Sherman Act, were the premier acts of Congress.[43] The Sherman Antitrust Act was a penal law carrying harsh penalties including imprisonment. These pre–New Deal antitrust laws were intended to supplement, not supplant, complementary state laws. They were to operate on interstate conspiracies considered beyond states' authority, leaving state law to deal with local internal commerce.[44] The Department of Justice had primary authority to enforce the Sherman Antitrust Act, and the Federal Trade Commission established in 1914 had jurisdiction for enforcement of the Clayton Antitrust Act. The Federal Reserve Board was created in 1913 to manage the banking and securities industries. This legislation was enacted despite vehement opposition from the leading targets, the robber barons, who also faced massive litigation and muckraker media blitzes. The 1887 Interstate Commerce Act, Interstate Commerce Commission, and Interstate Commerce Railroad Association that followed arose from the need to regulate ruinous competition among railroads that dated back to

Figure 6.2. Cartoon of Theodore Roosevelt, the trustbuster. *Source*: Granger Historical Picture Archive.

discussions in Congress starting in the early 1870s.[45] Moreover, the Federal Power Commission was established in 1920 to maintain competition in energy and electricity production.

From this period, notable litigation included the *United States v. E.C. Knight & Co.*[46] who had over a 98 percent monopoly on American sugar refining; the breakup of Rockefeller's Standard Oil monopoly resulting from muckraker Ida Tarbell's crusade[47]; the 1904 *Northern Securities v. United States*[48] case that broke up the Northern Securities Company's monopoly holding in trust many major railroad companies; and the 1911 American Tobacco breakup for their tobacco monopoly violating the Sherman Act.[49]

The antitrust litigation before the Supreme Court and the evils of price-fixing, the restraint of trade, cartels, monopsony and oligopsony, and industrial monopolies and trusts suffered upon the American public magnified the need for harsh controls on the perpetrators. The Supreme Court struggled for over two decades with the Sherman Antitrust Act to define the separation between state and federal authority in interstate commerce. Ripple effects from this long struggle were seen seventy-five years later in endangered species cases. Both debates—antitrust then and endangered species later—were over constitutional authority under the Interstate Commerce Clause and state authority under the Supremacy Clause and the Tenth Amendment. This same issue of federal versus state authority under these two constitutional clauses manifested itself in the wildlife context in the Lacey Act of 1900 and the Migratory Bird Treaty Act— which was first conceived in 1913 and finally became law in 1918. Hear the harsh words of the Supreme Court from this progressive antitrust era:

> When competition is left free, individual error or folly will generally find a correction in the conduct of others.[50]

> Public policy unquestionably favors competition in trade to the end that its commodities may be afforded to the consumer as cheaply as possible, and is opposed to monopolies which tend to advance market prices, to the injury of the general public. Monopoly in trade, or in any kind of business in this country, is odious to our form of government. Its tendency is destructive of free institutions, and repugnant to the instincts of a free people, and contrary to the whole scope and spirit of the federal Constitution.[51]

> The power over commerce with foreign nations and among the several states is vested in Congress as absolute.[52]

Similarly, early Progressive Era debates in Congress and the Supreme Court would also foreshadow the debate to come over endangered species later in the century.[53] These included debates over the environment, national legislation regulating wages, working conditions, eight-hour workdays, sanitation, and child labor. The Progressive Era also caused the nation to look at environmental impacts on a national scale and to resort to serious regulations for sewage disposal, to mitigate pollution of waterways, to preserve air quality, and to protect recreation in nature for its positive effects on emotional well-being.[54] From this era, regulations were developed to improve sanitation and public health, mitigate overcrowding in slums and tenant houses, and address other related issues, and thus began America's welfare movement. This new political platform for the federal government's preemption of state authority grew in complexity and breadth throughout the twentieth century because many of the growing social problems were national in scope. Following the Progressive Era, concerns regarding social welfare were later repeated and reflected in Franklin D. Roosevelt's New Deal, John F. Kennedy's New Frontier, and Lyndon B. Johnson's Great Society, thus becoming a major element of the Democratic Party's policies and principles throughout the twentieth century.

Industry's shortcomings were not the only social and economic ills exposed during the Progressive Era that precipitated federal legislation preempting state power. Driven in part by the Industrial Revolution, the Progressive Era produced more aggressive expansion of the federal government's intervention into and preemption of local and state authority than any other period of American history up to that point.[55] Between 1870 and 1920, twenty-six million immigrants came to the United States, coinciding with mass migration from the farms to the city and with the migration of Blacks from the South to Northern cities.[56] In 1840, the United States' urban population was only 11 percent (1.8 million); by the 1920 census, the urban population had reached fifty-four million—over 50 percent of the total population of 105,710,620.[57] That was a significant demographic shift for the nation when its urban population surpassed its rural, agrarian population. In one district of New York City alone, the density was one thousand people per acre.[58] The influx of unskilled workers into urban areas to staff the new factories and assembly lines exacerbated many existing social problems—including inadequate housing and sanitation, ongoing worker exploitation, the abuse of liquor and narcotic drugs, prostitution, and spousal abuse.[59] All of these conditions created demand for social reforms, raised environmental awareness, and mustered the growth in society and government of what was called "sewer socialism."[60]

The Woman's Christian Temperance Union (WCTU) was founded to address the liquor problem; Jane Addams established Hull House in Chicago to showcase a solution for poor immigrant slums, and Jacob Riis exposed the slums and social ills of New York City.[61] The media exposure from these social problems led to a variety of state and local welfare laws under the authority of their police power. Thereafter, many of these would be preempted by federal legislation when the reform efforts required a national scope.[62]

Such popular movements for social reform led to the creation of the US Public Health Service in 1912 (formed from the former Marine Hospital Service), whose mission included policing sewage, water, pollution, occupational-health hazards, general public sanitation, and epidemic diseases. A division of Industrial Hygiene and Sanitation was created by the Service in 1915, extending its oversight into industrial production facilities and toxins in the workplace. The Bureau of Mines was created in 1910 by the Department of the Interior to regulate health hazards and lead poisoning in mines. The Department of Labor evolved in 1913. In 1906 Congress had passed the Meat Inspection Act, followed by the Pure Food and Drug Act. Support for these two acts had been generated by Upton Sinclair's novel *The Jungle*, which focused attention on the poor, unsanitary conditions in slaughterhouses.[63] More than a half-century later, in 1970, the Environmental Protection Agency and the Occupational Safety and Health Administration were to be followed shortly by a plethora of new federal laws expanding federal authority and limiting state powers. These laws for over seventy years induced a massive expansion of federal bureaucratic expertise in a host of scientific, technical, welfare, and administrative fields that heretofore had been the sole province of the states, provoking new political cleavage between federal and state governments over authority.[64]

In 1890 Carrie Chapman Catt, a leading suffragette, established the National American Woman Suffrage Association, followed by Alice Paul's National Woman's Party in 1916, which led to the 1920 passage of the Nineteenth Amendment, granting a woman's right to vote.[65] Three other amendments to the US Constitution were passed during the Progressive Era. In 1913, the Sixteenth and Seventeenth Amendments were ratified.[66] The former created a revised federal income tax, and an estate tax enacted later. Further revisions to the tax code followed on a regular basis almost annually.[67] The latter required the direct election of US senators by popular vote, stripping the power of state legislatures to select senators.

While the Seventeenth Amendment reduced state power within the federal system, the Sixteenth dramatically increased the power within the federal system and the power and wealth of the national authority, including a vast expansion of the federal bureaucracy and the administrative state.

As an example, the number of IRS employees across the country between 1915 and 1925 rose from 4,690 to 16,160. The annual cost of operating the tax bureau in those same years went from $6,764,800 to $37,102,200. Total revenue collected from all sources in 1915 was $415,681,000; that rose to $2,548,140,300 by 1925. This provides some insight into another aspect of the magnitude of the federal bureaucracy created by the Sixteenth Amendment of 1913 amid the Progressive Era, which in turn exploded further with the Eighteenth Amendment's enactment of Prohibition five years later, in 1919.[68] The apotheosis of the administrative state began to rise during this period.

SUMMARY

The Progressive Era was a direct reaction to the Industrial Revolution, which had spawned social, political, and economic unrest across the nation stemming from the massive concentration of wealth and the corresponding poor and unhealthy living conditions of immigrant and working-class communities. When Upton Sinclair poignantly chronicled the oppressive conditions in *The Jungle*, he famously raised the eyebrows of President Theodore Roosevelt as he sat at his breakfast table. Indeed, problems existed, but the broader question about the *solution* remained unsettled. According to Progressives, the nation was unequipped to deal with new, unanticipated economic challenges using the dual-federalism blueprint of the past. Thus, they felt, the federal government would be required to exercise *more* power to solve problems. However, the *Lochner* Court had a different vision—one that protected individual liberty, expanded states' rights, and promoted an integrated market economy.

During the *Lochner* Era, the Supreme Court constitutionalized an integrated market economy while placing limits on the application of federal regulatory power. However, because of the *dynamic* forces that were changing the nation's interactions in the early part of the century, the Supreme Court was limited—at first—in its capacity to develop a coherent doctrine to adapt to these new economic challenges. The preemption doctrine—from *Savage v. Jones* (1912) and *Southern Railway v. Reid* (1913) to *Chicago, Rock Island & Pacific Railway Co. v. Hardwick-Farmers Elevator Co.* (1913)—manifested this institutional confusion as the Court wrestled with the manner in which federalism should work in a new, modern age. Finally, in *Mintz v. Baldwin* (1933) the Court adopted a clear, cognizable standard: Under the new preemption doctrine, there would be a presumption against preemption, allowing states—unless expressly stated by Congress or by actual conflict—to concurrently regulate activities under their police powers. Accordingly, while the *Lochner* Court was concerned with scaling back the federal government's regulatory reach in traditional areas of state regulatory authority, *Mintz* reflects a clear example of *cooperative federalism*: Congress had discretion to preempt state law but otherwise would not automatically subsume state regulatory authority.

Specifically, Congress played a cooperative role with states in regulating draconian corporate behavior: In dealing with the rise of the concentration of wealth, which had been the result of financial trusts and monopolies, Congress regulated a range of illegal commercial activities, such as price-fixing and restraints on trade. Notably, the Sherman Antitrust Act of 1890 as well as the Mann-Elkins Act of 1913 and the Clayton Anti-Trust of 1914 were federal laws intended to *supplement*—not supplant—state laws. Consistent with the general approach using cooperative federalism, the Executive Branch was authorized to employ the Department of Justice, the Federal Trade Commission, and the Interstate Commerce Commission, among others, to combat the rising problems posed by trusts and monopolies. Overall, the days in which the federal government had played a limited and nonexclusive role in governing private economic affairs were over. Congress, with the help of the executive, aimed to innovatively solve *national* issues using the entire apparatus of the federal government. Thus the model of cooperative federalism was now on deck to become the new national solution.

NOTES

1. *Lochner v. New York*, 198 U.S. 45 (1905).
2. *Mintz v. Baldwin*, 289 U.S. 346 (1933).
3. "Second Industrial Revolution," Britannica.com, accessed February 4, 2021, https://www.britannica.com/topic/Second-Industrial-Revolution; "Second Industrial Revolution," Wikipedia.
4. See generally White, *Railroaded*; Michael McGerr, *A Fierce Discontent: The Rise and Fall of the Progressive Movement in America, 1870–1920* (New York: Simon and Schuster, 2003); and Joshua B. Freeman, *Behemoth: A History of the Factory and the Making of the Modern World* (New York: W. W. Norton and Company, 2018).
5. McGerr, *Fierce Discontent*, 3–146.
6. McGerr, *Fierce Discontent*, 147–81.
7. Bryan was a candidate for the presidency with the Democratic and Populist nominations in 1896, 1900, and 1908. He was secretary of state in 1913. Throughout his career he advocated for economic reforms to control trust and monopolies; for labor reforms establishing the minimum wage, the eight-hour workday, and support for labor unions and workplace safety; and for political and policy reforms by way of the creation of health departments, access to education, defense of the rights of minorities, voting reforms, and regulation of political-campaign contributions.
8. McGerr, *Fierce Discontent*, 155–64; Richard N. L. Andrews, *Managing the Environment: Managing Ourselves* (New Haven: Yale University Press, 1999), 94–135.
9. *United States v. E. C. Knight Co.*, 156 U.S. 1, 11 (1895).

10. To give the reader an example of how fiercely President Hoover—a Republican—held the hard line on the separation of federal and state authority, when the Great Depression hit the country in 1929, Hoover believed no American should go hungry but refused federal assistance because he believed that "care for the needy was properly the responsibility of private organizations and of state and local officials." William J. Barber, *From New Era to New Deal: Herbert Hoover, the Economists, and American Economic Policy, 1921–1933* (Cambridge: Cambridge University Press, 1988). This same phenomenon again occurred in 2020 and 2021 when the Trump administration—also Republican—refused to assume responsibility for addressing of the COVID-19 crisis that gripped the nation, leaving it up to the states to both order and administer the vaccine required to quell rates of new infections.

11. Particularly see Gardbaum, "Breadth versus Depth," 48.

12. *Lochner v. New York*, 198 U.S. 45 (1905).

13. Peckham quoted in Stephen B. Presser, *Recapturing the Constitution: Race, Religion, and Abortion Reconsidered* (Washington, DC: Regnery, 1994), 139–43.

14. Lochner, 198 U.S. 45, 68 (1905).

15. Hoffer, Hoffer, and Hull, *Supreme Court*, 184–85.

16. Gardbaum, "Breadth versus Depth," 48 and then 57.

17. Presser, *Recapturing the Constitution*, 143–49. In 1912 Theodore Roosevelt even campaigned for president under the banner of "New Nationalism." See "New Nationalism (Theodore Roosevelt)," Wikipedia, last modified September 2, 2021, https://en.wikipedia.org/wiki/New_Nationalism_(Theodore_Roosevelt).

18. *Savage v. Jones*, 225 U.S. 501 (1912); *Southern Ry. Co. v. Reid*, 222 U.S. 424 (1912). *Reid v. People of State of Colorado* (187 U.S. 137 [1902]) was the precedent cited in *Savage v. Jones*, which coexisted with Southern Railroad and Hardwick throughout the Lochner era. See Gardbaum, "Breadth versus Depth," 63.

19. Gardbaum, "Breadth versus Depth," 57–58.

20. *Charleston & Western Carolina Ry v. Varnville Furniture Co.*, 237 U.S. 597, 604 (1915).

21. Gardbaum, "Breadth versus Depth," 58–62.

22. 226 U.S. 426 (1913).

23. Ernest A. Young, "'The Ordinary Diet of the Law': The Presumption against Preemption in the Roberts Court," *Supreme Court Review* 2011, no. 1 (2012): 266, https://scholarship.law.duke.edu/cgi/viewcontent.cgi?article=5297&context=faculty_scholarship.

24. *Chicago Rock Island & Pacific Railway Co. v. Hardwick-Farmers Elevator Co.*, 226 U.S. 426, 435 (1913).

25. *Missouri Pac. R.R. v. Stroud*, 267 U.S. 404, 408 (1925).

26. In a similar case following two years later, *Charleston & Western Carolina Ry v. Varnville Furniture Co.*, the Court concluded, under the prevailing doctrine in this period, that "preemption eliminates the need to consider the content of state laws on the subject, to lay the two laws side by side to ascertain whether or not they conflict." Stephen A. Gardbaum, "The Nature of Preemption," *Cornell Law Review* 79, no. 4 (1994): 776, 805, https://core.ac.uk/download/pdf/216737946.pdf, quoting Charleston & Western Carolina Ry, 237 U.S. 597, 604 (1915).

27. *New York Cent. R. Co. v. Winfield*, 244 U.S. 147, 169 (1917).
28. Gardbaum, "Breadth versus Depth," 66.
29. Young, "'Ordinary Diet of the Law,'" 259, and see notes 23–24, pages 257–59. Also see *Wickard v. Filburn*, 317 U.S. 111 (1942); and Stephen Gardbaum, "New Deal Constitutionalism and the Unshackling of the States," *University of Chicago Law Review* 483, no. 2 (1997): 483–566, https://chicagounbound.uchicago.edu/cgi/viewcontent.cgi?article=4956&context=uclrev (explaining how the New Deal revolution expanded the regulatory authority of *both* federal and state governments).

And see Corwin, "Passing of Dual Federalism," 17–23: "According to [the post–New Deal] conception," Corwin writes, "the National Government and the States are mutually complementary parts of a *single* governmental mechanism all of whose powers are intended to realize the current purposes of government according to their applicability to the problem at hand" (emphasis original).

30. 289 U.S. 346 (1933).
31. The *Mintz* opinion was reinforced later that same year by Justice Brandeis in *Dickson v. Uhlmann Grain Company* (288 U.S. 188, 189 [1933]).
32. Gardbaum, "Breadth versus Depth," 68, 77. The canonical statement appears in the later case of *Rice v. Santa Fe Elevator Corp.* (331 U.S. 218, 230 [1947]): "We start with the assumption that the historic police powers of the States were not to be superseded by the Federal Act unless that was the clear purpose of Congress."
33. Gardbaum, "Breadth versus Depth," 68, 73–74.
34. Gardbaum, "Breadth versus Depth," 69.
35. Epstein and Greve, "Introduction: Preemption in Context," 16.
36. Epstein and Greve, "Introduction: Preemption in Context," 11, 19.
37. Epstein and Greve, "Introduction: Preemption in Context," 16.
38. Epstein and Greve, "Introduction: Preemption in Context," 11.
39. Gardbaum, "Breadth versus Depth," 67. See also South Carolina Highway Dep't v. Barnwell Bros., Inc., 303 U.S. 177 (1938).
40. Gardbaum, "Breadth versus Depth," 67–68.
41. *Hines v. Davidowitz*, 312 U.S. 52 (1941); Rice, 331 U.S. 218 (1947).
42. The 1938 *Erie Railroad* case erased the use of federal common law—"one of the proudest and most central element in the evolution of the post New Deal order" that stands to this day as a statutory compromise over governmental architecture and federalism. *Erie R.R. Co. v. Tompkins*, 304 U.S. 64 (1938), as discussed in Epstein and Greve, "Introduction: Preemption in Context," 17.
43. McGerr, *Fierce Discontent*, 150–64.
44. Epstein and Greve, "Introduction: Preemption in Context," 317.
45. White, *Railroaded*, 355–65; Richard D. Stone, *The Interstate Commerce Commission and the Railroad Industry: A History of Regulatory Policy* (New York: Praeger, 1991); and "Interstate Commerce Commission," Wikipedia, last modified September 2, 2021, https://en.wikipedia.org/wiki/Interstate_Commerce_Commission.
46. 156 U.S. 1 (1895).
47. Ida M. Tarbell, "The History of the Standard Oil Company," *McClure's Magazine* 20, no. 2, December 1902, pp. 115–28, online at https://archive.org/details/sim_new-mcclures-magazine_1902-12_20_2/mode/2up; Ida M. Tarbell, *The History*

of the Standard Oil Company (New York: McClure, Phillips and Company, 1904); and *Standard Oil Co. of New Jersey v. United States*, 221 U.S. 1 (1911).

48. 24 S. Ct. 436 (1904).

49. *American Tobacco Co. v. United States*, 221 U.S. 106 (1911). See also *Addyston Pipe & Steel Co. v. United States*, 175 U.S. 211 (1899); *United States v. Trans-Missouri Freight Association*, 166 U.S. 290 (1897); and *Chicago Board of Trade v. United States*, 246 U.S. 231 (1918).

50. *Northern Securities Co. v. United States*, 24 S. Ct. 436, 458 (1904).

51. *E. C. Knight Co. v. United States*, 156 U.S. 1, 27, 31 (1895), quoting *Central Ohio Salt Co. v. Guthrie*, 35 Ohio St. 666, 672 (1880).

52. *Northern Securities Co. v. United States*, 24 S. Ct. 436, 460.

53. Major national events highlighted the need for uniform industrial regulations, including the 1892 Homestead Strike in which steelworkers protested wage cuts; the 1902 Anthracite Coal Strike for higher wages and an eight-hour workday; and the 1911 Triangle Shirtwaist Factory fire, which resulted in the death of 146 garment workers. In addition to the antitrust acts and the Interstate Commerce Act legislation cited above, the major federal legislation provoked by these national events and the reaction to the Progressive and Granger movements included the Revenue Act of 1894, the Federal Lottery Act of 1895, the Pure Food and Drug Act of 1906, the two Federal Employer Liability Acts of 1906 and 1908, and the White-Slave Traffic Act (the Mann Act) of 1910. Many labor unions were formed in the 1880s and '90s, the earliest being Samuel Gompers's American Federation of Labor (AFL). All of these were responses to the demands for national control of society's welfare and the economy. McGerr, *Fierce Discontent*, 21, 32–33, 118–21, 126, 129–32, 140–45, 272, 289–90; and Gardbaum, "Breadth versus Depth," 50.

54. Chad Montrie, *The Myth of Silent Spring: Rethinking the Origins of American Environmentalism* (Oakland: University of California Press, 2018), 62–98.

55. McGerr, *Fierce Discontent*, 315–19.

56. Montrie, *Myth of Silent Spring*, 66–68.

57. US Census Bureau, *Statistical Abstract of the United States: 1920* (Washington, DC: US Government Printing Office, 1921), , downloadable at https://www.census.gov/library/publications/1920/compendia/statab/23ed.html.

58. Andrews, *Managing the Environment*, 111.

59. Robert Gottlieb, *Forcing the Spring: The Transformation of the American Environmental Movement* (Washington, DC: Island Press, 1993), 47–75.

60. Montrie, *Myth of Silent Spring*, 66–67.

61. McGerr, *Fierce Discontent*, 52–59, 81–104.

Jacob Riis was a social reformer, political activist, and police reporter. In 1890, he shocked the conscience of his readers when he detailed slum conditions in New York City with the publication of *How the Other Half Lives: Studies among the Tenements of New York* (New York: Charles Scribner's Sons). He followed this book with publications of *The Children of the Poor* (New York: Scribner's Sons, 1892), *Out of Mulberry Street* (New York: The Century Co., 1898), *The Battle with the Slum* (New York: Macmillan Co., 1902), and his autobiography, *The Making of an American* (New York: Macmillan, 1901).

62. Samuel P. Hays, *Explorations in Environmental History* (Pittsburgh: University of Pittsburgh Press, 1998), 69–75.

63. Andrews, *Managing the Environment*, 131–33.

Upton Sinclair published a series of articles in the newspaper *Appeal to Reason* in 1905 on the evils of the meat-processing business, based on his investigations into the four major meatpacking companies in Chicago, which he then published as a book in 1906, *The Jungle*, a punishingly blunt polemic (New York: Doubleday, Page and Co.). The novel inspired President Theodore Roosevelt to further investigate, and the findings confirmed the conditions revealed in *The Jungle*, leading to the Meat Inspection Act, followed the same day in 1906 by the Pure Food and Drug Act. Sinclair, labeled a muckraker, wrote ninety novels on the social ills of industrial production, including, among others, *King Coal: A Novel* (New York: Macmillan Co., 1917), *Oil!* (New York: Albert and Charles Boni, 1927), and *The Flivver King* (Detroit: United Automobile Workers, 1937), the latter about Henry Ford's assembly lines.

64. Andrews, *Managing the Environment*, 133.

65. McGerr, *Fierce Discontent*, 52, 296.

66. US Constitution, Amend. 16, https://www.senate.gov/civics/constitution_item/constitution.htm#amdt_16_(1913), Art. 1, Sec. 9, https://www.senate.gov/civics/constitution_item/constitution.htm#a1_sec9; and US Constitution, Amend. 17, https://www.senate.gov/civics/constitution_item/constitution.htm#amdt_17_(1913), Art. 1, Sec. 8, https://www.senate.gov/civics/constitution_item/constitution.htm#a1_sec8.

Passage of the Sixteenth Amendment, reviving federal income tax, followed a sordid history of revenue-raising measures begun in 1862 when President Abraham Lincoln had signed a law to raise money to pay for the Civil War: a 3 percent tax had been levied on income between $600 and $10,000, and 5 percent on income over $10,000. This measure had created the first commissioner of internal revenue. Congress then cut the tax rate in 1867 and repealed it entirely in 1872. Ninety percent of all revenues thereafter came from taxes on liquor, beer, wine, and tobacco. In 1894, income taxes were again levied, but one year later the Supreme Court ruled them unconstitutional. Enacted in 1909 and ratified in 1913, the Sixteenth Amendment gave Congress the power to collect taxes on incomes, and it levied a flat 1 percent tax on net income above $3,000 and 6 percent on income above $500,000. In 1916 a federal estate tax was added to the income tax burden; in 1926 the estate tax became a credit—or offset—against state-inheritance taxes. In 1918, to raise money for World War I, a progressive income tax rate of up to 75 percent was codified.

67. Internal Revenue Service, "Historical Highlights of the IRS," IRS.gov, last modified December 18, 2020, https://www.irs.gov/newsroom/historical-highlights-of-the-irs.

The Bureau of Internal Revenue—initially BIR, later the IRS—began in 1862 with Lincoln's appointment of a commissioner of internal revenue within the Treasury Department. In addition to the collection of prescribed taxes, the bureau was responsible for collecting regulatory taxes on a variety of butters, oleomargarines, flours, cheeses, phosphorus matches, pistols and revolvers, futures trading contracts, cotton futures, foreign-built boats, and narcotics and a tax on the businesses of brewers, distillers, and retail and wholesale liquor dealers. Following the adoption of the

Eighteenth Amendment, establishing Prohibition, the IRS was responsible for tax and penalty revenues derived from the prohibition on the sale of liquor supplementary to the Bureau of Prohibition, created in 1927. See Carroll Hill Wooddy, *The Growth of the Federal Government, 1915–1932* (New York: McGraw-Hill, 1934), 38–39, 41.

68. Wooddy, *Growth of the Federal Government*, 41–43.

7

Prohibition and Reform: The Emergence of the Administrative State, 1919–1933

The most controversial attempt at preemption was Prohibition, which had been inspired by the Women's Temperance Movement and its respective social and moral aims to preserve the stability and continuance of the core family unit and curb "expensive idleness and gross debauchery."[1] This ambitious but ultimately failed attempt at federal control of alcohol sales included a pervasive role for the Treasury Department in enforcing Prohibition, and the modern administrative state emerged from the ashes of that failed project. While Section 2 of the Eighteenth Amendment permitted states to *concurrently* exercise their police power to enforce Prohibition's mandate, states largely refused to enforce it, as doing so violated the spirit of federalism. This acquiescence inadvertently ceded power to the federal government, leading to rapid ascent of the administrative state and the problems that follow when federal power is left unchecked by states exercising their independence as a sovereign balance.

THE TEMPERANCE MOVEMENT, THE SIXTEENTH AMENDMENT OF 1913, THE EIGHTEENTH AMENDMENT OF 1919, AND THE NINETEENTH AMENDMENT OF 1920

At this point in the story of the creep of federal preemption over the public trust doctrine and states' rights, just as US soldiers were returning home from World War I in 1918, a major change was sweeping the nation: Prohibition. The expansive forces of the Progressive Era exploded yet again with the Eighteenth Amendment in 1919, banning the production, sale, and distribution of alcohol. This greatly expanded federal police powers over state police authority—heretofore the exclusive province of state and local governments. Nationwide Prohibition had been actively promoted by the Women's Temperance Movement for over forty years. Despite its repeal by the Twenty-First Amendment in 1933, the federal bureaucratic expansion remained in place. Most historians have overlooked the substantial, continuing, and destructive effect the Eighteenth Amendment had on federalism, preemption, and state sovereignty.[2]

Dramatic industrial expansion followed the era of great prosperity from the robber barons' expansion of railroads and the rapid growth of technology. This had generated a new middle class, providing workers with family and leisure time, stable incomes, regulated hours, paid vacations, and lifestyles that afforded them time for vice and "the trinity of temptations—drink, prostitution, and divorce."[3] Theodore Roosevelt characterized it as the "life of foolishness and expensive idleness and gross debauchery."[4] From 1880 to 1900, the number of saloons—considered the public symbol of alcohol consumption—grew from 150,000 to 250,000.[5] Americans had drunk 590 million gallons of beer and malt liquor annually in 1885, which had risen to 1.2 billion gallons by 1900. The vices of prostitution and illegal narcotics followed the rise of alcohol consumption,[6] as did card playing, gambling, horse racing, off-track betting, dance halls, peep shows, and brothels. The divorce rate had risen from four in one thousand marriages in 1900 to four and a half in one thousand by 1910.[7]

To combat what some considered omnipresent vice, large armies of temperance and moral crusaders were mobilized. Rightly or wrongly, these self-righteous crusaders saw these vices as eating into American society, which they felt was centered on the stability and health of the family and middle-class values.[8] Prominent were the Woman's Christian Temperance Union and the Anti-Saloon League. These crusading groups were part of the much larger women's movement that finally achieved adoption of the Eighteenth Amendment, bringing about nationwide Prohibition in 1919.[9] "The Eighteenth Amendment's prohibition on the sale and manufacture of liquor prompted the greatest expansion of federal administrative regulatory authority since the days of Reconstruction."[10] This was quickly followed by the right of women to vote in 1920 with the Nineteenth Amendment, preempting state authority to restrict female voting. Expansion of preemption and of the Washington bureaucracy followed these three constitutional amendments, including the Sixteenth Amendment, which gave the federal government the right to levy income taxes, further enlarging the Treasury's Bureau of Internal Revenue.

Prohibition and Reform: The Emergence of the Administrative State, 1919–1933   77

Figure 7.1.   New York City Police oversee the pouring of liquor from a barrel down a sewer in a raid during Prohibition. *Source*: Ian Dagnell Computing/Alamay Stock Photo.

THE ROLE OF THE TREASURY DEPARTMENT TO ENFORCE PROHIBITION: THE GREATEST EXPANSION OF WASHINGTON BUREAUCRACY SINCE THE CIVIL WAR

Prior to 1919, the Treasury Department had been responsible for collecting excise taxes levied on alcoholic beverages. To enforce the National Prohibition Act of 1919 (the Volstead Act), the Prohibition Unit was created within the Department of Treasury's Bureau of Internal Revenue. Added to the unit from existing branches within Treasury were the Narcotics Division and the Technical Division, used to control the distribution of narcotic drugs and industrial alcohol. In 1927, the Prohibition Unit became the Bureau of Prohibition, an independent entity within Treasury. In 1930 the bureau was transferred to the Department of Justice, and in 1933, following repeal of the Eighteenth Amendment, part of its enforcement functions were merged into the Federal Bureau of Investigation at Justice, along with its 2,000 employees. The remaining regulatory body of the Bureau of Prohibition was once again transferred back to Treasury as the Alcohol Tax Unit of the Internal Revenue Service, the Bureau of Industrial Alcohol, and the Bureau of Narcotics (to enforce the Harrison Narcotic Law of 1914); thereafter, part of it evolved into the Bureau of Alcohol, Tobacco and Firearms (ATF).

Almost seventy years later, following the terrorist attacks of September 11, 2001, the Homeland Security Act of 2002 created the Department of Homeland Security, and within the same law ATF was transferred back to the Department of Justice, where it became the Bureau of Alcohol, Tobacco, Firearms, and Explosives (BATFE). However, in 2003 the BATFE regulatory functions relating to collecting revenue and excise taxes from the production and sale of tobacco and alcohol products were transferred to the newly created Alcohol and Tobacco Tax and Trade Bureau and moved back to the Treasury Department. With each transfer, the bureaucracy grew through accretion.

When the Prohibition Unit was founded in 1919, its enforcement functions included addressing illegal narcotics manufacturing and traffic. About 2,300 agents were appointed initially to enforce Prohibition; by 1925, that number had risen to 4,488. They were paid $2,500 a year and issued guns and vehicles but were given little to no training.[11] When Prohibition was repealed in 1933, the ranks of the agents totaled some 3,300.[12] The agents, however, were but a small part of the bureaucratic framework needed to support Prohibition. The number of arrests by agents had gone from 34,175 in 1921 to 78,383 in 1932. The total number of automobile seizures in connection with these arrests was 11,833 in 1932 alone. Moreover, the number of stills, distilleries, fermenters, and related manufacturing paraphernalia seized totaled 282,122 in 1930.[13]

These activities placed a high burden on the federal prison system and courts. About 80 percent of arrests for liquor violations terminated in guilty pleas, and half of all federal prisoners were serving liquor-related violations. In 1932 there were 13,698 federal prisoners incarcerated, at a maintenance cost of $14,966,500 annually. From Prohibition, the prison system was forced to expand, with the creation of six new facilities that included penitentiaries, reformatories, a hospital, six work camps, and two farms.[14]

The Department of Justice's attorney general and the courts were burdened with prosecuting all the enforcement arrests. In 1929 alone there were 74,723 prosecutions, and in 1931 there were 72,509 jury trials for liquor cases, which represented one-quarter of all federal trials. The massive number of Prohibition prosecutions forced federal courts "to perform the function of petty police courts."[15] One federal district judge in 1925 complained, "When I came on the bench ten years ago . . . The position was one of dignity and honor. Today . . . more than 50% [is like] a police court . . . swarming with samples of all the races . . . bootleggers, dope fiends, dope peddlers, white slaves, etc. The work and worry, the responsibility, are more than double what they were in 1915."[16] Salaries for all judges, retired judges, pensioners, court clerks, bailiffs, US Marshals, office expenses, printing and binding, jurors, and commissioners totaled a high of $5,369,000 in 1931, well over half of the total Department of Justice annual budget of $9,934,600.[17] The Coast Guard played a major role in liquor enforcement, due to offshore and border smuggling operations from the Caribbean, Canada, and Mexico. Their highest yearly cost of $15,377,000 in 1931 was 36 percent of the total cost of Prohibition enforcement that year.[18] The apotheosis of the administrative state arose from this massive bureaucracy.

The reach and breadth of the federal bureaucratic apparatus to manage and control the manufacture and sale of distilled spirits and to suppress illegal traffic in alcohol and narcotics had become enormous, all at the expense of federalism and state sovereignty. The expansion of the federal prohibition bureaucracy and of federal power over the states went well beyond just the investigation, apprehension, prosecution (via the Justice Department), and incarceration of criminals (with the Bureau of Prisons). It included seizure and forfeiture of illegal liquor and narcotics traffic and working with state law enforcement and their courts who had "concurrent" power to enforce the Eighteenth Amendment.[19] It also included control of the production of legal liquor and industrial alcohol for legitimate medicinal and antiseptic uses, sacramental wines, vinegar and sweet cider, flavoring extracts and syrups and control of bonded liquor warehouses and the administration of treaties with foreign countries regarding smuggling and legal importation.[20] The bureaucratic scope of enforcement was enormous.

THE APOTHEOSIS OF THE ADMINISTRATIVE STATE

The Eighteenth Amendment (Section 2) provided that the states have "concurrent power" to enforce Prohibition. This practically conscripted state law-enforcement agencies and courts into capturing and prosecuting illegal liquor criminals.[21] Ohio even created a series of "village liquor courts" throughout the state to generate supplemental revenue shared with the villages. However, when their enforcement, prosecutions, and fines grew so onerous, they created a "reign of terror" in Ohio, and the US Supreme Court declared the Ohio enabling statute unconstitutional.[22] Those state and local costs have never been quantified or even estimated. However, the federal government's total costs to enforce Prohibition, including all supporting bureaus, agencies, and departments, were calculated in a monumental 1934 study; the cost in 1930 was $39,691,000 million. In 1931, that cost had risen to $42,630,000.[23] Converted to 2020 dollars, that is equivalent to $680,387,589.

This confusing evolution of expanding Prohibition bureaucracy is but a small part of the regulatory and enforcement authority of the federal government. It is representative of how the opportunistic federal government started its vast expansion early in the Progressive Era by exploiting an opportunity. It continues to grow a century later in the same manner by exploiting opportunity and crisis.[24] One legal scholar characterizes the era: "Prohibition was in many ways the apotheosis of the administrative state, for it deployed a vast government apparatus to control intimate details of personal consumption."[25] The total cost of running the federal government in 1930 was $4,891,333,000, up from $1,047,492,000 in 1915.[26] The number of employees in federal executive civil service in 1915 had been 476,363, and in 1930 it had risen to 808,915 employees, creating 17,768 retirees with federal retirement benefits.[27] That offers some perspective on the cost of expanding the federal government to support all the programs put in place both during and later due to the Progressive Era.

The growth in the federal government from the Depression era and its social and economic relief programs in the 1930s added yet another vast bureaucratic structure on top of that created by those of the previous era from 1890 to 1933. This was the birth of the behemoth administrative state.[28] The new agencies created during the 1930s included the Federal Deposit Insurance Corporation, to protect and regulate US banking; the National Labor Relations Board, to protect workers; the Securities and Exchange Commission, to regulate the stock market; and the Civil Aeronautics Board, to regulate air travel. From it all, the federal government's control grew enormous, and state sovereignty lessened as preemption of state power accelerated. These conditions worsened once the US Supreme Court weighed in.

Following the tenure of Chief Justice White, the Supreme Court was led by former US President William Howard Taft from 1921 through 1930. "The Taft Court played a decentralization role of limiting the growth of national regulation under the enumerated powers doctrine. Its simultaneous imposition of due process limits on state regulation had the effect of creating a uniform national economic policy of *laissez faire*."[29] The Taft Court also addressed the enforcement of the Eighteenth Amendment of Prohibition with a fiercely divided Court because the amendment ceded to Congress unfettered authority.[30] Several key cases highlight how the Court strained to support enforcement of a law that lacked public support and was contrary to social norms and values.[31] These Prohibition cases strengthened the federal administrative state's power to preempt state laws, ignore social values, and pursue bureaucratic ends, notwithstanding its demoralizing effects on society.

The lessons learned from the adoption and repeal of Prohibition is that the American public will not accept the legitimacy of federal control of their personal habits or of their entrenched values; a law without such legitimacy will fail and will provoke flagrant defiance and distrust of federal authority. It will instead be seen as a form of "domestic imperialism," a "nationalistic invasion" of local and personal affairs.[32] The divided Taft Court, in the untenable position of having to navigate strong internal disagreements,[33] was viewed as a "potent symbol of the oppressive bureaucratic apparatus necessary to sustain Prohibition." While the Eighteenth Amendment gave the states concurrent powers of enforcement, the states saw this as merely an "option," not a "duty," and refused to participate.[34] The states viewed Prohibition as a repudiation of the spirit of federalism and a radical departure from the constitutional structure of our federal system.[35]

The effect of this usurpation was to transfer much of the states' police power of enforcement to the federal government and to conscript local police into federal service.[36] Congress compounded the damage to federalism by refusing to adequately fund a sufficient number of federal agents and by using until 1927 federal agents who were political patronage appointments of party hacks. They were incompetent and untrained, and many were dishonest, openly violating the law and creating their own crime wave by accepting bribes and by ignoring constitutional search and seizure requirements—all with the full support of the Supreme Court.[37] The combination of congressional stupidity, bureaucratic incompetence, and judicial complicity dealt a serious blow to the democratic legitimacy inherent in self-government, federalism, and state sovereignty. As the Supreme Court saw it (wrongly), this was all a matter of "positive dualism" and of "dual sovereignty"; in reality, it was federal usurpation of constitutional authority through abuse of the Supremacy Clause.[38]

By the time Prohibition was repealed in 1933, it had become apparent that the constitutional amendment had been a disastrous failure that had bred contempt for the rule of law and had invited corruption and anarchy, and badly undermined federalism and state sovereignty. The amendment had been meant to reform the entrenched social values and reshape the personal behavior of an entire nation.[39] But the nation lacked the institutional structure and congressional funding necessary to control and effectively implement the amendment.[40] It had endowed the federal government with comprehensive but ineffective police powers that demoralized the public.[41] It had been a demoralizing overreach, the price of which had been simply too high for the nation. It was aptly described as "a sumptuary law out of touch with the consciousness of the country . . . that was obeyed only as a result of an escalating spiral of repressive enforcement [that] was simply not sustainable."[42]

THE ASCENDENCY OF FEDERAL POWER OVER THE STATES

The federal supremacy represented by the Eighteenth Amendment is best seen in three Prohibition Era Supreme Court cases. In 1922, the Taft Court in *United States v. Lanza*[43] unanimously held that the defendant Lanza could be tried and convicted for the same crime of a liquor violation in both the state and federal courts since they were two separate sovereignties, each with separate laws. This formulation of "dual sovereignty" undermined the Double Jeopardy Clause.[44] This holding was reaffirmed four years later.[45] The 1924 case of *James Everard's Breweries v. Day*[46] unanimously upheld Congress's regulation prohibiting physicians from prescribing intoxicating malt liquors for medicinal purposes. In the 1926 case of *Lambert v. Yellowley*,[47] the Court upheld Congress's authority to regulate the prescription of vinous and spirituous liquors—a common and accepted medical practice—far more than prescribing malt liquors. The regulation of liquor in medical practice in *Lambert* was a direct intrusion into the police power of the states.[48] The dissent by Justice George Sutherland regarded it as a "transfer" of police power and loss of the democratic legitimacy inherent in federalism. Both decisions were ruthlessly nationalistic but reflected the ascendency of federal power, the administrative state, and federal preemption.[49]

The issue of warrantless search and seizure came before the Taft Court in 1925 after an automobile had been stopped that the police had recognized as previously being used to sell liquor.[50] Taft's opinion reinterpreted the Fourth Amendment doctrine and strained the reading of the Eighteenth Amendment in the pragmatic need of local law enforcement to enforce federal Prohibition.[51] The decision was criticized for "awarding" carte blanche to Prohibition officers.[52] Chief Justice Taft's crusade for stricter enforcement of Prohibition reached its zenith in *Olmstead v. United States*, in which the Court held that the wiretapping of a liquor dealer's phone line outside his house had not been search and seizure under the Fourth Amendment, despite Washington State's law prohibiting such action.[53] The *Olmstead* opinion carried "still further the progress of creating a governmental bureaucracy equipped with almost unlimited powers of espionage for purposes of attempting to enforce Prohibition."[54]

Similarly, the Taft Prohibition Court repeated by ratification federal usurpation and law breaking by federal officials. In *Hester v. United States*, the Court held that the Fourth Amendment didn't apply to liquor discovered in an open field onto which the police had unlawfully trespassed; the distinction made was that an open field isn't a "house" contemplated by the words of the Fourth Amendment.[55] Also, according to the compliant Prohibition Court, the Coast Guard's use of a searchlight to examine the deck of a ship seized on the high seas did not constitute an illegal search.[56] The same year, the case of *Gambino v. United States* held that restrictions of the Fourth and Fifth Amendments on search and seizure did not apply to the states since New York state troopers had made the arrest and had been enforcing state law.[57] The admissibility of evidence was not affected by the illegality of the means by which it was obtained.[58] Thus, to get around the Fourth and Fifth Amendments, federal officers increasingly commandeered state police to illegally gather evidence, which they could then use in federal court without constitutional challenges. This nefarious practice became known as the "silver platter doctrine."[59] After almost forty years of harm to federalism, the 1928 *Olmstead* holding was finally overturned in 1967 when the Supreme Court adopted the theory of Justice Louis Brandeis's dissent in *Olmstead*.[60]

Prohibition became the biggest political issue since the Civil War[61] and was undoubtedly the largest, most controversial federal preemption effort ever attempted in American history. Prohibition jurisprudence had empowered federal preemption as a politically feasible option of governance and helped give birth to what legal historian Robert Post characterizes as the emergence of the American administrative state.[62]

SUMMARY

The nation's most controversial attempt at preemption was Prohibition. Inspired by the Women's Temperance Movement, which had admirable ends to curb what Theodore Roosevelt identified as "expensive idleness and gross debauchery" and to ensure the health and stability of the family unit, the Prohibition movement—according to its crusaders—necessitated comprehensive *federal* action. However, despite its social and moral objectives at reform, the ratification of the Eighteenth Amendment and the adoption of the National Prohibition Act of 1919 (the Volstead Act) presented new problems for the nation between 1919 and 1933: Under its newly prescribed mandate to prohibit the sale of liquor, the federal government acquired greater regulatory authority over the private conduct of its citizenry. In addition, Section 2 of the Eighteenth Amendment allowed for the states to concurrently exercise power to regulate and enforce Prohibition's mandate. Structurally, the Eighteenth Amendment modeled cooperative federalism.

The Department of the Treasury's Prohibition Unit established in 1919 was designed for the principal purpose of using federal government powers to seize and forfeit illegal liquor, as well as intercept narcotics traffic. However, states—viewing Prohibition as a refutation of the basic purpose of federalism, and being what Louis Brandeis once called the "laboratories of democracy"—largely refused to exercise concurrent enforcement powers for Prohibition. Hence, states *inadvertently* ceded greater authority to the federal government. Overall, because of the increasing administrative burden that had been strapped on the federal government and its agents to execute its promise of Prohibition, the costs of enforcement and compliance became prohibitive.

Meanwhile, under the leadership of Chief Justice Taft, the Supreme Court empowered the federal government to rigorously regulate and enforce Prohibition. In a line of cases, ranging from regulating the use of liquor for medicinal purposes—for example, *James Everard's Breweries v. Day* (1924) and *Lambert v. Yellowley* (1926)—to extending its regulatory reach to search and seizures under the Fourth Amendment—for example, *Olmstead v. United States* (1925) and *Gambino v. United States* (1927)—the federal government "deployed a vast government apparatus to control intimate details of personal consumption."[63] Accordingly, these flagrant attempts at regulation demonstrate the "apotheosis" of the administrative state and the length to which the federal government will go when unchecked by state power. Overall, while Prohibition had aimed for both the federal government and states to concurrently exercise their respective powers, the effects were abysmal and breached the public trust. However, while federal preemption of the prohibition of liquor ultimately failed in its aims, fertile ground had been laid for the future modern administrative state to grow.

NOTES

1. William Henry Harbaugh, *Power and Responsibility: The Life and Times of Theodore Roosevelt* (New York: Farrar, Straus and Cudahy, 1961), 52.

2. Robert Post, "Federalism, Positive Law, and the Emergence of the American Administrative State: Prohibition in the Taft Court Era," *William and Mary Law Review* 48, no. 1 (2006): 2, 4, https://scholarship.law.wm.edu/cgi/viewcontent.cgi?article=1100&context=wmlr.

3. McGerr, *Fierce Discontent*, 84.

4. Harbaugh, *Power and Responsibility: The Life and Times of Theodore Roosevelt*, 52.

5. McGerr, *Fierce Discontent*, 85.

6. McGerr, *Fierce Discontent*, 84.

7. McGerr, *Fierce Discontent*, 92.

8. McGerr, *Fierce Discontent*, 84, 86, 91.

9. McGerr, *Fierce Discontent*, 296; and Eleanor Flexner and Ellen Fitzpatrick, *Century of Struggle: The Woman's Rights Movement in the United States* (Cambridge: Harvard University Press, 1996), 241–317.

10. Post, "Federalism, Positive Law," 2, 4.

11. Bureau of Alcohol, Tobacco, Firearms and Explosives, "Fallen Prohibition Agents," ATF.gov, accessed February 4, 2021, https://www.atf.gov/our-history/fallen-agents; and Bureau of Alcohol, Tobacco, Firearms and Explosives, "ATF's Legacy of Diversity," ATF.gov, last reviewed September 22, 2016, https://www.atf.gov/our-history/atfs-legacy-diversity.

12. Wooddy, *Growth of the Federal Government*, 98, 102.

13. Wooddy, *Growth of the Federal Government*, 102.

14. Wooddy, *Growth of the Federal Government*, 95–96, 102; Post, "Federalism, Positive Law," 28, n. 92.

15. "Prohibition and Federal Judges," *New York Times*, May 29, 1925, p. 16, https://timesmachine.nytimes.com/timesmachine/1925/05/29/104174646.html.

16. Post, "Federalism, Positive Law," 27, 89.

17. Wooddy, *Growth of the Federal Government*, 83, 105.

18. Wooddy, *Growth of the Federal Government*, 105.

19. Post, "Federalism, Positive Law," 24–27, 29–33.

20. Wooddy, *Growth of the Federal Government*, 98–99.

21. Post, "Federalism, Positive Law," 24–26.

22. Post, "Federalism, Positive Law," 113–14; and see *Tumey v. Ohio*, 273 U.S. 510 (1927).

23. Wooddy, *Growth of the Federal Government*, 577, and then 105.

24. Wooddy, *Growth of the Federal Government*, 97–112; and Laurence F. Schmeckebier, *The Bureau of Prohibition: Its History, Activities and Organization* (Washington, DC: Brookings Institution, 1929). And see "Bureau of Prohibition," Wikipedia, last modified September 1, 2021, https://en.wikipedia.org/wiki/Bureau_of_Prohibition.

25. Post, "Federalism, Positive Law," 18.

26. Wooddy, *Growth of the Federal Government*, 544.

27. Wooddy, *Growth of the Federal Government*, 48, 55.

28. Post, "Federalism, Positive Law," 1–4.

29. Young, "Making Federalism Doctrine," 1733, 1751.

30. Post, "Federalism, Positive Law," 12, 13, 58.

31. Hoffer, Hoffer, and Hull, *Supreme Court*, 217–51; and Post, "Federalism, Positive Law," 7, 12–13, 68–70, 82, 103–59.

32. Post, "Federalism, Positive Law," 50, 52, 57.

33. Post, "Federalism, Positive Law," 10.

34. Post, "Federalism, Positive Law," 29–31.

35. Post, "Federalism, Positive Law," 25–26, 50, 74.

36. Post, "Federalism, Positive Law," 65–66.

37. Post, "Federalism, Positive Law," 24–27, 103–109, 159. See Post's footnote 348 at page 103 for a detailed bibliography of the crime wave history.

38. Post, "Federalism, Positive Law," 67.

39. Post, "Federalism, Positive Law," 7, 11 12, 13 159.

40. Post, "Federalism, Positive Law," 6, 10.

41. Post, "Federalism, Positive Law," 11, 12, 13.

42. Post, "Federalism, Positive Law," 172.

43. Hoffer, Hoffer, and Hull, *Supreme Court*; Post, "Federalism, Positive Law," 37; and *United States v. Lanza*, 260 U.S. 377 (1922).

44. Post, "Federalism, Positive Law," 38–42.

45. *Hebert et al. v. Louisiana*, 272 U.S. 312 (1926).

46. 124 U.S. 545 (1924).

47. 272 U.S. 581 (1926); and Post, "Federalism, Positive Law," 57, 60, 67.

48. Post, "Federalism, Positive Law," 60–67.

49. Post, "Federalism, Positive Law," 57.

50. *Carroll v. United States*, 267 U.S. 132 (1925).

51. Post, "Federalism, Positive Law," 120.

52. Post, "Federalism, Positive Law," 135.

53. Post, "Federalism, Positive Law," 137, 138. And see *Olmstead v. United States*, 277 U.S. 438 (1928).

54. Post, "Federalism, Positive Law," 170.

55. Post, "Federalism, Positive Law," 154. And see *Hester v. United States*, 265 U.S. 57 (1924).

56. Post, "Federalism, Positive Law," 138. And see *United States v. Lee*, 274 U.S. 559 (1927).

57. Post, "Federalism, Positive Law," 34–36. And see *Gambino v. United States*, 275 U.S. 310 (1927).

58. Post, "Federalism, Positive Law," 129–59, 166, 167.

59. Post, "Federalism, Positive Law," 34–36, and 34 n. 113. Also see *Weeks v. United States*, 232 U.S. 383, 398 (1913).

60. Post, "Federalism, Positive Law," 156. And see *Katz v. United States*, 389 U.S. 347 (1967).

61. Post, "Federalism, Positive Law," 11.

62. Post, "Federalism, Positive Law," 1–4.

63. Again, as seen in Post, "Federalism, Positive Law," 18.

8

The Great Depression, FDR's New Deal, and a "New" Supreme Court Overwhelms States' Rights, 1933–1941

The greatest economic challenge the United States faced in the twentieth century was the Great Depression. During this period, spanning 1933 and 1941, the nation faced unemployment rates that hovered above 25 percent as well as a gross depletion of savings and investments. President Roosevelt called for a *national* economic solution—one requiring an extension of the Commerce Clause's reach to regulatory activities that had traditionally been reserved to states to regulate. Roosevelt's revolutionary agenda and failed "court packing" scheme together spawned a seismic shift in the Court's jurisprudence in 1937. Thus, moving forward during this period, the Court would begin to subscribe to a broader, more expansive interpretation of the Commerce Clause—one that saw it as an affirmative grant of federal power and not merely a limitation on federal authority. Because of its shift, the Court fully ushered in a new era of *cooperative federalism*, wherein the national government would play a direct and pervasive role in regulating private conduct that had traditionally been within the ambit and scope of state control.

THE GREAT DEPRESSION BRINGS ABOUT A NATIONALIST GOVERNMENT

The 1920s were characterized by the continuing robust expansion of industrial America. Notwithstanding Prohibition, it was the age of the robber barons (notwithstanding the antitrust efforts to reign them in), the Great Gatsby both in myth and reality, speakeasies, jazz, Vaudeville, and flamboyant wealth and extravagant luxuries for the rich and famous. But on October 29, 1929, Black Tuesday, the stock market failed, and with its crash, massive losses of wealth and economic power followed. The country had undergone a massive economic expansion during the 1900s through the 1920s, much of it on excessive credit margins in the stock market and with debt based on irrational optimism and overconfidence. Overproduction of consumer goods had created massive inventories that couldn't be sold at any price following the crash. The Federal Reserve wasn't prepared for the run on banks during which account holders withdrew their savings. Nine thousand banks failed during the 1930s, and with them $140 billion in savings. The country was illiquid, and bankruptcies were at their all-time high. The unemployment rate was 25 percent by 1933. A prolonged drought lasting much of the 1930s created a "dust bowl" out of the Midwest and West, triggering farms and ranches to be abandoned as part of the decade-long economic catastrophe.[1]

Herbert Hoover, sworn in as the country's thirty-first president on March 4, 1929, was not prepared to manage the crisis that engulfed the country seven months after his inauguration, even though he had served as secretary of Commerce in the Republican administrations of Presidents Harding and Coolidge. The Great Depression was national in scope and required national solutions originating from the federal government. President Hoover's administration miserably failed to manage the crisis, chasing the phantom of recovery, as historian David M. Kennedy so characterizes it.[2] The magnitude and immediacy of human despair and suffering caused the following administration under Franklin Delano Roosevelt to overreach in its initial responses to the crisis. The nationalistic approach, however, became the incubator for preemption to override state authority and historic police powers in the desperate and revolutionary attempt to rescue the American people from an overwhelming crisis by overhauling government and dismantling federalism. Roosevelt thought he was acting in the national interest in the name of the people's welfare. Charles Evans Hughes had became Chief Justice of the Supreme Court on February 24, 1930, upon appointment by President Hoover.

Franklin Delano Roosevelt succeeded Hoover in March 1933. His strategy of immediate relief to stabilize the country included a flurry of relief programs included in the Agricultural Adjustment Act, the National Industrial Recovery Act, the Railroad Retirement Act, the Bituminous Coal Conservation Act of 1935, the Municipal Bankruptcy Act of 1934, the Frazier-Lemke Act, and the New York Minimum Wage Law.[3] All of these were struck down by the Supreme Court, holding they were not within the four corners of Congress's enumerated constitutional authority, compromising state jurisdiction and the private sphere in manufacturing, employment, wages and price controls, and commercial relations. This business sphere had been an area long protected against government intrusion, articulated in the opinions of the Fuller, White, and Taft Courts going back to the 1880s. Roosevelt referred to his four

Figure 8.1. Unemployed men line up outside a soup kitchen at 935 South State Street, Chicago, Illinois, in late 1930 or early 1931. *Source*: Everett Collection Inc./Alamy Stock Photo.

chief adversaries on the Supreme Court—Pierce Butler, James McReynolds, George Sutherland, and Willis Van Devanter—as "The Four Horsemen" after the allegorical figures of the apocalypse in the biblical book of Revelation, representing death and destruction. Later they were joined by Justice Owen Roberts, who often cast the swing vote to create a conservative majority.[4]

After Roosevelt won an overwhelming reelection victory in 1937, he planned to reconstitute the Supreme Court's membership, adding justices for every member over age seventy, thus "packing" the high court.[5] The Senate quashed the initiative, but the retirement of nine primarily conservative justices between 1937 and 1941 gave Roosevelt ample opportunity to appoint New Deal supporters who created an entirely new federalism and constitutional jurisprudence, both to the determent of state sovereignty.[6] Thus the Hughes Court had two faces, one before and one after 1937. The early Hughes Court was decidedly a protector of nation-state equality and a guardian of federalism, and the later court quite the reverse.

THE "NEW" SUPREME COURT OF 1937 AND A CONSOLIDATION OF NATIONAL POWERS

The "new" Supreme Court in 1937 altered the fundamentals of federalism jurisprudence of the previous hundred years.[7] The "dual federalism" doctrine of nation-state equality, "a highly complicated fabric of constitutional exegesis," had prevailed since the Taney Court, starting in 1836.[8] The 1938 *Barnwell Brothers*[9] case marked the emergence of the new Supreme Court, which scaled back the Commerce Clause, because of its strong nationalist concept mandating a single national market, one country, one market; this reduction of the reach of the Commerce Clause enhanced state authority.[10] Legal scholars Richard Epstein and Michael Greve characterize the *Barnwell Brothers* case as the watershed decision for the New Deal's 1937 Supreme Court. Justice Harlan Stone's opinion characterized the Commerce Clause as follows: "The commerce clause, by its own force, prohibits discrimination against interstate commerce, whatever its form or method, and the decisions by this Court have recognized that there is scope for its like operation when state legislation nominally of local concern is in point of fact aimed at interstate commerce, or *by its necessary operation is a means of gaining a local benefit by throwing the attendant burdens on those without the state.*"[11] Epstein and Greve conclude the New Deal's Commerce Clause "turns on specific constitutional federalism risks: state discrimination and balkanization." The "old" Commerce Clause focused on balance and history versus "risks."[12]

The prevailing historical consensus of scholars is that the new 1937 Court marked the end of dual federalism.[13] To confuse the issue, a well-documented case has been made by Professor Joseph Zimmerman that the end of dual federalism actually began in 1913 with a broad clutch of federal grants-in-aid to state and local governments that carried with them federal controls over state policies and regulations.[14] While Zimmerman doesn't mention them, the Sixteenth Amendment in 1913 establishing an income tax system, the Eighteenth Amendment in 1919 prohibiting liquor, and the Social Security Act of 1935 all carried with them an immense amount of federal control, prescient of the future administrative state. The Seventeenth Amendment, moreover, constituted a major change in the politics of federalism and state sovereignty.

Federal preemption first occurred in 1790, with enactment of the federal Copyright Act and the Patent Act.[15] Prior to 1900, twenty-seven additional preemption statutes had been enacted, including the Civil Rights Act of 1870, and amendments thereto in 1871, based on the Fifteenth Amendment in 1870.[16] Zimmerman concludes that, while the new FDR Court in 1937 officially marked the demise of dual federalism,[17] 1965 was also a major milestone for the issue, when Congress enacted a national policy for minimum clean water standards. After 1975, deregulation of state sovereignty over the banking and transportation industries followed. The Telecommunication Act of 1996 was another major mile marker, removing all state regulation of telecommunication services. The 1996 Health Insurance Act followed, regulating private health insurance and establishing minimum national standards.

Zimmerman brackets the period spanning 1935 through 1970 as the transition of cooperative federalism and the period spanning 1970 through 1982 as the conversion of the federal system to "coercive federalism." exhibiting the characteristics of a unitary system of government.[18] The entire journey from the Taney Court to today has been one of a slow but inexorable metamorphosis, arguably caused by the pressures of an ever-expanding, ever-demanding population and unbridled economic growth. The Hughes Court in 1937 ushered in the doctrine of cooperative federalism fabricated as part of a "constitutional revolution"[19] by the new members of the Supreme Court appointed by President Roosevelt.

The Great Depression in the 1930s had wrought unprecedented financial disaster, staggering unemployment, anarchy, social violence, labor and civil-rights unrest, constitutional turmoil, and a plethora of sweeping New Deal relief legislation. The maelstrom overwhelmed the Supreme Court's docket and forced the Court after 1937 into a new policy charitably called "cooperative federalism," with the federal government dictating the terms of the states' dependency. The dynamics of federalism went from one of cooperation to tension.[20] "In contrast to a dual federalism, cooperative federalism envisions a sharing of regulatory authority between the federal government and the states that allows states to regulate within a framework delineated by federal law."[21]

The new Court after 1937 replaced the "Constitution of Rights" with a "Constitution of Powers," with national power consolidated in the Congress and the president at the expense of the states.[22] The two sovereign centers of government went from collaboration to tension. The Hughes Court began to interpret the Commerce Clause expansively as a "grant of power," not as a limitation on Congress to implement economic enterprise, considered untouchable. The Tenth Amendment was relegated to just a truism, a mere guide to interpretation. No judicial consideration of states' reserved powers under the Tenth Amendment was given by the Court. With the advent of cooperative federalism, the Court's view of the Tenth Amendment shifted significantly. In *United States v. Darby*, the Court found that "The [Tenth A]mendment states but a truism that all is retained which has not been surrendered. There is nothing in the history of its adoption to suggest that it was more than declaratory of the relationship between the national and state governments as it had been established by the Constitution before the amendment or that its purpose was other than to allay fears that the new national government might seek to exercise powers not granted, and that the states might not be able to exercise fully their reserved powers."[23]

State parity with the federal government was no longer an issue after 1937, and Congress was free to pursue its objectives without regard to the powers reserved to the states.[24] As Professor Ernest A. Young characterizes it, "The Court unshackled both [the Executive and Congressional] levels of government, while laying the groundwork for an overall shift towards national authority through its seeming refusal to recognize *any* limits on Congress's power."[25]

Furthermore, the Hughes Court extended the federal judiciary's authority into areas of jurisprudence that had formerly been exclusively state authority, thus liberally expanding the federal power of the Supreme Court. The Hughes Court overturned state laws infringing on the First Amendment and the Privileges or Immunities Clause of the Fourteenth Amendment; on constitutional grounds, the Court overturned two highly publicized, racially charged state convictions of eight Black teenagers for rape in Scottsboro, Alabama. The dissent correctly called this "an extension of federal authority into a field hitherto occupied exclusively by the several states."[26]

Most importantly as it relates to the focus of this book, the Supreme Court's new propensity to extend federal authority at the expense of states also occurred in the area of wildlife management. Over North Carolina's objection, in 1940 the US Court of Appeals for the Fourth Circuit held in *Chalk v. United States* that the federal government could remove deer from the Pisgah National Forest to protect the habitat from being overgrazed.[27] This decision was similar to a 1928 Supreme Court case involving the removal of excess deer from the Kaibab National Forest over the objections of Arizona—as will be more fully discussed in chapter 9.[28] What had begun in 1932 as merely the authority of the US Forest Service to control the deer population and exempt hunters from the state's licensing requirements led quickly to the Forest Service promulgating regulation G-20-A, empowering the secretary of agriculture with the sole right to require a license to hunt or fish in any national forest, to set seasons and bag limits, and to prohibit hunting to protect the habitat. North Carolina saw the Forest Service's power grab as a total usurpation of state authority over wildlife. The new Supreme Court disagreed, giving the federal government the right to protect its federal property.[29] This grant of unilateral bureaucratic power to a federal forester essentially preempted state authority and generated serious friction with states across the country.[30] Thus, by virtue of judicially sanctioned bureaucratic fiat, an exception to the presumption against preemption doctrine was established for all federal lands.

SUMMARY

The Great Depression presented the greatest challenge to the bedrock principle of federalism since the nation's inception. With unemployment rates soaring to never-before-seen heights and savings and investments depleting, the United States faced a crisis that arguably *required* a national solution. By this point, the Supreme Court's dual federalism framework had already begun to slowly deteriorate under the economic pressures created by the Progressive Era. However, *before* 1937, the Court had upheld limits on federal regulatory power, holding unconstitutional the Roosevelt administration's signature pieces of legislation—ranging from the Agricultural Adjustment Act to the National Industrial Recovery Act, which were directed at mitigating the deleterious effects of the Depression.

In 1937, the Court underwent a famous jurisprudential shift with the "switch in time that saved nine."[31] Instead of upholding the mutual exclusivity of federal and state power under the Commerce Clause—a method of interpretation fundamental to preserving its *dual* federalism framework, which would define clear lines for federal and state authority—during the Depression the Supreme Court fully adopted *cooperative* federalism as its model. Because the Commerce Clause now embraced a broader interpretation as an affirmative grant of power—not merely a limitation on government, the Tenth Amendment—and its secured promise of reserving power *not already delegated* to the federal government, the clause became a nullity in the eyes of the Court. In 1937, the era of the dual-federalism doctrine had most visibly come to a close, more palpably replaced with cooperative federalism. Now the future of the federalism doctrine pointed in a certain, biased direction: the *federal* government—not the states—would have broad regulatory authority under the Commerce Clause.

NOTES

1. See generally David M. Kennedy, *Freedom from Fear: The American People in the Great Depression* (New York: Oxford University Press, 1999).
2. Kennedy, *Freedom from Fear*, 190–217.
3. Hoffer, Hoffer, and Hull, *Supreme Court*, 252–63.
4. Hoffer, Hoffer, and Hull, *Supreme Court*, 257–63; William E. Leuchtenburg, *The Supreme Court Reborn: The Constitutional Revolution in the Age of Roosevelt* (New York: Oxford University Press, 1995), 1187–1204; G. Edward White, *The Constitution and the New Deal* (Cambridge: Harvard University Press, 2000); Arthur M. Schlesinger, *The Politics of Upheaval: The Age of Roosevelt, 1935–1936* (New York: Houghton Mifflin Harcourt, 2003); and William E. Leuchtenburg, "Charles Evans

Hughes: The Center Holds," *North Carolina Law Review* 83, no. 5 (June 2005): 1187, https://scholarship.law.unc.edu/cgi/viewcontent.cgi?referer=&httpsredir=1&article=4160&context=nclr.

5. Hoffer, Hoffer, and Hull, *Supreme Court*, 254–57, 265–69.
6. Hoffer, Hoffer, and Hull, *Supreme Court*, 253–82.
7. Hoffer, Hoffer, and Hull, *Supreme Court*, 265–69.
8. Corwin, "Passing of Dual Federalism," 15.
9. *South Carolina Highway Dep't v. Barnwell Bros., Inc.*, 303 U.S. 177 (1938).
10. Gardbaum, "Breadth versus Depth," 48, 67.
11. South Carolina Highway Dep't, 303 U.S. 177, at 185–86 (emphasis added).
12. Epstein and Greve, "Conclusion: Preemption Doctrine and Its Limits," 318–19.
13. Ernest A. Young, "The Puzzling Persistence of Dual Federalism: A Bad Idea, but Not Self-Defeating," in *Federalism and Subsidiarity*, Nomos LV, American Society for Political and Legal Philosophy, ed. James E. Fleming and Jacob T. Levy (New York: New York University Press, 2014), 41, https://scholarship.law.duke.edu/cgi/viewcontent.cgi?article=5365&context=faculty_scholarship; Joseph F. Zimmerman, "National-State Relations: Cooperative Federalism in the Twentieth Century," *Publius* 31, no. 2 (Spring 2001): 28; and Epstein and Greve, "Conclusion: Preemption Doctrine and Its Limits," 318–19.
14. Zimmerman, "National-State Relations," 28.
15. Zimmerman, "National-State Relations," 28.
16. Zimmerman, "National-State Relations," 28.
17. Zimmerman, "National-State Relations," 28.
18. Zimmerman, "National-State Relations," 28–29.
19. See generally Robert L. Fischman, "Cooperative Federalism and Natural Resource Law," *NYU Environmental Law Journal* 14, no. 1 (2005): 179; Leuchtenburg, *Supreme Court Reborn*; Corwin, "Passing of Dual Federalism"; Zimmerman, "National-State Relations"; and Young, "Puzzling Persistence."
20. Miller, "Burger Court's View," 576, 580; Corwin, "Passing of Dual Federalism," 2, 21. Also see Philip J. Weiser, "Towards a Constitutional Architecture for Cooperative Federalism," *North Carolina Law Review* 79, no. 3 (2001): 663–65.
21. Weiser, "Towards a Constitutional Architecture," 665.
22. Miller, "Burger Court's View," 573–76; Corwin, "Passing of Dual Federalism," 2.
23. *United States v. Darby*, 312 U.S. 100, 124 (1941).
24. Miller, "Burger Court's View," 576–79.
25. Young, "Making Federalism Doctrine," 1733, 1752.
26. Hoffer, Hoffer, and Hull, *Supreme Court*, 269–78, 271.
27. *Chalk v. United States*, 114 F.2nd 207 (4th Cir. 1940).
28. *Hunt v. United States*, 278 U.S. 96 (1928).

See also *New Mexico State Game Commission v. Udall*, 410 F.2d 1197 (10th Cir. 1969). This decision further expanded the right of the federal government to regulate wildlife on federal property, as did *Kleppe v. New Mexico* (426 U.S. 529 [1976]). This right was further raised to the level of a federal property interest in *Palila v. Hawaii Department of Land and Natural Resources* (471 F.Supp. 995 (D. Haw. [1979]).

29. The states—working collectively through their national organization, the Association of Fish and Wildlife Agencies (AFWA)—later prevailed upon the Forest Service to repeal Regulation G-20-A and replaced it with Regulation W-2, which gave the states the opportunity to participate in determining wildlife populations. Belanger and Kinnane, *Managing American Wildlife*, 53–58.

30. Hunt, 278 U.S. 96 (1928).

31. A quip attributed to humorist Cal Tinney in 1937, regarding the Court's sudden shift in philosophy.

9

The Competing Ideologies that Characterized the Progressive Movement and Beyond, 1890–1940

The philosophical principles and ideas supporting the Progressive Movement in the early 1900s had a significant impact on wildlife conservation. President Theodore Roosevelt's "Conservation Movement" was the intellectual product of environmental "expertise" that had been designed to create better, more sustainable policies and solutions to emergent national wildlife problems. The central role of expertise that was at the heart of the Progressive vision provided a rationale for preemption—based on ecology, science, and education—that was clearly displayed in cases where the federal government expressed its preference for federal involvement, ranging from the Supreme Court's decision in *Foster-Fountain Packing Co. v. Haydel* (1928) to the Pittman-Robertson Act, which provided federal funding to states requiring the cooperative management of wildlife.[1]

ROOSEVELT'S PROGRESSIVE CONSERVATION MOVEMENT

Since the waning decades of the twentieth century, historians and social and political scientists have been forensically examining the impetus and factors that gave rise to the Progressive movement and the byproducts of the era's legacy that continued to influence the twenty-first century. Few historians, however, have explored the influence of Progressives on the conservation and natural resources movement.

Environmental historian Samuel P. Hayes has called the movement to protect vanishing species "Progressive conservation," a movement most notably led by Theodore Roosevelt and that included George Bird Grinnell, Gifford Pinchot,[2] and a cadre of colleagues who formed a brain trust to promote wildlife conservation around 1900.³ This group of visionaries whose philosophy was a reflection of the Good Government Guys Movement (aka the "Goo-Goo Guys"⁴), comprised of liberal, well-educated, members of the New York social elite. The Goo-Goo Guys were intent on reforming the tyranny of the Tammany Hall political bosses who ran New York City while ignoring the societal ills brought on by the Industrial Revolution—like the harsh, toxic, and dangerous working conditions, overcrowded slum housing, poor sanitation, alcoholism, prostitution, and gambling. The group and its zealous followers were driven by an almost-religious belief that societal reform was indispensable to restoration of a moral compass in New York City—and indeed all of society.[5]

That ideology strongly influenced the mentality of those committed to wildlife conservation. Given that species migrate over state lines and international boundaries, Roosevelt and his cadre of confidants firmly believed that federal wildlife protection was necessary and that state laws were insufficient. They shared a utilitarian philosophy that wildlife was a national resource to be managed in trust by the federal government to achieve the greatest good for the greatest number of citizens by the wise and sustainable use of the nation's natural resources. They believed that the efficiency and science necessary for this task would be established through agencies of the federal government managed by professionals.

Historian Clayton R. Koppes has concluded that for the rest of the twentieth century, the policies and ideology of Roosevelt's Progressive Era became self-sustaining ideas. A strong centralized government was key to protecting not just natural resources but also the other major essentials of the public, like transportation, housing, public health and welfare, and major public works projects, and the changing demands of the public through differing political transitions.[6]

Environmental historian Samuel P. Hays, in defining the ideology of what he calls the "Progressive conservation" era, has concluded that "conservation, above all, was a scientific movement, and its role in history arises from the implications of science and technology in modern society."[7] Other historians have viewed conservation as a patriotic cause in the public's best interest based on US spiritual and moral values.[8] Still others, such as historian Richard Andrews, have come to view environmental politics as interwoven with broader forces at work throughout the nineteenth century, including transportation, industrialization, urbanization, trade, water resources, and the disposition and dedication of public lands.[9]

Federal preemption is more readily understood[10] as integral to understanding the conservation movement and within that broader reform context. The concept of federal preemption, moreover, fits better within this rubric and transcends Hays's narrow viewpoint. Industrial growth in the early 1900s led to Progressive reform responses and laws regulating human health, waste, air and water pollution, economic exploitation, and social inequality, all of which became part of the environmental "reform" rubric. All of the competing reform themes relate directly to the ideology of federal preemption over the states' constitutional right to control their wildlife. It started with the federalist view that a strong federal government would be central to governing the use of the nation's natural resources from the top down, which in turn mandated preemption.

We can see the actual physical manifestation of expansionist public policy in the encouraged development of the railroads across the United States. Railroad development was, in essence, a project of the federal government that gave free land for rights-of-way, subsidized every mile of tracks, and allowed federal lands to be used for harvesting wood for railroad ties and the construction of new towns and cities along the track. The General Mining Law of 1872 encouraged mineral exploration, which led to mining iron ore, which was then used to make iron and steel, and coal, used for smelter furnaces and people's stoves. Industrial production employed men for vast assembly lines, which in turn led to urban cities, dams for hydroelectric power to sustain industrial expansion and lighting towns and cities, and extensive agricultural irrigation to feed the burgeoning masses.[11] All of this expansion was funded or encouraged by the federal government at the cost of diminished wildlife and habitat. This in turn altered reform thinking regarding wildlife conservation and turned it toward federal control and preemption—and ultimately the destruction of state sovereignty over conservation and wildlife.

ECOLOGY, SCIENCE, EDUCATION, AND FEDERAL AID FOR STATE WILDLIFE CONSERVATION BECOMES THE TROJAN HORSE OF PREEMPTION: THE LEOPOLD YEARS

The ideological origins of the underlying philosophy regarding the extinction of game are to be found in the writings of George Perkins Marsh, Ernst Haeckel, Charles Darwin, and earlier naturalists and scientists, such as Alexander von Humboldt and Carolus Linnaeus in the eighteenth century, who collectively began developing the science of ecology. Their writings influenced major conservation policymakers such as George Bird Grinnell, Theodore Roosevelt, Gifford Pinchot, and, later, Aldo Leopold. Indeed, the word "ecology" was first coined in 1866 as Ökologie by German biologist Ernst Haeckel, derived from the Greek word *oikos*, meaning "house," and *logos*, meaning "study."[12] In the Progressive period in the early 1900s were the beginnings of the scientific study of wildlife under the broad rubric of ecology.

Early approaches to stopping the extinction of species included the creation of game refuges and sanctuaries and of national park and forest reserves, along with prohibitions on hunting, especially commercial market hunting; hunting seasons and bag limits followed. But study of species population, predator control, and inconsistent state game laws was the only action undertaken by early policymakers. These early actions are characterized as the study of natural history and early ecology principles and descriptive observation, with individual species being studied and manipulated. In 1920, the president of the Ecological Society of America, Barrington Moore, described the group's interest as "primarily in the relations between living organisms and their environment . . . to learn how plants and animals have developed and become established . . . [and] to know the environment of each, and the response to the various factors of this environment."[13] Applied ecology utilizing quantitative science for wildlife management followed much later when the focus of study had shifted to entire ecosystems and the community of species it supported.[14]

The only conservation measures that early naturalists knew to stem the extinction of certain species in the late 1800s and early 1900s were hunting prohibitions, game laws on hunting seasons and bag limits, and harvest rules on the sex of an animal taken. The Boone and Crockett Club—the oldest wildlife-management organization in the United States, created in 1887 by Theodore Roosevelt—recognized the deficiency in this approach to wildlife management in a 1912 policy statement:

> Population and industrialism are increasing faster than game. Is there any fundamental policy which, if it can be adopted, will meet such a situation and conserve game? We think there is. . . . The policy needed is one which calls for the complete administration of the game together with the responsibility which goes with it. Heretofore most of our legislation on behalf of saving game has dealt with the protective side of game conservation.
>
> Game protection, rather than game administration, has been our habit of thought. So long as we continue both in thought and by legislation to hold to this attitude, we cannot make wise laws fast enough to meet the changing situations, nor can we quickly adopt methods which will prevent the destruction of the breeding stock of game.[15]

As the science and discipline of wildlife biology developed, the field's professionals began to look at predator-prey relationships, habitat and ecosystem health and carrying capacity, domestic livestock interactions with wildlife disease, and invasive species. Hence the discipline of applied ecology evolved to develop other conservation methods to protect species and reverse their declining populations. Paralleling the developing science of ecology, the creation of federal game refuges and wildlife sanctuaries, parks, and national forests beginning in the late 1880s and early 1900s produced wildlife nurseries and increasing game populations.

When federal forester Aldo Leopold (1887–1948) observed in the 1920s a low and unhealthy mule deer population in the Kaibab Plateau, a federal game preserve in northern Arizona, he surmised it was because of the large predator population. To prove his theory, he carried out an extermination program of predator control of coyote, mountain lion, wildcat, wolf, and bear populations. This caused the mule deer population to expand dramatically, to the detriment of the herd's health. The plateau's carrying capacity was exceeded, the 30,000 deer were starving, and the population needed to be greatly reduced. Henry C. Wallace, Secretary of Agriculture, directed immediate reduction of the deer population to an appropriate manageable size without regard to Arizona law.[16] "Since this is the first attempt of the government to install scientific game management plans on a large scale," Wallace said, "it has been the desire of the Department to approach the matter cautiously and work out in the light of experience the right number of deer which should be removed . . . and will make the [Kaibab] Game Preserve a real demonstration of what scientific game management plans can secure in the perpetuation and utilization of our wildlife."[17]

Wallace's decision caused the state to sue the federal government for intervening in the management of their resident wildlife, preempting their state authority. In an opinion written by Justice Sutherland in 1928, the Taft Supreme Court held that the federal government had the right to protect federal lands and property, notwithstanding any state laws, based on the Property Clause of the US Constitution.[18] The rationale for wielding the weapon of federal preemption was driven by the science of wildlife biology[19] and by the federalist orthodoxy throughout the Taft Supreme Court.

In 1928, the Taft Court extended both the reach of the Commerce Clause and constraints on "a state's absolute control over the use of wildlife once it permits part or all of its wildlife to enter the stream of commerce."[20] In this case, the Louisiana Department of Conservation attempted to enforce a state law that made it unlawful to ship shrimp out of state unless and until the heads, shells, and hulls were removed, which made the shrimp ready for human consumption. The law was intended to keep the shrimp packing and canning industry in Louisiana rather than in Biloxi, Mississippi, where the center of the industry had been developed and which relied on Louisiana shrimp for 95 percent of its supply. Louisiana argued that their law was beyond the reach of the Commerce Clause, based on *Geer*. Since the Louisiana law anticipated the shrimp being sold across state lines once they had been prepared as prescribed in the law, the Supreme Court distinguished the case from *Geer* (1896), since the shrimp were intended for sale and not a food supply necessary for the exclusive benefit of the people of Louisiana. The Court narrowed the *Geer* holding and held: "Interstate commerce includes more than transportation; it embraces all the component parts of commercial intercourse among states. And a state statute that operates directly to burden any of its essential elements is invalid. *Dahnke-Walker Co. v. Bondurant, Shafer v. Farmers' Grain Co.* A state is without power to prevent privately owned articles of trade from being shipped and sold in interstate commerce on the ground that they are required to satisfy local demands or because they are needed by the people of the state. *Penna. v. West Virginia.*"[21]

In a later 1948 case, Justice Felix Frankfurter expounded further on the constitutional limitations imposed on a state's sovereign right over its fish and wildlife. "When a State regulates the sending of products across State lines, we have commerce among the States as to which State intervention is subordinate to the Commerce Clause. That is the nub of the decision in *Foster-Fountain Packing Co. v. Haydel*. South Carolina has attempted such regulation of commerce in shrimp among the States. In doing so she has exceeded the restrictions of the Commerce Clause."[22]

Aldo Leopold became the nation's leading wildlife authority and a land and wildlife philosopher who developed an ecological ethic for the web of life, respecting each of its components. This became known as Leopold's "land ethic" philosophy.[23] His 1933 *Game Management* remains a classic text, as does his *Sand County Almanac*, published posthumously in 1949, followed by *Round River* in 1953.[24] The latter two works represent the highest expression of human environmental responsibility to the land and its species and made Leopold the leading influence in wildlife management. His ideology reflected the works of eighteenth- and nineteenth-century thinkers like Francis Bacon, Linnaeus, von Humboldt, Marsh, Haeckel, and Darwin, reflecting the complex interactions and struggle for existence in nature. Leopold saw the natural world as one integrated holistic system, wherein each organism relates to all others and all work together as a unified supporting network—a holistic web of life. No part could be discarded, each an essential component.[25]

Because of Leopold's developing reputation, in 1928 the Sporting Arms and Ammunition Manufacturers' Institute (SAAMI), an industry-science consortium, hired Leopold to do a national survey of game conditions. The game conservation system of the day focused on huntable game animals without any focus on their management, environment, or habitat. For Leopold, the challenge was to foster social and economic forces (including financial inducements and predator controls) that would conserve habitats without

Figure 9.1. Aldo Leopold, America's revered leading philosopher on land and wildlife conservation. *Source*: Aldo Leopold Foundation and University of Wisconsin-Madison Archives.

interfering with farmers and their systems of land use. This would in turn increase the stock of game populations favorable to hunting. Thereafter, Leopold chaired a committee whose findings were presented at the Seventeenth American Game Conference of the Wildlife Management Institute and became known as the American Game Policy of 1930. This was transformative in its approach, establishing the overarching wildlife management model for much of the twentieth century.[26]

The 1930 policy was a pivotal moment in wildlife management. In essence, it said the existing conservation approach was failing and that the United States needed to focus on restoration. The policy called for the creation of a formal wildlife profession, the application of science to wildlife problems, the hiring of trained people to do the science and implement conservation measures, and stable, equitable funding. It also called for collaboration among the stakeholders—hunters, landowners, and other conservationists. The impact of the policy was profound, leading to the creation of the Cooperative Wildlife Research Units, the passage of the Fish and Wildlife Coordination Act, the Pittman-Robertson Act, and the creation of The Wildlife Society. It created the foundation for what came after—and insistence that landowners, conservationists, and hunters all needed to work together, which was finally realized in the cooperative conservation efforts the United States is seeing today. The 1934 Fish and Wildlife Coordination Act[27] followed and directed the secretaries of agriculture and commerce to develop a nationwide program to protect and rehabilitate wildlife habitats from the effects of domestic sewage, industrial wastes, and water pollution in consultation with the US Fish and Wildlife Service (FWS).[28]

The 1930 policy led to the 1973 North American Wildlife Policy (also a product of the Wildlife Management Institute), which refined the policy to reflect the demands of the contemporary United States, including consideration of all species of wildlife, both game and nongame, fish, plants, their related societal values, and the need for greater conservation funding. The 1973 policy update was an acknowledgment of the changes that had occurred in the forty-three years since the 1930 policy. It spoke of the impacts of human population growth and resource consumption rates; the loss of species, populations, and communities of wildlife; and cultural loss due to an urbanizing society; and it called for an expanded federal role, which was realized with the Endangered Species Act, the Clean Water Act, and the Clean Air Act.[29]

The lead author of the policy update was Dr. Durward Allen (of Purdue University), who defined its goal as advancing universal ecology.[30] Much of the 1973 wildlife policy was reflected later that same year when the Endangered Species Act was enacted by Congress. Both were prepared in the early 1970s and developed simultaneously along with the Convention on International Trade in Endangered Species of Wild Fauna and Flora (CITES), adopted by a world wildlife conference of nations in Washington, D.C., in the summer of 1973.

EDUCATION, FUNDING, AND FEDERAL AID

The 1930s witnessed the fruition of several other events, including the development of ecology as an independent discipline covering all species and ecosystems (i.e., biodiversity), which foreshadowed the further expansion of federal preemption of state authority. The 1934 Migratory Bird Hunting Stamp Act (the "Duck Stamp")[31] placed a one-dollar tax on every waterfowl hunting license. This generated a revenue stream used by the federal government to acquire, expand, maintain, and manage waterfowl refuges, including many areas that up until then had been subject to state authority. The hunting licenses had been the sole revenue sources for each state to support their wildlife management programs. The expansion of waterfowl refuges created a much larger federal footprint of land control and wildlife management authority in affected states.

After the stock market crash in 1929, followed by the Great Depression, funding for the science and management of wildlife became a major challenge,[32] leading to yet more federal authority, this time in higher education.[33] The federal government's first response in 1935 was to create a nationwide series of university science courses and PhD research programs, housed in land-grant universities, known as the Cooperative Wildlife Research Units program. These ventures were cooperatively managed by the state, the federal government, and the host university.[34] Today forty units exist, primarily controlled by the federal government. The Bureau of Biological Survey, which oversaw the Cooperative Research Units Program (Coop Program), was first created within the Department of Agriculture in 1896 but was reorganized and expanded in its focus in 1934 and given the mission of overseeing development of the broad science of ecology and wildlife management in the United States.[35] The bureau became the US Fish and Wildlife Service in 1940 and was moved into the Department of the Interior.[36]

This national education program dramatically advanced the scientific management skills and numbers of federal and state career professionals with an enlightened perspective[37] and a view toward a collaborative working relationship between federal and state wildlife managers beginning with the Coop Program in preparing biologists to set and implement policy.[38] Future generations of state and federal government wildlife biologists and senior scientists were educated together in these university settings, forging lifelong friendships that helped bridge the federal-state divide. Generations later, the collegial culture fostered by this educational program fostered federal-state dispute resolution.[39]

What does the university Coop Program have to do with the issue of federal preemption of state authority? The better informed and educated the wildlife biologists are, the sounder and more science-based their decisions.[40] Moreover, the better connected they are through the collegial Coop Program network, the easier disputes are to resolve, thus avoiding preemption challenges. The Cooperative Research Units are staffed by federal biologists who serve their state fish and wildlife agency cooperators, and students mentored in the system develop an appreciation for both state and federal roles. It is a model of state-federal collaboration, with deference to state priorities.

THE PITTMAN-ROBERTSON ACT

At this point in the chronology of federal preemption, Congress passed the 1937 Pittman-Robertson Act (P-R Act), which provided federal funding for wildlife conservation.[41] This was the largest piece of federal legislation incentivizing the states and federal government to share in wildlife management. The P-R Act directed funds from an existing federal excise tax on sporting arms and ammunition (originally imposed in 1918 to fund the Migratory Bird Treaty Act, although funds went into the general treasury), thence to the states to fund wildlife restoration, the need of which had been identified in the 1930 American Game Policy. The US Fish and Wildlife Service annually determines how much funding each state gets based on a specific formulae.[42] Even though these are dedicated funds by law, early on Congress would not appropriate all of the monies sportsmen paid back to the states. It took an act of Congress in 1955 to bypass the appropriations process so that all funds in the account could go to the states. As a result, the unfunded surplus of $13.5 million from 1945 was released to the states. Today Congress requires that the unfunded surpluses go into the FWS's Migratory Bird Conservation Act fund, and the interest on the fund is put into the North American Wetlands Conservation Fund, all of which ultimately benefits migratory birds.[43] In fiscal year 2021, from the Pittman-Robertson and Dingell-Johnson fund, $1,093,154,901 was distributed to the states. Since its inception, a total of $22.9 billion has been distributed.[44]

The 1937 P-R Act allowed states to grow their conservation programs based on identified state priorities, which the FWS honors. This has created a state dependency on federal money for wildlife-conservation programs governed by the checks and balances of the FWS and the performance assurances required of the states, which over time has occasionally created stress in state-federal relations. Prior to 1937, the sale of licenses to hunt, trap, or fish provided sufficient revenue to support the budget of each state's wildlife management agency.[45] Thereafter, the states had a choice: they could receive federal funds based on the matching requirements of 25/75 percent, or they could opt out of participation in the program entirely. However, as license sales dropped, federal funding became critical and rendered the state agencies dependent on federal largesse if they were to do effective conservation work.

What do these federal funding sources have to do with preemption? As early as 1938, distinguished legal historian Edward S. Corwin[46] began addressing the state-dependency problems created by laws that required federally generated funds be shared with the states, and how this strengthens national power at the expense of state authority. The culmination of this was reached in the Social Security Act. "When two cooperate, it is the stronger member of the combination who calls the tune."[47] However, this cost sharing began as early as 1911, during the Progressive Era, with congressional funding subsidizing forest protection and reforestation, vocational rehabilitation, maintenance of nautical schools, highway construction, and education in agricultural, industrial, and home economics, all on a cost-sharing basis with the states, pursuant to regulations established by Congress.[48]

The grants-in-aid expenditures by the federal government in 1915 amounted to $6 million; in 1930, that had grown to $109 million; in 1931, it was $198 million; and in 1932, it had grown to $234 million.[49] Thence the Pittman-Robertson fund kicked in after 1937. Professor Corwin asserts that "'grants-in-aid' tends to break down state initiative and devitalize state policies." Furthermore, he writes, "'Cooperative Federalism' spells farther aggrandizement of national power . . . Cooperative Federalism has been to date, a short expression for a constantly increasing concentration of power at Washington in the instigation and supervision of local policies."[50] It moreover embodies the talisman of preemption when grants-in-aid are involved.[51]

Professor Joseph Zimmerman concludes that Congress directly influences the nature of services provided by states and local governments through the many conditions it attaches to federal grants-in-aid to the states. Zimmerman also argues that this subsidization, beginning as early as 1911, actually ended the period of dual federalism, which had dated back to the early Taney Court after 1836.[52] Professor William Anderson contrasts 1789 and 1942: "*Then* (before 1789) state grants *to* the Congress of the United States [were] for defense and debt purposes. *Now* grants-in-aid *by* the national government [are] to the states in increasing amounts and with steadily tightening national controls over state action."[53] This financial relationship created by the states' critical need for wildlife-conservation funding to keep up with the demands of the loss of habitat as the country continues to grow, putting greater pressure on species survival, will forever remain a source of tension. It is further exacerbated by the occasional state director driven by their governor's propensity to seek "free" federal money, thus creating pressures that undermine enforcement of the P-R Act and the Endangered Species Act.[54] Alternatively, states can simply choose to not participate in the federal-funding programs and can instead utilize their own funds for wildlife conservation; the alternative is a mirage, however, because of states' absolute need for federal funding to supplement state revenues. The states are caught in a catch-22.

SUMMARY

At this point in our exploration of US history, the Progressive Movement had become the dominant, central philosophical posture of the government. Crucially, the heart of its ethos was a belief that the federal government was primarily responsible for solving impending national problems with *national* legislation. Under Theodore Roosevelt's Progressive conservation coalition, wildlife constituted a national treasure to be safeguarded by a national coalition of experts. Therefore, in order to properly protect the sanctity and integrity of America's wildlife, professional experts would need the knowledge, foresight, and intellectual horsepower to tackle emergent issues with cutting-edge solutions, such as the creation of game refugees and sanctuaries, along with national parks and forest reserves.

At its core, the policy rationale for preemption derived, in large measure, from the science and educational advancements that developed in the academia with respect to wildlife biology and ecology, which pinpointed glaring national issues. With science identifying the problem, the federal government offered a solution—*more* central government from Washington. For example, in 1928, the Supreme Court aptly captured this reasoning in *Foster-Fountain Packing Co. v. Haydel*: "Interstate commerce includes more than transportation; it embraces all the component parts of commercial intercourse among states. And a state statute that operates directly to burden any of its essential elements is invalid."[55] Within the Progressive Movement, the size and scope of the federal government grew. Critically, the impulse for greater preemption over state laws became clear. In recognizing the science about the current state of wildlife across the nation, the federal government realized it needed to play "Night Watchman" over wildlife.

This Progressive vision also impacted the federalism balance that was tipping toward greater cooperative federalism among the federal government and state governments. Notably, the American Game Policy of 1930 was pivotal and transformative in establishing the wildlife-management model for much of the twentieth century. It was followed by the Fish and Wildlife Coordination Act in 1934, which developed a nationwide program to protect and rehabilitate wildlife habitats from the deleterious effects of pollution, and then by the Pittman-Robertson Act of 1937, which furnished federal funding (thus creating state dependency on federal money) for wildlife conservation. Indeed, Progressives placed a premium on federal funding for conservation because they viewed subsidies as *necessary* to producing greater knowledge; in turn, greater knowledge—cultivated in universities—would generate better policymakers. Overall, the cooperative vision of federalism had become dominant. With Progressives recognizing the role of science and expertise in the new, developing area of environmental policymaking—and the centrality of federal funding to incentivize better, more creative solutions to protect wildlife—the future of wildlife authority became abundantly clear: regulation would be coming from Washington.

NOTES

1. *Foster-Fountain Packing Company v. Haydel*, 278 U.S. 1 (1928).

2. Samuel P. Hays, *Conservation and the Gospel of Efficiency: The Progressive Conservation Movement, 1890–1920* (Cambridge: Harvard University Press, 1959), 122–33, 261–71.

3. They affiliated in an organization called the Boone and Crockett Club, established in 1887 by Theodore Roosevelt and George Bird Grinnell. For a history of the club following, see George Bird Grinnell, ed., *A Brief History of the Boone and Crockett Club* (New York: Forest and Stream Publishing Company, 1910); Reiger, *American Sportsmen*, 146–74; George Bird Grinnell, ed., *Hunting at High Altitudes* (New York: Harper and Brothers, 1913), 433–91; Douglas Brinkley, *The Wilderness Warrior: Theodore Roosevelt and the Crusade for America, 1858–1919* (New York: Harper Perennial, 2010), 201–16; and Lowell E. Baier, *Records of North American Big Game*, 10th ed., ed. Jack Reneau and Susan Reneau, The Boone and Crockett Club: A 106 Year Retrospective (Missoula: Boone and Crockett Club, 1993), 3–28.

4. James L. Merriner, *Grafters and Goo Goos: Corruption and Reform in Chicago, 1833–2003* (Bristol, UK: Policy Press, Southern Illinois University Press, 2004).

5. See generally Merriner, *Grafters and Goo Goos*; and Jon C. Teaford, s.v. "Good Government Movements," *The Encyclopedia of Chicago*, accessed May 10, 2001, http://www.encyclopedia.chicagohistory.org/pages/527.html.

6. Clayton R. Koppes, *JPL and the American Space Program: A History of the Jet Propulsion Laboratory* (New Haven: Yale University Press, 1982).

7. Hays, *Conservation and the Gospel of Efficiency*, 2.

8. Hays, *Conservation and the Gospel of Efficiency*, 1–4, 141–46, 261–76; Petersen, "Modern Ark," 25–29.

9. See generally Andrews, *Managing the Environment*.

10. For this perspective, consider Gottlieb, *Forcing the Spring*; or historian Montrie, *Myth of Silent Spring*. Moreover, historian Joshua B. Freeman provides a critical view of the harshness of industrial factories on its workers and their families in *Behemoth*.

11. An overlooked book on the economic forces at work in the nineteenth century, defining the physical manifestations of that period, was published as part of the Weyerhaeuser Environmental Books series in 2012: Mark Fiege, *The Republic of Nature: An Environmental History of the United States* (Seattle: University of Washington Press, 2012). A similar book that explores the nineteenth and twentieth centuries and up to 2012 focuses on how land and natural resource uses influence American culture and politics and what consequences are realized from conflicting policies and shifting perspectives: Jeff Crane, *The Environment in American History: Nature and the Formation of the United States* (New York: Routledge, 2015).

12. Ernst Haeckel, *Generelle Morphologie der Organismen*, 2 vols. (Berlin: Reimer, 1866); and "Ecology," Wikipedia, last modified September 20, 2021, https://en.wikipedia.org/wiki/Ecology.

13. Barrington Moore to Dr. George Bird Grinnell, August 3, 1920, archived as microfilm, reel 39, box 25, folder 106, of the George Bird Grinnell Papers, Sterling Memorial Library, Yale University Library.

14. Shannon Peterson has a very different view of how the science of ecology influenced wildlife management. He postulates that "the emergence of ecology provided scientific rationale for the expansion of federal power [i.e. preemption]." Petersen, "Modern Ark," 43–45. Also see Shannon Petersen, "Bison to Blue Whales: Protecting Endangered Species before the Endangered Species Act of 1973," *Environs: Environmental Law and Policy Journal* 22, no. 2 (Spring 1999): 71–106, 92–95, https://environs.law.ucdavis.edu/volumes/22/2/articles/petersen.pdf. Petersen doesn't quote Samuel Hays's *Conservation and the Gospel of Efficiency: The Progressive Conservation Movement*, but that is Hays's narrow view, which Petersen has co-opted.

15. Boone and Crockett Club Game Preservation Committee Policy Report of 1912, archived in box 85, folder 14, 1909–1929, Mansfield Library Special Collections, University of Montana, Missoula, Montana, searchable at http://archiveswest.orbiscascade.org/ark:/80444/xv46765.

16. Belanger and Kinnane, *Managing American Wildlife*, 40–43.

17. Henry C. Wallace to George Bird Grinnell, February 18, 1924, archived as microfilm in reel 40, box 39, folder 133, of the George Bird Grinnell Papers, Sterling Memorial Library, Yale University Library, https://archives.yale.edu/repositories/12/archival_objects/1248823.

18. *Hunt v. United States*, 278 U.S. 96 (1928).

19. Belanger and Kinnane, *Managing American Wildlife*, 42–44.

20. Bean and Rowland, *Evolution of National Wildlife Law*, 23 (citing *Foster-Fountain Packing Company v. Haydel*, 278 U.S. 1, 5 [1928]).

21. *Foster-Fountain Packing Co.*, 278 U.S. 1, 10 (1928) (internal citations omitted).

22. *Toomer v. Witsell*, 334 U.S. 385, 409 (1948).

23. Belanger and Kinnane, *Managing American Wildlife*, 43; and Reiger, *American Sportsmen*, 188–95.

24. Aldo Leopold, *Game Management* (New York: Charles Scribner's Sons, 1933); Aldo Leopold, *Sand County Almanac* (New York and Oxford: Oxford University Press, 1949); and Aldo Leopold, *Round River* (New York and Oxford: Oxford University Press, 1953).

25. For a well-researched and masterful text on Aldo Leopold's career, writing, ideas, and philosophy of human stewardship and ethical responsibilities toward wildlife and the land, read the articulate and complete biography by Curt Meine: *Aldo Leopold: His Life and Work* (Madison: The University of Wisconsin Press, 1988). Also see Julianne Lutz Newton, *Aldo Leopold's Odyssey* (Washington, DC: Island Press, 2006); and Belanger and Kinnane, *Managing American Wildlife*, 63.

26. John F. Organ, Robert M. Muth, Jan E. Dizard, Scot J. Williamson, and Thomas A. Decker, "Fair Chase and Humane Treatment: Balancing the Ethics of Hunting and Trapping," presentation made at the 63rd North American Wildlife and Natural Resources Conference, Orlando, Florida, March 20–24, 1998; and John F. Organ, Valerius Geist, Shane P. Mahoney, et al., *The North American Model of Wildlife Conservation*, The Wildlife Society and the Boone and Crockett Club Technical

Review 12–04, ed. Theodore H. Bookhout (Bethesda, MD: The Wildlife Society, 2012), chap. 16, 530–32, https://perma.cc/68VB-FJ7F.

27. US Congress, Fish and Wildlife Coordination Act, Pub. L. No. 73–121, 48 Stat. 401 (1934) (codified as amended at 16 U.S.C. §§ 661–67, https://www.govinfo.gov/content/pkg/USCODE-2013-title16/html/USCODE-2013-title16-chap5A.htm).

28. Alston Chase, *In a Dark Wood: The Fight over Forests and the Rising Tyranny of Ecology* (New York: Houghton Mifflin Company, 1995), 84.

Consultation later became the heart of the 1973 ESA, "designed to slow down headlong rushes to complete ill-considered projects and to provide an outside opinion on possible consequences for biological resources. . . . This common management tool of consultation to improve decision making achieved its apotheosis in the National Environmental Policy Act (NEPA)." This led to investigating wildlife problems in each state, later reflected in Sections 6 and 7 of the Endangered Species Act. Robert L. Fischman, "Predictions and Prescriptions for the Endangered Species Act," *Environmental Law* 34 (2004): 451, 455–56, https://www.repository.law.indiana.edu/cgi/viewcontent.cgi?article=1224&context=facpub.

29. Fischman, "Predictions and Prescriptions," 451, 455–56.

30. Durward Allen, "Report of the Committee on North American Wildlife Policy," *Wildlife Society Bulletin* 1, no. 2 (Summer 1973): 73–92.

31. US Congress, Fish and Wildlife Coordination Act; and Belanger and Kinnane, *Managing American Wildlife*, 39–40.

32. Kennedy, *Freedom from Fear*, 65–68, 77, 135–36, 163–67.

33. Chase, *In a Dark Wood*, 74.

34. See generally W. Reid Goforth, *The Cooperative Fish and Wildlife Research Unit Program* (Reston, VA: US Geological Survey, 2006). The Wildlife Management Institute is also a supporting partner, known as a "cooperator."

35. For a great summation of the state of the wildlife biologists and scientists' profession, their responsibilities and obligations, and essays written during the period spanning 1930 to 1950 by Coop Program professionals, see James A. Bailey, William Elder, and Ted D. McKinney, *Reading in Wildlife Conservation* (Washington, DC: The Wildlife Society, 1974), 393–428.

36. Belanger and Kinnane, *Managing American Wildlife*, 248; and Peterson, *Acting for Endangered Species*, 12–15.

37. The origins of this expanded emphasis on developing greater technical and scientific skills flowed directly from the early Progressive Era at the beginning of the century. Hays, *Conservation and the Gospel of Efficiency*, 121–46; and Belanger and Kinnane, *Managing American Wildlife*, 62–63.

38. Abbe R. Gluck, "Intrastatutory Federalism and Statutory Interpretation: State Implementation of Federal Law in Health Reform and Beyond," *Yale Law Journal* 121 (2011): 534, 552, https://docs.google.com/viewerng/viewer?url=https://www.yalelawjournal.org/pdf/1032_qcrpe69v.pdf.

39. Gluck, "Intrastatutory Federalism," 534, 552; and Belanger and Kinnane, *Managing American Wildlife*, 167, 168.

40. Martin Nie, Christopher Barns, Jonathan Haber, Julie Joly, Kenneth Pitt, and Sandra Zellmer, "Fish and Wildlife Management on Federal Lands: Debunking State Supremacy," *Environmental Law* 47, no. 4 (2017): 808–809.

While state fish and wildlife agencies are structured in numerous ways, a commonality that most share is that the director or head of the agency is responsible to some sort of politically appointed fish and wildlife commission, board, or advisory council. The powers granted to state wildlife commissions vary, from setting fish and game seasons and bag limits to charting broader management goals and objectives for the states. Members are typically appointed by the governor and subject to state legislative approval. Most states also have requirements for commission membership, such as a general knowledge of wildlife issues, political and geographic balance, or requiring that they hold a sporting license. The commission framework stems from sport hunters and conservationists wanting to secure their hard-fought protections for fish and game; thus, commissions were created so that sport hunters had a voice in preventing a return of widespread market hunting. More recently, however, state wildlife commissions have been criticized, mostly because some interests believe that their memberships do not adequately represent the diverse values and interests of those people who do not hunt, fish, or trap.

41. US Congress, Federal Aid in Wildlife Restoration Act of 1937, Pub. L. No. 75–415, 50 Stat. 917, 16 U.S.C. 669–69(i) (1937), https://www.ssa.gov/OP_Home/comp2/F075-412.html.

42. The P-R program works this way: The act imposed an 11 percent excise tax on rifles, ammunition, bows, and archery equipment, and 10 percent on handguns, all of which went into the US Treasury. Those dedicated tax revenues were then distributed by the FWS to the states for wildlife conservation, including nongame species and at-risk- and endangered-species projects, habitat restoration, and recreational projects, utilizing a formula based on a state's land mass and the number of state hunting and fishing licenses sold. The federal government funds 75 percent of project costs, but the states must first fund 25 percent of the cost. The real federal control results from the requirement that before being eligible to participate in the Pittman-Robertson program, every five years each state is required to submit to the FWS a comprehensive fish and wildlife–management plan detailing how they will manage their resident wildlife, and the federal government must approve each plan.

In 1950 the Dingell-Johnson Act, and later the 1984 Wallop-Breaux Federal Aid in Sport Fish Restoration Act, was added to the P-R revenues. These later two laws placed an excise tax on fishing tackle, rods, reels, lines, outboard engines, and motorboat fuel.

A totally separate funding program created in 2000 is the State Wildlife Action Plans (SWAP), which "have proven to be an effective means for states and their partners to target science-based conservation actions on behalf of the nation's declining wildlife resources" at a time when "as many as one-third of America's species are vulnerable" due to habitat loss and degradation, invasive species, climate change, disease, and pollution. SWAPs are a significant component in minimizing further losses in biodiversity. Programs to manage and restore ecosystem functions damaged by anthropogenic climate change and its attendant effects—including invasive species, wildfires, and extreme weather events like droughts and floods—can make extensive use of state capabilities in tracking and preserving ecosystem functions and carrying out translocations for species most at risk where in situ conservation may not be otherwise feasible. SWAPs and other state-wise strategies have been in use for a long time and are expected to be a central instrument in minimizing further losses in biodiversity. Jonathan R. Mawdsley, Robin O'Malley, and Dennis S. Ojima, "A Review of Climate-Change Adaptation Strategies for Wildlife Management and Biodiversity Conservation," *Conservation Biology* 23, no. 5 (2009): 1083–84, https://conbio.onlinelibrary.wiley.com/doi/epdf/10.1111/j.1523-1739.2009.01264.x.

And also see Lane Kisonak, "Fish and Wildlife Management on Federal Lands: The Authorities and Responsibilities of State Fish and Wildlife Agencies," *Environmental Law* 50, no. 4(2021): 935–71.

Each state is assigned by the FWS a federal aid coordinator who administers the funding, and beyond that a joint task force comprised of federal and state officials arbitrates disputes. Bruce A. Stein, Naomi Edelson, Lauren Anderson, John J. Kanter, and Jodi. Stemler, *Reversing America's Wildlife Crisis: Securing the Future of our Fish and Wildlife* (Washington, DC: National Wildlife Federation, 2018), ii, 4, 10, https://www.nwf.org/-/media/Documents/PDFs/NWF-Reports/2018/Reversing-Americas-Wildlife-Crisis_2018.ashx.

43. An amendment to the 1937 Pittman-Robertson Act enacted in 2000, separate and apart from the dedicated revenues listed above, further provides for State Wildlife Grants (US Congress, Fish and Wildlife Programs Improvement and National Wildlife Refuge System Centennial Act of 2000, Pub. L. No. 106–408, 114 Stat. 1763 [2000], https://uscode.house.gov/statutes/pl/106/408.pdf.) to the states from FWS for wildlife species of greatest conservation need, including nongame species such as song birds, small mammals, and so on. These include "candidate species," a classification that comes before a threatened or endangered listing. See Temple Stoellinger, "Wildlife Issues Are Local—So Why Isn't ESA Implementation?" *Ecology Law Quarterly* 44, no. 3 (2017): 681–25, https://www.ecologylawquarterly.org/wp-content/uploads/2020/03/Wildlife-Issues-Are-Local----So-Why-Isnt-ESA-Implementation.pdf (citing US Congress, Fish and Wildlife Programs Improvement . . .).

Federal taxpayer money for these nongame species is essential, because state wildlife management budgets are based primarily on hunting and fishing license fees, and sport hunters generally don't want their license dollars going for conservation of species they can't hunt. This attitude of sport hunters by necessity establishes a basis for broader federal oversight and authority over nongame species, which are most of the other species within nature's biota.

In the federal budget for fiscal year 2020, $51,111,386 million was included for State Wildlife Grants, which is discretionary and must be appropriated annually. In fiscal year 2021, $54,849,080 was provided under this program. Conversely, $971,552,178 of dedicated funds under the primary Pittman-Robertson fund were distributed to the states for fiscal year 2020. In fiscal year 2021, $1,093,154,901 was provided under the Pittman-Robertson program. These two separate revenue sources under Pittman-Robertson (as amended), combined with grants annually appropriated from general revenues and the funds states receive from the sale of fishing and hunting licenses, are the primary funding sources that state wildlife agencies have to fund their operations. The number of sport hunters buying licenses has dramatically decreased, and people are disconnecting with the natural world because of the computer age. The revenues that solely supported the state agencies in the past from license sales today make up a small percentage of their annual budgets. Hence reliance on federal funding has become critical for state agencies to survive and fulfill their mandate of wildlife conservation. The added burden of inadequate congressional funding for ESA has exacerbated the states' growing budget crises and increased their dependency on the federal government for money.

44. US Fish and Wildlife Service, "1939 through 2021 Wildlife Restoration Apportionments (Includes Hunter Ed)," Wildlife and Sport Fish Restoration Program, last modified February 24, 2021, downloadable from https://www.fws.gov/wsfrprograms/subpages/grantprograms/wr/wr_funding.htm; and US Fish and Wildlife Service, "1952 through 2021 Sport Fish Restoration Apportionments," Wildlife and Sport Fish Restoration Program, last modified February 24, 2021, downloadable from https://www.fws.gov/wsfrprograms/subpages/grantprograms/sfr/sfr_funding.htm.

45. Chase, *In a Dark Wood*, 85.

Funding for state wildlife management generally comes from the sale of hunting, fishing, and trapping licenses at the state level and from federal funds generated through targeted excise taxes. The result is that hunting, fishing, and trapping-derived revenue "comprise between 60 and 90 percent of the typical state fish and wildlife agency budget." This arrangement is often referred to as a "user-pay, user-benefit" funding model because states apply most of these funds to the management of sport fish and game species. This funding mechanism serves to reinforce the complaint of non-hunters that their values and interests are not adequately considered in management decisions.

Nie et al., "Fish and Wildlife Management," 809, citing Organ, Geist, Mahoney, et al., *North American Model*.

46. Edward S. Corwin, *Court over Constitution: A Study of Judicial Review as an Instrument of Popular Government* (Princeton: Princeton University Press, 1938).

The Supreme Court even took notice of the massive federal aid programs during the later part of twentieth century:

The effectiveness of the federal political process in preserving the States' interests is apparent even today in the course of federal legislation. On the one hand, the States have been able to direct a substantial proportion of federal revenues into their own treasuries in the form of general and program-specific grants in aid. The federal role in assisting state and local governments is a longstanding one; Congress provided federal land grants to finance state governments from the beginning of the Republic, and direct cash grants were awarded as early as 1887 under the Hatch Act. In the past quarter-century alone, federal grants to States and localities have grown from $7 billion to $96 billion. As a result, federal grants now account for about one-fifth of state and local government expenditures. The States have obtained federal funding for such services as police and fire protection, education, public health and hospitals, parks and recreation, and sanitation. Moreover, at the same time that the States have exercised their influence to obtain federal support, they have been able to exempt themselves from a wide variety of obligations imposed by

Congress under the Commerce Clause. For example, the Federal Power Act, the National Labor Relations Act, the Labor-Management Reporting and Disclosure Act, the Occupational Safety and Health Act, the Employee Retirement Income Security Act, and the Sherman Act all contain express or implied exemptions for States and their subdivisions.

Garcia v. San Antonio Transit Authority, 469 U.S. 528, 553–54 (1985).

47. Corwin, *Court over Constitution*, 21.

48. Corwin, "Passing of Dual Federalism," 20; also see generally Corwin, *Court over Constitution*.

49. Wooddy, *Growth of the Federal Government*, 552.

50. Corwin, "Passing of Dual Federalism," 20–21.

51. William W. Bratton, "Preemption Doctrine: Shifting Perspectives on Federalism and the Burger Court," *Columbia Law Review* 75, no. 3 (1975): 623, 643; and *New York State Department of Social Services v. Dublino*, 413 U.S. 405 (1973).

52. Zimmerman, "National-State Relations," 15, 20, 28.

53. William Anderson, "Federalism, Then and Now," *State Government* 16 (1943): 107–12, emphasis original.

54. The issue of federal assistance grants and their hidden dangers is far beyond the scope of this chapter or book. Called by legal and constitutional scholar Mario Loyola the "Trojan horse of cooperative federalism," because it is not readily discernible or easy to see, these federal grants implicitly carry within a "conditional preemption" because the money is conditioned on complying with accompanying federal regulations and direction of applying the funds, diminishing the state's autonomy. If spent inconsistently with the accompanying federal regulations or standards, there are penalties. The Clean Air Act, the Federal Aid Highway Act, and the Affordable Care Act are notable examples. Mario Loyola, "Federal-State Crack Up," *The American Interest* 8, no. 3, December 12, 2012, https://www.the-american-interest.com/2012/12/12/the-federal-state-crack-up/.

Congress and the federal agencies cross the constitutional line when they fail to distinguish between encouragement and coercion. See *New York v. United States*, 505 U.S. 144 (1992); and *Printz v. United States*, 521 U.S. 898 (1997). As it applies directly to states, their residents pay federal income and estate taxes. If states refuse grants-in-aid-because of the conditions attached, their federal taxes are simply transferred to other states and they lose the benefits.

For more on this subject, read the writings of attorney and scholar Michael S. Greve: *The Upside-Down Constitution* (Cambridge: Harvard University Press, 2012; and see Richard A. Epstein and Michael Greve, eds., *Federal Preemption: States' Powers, National Interests* (Washington, D.C.: AEI Press, 2007). Or read Mario Loyola, who publishes in *The Atlantic*, *The American Interest*, and *National Review*. Also see Samuel P. Hays, *Beauty, Health, and Permanence: Environmental Politics in the United States, 1955–1985* (Cambridge: Cambridge University Press, 1987), 443–48.

55. *Foster-Fountain Packing Company v. Haydel*, 278 U.S. 1, 10 (1928).

10

The Stone Court and the Development of the Presumption against Preemption in *Rice*, 1941–1946

The doctrinal codification of the "presumption against preemption" put a greater burden on the federal government in preemption disputes. Specifically, the Stone Court's landmark decision in *Rice v. Santa Fe Elevator Corp.* (1947) established the modern preemption doctrine and *explicitly* ensured that the canon of interpretation—*presumption against preemption*—would prevail in wildlife cases and controversies.[1] While the growth of the federal government had expanded substantially under the Supreme Court's Commerce Clause jurisprudence beginning with the ideological shift in 1937, the Stone Court erected a higher hurdle and burden that would require Congress to sufficiently articulate a "clear and manifest purpose" when attempting to preempt state laws that regulated the respective health, safety, and welfare of its citizens.

* * *

Harlan Stone succeeded Hughes as Chief Justice of the Supreme Court (1941–1946) and built on the liberalization of the Hughes Court's extension of federal authority into states' rights jurisdiction. The Stone Court addressed myriad matters affecting state powers, including wartime dissent, freedom of speech and the press, civil liberties, sabotage, disloyalty, detention of German and Japanese nationals, legal equality for working-class minorities and organized labor groups, insular and isolated minorities, civil rights, and criminal law.[2] The Stone Court developed a broad conception of individual rights and imposed portions of the Bill of Rights on the states. The Taft Court had glanced in this direction, and the Hughes Court taken a tentative step or two, but the Stone Court saw fit to strictly scrutinize state officials when it felt that "preferred freedoms are threatened."[3] The separate sovereignty of the state and federal governments became moribund with the emergence of "cooperative federalism."[4] However, the Depression-era federal relief programs and the Social Security Act of 1935—the paramount program and the forerunner of the era of "cooperative federalism"[5]—called for a sharing of regulatory authority between the federal government and the states. This allowed the states to regulate within a framework delineated by federal law.[6]

Cooperative federalism regarded federal and state governments as "mutually complementary parts of a single governmental mechanism . . . whose powers are intended to realize the purposes of government."[7] Early in the 1930s, the "old" FDR Court had created a presumption favoring the validity of state laws in the exercise of their police powers. As discussed earlier, the 1933 *Mintz* case had memorialized this presumption—that state powers prevailed unless a congressional statute clearly preempted state authority.[8] In 1941, *Hines v. Davidowitz* reformulated the judicial review function of the preemption doctrine and principles of federalism and made the new concurrent approach irreconcilable with the state-directed model of the early 1930s. In his dissenting opinion, Justice Stone admonished: "At a time when the exercise of the federal power is being rapidly expanded through Congressional action . . . it is difficult to overstate the importance of safeguarding against such diminution of state power by vague inferences as to what Congress might have intended . . . or by reference to our own conceptions of a policy which Congress has not expressed."[9]

The objective was for the "new" Supreme Court to determine whether or not a state statute stands as an obstacle to the full purposes and objectives of Congress, a retreat from the earlier rigorous intent standards of a congressional statute. Under *Hines*, a clear implication of intent by inference sufficed to achieve preemption—that is, *implied preemption*. However, six years later, in the *Rice* case, the Court rejected the doctrine of implied preemption.[10]

When the milestone case *Rice v. Santa Fe Elevator Corp.* reached the Court's docket six years later, the decision defined a new standard in preemption jurisprudence—that is, the presumption against preemption—which turned the spotlight squarely on congressional intent. Professor Ernest A. Young characterizes the case, writing that "it is now settled doctrine that the purpose of Congress is the ultimate touchstone in every preemption case."[11] Professor Stephen Gardbaum further describes the case as "the *locus classicus* of modern preemption doctrine."[12] Professor Gardbaum places the origins of the preemption doctrine at the time after 1937 when the Supreme Court gave Congress plenary lawmaking power under the Commerce Clause. This deeply threatened the intent of the framers of the Constitution for the federal government, who'd given only enumerated powers to Congress, with the remaining legislative authority left to the states. "The Court developed the presumption against preemption at the same time that it gave Congress broader Commerce Clause authority," Gardbaum writes, "and the initial purpose of the presumption appears to have been to protect some measure of state authority in light of Congress's newly recognized power to legislate in virtually any field."[13]

Rice v. Santa Fe Elevator Corp. (1947) articulated and broadened the new Court's intent standard (following the *Hines* and *Cloverleaf Butter Co. v. Patterson* cases).[14] A clear and manifest purpose is required when a state's police power is in question.[15] Even in redefining the criteria to be used in ascertaining congressional intent in *Rice,* Justice William O. Douglas observed, "We start with the assumption that the historic police powers of the States were not to be superseded by the Federal Act unless that was the clear and manifest purpose of Congress."[16] The Court took a restrained approach to federalism and preemption.

The *Rice* holding was that Congress's intent to supersede a state's police powers must be manifest (clear and distinct) to overcome the presumption against preemption. Scholars and jurists in applying the principles of the *Rice* case later reflected that it was "the canonical statement of the modern preemption doctrine"[17] that has prevailed for over half a century to this day:

> Congress legislated here in a field which the States have traditionally occupied. So, we start with the assumption that the historic police powers of the States were not to be superseded by the Federal Act unless that was the clear and manifest purpose of Congress. Such a purpose may be evidenced in several ways. The scheme of federal regulation may be so pervasive as to make reasonable the inference that Congress left no room for the States to supplement it. Or the Act of Congress may touch a field in which the federal interest is so dominant that the federal system will be assumed to preclude enforcement of state laws on the same subject. Likewise, the object sought to be obtained by the federal law and the character of obligations imposed by it may reveal the same purpose. Or the state policy may produce a result inconsistent with the objective of the federal statute. It is often a perplexing question whether Congress has precluded state action or by the choice of selective regulatory measures has left the police power of the States undisturbed except as the state and federal regulations collide.[18]

In 2002, one author looking back on the evolution of the preemption doctrine over the first half of the twentieth century, summarized the preemption doctrine as having "evolved over the last century from one based on an assumption of congressional legislative exclusivity and almost certain preemption of state regulation to a doctrine, in the mid-part of the century, based on a search for [clear and distinct] congressional intent to preempt so that state laws, particularly those based on historical police powers, were not needlessly displaced."[19]

SUMMARY

Beginning in 1937, the Supreme Court had adopted an expansive interpretation of the federal government's authority under the Commerce Clause. However, while congressional power in the area of commerce increased exponentially during this historical period, at the same time the Stone Court provided greater clarity to the preemption doctrine and supplied its famous statutory canon and constitutional principle in *Rice v. Santa Fe Elevator Corp.* (1947). In that landmark preemption decision, the Court explicitly pronounced its "presumption against preemption," which had been conceptually introduced in *Mintz* (1933) but now was formally constitutionalized. Because the intent and purpose of Congress remained the "ultimate touchstone in every case," the Stone Court required that a "clear and manifest purpose" be articulated and ascertained before federal preemption could be activated over state laws. This placed a greater burden on the federal government, which had been assumed to legislate predominantly over a number of subject areas.

NOTES

1. *Rice v. Santa Fe Elevator Corp.*, 331 U.S. 218 (1947).
2. Hoffer, Hoffer, and Hull, *Supreme Court*, 281–305.
3. Hoffer, Hoffer, and Hull, *Supreme Court*, 305.
4. Corwin, "Passing of Dual Federalism," 17.
5. Corwin, "Passing of Dual Federalism," 20–21.
6. Weiser, "Towards a Constitutional Architecture," 665.
7. Deil S. Wright, "The Advisory Commission on Intergovernmental Relations: Unique Features and Policy Orientation," *Public Administration Review* 25, no. 3 (1965): 193–202.
8. *Mintz v. Baldwin*, 289 U.S. 346 (1933) (see the discussion in chapter 6 on page 62).
9. *Hines v. Davidowitz*, 312 U.S. 52, (1941) (see also chapter 12 at 160n107), at 75 (J. Stone, dissenting).
10. Gardbaum, "Breadth versus Depth," 70.
11. Young, "'Ordinary Diet of the Law,'" 269 (quoting *Medtronic, Inc. v. Lohr*, 518 U.S. 470, 485 [1996]).
12. Gardbaum, "Nature of Preemption," 807, emphasis original.
13. Stephen A. Gardbaum, "New Evidence on the Presumption against Preemption: An Empirical Study of Congressional Responses to Supreme Court Preemption

Decisions," *Harvard Law Review* 120, no. 6 (2007): 1604, direct quotation at 1609, https://harvardlawreview.org/wp-content/uploads/pdfs/new_evidence_on_the_presumption.pdf; and see Gardbaum, "Nature of Preemption," 767, 806–07.

14. *Rice v. Santa Fe Elevator Corp.*, 331 U.S. 218 (1947). And see *Hines v. Davidowitz*, 312 U.S. 52 (1941); and *Cloverleaf Butter Co. v. Patterson*, 315 U.S. 148 (1942). Note the extensive list of prior cases cited articulating the Court's expansive standards in applying the Commerce Clause at 154–59 and their footnote 3.

15. Presumption in favor of preemption, however, followed with constitutional backing when foreign affairs was involved. Bratton, "Preemption Doctrine," 633, 637; and see generally Wright, "Advisory Commission."

16. Rice, 331 U.S. at 230.

17. Epstein and Greve, "Conclusion: Preemption Doctrine and Its Limits," 309.

Epstein and Greve, however, argue that *Rice* is not a true preemption case but a case about exclusive jurisdiction: "The perceived blow to state authority had nothing to do with the Supremacy Clause" (315). Rather, it had to do with the federal government's decision to offer a regulatory option in competition with those of the states. See Rice, 331 U.S. at 316.

18. Rice, 331 U.S. at 230. And see Epstein and Greve, *Federal Preemption*; and Bratton, "Preemption Doctrine," 626, 632–37.

19. Mary J. Davis, "Unmasking the Presumption in Favor of Preemption," *South Carolina Law Review* 53, no. 4 (2002): 967, 971.

11

The End of the State Wildlife Ownership Doctrine following World War II, 1946-1969

The Supreme Court performed a doctrinal evisceration of the long-standing principle of state "ownership" over its wildlife in two decisions in 1948: *Takahashi v. Fish and Game Commission* and *Toomer v. Witsell*.[1] Crucially, however, the Warren Court displayed a jurisprudential shift in placing greater independent *limitations* on the scope of state sovereignty—most notably in a range of cases in the 1960s that expanded individual rights and incorporated the Bill of Rights against the states. The cultural and political forces at play during the 1960s and 1970s, which influenced the environmental movement and the Warren Court, set the stage for the pendulum to shift back toward a more conservative jurisprudence, beginning with the Burger Court in 1969.

* * *

Following World War II (1939–1945), the United States enjoyed a long period of comparative peace. The economy was robust and vibrant as returning troops started families and sought housing and jobs; Europe needed massive rebuilding, supplied by the United States under the Marshall Plan. The Truman administration (1945–1953) was dominated by the beginning of the Cold War, the Korean War, a policy of containment of Russia (1946–1951), and the haunting threat of Communists infiltrating many aspects of US society, including the federal government. The United Nations was created in 1945 to assist in keeping world peace. This period was followed by the Eisenhower administration (1953–1961), which was preoccupied with the prospects of a nuclear war with Russia. Pollution and degradation of the environment and wildlife were largely ignored during the wartime production of munitions, ships, planes, and supplies and thereafter as the nation busied itself with retooling factories for peacetime industrial production.[2]

The postwar era, moreover, witnessed mass migration out of major cities, creating urban sprawl and the development of suburbs and tract housing. Environmental consequences followed the bulldozers and new suburbanites. Two historians have ably documented that the rise of the environmental movement in the 1960s and '70s originated in the suburbs.[3]

When the national park system had been developed back in the early part of the twentieth century, up to this point, access had been primarily by railway. Cars were cost prohibitive for the average family, and the road system as we know it today was then nonexistent. During the Great Depression, a national US highway system had been developed as a public-works project. By the time the troops were returning from World War II, automobiles were affordable, and the state and national federal parks and forests offered an affordable escape into the outdoors.[4] The high visitation rate forced the National Park Service (NPS) into a ten-year billion-dollar expansion and rehabilitation program for their old park structures. Mission 66 (1956–1966), as it came

Figure 11.1. Urban sprawl defined the growth of the United States following World War II and set in motion many of the environmental concerns that would come to dominate the 1960s and 1970s. *Source*: iofoto/Shutterstock.

to be known, was to be completed on the fiftieth anniversary of the NPS.[5] A parallel program started the same year during the Eisenhower administration was the development of the interstate highway system.[6]

These two major programs dramatically elevated outdoor recreation and park visitation in the United States, creating an opportunity for Americans to rediscover the natural world and outdoors. The kids that were in the back seats of cars touring the parks throughout America in the late 1940s and 1950s became the young adults and student environmental activists of later decades. They matured with a broadened appreciation of and connection to the natural world from their childhood experience in the parks. These experiences planted the seed that inspired their energies in the 1960s and '70s to promote an abundance of environmental legislation.

Following World War II, in 1948 the Supreme Court decided two wildlife cases relating to the federal preemption of state authority, both under the aegis of Chief Justice Fred M. Vinson. In June 1948, the Court heard the case of *Takahashi v. Fish and Game Commission*,[7] which involved denial of a commercial fishing license to a Japanese-American who had come to California in 1907 and been a commercial fisherman, properly licensed from 1915 up to 1942, when he and his family had been interned during the war. Both before and especially after World War II, anti-Japanese antagonistic sentiment and discrimination had reached its zenith in US public opinion on the West Coast, and the California legislature enacted many discriminatory laws and regulations, taxes, licenses, exactions, and punishments in an attempt to drive aliens and people of Japanese descent out of the state. The US Supreme Court selected this wildlife-law case to address outrageous Fourteenth Amendment equal protection violations. California argued that the state had "a proprietary interest in fish in the ocean waters within three miles of the shore to protect the special interests of its citizens."[8] The state argued that California owned the fish as trustee for its citizens and that it had the power to deny licenses for aliens as a means of conserving the supply of fish. Denying certain licenses "tends to reduce the number of commercial fishermen and therefore is a proper fish conservation measure."[9]

Justice Black, writing for the majority, and citing Justice Oliver Wendell Holmes in the *Missouri v. Holland* decision of 1920, stated that California's claim of ownership of fish "is to lean upon a slender reed" and constitutes "the very negation of all ideals of the equal protection clause" of the US Constitution.[10]

> To whatever extent the fish in the three-mile belt off California may be "capable of ownership" by California, we think that "ownership" is inadequate to justify California in excluding any or all aliens who are lawful residents of the State from making a living by fishing in the ocean off its shores while permitting all

others to do so. . . . It denies them commercial fishing rights not because they threaten the success of any conservation program, not because their fishing activities constitute a clear and present danger to the welfare of California or of the nation, but only because they are of Japanese stock, a stock which has had the misfortune to arouse antagonism among certain powerful interests . . . the very negation of all the ideals of the equal protection clause.[11]

Two months after the *Takahashi* opinion, the case of *Toomer v. Witsell*[12] was decided in June 1948, with Chief Justice Vinson writing the majority opinion. Based on the Privileges and Immunities Clause of the US Constitution (Art. IV, Sec. 2), the majority concluded that South Carolina lacked appropriate justification or special property interests to justify discrimination against nonresident boats in licensing fees on commercial shrimp boats of twenty-five dollars for resident-owned boats and $2,500 for nonresident boats operating within the three-mile maritime belt. Moreover, the state could not require nonresidents to dock at a South Carolina port and unload, weigh, pack, and stamp their catch and pay a special tax of one-eighth cent per pound on shrimp taken within the state's waters before transporting their catch to another state. The purpose of the South Carolina regulations had purely been to create a commercial monopoly for state residents—not to conserve shrimp for their citizen's consumption. The Court held:

> By that statute South Carolina plainly and frankly discriminates against non-residents, and the record leaves little doubt but what the discrimination is so great that its practical effect is virtually exclusionary . . . the purpose of that clause [Privilege and Immunities], which, as indicated above, is to outlaw classifications based on the fact of non-citizenship unless there is something to indicate that non-citizens constitute a peculiar source of the evil at which the statute is aimed.
>
> However satisfactory the ownership theory explains the *McCready* case, the very factors which make the present case distinguishable render that theory but a weak prop for the South Carolina statute. That the shrimp are migratory makes apposite Mr. Justice Holmes' statement in *Missouri v. Holland*, that "To put the claim of the State upon title is to lean upon a slender reed. Wild birds are not in the possession of anyone; and possession is the beginning of ownership." Indeed, only fifteen years after the *McCready* decision, a unanimous Court indicated that the rule of that case might not apply to free-swimming fish. The fact that it is activity in the three-mile belt which the South Carolina statute regulates is of equal relevance in considering the applicability of the ownership doctrine. . . . The whole ownership theory, in fact, is now generally regarded as but a fiction expressive in legal shorthand of the importance to its people that a State have power to preserve and regulate the exploitation of an important resource. And there is no necessary conflict between that vital policy consideration and the constitutional command that the State exercise that power, like its other powers, so as not to discriminate without reason against citizens of other States.

See e.g., Roscoe Pound, *An Introduction to the Philosophy of Law* (New Haven: Yale University Press, 1930), 197–202. The fiction apparently gained currency partly as a result of confusion between the Roman term imperium or governmental power to regulate, and dominium, or ownership. Power over fish and game was, in origin, imperium.[13]

Justice Felix Frankfurter concurred with the majority but found that South Carolina's regulations only violated the Commerce Clause of the Constitution:

> While I agree that South Carolina has exceeded her power to control fisheries within her waters, I rest the invalidity of her attempt to do so on the Commerce Clause. . . . Like other provisions of the Constitution, the Clause whereby "The Citizens of each State shall be entitled to all Privileges and Immunities of Citizens in the several States" must be read in conjunction with the Tenth Amendment to the Constitution. This clause presupposes the continued retention by the States of powers that historically belonged to the States, and were not explicitly given to the central government or withdrawn from the States. . . . When the Constitution was adopted, such, no doubt, was the common understanding regarding the power of States over its fisheries, and it is this common understanding that was reflected in *McCready v. Virginia*. The *McCready* case is not an isolated decision to be looked at askance. It is the symbol of one of the weightiest doctrines in our law. It expressed the momentum of legal history that preceded it, and around it in turn has clustered a voluminous body of rulings. Not only has a host of State cases applied the *McCready* doctrine as to the power of States to control their game and fisheries for the benefit of their own citizens, but in our own day this Court formulated the amplitude of the *McCready* doctrine by referring to "the regulation or the distribution of the public domain, or of the common property or resources of the people of the state, the enjoyment of which may be limited to its citizens as against both aliens and the citizens of other states." *Truax v. Raich*.
>
> But a State cannot project its powers over its own resources by seeking to control the channels of commerce among the States. It is one thing to say that a food supply that may be reduced to control by a State for feeding its own people should be only locally consumed. The State has that power and the Privileges and Immunities Clause is no restriction upon its exercise. It is a wholly different thing for the State to provide that only its citizens shall be engaged in commerce among the States, even though based on a locally available food supply. That is not the exercise of the basic right of a State to feed and maintain and give enjoyment to its own people. When a State regulates the sending of products across State lines we have commerce among the States as to which State intervention is subordinate to the Commerce Clause. That is the nub of the decision in *Foster-Fountain Packing Co. v. Haydel*. South Carolina has attempted such regulation of commerce in shrimp among the States. In doing so she has exceeded the restrictions of the Commerce Clause.[14]

Clearly, the Supreme Court eliminated the grounds of its earlier doctrine of state sovereignty over fish and wildlife to be conserved for the exclusive benefit and consumption by its residents. However, the *Takahashi* and *Toomer* decisions were not surprising, given the growing trend beginning in 1937 well into and beyond the Vinson Court on issues regarding alleged violation of constitutionally protected individual rights under the Fourteenth Amendment. This trend imposing the Bill of Rights on states while diminishing traditional state authority would continue into the 1950s with the Warren Court's school-desegregation decision in *Brown v. Board of Education*[15] and then accelerate dramatically in the 1960s and 1970s with the Court's expanding role in defining constitutional civil liberties.

THE EXPLOSIVE ETHOS OF THE 1960S AND 1970S AND THE ENVIRONMENTAL AWAKENING OF AMERICA

The quietude of the post–World War II era came to an abrupt end with the chaos and counterrevolutionary forces of the 1960s and '70s. The challenging and ever rending of societal norms fostered a growing uneasiness and mistrust of the federal government, an estrangement not widespread within American society since the Civil War.[16] Four seminal events defined this period, each weakening public confidence in government. First, the highly unpopular Vietnam War (with Kennedy's escalation starting in 1961, and fighting continuing through 1975) in Southeast Asia injured 304,000 and took the lives of 58,220 American soldiers. Second, forced integration in the public schools of the American South further agitated the civil rights (and thereafter the social justice) movement. Third, a series of major environmental disasters resulted from industrial disregard of the environment before, during, and after World War II. These national troubles, moreover, provided grist for the media, which had grown to twenty-four-seven news and TV coverage, bringing them directly into the public's living room.[17]

Alongside the natural disasters of the 1960s and '70s was a growing national awareness of the manufacture and use of toxic chemicals and pesticides polluting the nation's food supply, air, and water. Rachel Carson's book *Silent Spring* publicized this, provoking a national dialogue.[18] Historian Samuel P. Hayes would add scientific inquiry as a reason for this growth of national concern, as it informed the public of the science underlying environmental changes.[19] Secondary events that further contributed to the loss of confidence in the federal government's ability to protect its citizens included the race riots following the assassination of Martin Luther King Jr. in 1968, the Kent State massacre of armed troops' killing of college students, the energy crisis and oil embargo that produced a massive gas shortage and miles-long lines of cars at gas stations, and abandonment of the gold standard. The latter two demonstrated the American economy's growing estrangement from the world economy during this period.[20]

The fourth class of events defining this period of American history and the public's moral outrage was the national response of civil, nonviolent disobedience and orchestrated protests that mobilized the environmental community to follow the playbook of the war protestors and civil rights activists to realize their legislative objectives and achievements.[21] Added to this fourth class would be the organized growth of the environmental community and their growing public advocacy including an aggressive litigation strategy. Older conservation organizations like the Sierra Club, the Wilderness Society, the National Audubon Society, and the National Wildlife Federation revised their historic mission and focus to address contemporary issues. New groups emerged, such as the Environmental Defense Fund, Friends of the Earth, and the Natural Resources Defense Council. Highly litigious, radicalized groups, moreover, emerged during this period, such as People for the Ethical Treatment of Animals, the Center for Biological Diversity, WildEarth Guardians, and the Western Watersheds Project.[22] Environmental organizations swelled in membership from 125,000 in 1960 to one million in 1970, two million in 1980, and six million in 1990.[23] Amid the social upheaval and political chaos of the era, the 1960s and '70s produced the largest number of conservation and environmental laws and consumer-protection legislation ever realized in the United States in two centuries.[24] These were truly the decades of the environment, with the first Earth Day celebrated on Wednesday, April 22, 1970.

A product of these two growling decades was the public's demand for more environmental protection and greater safety from faulty product design and manufacturing, which led to the enactment of some sixty-seven laws. (See Appendix I)[25] Significant particularly to the environmental movement were the National Environmental Policy Act, the Clean Air Act, the federal Water Pollution Control Act, the Marine Mammal Protection Act, the Noise Control Act, and the Endangered Species Act, this latter the first legislation exclusively designed to protect endangered species.[26]

The broad rubric of ecology[27] popularized in the wildlife sciences in the 1930s by Aldo Leopold had become splintered throughout the twentieth century into a host of independent science disciplines. These included human ecology, human dimension science, conservation biology, wildlife biology, environmental science, ecosystem science, anthropology, ethnology, and zoology.[28] Science consumed America's focus after World War II and became the new "God" by which humans and human ingenuity could control and improve upon nature. The hydrogen bomb proved humans could destroy nature and humanity. Rachel Carson's *Silent Spring* challenged the paradigm of the day and was branded revolutionary.[29] The science of conservation biology and biodiversity emanated from a 1978 conference held at the University of California San Diego and led by Dr. Tom Lovejoy,[30] which added a whole new dimension to how the world viewed the conservation and community of species. A full decade would pass, however, before Congress and the courts would catch up with the state of scientific understanding.[31]

These new disciplines dominated the conscience of the environmental community in the area of wildlife science and began to be recognized by the judiciary.[32] Environmental scholar and philosopher Dr. Alston Chase copiously describes the development of this new consciousness in his landmark book, *In a Dark Wood: The Fight over Forests and the Rising Tyranny of Ecology*.[33] Today the more popular nomenclature is "comprehensive wildlife conservation" or "landscape conservation," since its focus ranges far beyond one ecosystem and its community of species. The ideology underlying each of these successive disciplines can be traced directly back to the philosophers and scholars of the eighteenth and nineteenth centuries. The emergence of ecology and its multiple disciplines provided scientific rationale for expanding federal power over the environment throughout the twentieth century,[34] as the courts began to incorporate science into their decisions based on the Commerce and Property Clauses of the Constitution. This further eroded state authority and expanded federal preemption.[35]

The Supreme Court during this postwar period was managed by Chief Justice Earl Warren, appointee of President Dwight D. Eisenhower, who later conceded that the appointment "was the worst mistake I've ever made."[36] Warren's tenure spanned from 1953 to 1969 and ushered in the civil rights revolution, beginning with an early decision in *Brown v. Board of Education* (1955).[37]

The Warren's Court's expansion of civil rights and civil liberties profoundly changed American constitutional law, especially federalism, as the Court led the federal government in this politically supercharged period on a decades-long diminution of states' rights and powers. The Warren Court's decisions reflected societal changes and the violent ethos of the 1960s and '70s. Warren had an expansive concept of an individual's constitutional rights, accompanied by a correspondingly expansive concept of judicial authority to vindicate those rights.[38] One legal scholar characterizes this period of the Court as "enlightened gradualism in . . . the nationalization of American law [reflecting] . . . the immense increase in the power of the national government."[39] Warren saw no special position for states within the federal system. In his opinion, states surrendered a portion of their sovereignty when they ratified the Constitution and granted Congress enumerated powers.[40]

Concerns over the protections afforded by the Tenth Amendment evaporated as the Court took a revisionist rather than an originalist approach to interpreting the Constitution. Warren liberally utilized preemption of states' rights under the guise of protecting an ever-expanding list of "civil liberties" without regard to constitutional language and precedent. Warren identified the outcome he wanted and interpreted the law to support it.

The Warren Court's idiosyncratic approach to case outcomes, jurisprudential consistency, and lack of judicial restraint truly reflected the strife and chaos ongoing across America during its tenure. Palpable conflict surfaced among the justices and judicial alignments mirroring the diverse and fluctuating political ideologies of the era and growing judicial contempt for state authority. No major wildlife cases were decided during the Warren Court's sixteen years, but its contempt for state authority and the Court's own precedents would spill over and influence the Burger Court, which followed. The Burger Court would reach a zenith of definitive jurisprudence on wildlife law, preemption, and the federal presence in the wildlife arena, rewriting historic judicial doctrines. The states would thereafter have definitive guidelines on their authority. Moreover, under the Burger Court the judicial pendulum would begin to swing back to a conservative Court.

SUMMARY

The constitutional notion of state "ownership" over wildlife was eviscerated by the Supreme Court in 1948, beginning first with *Takahashi v. Fish and Game Commission*, which held that California's claim to "ownership" over fish wildlife was squarely "inadequate" to justify the exclusion of fisherman on the basis of race, as proscribed under the Equal Protection Clause of the Fourteenth Amendment. Similarly, the Court in *Toomer v. Witsell* held that South Carolina lacked power to discriminate against nonresidents under the Privileges and Immunities Clause. Most fundamentally, both cases imposed *independent* limitations on the overall size, scope, and application of state sovereignty to individual cases and controversies. These two cases, however, told a broader, more important story about the future trajectory of federalism and preemption: The Supreme Court would *significantly* scale back the power of state authority through the 1960s with the Warren Court using the expansion of individual rights to impose independent limits on state police powers.

The political, cultural, and social unrest during this time period greatly influenced the Supreme Court's individual-rights jurisprudence. From the explosive controversies surrounding the Vietnam War to the racial battles over Southern integration, individual public-interest advocacy groups emerged to combat the glaring problems of the 1960s. Specifically, from the environmental movement aggressive, *impact litigation* campaigns emerged to ensure environmental safety and curb harmful pollution. In particular, beginning with the Progressive Movement during the early 1900s, the discipline of ecology had continued to furnish sound justifications for the federal government to expand its reach into environmental regulation and preemption. However, these justifications were evolving: Under the Warren Court, which maintained an expansive federal view of individual rights, the Court rendered a number of decisions hostile to the notion of state sovereignty. While the Warren Court did *not* specifically issue any landmark rulings that touched on the intersection between federalism, preemption, *and* wildlife authority, the Court's contempt for state authority was evident from its rulings. Accordingly, the Warren Court's adopted justification during the 1960s—the notion of individual rights as an independent *limitation* on state power—became controversial and soon became subject to intense review under the Burger Court.

NOTES

1. *Takahashi v. Fish and Game Commission*, 334 U.S. 410 (1948); *Toomer v. Witsell*, 334 U.S. 385 (1948).

2. Historian James T. Patterson does a very competent history of the postwar era in his book *Grand Expectations: The United States, 1945–1974* (New York: Oxford University Press, 1996). For a well-edited and very informative overview during the 1950s and '60s on the state of wildlife management primarily from the states' perspective, see Bailey, Elder, and McKinney, *Readings in Wildlife Conservation*. Moreover, Hal K. Rothman does a very credible overview of environmental politics and policies after 1945 in *The Greening of a Nation? Environmentalism in the United States since 1945* (Fort Worth: Harcourt Brace College Publishers, 1998). His 2000 book, *Saving the Planet: The American Response to the Environment in the Twentieth Century* (Chicago: Ivan R. Dee Publishing), is likewise a journalistic approach to a survey of the development of environmentalism from the 1890s into the 1990s.

3. Adam Rome, *The Bulldozer in the Countryside: Suburban Sprawl and the Rise of American Environmentalism* (Cambridge: Cambridge University Press, 2001); and Christopher C. Sellers, *Crabgrass Crucible: Suburban Nature and the Rise of Environmentalism in Twentieth-Century America* (Chapel Hill: The University of North Carolina Press, 2012).

4. Paul S. Sutter, *Driven Wild: How the Fight against Automobiles Launched the Modern Wilderness Movement* (Seattle: University of Washington Press, 2002), 255–63. 5. Alston Chase, *Playing God in Yellowstone: The Destruction of America's First National Park* (San Diego and New York: Harcourt Brace Jovanovich, 1987), 203–208; Sutter, *Driven Wild*, 256; and Christopher W. Wells, *Car Country: An Environmental History* (Seattle: University of Washington Press, 2012), 273–75.

6. See Wells, *Car Country*, 273–74; and Sutter, *Driven Wild*, 256.
7. *Takahashi v. Fish and Game Commission*, 334 U.S. 410 (1948).
8. *Takahashi*, 334 U.S. at 414.
9. *Takahashi*, 334 U.S. at 418.
10. *Takahashi*, 334 U.S. at 421, and then at 427 (J. Murphy, concurring).
11. *Takahashi*, 334 U.S. at 427 (J. Murphy, concurring).
12. *Toomer v. Witsell*, 334 U.S. 385 (1948).
13. *Toomer*, 334 U.S. at 394, 396, 397, 401, 402 n. 37 (internal citations omitted).
14. *Toomer*, 334 U.S. at 407–409 (J. Frankfurter, concurring; internal citations omitted).
15. 347 U.S. 483 (1954).
16. For an interesting global perspective on the 1960s and '70s, see Jon Agar, "What Happened in the Sixties?" *The British Journal for the History of Science* 41, no. 4 (2008): 567–600. For a history of the Kennedy-Johnson administration's management of the first and third classes of events following, see Robert A. Divine, ed., *The Johnson Years* (Lawrence: The University Press of Kansas, 1987), 23–53, 113–80.
17. Dr. Lee M. Talbot, interview by Lowell E. Baier, March 29, 2016.
18. Rachel Carson, *Silent Spring* (Boston: Houghton Mifflin Company, 1962).

Shannon Petersen argues the whole matter of environmental awareness and consciousness of this era sprung from Carson's *Silent Spring*. He appears to completely discount the context of the era as explained herein. See Petersen, *Acting for Endangered Species*, 21. Moreover, for the underlying themes of societal unrest throughout the twentieth century leading up to this era of environmental awareness, see Chad Montrie, *Myth of Silent Spring*; and see his earlier book, *A People's History of Environmentalism in the United States* (New York: Continuum Press, 2011). Also see James Fisher, Noel Simon, and Jack Vincent, *Wildlife in Danger* (New York: Viking Press, 1969).

19. Samuel P. Hays, *A History of Environmental Politics since 1945* (Pittsburgh: University of Pittsburgh Press, 2000), 5, 137–53.
20. Lowell E. Baier, *Inside the Equal Access to Justice Act: Environmental Litigation and the Crippling Battle over America's Lands, Endangered Species, and Critical Habitats* (Lanham, MD: Rowman & Littlefield, 2016), 40–43. And see generally David Frum, *How We Got Here: The 70's; The Decade That Brought You Modern Life (For Better or Worse)* (New York: Basic Books, 2000).
21. For a well researched and thoroughly documented article on this subject, see Lincoln L. Davies, "Lessons for an Endangered Movement: What a Historical Juxtaposition of the Legal Response to Civil Rights and Environmentalism," *Environmental Law* 21, no. 2 (Spring 2001): 229–370; see also Dorceta E. Taylor, "American Environmentalism: The Role of Race, Class and Gender in Shaping Activism, 1820–1995," *Environmentalism and Race, Gender, Class Issues* 5, no. 1 (1997): 16, 39–47.

Shannon Petersen dates the beginning of the litigation strategy of the environmental community to the 1980s. Court records clearly indicate it began in the late 1960s and early 1970s, however, following the enactment of the National Environmental Policy Act. But it intensified during the antienvironmental period of the Reagan administration (1981–1988). Petersen, "Modern Ark," 153; Baier, *Inside the Equal Access to Justice Act*, 137–59. Samuel Hays dates the beginning of legal action to the 1960s. Hays, *History of Environmental Politics*, 104.

22. Baier, *Inside the Equal Access to Justice Act*, 135–269.

23. Hays, *History of Environmental Politics*, 5, 22–26, 94–108; James T. Patterson, *Restless Giant: The United States from Watergate to "Bush v. Gore"* (Oxford: Oxford University Press, 2005), 117. For the development of the representative NGOs, see Baier, *Inside the Equal Access to Justice Act*, 135–270; see also James A. Tober, *Wildlife and the Public Interest: Nonprofit Organizations and Federal Wildlife Policy* (New York: Praeger Publishers, 1989), 1–58, 159–97.

24. For a timeline, see appendix 1 of this book.

25. Again, refer to appendix 1 for specifics.

26. US Congress, National Environmental Policy Act of 1969, Pub. L. No. 91–190, 83 Stat. 852 (1970), https://www.govinfo.gov/content/pkg/STATUTE-83/pdf/STATUTE-83-Pg852.pdf; US House of Representatives, Clean Air Act Amendments of 1970, Pub. L. No. 91–604, 84 Stat. 1705 (1970), https://www.govinfo.gov/content/pkg/STATUTE-84/pdf/STATUTE-84-Pg1676.pdf; US Congress, Federal Water Pollution Control Act Amendments of 1972, Pub. L. No. 92–500, 86 Stat. 816 (1972), https://www.govinfo.gov/content/pkg/STATUTE-86/pdf/STATUTE-86-Pg816.pdf; US Congress, Marine Mammal Protection Act of 1972, Pub. L. No. 92–522, 85 Stat. 1027 (1972), https://www.fws.gov/international/pdf/legislation-marine-mammal-protection-act.pdf; US Congress, Noise Control Act of 1972, Pub. L. No. 92–574, 86 Stat. 1234 (1972), https://www.govinfo.gov/content/pkg/STATUTE-86/pdf/STATUTE-86-Pg1234.pdf; and US House of Representatives, Committee of Conference. Endangered Species Act of 1973, Pub. L. No. 93–205, 87 Stat. 884 (1973), https://www.govinfo.gov/content/pkg/STATUTE-87/pdf/STATUTE-87-Pg884.pdf.

27. For a renowned scientist's brilliant and illuminating evaluation of the state of the environment from the ecological perspective in the 1960s and '70s, see Barry Commoner, *The Closing Circle: Nature, Man, and Technology* (New York: Alfred A. Knopf, 1971).

28. Support for what was referred to as the "Neo-Darwin Theory of Evolution and Ecology" was led by Julian Huxley (1887–1975), Theodosuis Dobzhansky (1900–1975), George Gaylord Simpson (1902–1984), George Ledyard Stebbins Jr. (1906–2001), and Ernst Mayr (1904–2005).

29. William Souder, *On a Farther Shore: The Life and Legacy of Rachel Carson* (New York: Crown Publishers, 2012), 13–14, 320–21, 330–33, 335–36, 339, 345–46, 348–55, 365–66; and Linda Lear, *Rachel Carson: Witness for Nature* (New York: Houghton Mifflin, 1997), 323, 422, 425–26, 428–38, 448–52, 461–62, 468.

30. Dr. Tom Lovejoy, interview by Lowell E. Baier, May 8, 2018. Petersen misplaces the origin of the concept of biodiversity, placing it in the mid-1930s and mistakenly confusing it with Aldo Leopold's writings and the development of the science of ecosystems, a concept he attributes to biologist Arthur Tansley. See Petersen, *Acting for Endangered*. For a complete review of the concepts of biodiversity and conservation biology, see Dale D. Goble, J. Michael Scott, and Frank W. Davis, eds.,

The Endangered Species Act at Thirty, vol. 2 (Washington, DC: Island Press, 2006), 49–60, 275–90.

31. Petersen, *Acting for Endangered Species*, 19–20; Petersen, "Congress and Charismatic Megafauna," 20–23.

32. Petersen, "Congress and Charismatic Megafauna," 20–23.

33. Chase, *In a Dark Wood*; See especially pp. 105–202.

34. Petersen, *Acting for Endangered Species*, 17–18.

35. Petersen, "Modern Ark," 48. Steven L. Yaffee argues that science-based policy and technical expertise in policymaking need to have limits due to their impact on bureaucratic behavior. Yaffee, *Prohibitive Policy*, 1–16, 149–62.

36. Hoffer, Hoffer, and Hull, *Supreme Court*, 355.

37. Hoffer, Hoffer, and Hull, *Supreme Court*, 355.

That decision and others that followed did not explicitly overrule the seminal 1896 case of *Plessy v. Ferguson* (163 U.S. 537 [1896]). *Plessy* had been decided during the eugenics movement, which had sought to preserve a perceived purity and integrity in the Anglo-Saxon race. That period in history has most recently come under scrutiny with the Black Lives Matter movement and the protests of 2020 and 2021, and many streets, buildings, and monuments dedicated to national figures who were also prominent leaders of the eugenics movement have subsequently been renamed in response to the cancel culture of the day, which seeks to silence or "cancel" the voices and influence of those deemed insufficiently virtuous or in-step with contemporary mores.

38. Henry Paul Monaghan, "The Burger Court and 'Our Federalism,'" *Law and Contemporary Problems* 43, no. 3 (1980): 43–44, https://scholarship.law.columbia.edu/cgi/viewcontent.cgi?article=1772&context=faculty_scholarship.

39. Hoffer, Hoffer, and Hull, *Supreme Court*, 356, 368. And see Monaghan, "Burger Court," abstract:

> Historically, the major "legal" issue in "Our Federalism" has been substantive in nature, i.e., the extent to which the basic charter mandates a clear division of powers, one that both protects *and confines* the central and state governments in their respective spheres. That issue is devoid of current significance. The radical transformation that has occurred in the structure of "Our Federalism" in the nearly two centuries of our existence has emptied the concept of nearly all legal content and replaced it with a frank recognition of the legal hegemony of the national government. This occurred well before the arrival of the Burger Court, and that Court shows no signs of attempting to undo the past.
>
> In recent years, attention has been drawn to a second, process-oriented dimension of "Our Federalism": we have come to accept as an article of faith that adequate federal judicial and administrative mechanisms should exist to enforce federally secured rights. The Burger Court has been the object of much criticism at this level, some of it of an inflamed character. I think that the criticisms have been vastly overstated and that the Burger Court has done little to impair the Warren Court's legacy of strong federal enforcement of federal rights.

40. Miller, "Burger Court's View."

12

The Burger Court: State Ownership of Wildlife Declared a Legal Fiction and Anachronism, 1969–1986

The doctrinal landscape of wildlife law shifted dramatically under the Burger Court. Notably, Congress passed its landmark Endangered Species Act in 1973, which today remains the primary law for protecting imperiled species. In *Tennessee Valley Authority v. Hill* (1978) the Court described the act as "the most comprehensive legislation for the preservation of endangered species enacted by any nation."[1] The Endangered Species Act's core provisions were later construed in the context of federal preemption and federalism, where the Court would attempt to strike a delicate balance between expansive federal authority and traditional police powers under state sovereignty.

* * *

During the seventeen-year period in which the Supreme Court was led by Chief Justice Warren Burger—from 1969 to 1986—the Court made fifty-seven preemption decisions regarding state authority (more than all the forty-one combined preemption Supreme Court cases that had come before), of which twelve revolved around a state's sovereign authority over its resident wildlife.[2] In a book published in 2016 that struggles to summarize seventeen years of the decisions of the Burger Court, *The Burger Court and the Rise of the Judicial Right*,[3] one reviewer graciously concluded, "the authors assigned themselves a very heavy lift, and if they did not fully succeed it is in part because of their ambitious goal."[4] That conclusion reflects how difficult it is to define the Burger Court's jurisprudence on the state sovereignty issue over its resident wildlife. It was one of US history's most divided Courts, reflecting the absence of a national consensus on contested social and political issues.[5] Sensitive to public opinion, the Court's cases stretched across the spectrum—from abortion and women's rights to civil rights and ethnic discrimination, religious freedom, criminal law and the death penalty, and presidential executive privilege. And it imposed a wide variety of individual rights–based restrictions on state policy.[6]

Upon naming Warren Burger chief justice, President Richard Nixon called the appointment a symbol of conservative retrenchment. This Court has been referred to as a "transitional court," since it followed the very liberal Court of Chief Justice Earl Warren (1953–1969) and preceded the ultraconservative Court of Chief Justice William Rehnquist (1986–2005). The Burger Court dramatically diminished the scope and impact of the Warren Court's liberal precedents. For the Rehnquist Court that followed, the Burger Court established a conservative legal foundation.[7] In spite of being dominated by liberal judges, the Court collectively acted as strict constructionists on constitutional and legislative issues and practitioners of judicial restraint.[8]

In rapid succession, in a series of nine cases the Court adjudicated between 1976 and 1984—all within less than a decade of the seventeen-year Burger Court—through expansive rulings on Congress's enumerated powers, the US Supreme Court and US Courts of Appeal repeatedly redefined, limited, and narrowed state sovereign authority over its resident wildlife. In 1979's *Hughes v. Oklahoma*[9] the Court finally characterized it as a legal anachronism and a nineteenth-century legal fiction. However, in balancing federalism, the Burger Court also developed further the doctrine of *presumption against preemption*, permitting states to regulate when federal legislation has not been established. Starting in June 1976, the Wild Free-Roaming Horse and Burros Act was upheld in an opinion by Justice Thurgood Marshall in *Kleppe v. New Mexico*,[10] based on the Property Clause and the right of the federal government to protect wildlife and visitors on public lands. Justice Marshall deferred to what he called the "paramount power" of the United States over state wildlife authority on federal lands under the Property Clause of the Constitution. "The 'complete power' that Congress has over public lands necessarily includes the power to regulate and protect the wildlife living thereon . . . And when Congress so acts, the federal legislation necessarily overrides conflicting state laws under the Supremacy Clause . . . We hold today that the Property Clause also gives Congress the power to protect wildlife on public lands, state law notwithstanding."[11]

During the Burger Court, following *Kleppe*, two lower federal court cases addressed the reach of the Property Clause to regulate and protect wildlife thereon.[12] "Whereas the Privileges and Immunities Clause, (Article IV, s 2, cl. 1), places a limitation on the power of the States, there is no question that the complete power Congress has over public lands under the Property Clause of the Constitution, (Article IV, s 3, cl. 2), necessarily includes the power to regulate and protect the wildlife living there. *Kleppe v. New Mexico* (1976)."[13]

In January 1977, Justice Marshall, again writing for the Supreme Court, stated that the Interstate Commerce Clause protected the right of federally licensed fishing vessels to move unrestricted from the waters of one state to another following migrating fish.[14] "Justice Marshall declared '... it is pure fantasy to talk of 'owning' wild fish, birds or animals ... [No one] has title to these creatures until they are reduced to possession by skillful capture. The 'ownership' language of cases such as those cited by appellant must be understood as no more than a 19th century *legal fiction* expressing 'the importance to its people that a state have power to preserve and regulate the exploitation of an important resource' *Toomer v. Witsell*. ... Our decision is very much in keeping with sound policy considerations of federalism.'"[15]

In May 1978, the State of Montana's imposition of a higher license fee for nonresidents to hunt elk than that it charged its residents was brought before the Court in *Baldwin v. Fish and Game Commission of Montana*. Justice Blackmun, speaking for the Supreme Court, held the discriminatory higher fee for nonresidents violated neither the Privileges and Immunities Clause nor the Equal Protection Clause of the US Constitution.[16] His opinion repeated the language Justice Marshall had used in *Kleppe* a year earlier—that state "ownership" of wildlife "was no more than a nineteenth century legal fiction."[17] "Many of the early cases," Justice Blackmun continued,

> embrace the concept that the States had complete ownership over wildlife within their boundaries, and, as well, the power to preserve this bounty for their citizens alone. ... This holding, and the conception of state sovereignty upon which it relied, formed the basis for similar decisions during later years of the 19th century. ... In more recent years, however, the Court has recognized that the States' interest in regulating and controlling those things they claim to "own" including wildlife, is by no means absolute. States may not compel the confinement of the benefits of their resources, even their wildlife, to their own people whenever such hoarding and confinement impedes interstate commerce (citations omitted). *Foster-Fountain Packing Co. v. Haydel* (1928). Nor does a State's control over its resources preclude the proper exercise of federal power. *Douglas v. Seacoast Products, Inc.* (1977), *Kleppe v. New Mexico* (1976), *Missouri v. Holland* (1920). And a State's interest in its wildlife and other resources must yield when, without reason, it interferes with a nonresident's right to pursue a livelihood in a State other than his own, a right that is protected by Privileges and Immunities Clause. *Toomer v. Witsell* (1948), *Takahashi v. Fish and Game Commission* (1948).[18]

In his concurring opinion, Chief Justice Warren Burger noted,

The doctrine that a state "owns" the wildlife within its borders as trustee for its citizens (see *Geer v. Connecticut*) is admittedly a legal anachronism of sorts. See *Douglas v. Seacoast Products, Inc.* (1977). A State does not "own" wild birds and animals in the same way that it may own other natural resources such as land, oil, or timber. But, as noted in the Court's opinion [*Douglas*], *ante*, at 1861, and contrary to the implications of the dissent, the doctrine is not completely obsolete. It manifests the State's *special interest* in regulating and preserving wildlife for the benefit of its citizens. See *Douglas v. Seacoast Products, Inc.* (1978).[19]

In their dissenting opinion, Justices William J. Brennan Jr., White, and Marshall repeated Justice Blackmun's language regarding the nineteenth-century legal fiction. The dissenters then concluded with this terse statement: "The lingering death of the *McCready* [state ownership] doctrine as applied to a State's wildlife, begun with the thrust of Mr. Justice Holmes' blade in *Missouri v. Holland* '([t]o put the claim of the State upon title is to lean upon a slender reed') and aided by increasingly deep twists of the knife in *Foster Fountain Packing Co. v. Haydel, Toomer v. Witsell, Takahashi and Kleppe* [which] . . . finally became a reality in *Douglas v. Seacoast Products, Inc.*"[20]

In a 1982 case, a federal district court judge elaborated on Justice Burger's *Baldwin* opinion with a focus on the limitations of the Privileges and Immunities Clause as it relates to a state's wildlife regulations within the constitutional limits of its police power and interstate commerce. Burger, the district court found,

> emphasized that *Corfield* and *McCready* were still good law insofar as their result was concerned, and that "*McCready v. Virginia, supra*, made it clear that the Privileges and Immunities clause does not prevent a State from preferring its own citizens in granting public access to natural resources in which they have a special interest." Burger noted that while the Privileges and Immunities clause had not been interpreted to prevent a State from preferring its own citizens in allocating access to wildlife within the State, a State does not have absolute freedom to regulate the taking of wildlife within its borders or over its airspace and that "once wildlife becomes involved in interstate commerce, a State may not restrict the use of or access to that wildlife in a way that burdens interstate commerce," *Douglas v. Seacoast Products, Inc.* (1978), *Foster-Fountain Packing Co. v. Haydel* (1928). . . . The Supreme Court has relegated the "ownership" of natural resources as standing for nothing more than an assurance that the State has power to preserve and regulate the exploitation of an important resource within the constitutional limitations of police power. *Hughes v. Oklahoma* (1979).[21]

While both the majority and dissenting justices in the *Baldwin* case explored the issue of recreational sport hunting as a fundamental right, a federally protected interest under the Privilege and Immunity Clause, their reasoning is somewhat obscure. The issue was thought to be irrelevant by the minority, which did not dispute the majority's conclusion that recreational sport hunting was a non-fundamental right. This suggests to one distinguished legal scholar that in the nation's early history, preserving access to wildlife "owned" by each colony or state to preserve their food supply was not considered a fundamental right. While these cases have all been overruled, the scholar suggests they are instructive in determining whether a federally protected interest is at stake in fact-finding.[22]

THE BURGER COURT AND THE ENDANGERED SPECIES ACT

On December 28, 1973, President Richard Nixon signed into law the Endangered Species Act of 1973.[23] The ESA amended the earlier 1966 and 1969 Endangered Species Acts, which had proved ineffective, notwithstanding the federal government's recognition that it was responsible to address the extinction crisis.[24] This new ESA established federal authority over *all* threatened and endangered species, dramatically expanding the federal role in wildlife conservation and setting the stage for a number of cases that expanded the doctrine of preemption. The 1973 act was part of a broader reelection strategy by Nixon to woo the environmental bloc of voters that had coalesced during the 1960s and early 1970s around the blitzkrieg of environmental legislation enacted. "Cooperative federalism," the contemporary metaphor in state-federal wildlife relations, was then being implemented through issue-by-issue environmental regulations. It was envisioned that the ESA would be implemented under a cooperative federalism model, similar to the Clean Water Act that had been enacted just one year earlier, or the Migratory Bird Treaty Act of 1918.[25] It was acknowledged the states had more field personnel and day-to-day species-management experience, including enforcement of laws and regulations, and that they were far better equipped to protect endangered species than was the federal government—later proven a mistaken assumption.[26] However, the cooperative-federalism model unfortunately wasn't followed in implementation or regulatory approach by the administrative agency responsible, the US Fish and Wildlife Service.[27]

The ESA was passed in the Senate by a unanimous vote and a 355 to 4 vote in the House, championed by Representative John D. Dingell Jr. (D-MI). But few in Congress truly understood the law. Most considered it a largely symbolic gesture toward the ideal of saving endangered, iconic species symbolic of national heritage, such as the bald eagle and grizzly bear. Overlooked in the act's language were the changes in tone, the omissions of several key words, and the deletion of fundamental concepts that the two earlier endangered species laws of 1966 and 1969 had included. Among these was a recognition that conservation of species by federal agencies was to be pursued "insofar as in practical" or "to the extent practicable"; both phrases were deleted in the new act. The 1973 version of the ESA abandoned practicability as a standard, replacing it with an *absolute* prohibition on harming listed species or their habitat by federal agencies and by private citizens on public or private lands, making this prohibition superior to the rights of private property owners.[28]

The enactment of the 1973 Endangered Species Act was a watershed moment in the history of wildlife conservation. It produced a sea change in federal law and the law and politics of federalism, federal power, and states' rights. The polestar—the Ursa Major—of American wildlife law had changed places in the galaxy. Federal authority now replaced state authority over threatened and endangered species. Among listed species, two-thirds occur on private lands, as do hundreds more at risk of being listed. Federal authority moved from protecting a few individual species to protecting all species at risk and to ecosystem protection. The ESA imposed endangered species conservation as an affirmative obligation of the federal government, elevated federal power above state authority, and made wildlife conservation as a federal policy more important than economic development. "The ESA provides a floor, not a ceiling, for species protection, and it preempts inconsistent or less restrictive state laws."[29] Inconsistent state law is preempted notwithstanding the Tenth Amendment. The ESA finds its constitutional basis in part in the Treaty Clause of the Constitution, specifically the Convention on International Trade in Endangered Species of Wild Fauna and Flora (CITES), which resulted from a provision in the 1969 Endangered Species Act calling for international cooperation in the protection of endangered species. The new ESA cited as legal support seven treaties in its findings and purposes clause.[30] Other provisions of the ESA are founded primarily on the Supremacy Clause, the Commerce Clause, and the Property and Spending Clauses.[31]

It has been over one hundred years since Congress enacted its earliest intervention into state wildlife authority with the Lacey Act of 1900 and later the Migratory Bird Treaty Act of 1918. Those laws had been passed within the larger context of trustbusting, when the Supreme Court and Congress were both facing down the financial trusts, monopolies, and robber barons that had a stranglehold on the nation's economy and well-being. During the Gilded Age of the Progressive Era, Congress, supported by the Supreme Court, used the Supremacy and Commerce Clauses of the Constitution to articulate its claim to absolute authority over price fixing, restraint of trade, cartels, and the industrial monopolies. These constitutional and legal precedents of the Progressive Era echoed throughout the twentieth century, expressing themselves in a variety of contexts, including an increased federal role in what traditionally had been state wildlife management. The Endangered Species Act constituted a major expansion of federal supremacy under the Commerce and Supremacy Clauses in the new national policy of protecting endangered species and preempting state laws.

Commerce moves freely throughout the states to its final destination, the consumer's use—its ultimate purpose and goal. Monopolies and restraints on trade interrupt that flow of commerce to its end market and depress competition—evils the antitrust statutes as a national policy attempt to deter. Animals, birds, and endangered species are like interstate commerce: they too move and propagate freely throughout the country in search of food and seasonal habitats. As a national policy, they are to be protected for the enhancement of biodiversity and their survival promoted for the welfare of the people. Restraint or interference in their free migration, and destruction of their habitat or the species themselves, are evils like monopolies and restraint of trade that are to be prevented.

That is what Congress's constitutional exercise of the Supremacy and Commerce Clauses did in antitrust legislation and in the Endangered Species Act. Both share the same constitutional footings of supremacy and commerce, and both serve a national interest. The congressional embrace of federal supremacy and interstate commerce remains a deterrent against the concentration of economic power today and in the protection of endangered species, just as it did against the robber barons of yesteryear.[32]

The Endangered Species Act of 1973 has been significantly amended six times. It is the most contested wildlife conservation law ever adopted in US history and the least understood of all conservation laws. It was twenty pages long in 1973; today it is fifty pages. Congressional proposals for amendment have ranged from neutering its objectives to a complete rewrite to total repeal. Historian Roderick Nash calls the ESA "the strongest American legal expression to date of environmental ethics." Senator Bob Graham (D-FL) once characterized it as both "the crown jewel of the nation's environmental laws" and the "pit bull of environmental laws."[33]

Senator Ted Stevens (R-AK) lamented that "the bill is drawn on the basis of making the federal law preemptive [of state laws]," but he nevertheless supported enactment, because Section 6 required management through federal-state cooperation, not federal control. Stevens called Section 6 "the major backbone" of the ESA.[34] Yet during congressional hearings on the act's passage, the *Washington Post*'s lead editorial of June 26, 1973, argued that "the ultimate authority" for species protection *should* rest with the federal government rather than the states.[35] Congress and the nation recognized the seriousness of the extinction crisis and accepted that it could only be addressed uniformly by the federal government on a national scale, not individually by the states.[36] To many politicians, the ESA seemed to be a "win-win" opportunity.[37] Yet in a 2014 survey of its fifty state members, the Association of Fish and Wildlife Agencies said the most challenging law to the states was the Endangered Species Act. It was perceived by some state agency directors "as a vehicle for federal overreach, or of inappropriate reallocation of states' wildlife management duties into federal hands."[38] The law's very strength and unanticipated consequences, however, have threatened its future. The major "unanticipated consequence" has been Congress's failure to fully fund the costs of its absolute mandate to protect and conserve *all* endangered species.

The obvious retrospective question remains: *Why would Congress enact such a controversial bill?* The answer is twofold. First, the ESA arrived on "the peak of the environmental wave." It represented "the quintessential environmental issue" of its day, according to historian Steven Yaffee, with strong public sentiment supporting increased protection for endangered species.[39] A strong voting bloc of conservationists had emerged through accretion during the 1960s and early 1970s. Second, at the time of the law's enactment in 1973, the country was being roiled by the civil rights movement, anti–Vietnam War protests, and the Watergate scandal—which would soon lead to Nixon's resignation on August 8, 1974. Looking for a point of unity, politicians broadly supported the ESA—not out of a sincere commitment to species preservation but for self-serving reasons to get reelected.

TENNESSEE VALLEY AUTHORITY V. HILL: UNINTENDED CONSEQUENCES REALIZED

If the promise of the Endangered Species Act had been a watershed moment in federalism and a shift in federal power, the Supreme Court's first interpretation of the act, in *Tennessee Valley Authority v. Hill*,[40] fulfilled many fears of the legislation's unintended consequences. This case is important for four reasons: First, the United States had not realized the reach and magnitude of the 1973 law prior to this decision. Second, since two-thirds of all listed endangered species occur on the country's private lands, the Court's decision traumatized the industrial timber and agricultural sectors of land users across the country by adding another layer of federal control and prohibitions to their operations. Third, the decision added wildlife jurisprudence in unequivocal terms to the doctrine of federal preemption. Fourth, the decision signaled how the Supreme Court in its future opinions would view and value wildlife nationwide through the lens of the ESA.

Tennessee Valley Authority v. Hill addressed the questions of whether Section 7 of the ESA "encompassed the terminal phases of ongoing [construction] projects" begun before the ESA had become law. Moreover, the US Fish and Wildlife Service's duties under Section 7 were purely discretionary and advisory, with the ultimate decision to be left to the development agency, which in this case was the Tennessee Valley Authority.[41] The Supreme Court applied the standards of the doctrine of express preemption—a clear, plain, and manifest expressed intent of Congress—to decide the case based on the new law's legislative history, declaration of national policy, floor debate, and wording. They concluded that Section 7 was an absolute and substantive command of Congress with no room for exception or compromise.[42] Chief Justice Warren Burger, in a blistering opinion on the powers of federal authority regarding the "incalculable value" of all species and the need to protect them, made it abundantly clear how, going forward, the Supreme Court would view threatened wildlife nationwide through the lens of the ESA and the expressed intent of Congress:

"Man and his technology has [sic] continued at any ever-increasing rate to disrupt the natural ecosystem. This has resulted in a dramatic rise in the number and severity of the threats faced by the world's wildlife. The truth in this is apparent when one realizes that half of the recorded extinctions of mammals over the past 2,000 years have occurred in the most recent 50-year period." 1973 House Hearings 202 (statement of Assistant Secretary of the Interior).

In shaping legislation to deal with the problem thus presented, Congress started from the finding that "[t]he two major causes of extinction are hunting and destruction of natural habitat." S.Rep.No.93–307, p. 2 (1973) U.S. Code Cong & Admin. News 1973, pp. 2989, 2990.

As it was finally passed, the Endangered Species Act of 1973 represented the most comprehensive legislation for the preservation of endangered species ever enacted by any nation. Its stated purposes were "to provide a means whereby the ecosystems upon which endangered species and threatened species depend may be conserved," and "to provide a program for the conservation of such ... species."

The plain intent of Congress in enacting this statute was to halt and reverse the trend toward species extinction, *whatever the cost*. This is reflected not only in the stated policies of the Act, but in literally every section of the statute.

In addition, the legislative history undergirding § 7 reveals an explicit congressional decision to require [federal] agencies to afford first priority to the declared national policy of saving endangered species. The pointed omission of the type of qualifying language previously included in endangered species legislation reveals a conscious decision by Congress to give endangered species priority over the "primary missions" of federal agencies.[43]

In their dissents, Justices Rehnquist and Powell characterized the majority six-to-three opinion as an extreme example of the dark arc of literalist, statutory construction contrary to the intent of Congress.

Hill remains the best known case in environmental law, but one scholar argues that it has become the outlier in ESA jurisprudence. Over time, the ESA has become similar to many of the major pollution-control statutes—such as the Clean Air Act and the Clean Water Act. Its qualities have included expansive jurisdiction over land use with little connection to public health or welfare, complex regulations, time-consuming permitting, weak foundations in cost-benefit and cost-effective analysis, an inequitable distribution of benefits and burdens, and a gristmill of environmental litigation.[44] Environmental law scholar and professor J. B. Ruhl contends that *Hill* has methodically been eviscerated by four cases over the ensuing thirty years, largely in the opinions of Justice Antonin Scalia[45]: *Lujan v. Defenders of Wildlife*, *Babbitt v. Sweet Home Chapter of Communities for a Great Oregon*, *Bennett v. Spear*, and *National Assn. of Home Builders v. Defenders of Wildlife*.[46] All of these cases, like Hill, were initiated as citizen suits. All of the four, moreover, were decided in favor of prevailing probusiness interests.[47]

Professor Ruhl reasons that *Hill* has become an outlier because the Supreme Court's composition has changed in the decades since that decision was handed down. The Court has become more probusiness in its orientation

Figure 12.1. The snail darter (*Percina tanasi*) was the subject of the landmark 1978 US Supreme Court case *Tennessee Valley Authority v. Hill*, which held that under the Endangered Species Act of 1973 the survival of a tiny species of fish was more important than a $116 million federal dam that had almost been completed. *Source:* Joel Sartore, FIS005-00003, https://www.joelsartore.com/fis005-00003/?context=snail+darter&index=5.

and anti-environmentalism.[48] Further, Congress has since made several major amendments to the ESA, and the FWS has expanded its administrative agenda dramatically to reform its regulatory programs, opening the agency up to litigation.[49] The financial burdens on private landowner interests is the major issue that has turned the Supreme Court away from endorsing the environmental values embodied in the ESA back in 1973. There is no check on the FWS's limited attention to the cost of their decisions or mechanisms to ensure cost-benefit analysis or cost-effective regulations[50] to avoid an inequitable distribution of costs and benefits.[51]

Justice Scalia, in his dissent in *Sweet Home*, criticized the majority's reasoning in *Hill*, which, he said, "imposes unfairness to the point of financial ruin—not just upon the rich, but upon the simplest farmer who finds his land conscripted to national zoological use." For Scalia, the "cost of preserving the habitat of endangered species [should be] place[d] upon the public at large, rather than upon fortuitously accountable individual landowners."[52] Professor Robert Adler, however, argues that Justice Scalia's dissent evidences a lack of grounding in ecology and a great disconnect between science and the Court's understanding of ecosystems.[53]

THE PROGENY OF *TENNESSEE VALLEY AUTHORITY V. HILL*: THE SLENDER REED OF *GEER* OVERRULED AS A LEGAL FICTION

Following the *Hill* case, four wildlife cases were decided by the Supreme Court in 1979 alone. In April, the case of *Hughes v. Oklahoma* reversed the landmark precedent of the *Geer* case, which had stood as the law of the land since 1896.[54]

The decision in *Geer v. Connecticut* had for eighty-three years been a major milestone foundation in wildlife conservation law. It held that control over wildlife resided in the state as a public trust for the benefit of the people and the future of its citizens. *Geer* had been built on the 1842 *Waddell* case, which established the public trust doctrine in American jurisprudence.[55] *Waddell* had been followed by *McCready v. Virginia* in 1876.[56] Twenty years after that case, *Geer* became the single strongest precedent and foundational bulwark for a state's sovereign authority to manage its resident wildlife—legally, intellectually, and emotionally. From the states' perspective, their wildlife was theirs to manage in their sole discretion; they actually "owned the wildlife." The states' wildlife management systems and organizational structures had been built on this premise.[57] The jurisprudential foundation for this belief had been annihilated between the ESA and the Supreme Court's decisions in *Tennessee Valley Authority v. Hill* and *Hughes v. Oklahoma*. The states' whole belief system in their wildlife authority was erased by the Congress and the Supreme Court. However, it took time for this to sink in with the states, while the federal administrators charged with enforcement of the ESA, meanwhile, immediately recognized their newfound authority, eventually leading to bitter federal-state acrimony.[58] Once this precedent was overruled, state authority and management went adrift, and the states were sent into a free fall for lack of authority.

Historic glacial erosion of state control had really begun at the turn of the century with the Lacey Act of 1900 and the Migratory Bird Treaty Act of 1918. These had been followed through the century by *Hunt v. United States* (1928), *Foster-Fountain Packing Co. v. Haydel* (1928), *Chalk v. United States* (1940), *Takahashi v. Fish and Game Commission* (1948), *Toomer v. Witsell* (1948), *Kleppe v. New Mexico* (1976), *Douglas v. Seacoast Products, Inc.* (1977), and *Baldwin v. Fish and Game Commission of Montana* (1978).[59] Then came *Tennessee Valley Authority v. Hill* in 1978, followed ten months later by *Hughes v. Oklahoma* in 1979, which sealed the enlargement of federal authority at the expense of state autonomy and the federalist balance. In historical perspective, *Geer*'s magnitude over the twentieth century was as big as the *Hill* case: they were bookends, as were *Hughes* and *Hill*. The issue of states' authority was dramatically memorialized between these last two cases. Federal power was enhanced with the continuing "federalization" of wildlife, and the states' sovereign authority over its wildlife further eroded.

Justice Brennan's opinion in *Hughes v. Oklahoma*, which turned on a question of impeding interstate commerce, reflected how changing times and attitudes were governed by the originality of the US Constitution's language; yet time, Brennan wrote, had revealed the error of the Court's nineteenth-century decision. In other words, now "the Court was unwilling to continue to regard wildlife as conceptually different from other natural resources in a state."[60] While Justice Brennan's opinion is lengthy, its historical reflections are significant to understanding how wildlife jurisprudence evolved throughout the twentieth century. "The few simple words of the Commerce Clause," Brennan wrote in his *Hughes* decision, that "'The Congress shall have Power . . . To regulate Commerce . . . among the several States . . .'—reflected a central concern of the Framers that was an immediate reason for calling the Constitutional Convention: The conviction that in order to succeed, the new Union would have to avoid the tendencies toward economic Balkanization that had plagued relations among the Colonies and later among the States under the Articles of Confederation."[61] Brennan continued:

> The cases defining the scope of permissible state regulation in areas of congressional silence reflect an often controversial evolution of rules to accommodate federal and state interests. *Geer v. Connecticut* was decided relatively early in

that evolutionary process. We hold that time has revealed the error of the early resolution reached in that case, and accordingly *Geer* is today overruled.

Mr. Justice Field and the first Mr. Justice Harlan dissented [in the *Geer* case], rejecting as artificial and formalistic the Court's analysis of "ownership" and "commerce" in wild game. They would have affirmed the State's power to provide for the protection of wild game, but only "so far as such protection . . . does not contravene the power of Congress in the regulation of interstate commerce." Their view was that "[w]hen any animal . . . is lawfully killed for the purposes of food or other uses of man, it becomes an article of commerce, and its use cannot be limited to the citizens of one State to the exclusion of citizens of another State." . . .[62]

The view of the *Geer* dissenters increasingly prevailed in subsequent cases. Indeed, not only has the Geer analysis been rejected when natural resources other than wild game were involved, but even state regulations of wild game have been held subject to the strictures of the Commerce Clause under the pretext of distinctions from *Geer*. The erosion of *Geer* began only 15 years after it was decided. . . .[63]

The *Geer* analysis has also been eroded to the point of virtual extinction in cases involving regulation of wild animals. The first challenge to Geer's theory of a State's power over wild animals came in *Missouri v. Holland* (1920). The State of Missouri, relying on the theory of state ownership of wild animals, attacked the Migratory Bird Treaty Act on the ground that it interfered with the State's control over wild animals within its boundaries. Writing for the Court, Mr. Justice Holmes upheld the Act as a proper exercise of the treatymaking power. He commented in passing on the artificiality of the Geer rationale: "To put the claim of the State upon title is to lean upon a slender reed." . . .[64]

Foster-Fountain Packing's implicit shift away from *Geer's* formalistic "ownership" analysis became explicit in *Toomer v. Witsell* (1948), which struck down as violations of the Commerce Clause and the Privileges and Immunities Clause certain South Carolina laws discriminating against out-of-state commercial fishermen: "The whole ownership theory, in fact, is now generally regarded as but a fiction expressive in legal shorthand of the importance to its people that a State have power to preserve and regulate the exploitation of an important resource." . . .[65]

Seacoast Products explicitly embraced the analysis of the Geer dissenters:

"A State does not stand in the same position as the owner of a private game preserve and it is pure fantasy to talk of 'owning' wild fish, birds, or animals. Neither the States nor the Federal Government, any more than a hopeful fisherman or hunter, has title to these creatures until they are reduced to possession by skillful capture. . . . *Geer v. Connecticut* (1896) (Field, J., dissenting). The 'ownership' language of cases such as those cited by appellant must be understood as no more than a 19th-century legal fiction expressing 'the importance to its people that a State have power to preserve and regulate the exploitation of an important resource.' [Citing *Toomer*.] Under modern analysis, the question is simply whether the State has exercised its police power in conformity with the federal laws and Constitution." . . .[66]

The case before us is the first in modern times to present facts essentially on all fours with *Geer*. We now conclude that challenges under the Commerce Clause to state regulations of wild animals should be considered according to the same general rule applied to state regulations of other natural resources, and therefore expressly overrule *Geer*.[67] . . .

A State may no longer "keep the property, if the sovereign so chooses, always within its jurisdiction for every purpose." *Greer v. Connecticut*. The fiction of state ownership may no longer be used to force those outside the State to bear the full costs of "conserving" the wild animals within its borders when equally effective nondiscriminatory conservation measures are available.[68]

Contrast the dissent of Justices Rehnquist and Burger with Brennan's majority opinion. The dissenters could not restrain themselves at the overturning of a rule that had stood for eighty-three years:

This Court's seeming preoccupation in recent years with laws relating to wildlife must, I suspect, appear curious to casual observers of this institution. It is no more curious, however, than this Court's recent pronouncements on the validity of *Geer v. Connecticut* (1896). For less than one year ago we unreservedly reaffirmed the principles announced in *Geer*. *Baldwin v. Montana Fish & Game Comm'n* (1978). . . .[69]

Admittedly, a State does not "own" the wild creatures within its borders in any conventional sense of the word. *Baldwin v. Montana Fish & Game Comm'n* (1861); *Douglas v. Seacoast Products, Inc.* (1977); *Toomer v. Witsell* (1948); *Missouri v. Holland* (1920). But the concept expressed by the "ownership" doctrine is not obsolete. *Baldwin v. Montana Fish & Game Comm'n* (1864). This Court long has recognized that the ownership language of *Geer* and similar cases is simply a shorthand way of describing a State's substantial interest in preserving and regulating the exploitation of the fish and game and other natural resources within its boundaries for the benefit of its citizens. *Douglas v. Seacoast Products, Inc.*; *Toomer v. Witsell*.[70] . . .

To be sure, a State's power to preserve and regulate wildlife within its borders is not absolute. But the State is accorded wide latitude in fashioning regulations appropriate for protection of its wildlife.[71] . . .

The right to preserve game flows from the undoubted existence in the State of a police power to that end, which may be none the less efficiently called into play, because by doing so interstate commerce may be remotely and indirectly affected. *Kidd v. Pearson*; *Hall v. De Cuir*; *Sherlock v. Alling*; *Gibbons v. Ogden*. Indeed, the source of the police power as to game birds (like those covered by the statute here called into question) flows from the duty of the State to preserve for its people a valuable food supply.[72]

BURGER CONTINUED: CONGRESSIONAL INTENT AND THE PRESUMPTION AGAINST PREEMPTION

In June 1979, three months after Hughes, the US District Court for the District of Hawaii decided a case involving the destruction of the habitat of a rare six-inch-long bird called the palila (*Psittirostra bailleui*). About 1,500 of these were living on the forested slopes of Mauna Kea in the Hawaiian island chain. The palila had evolved in the *māmane-naio* ecosystem over centuries and were uniquely adapted to feeding, sheltering, and nesting in the *māmane* trees. Hawaii's Department of Land and Natural Resources owned the habitat and permitted a population of 550 feral mouflon sheep, goats, and pigs to live in the bird's habitat. They were destroying the vegetation the palila needed to survive. These feral animals were maintained solely for recreational sport–hunting purposes. The federal court ruled that Hawaii did not have exclusive control over wildlife in the face of federal law and regulations. The state's failure to control the feral animals that endangered the critical habitat of a bird protected by two international treaties, the Migratory Bird Treaty Act, and the Endangered Species Act, was clearly beyond its rights of sovereignty under the Tenth Amendment to the US Constitution[73] and violated the Endangered Species Act's "take" provisions in Section 9. "Congress has determined that protection of any endangered species anywhere is of the utmost importance to mankind, and that the major cause of extinction is destruction of natural habitat," the Court's opinion states.

> In this context, a national program to protect and improve the natural habitats of endangered species preserves the possibilities of interstate commerce in these species and of interstate movement of persons, such as amateur students of nature or professional scientists who come to a state to observe and study these species, that would otherwise be lost by state inaction. . . .[74]
>
> I am therefore of the opinion that the Tenth Amendment does not restrict enforcement of the Endangered Species Act, both because of the power of Congress to enact legislation implementing valid treaties and because of the power of Congress to regulate commerce. . . .[75]
>
> The "threshold fact of Congressional authorization" is found where a Congressional enactment "by its terms authorize(s) suit by designated plaintiffs against a general class of defendants which literally include(s) States or state instrumentalities." . . .[76]
>
> Here, Congress has spoken clearly. Section 11(g) of the [Endangered Species] Act expressly authorizes private citizens to bring suit enjoining a general class of defendants who violate the Act, including "the United States and any other governmental instrumentality or agency (to the extent permitted by the eleventh amendment to the Constitution). . . ."[77]

... the State consents to be sued under the Endangered Species Act when its wildlife management activities extend to areas regulated under the federal government's commerce and treaty-making powers. The State of Hawaii has actively attempted to participate in the conservation scheme contemplated under the Act by taking advantage of the "cooperative agreement" provisions of [Section 6 of the act]. In 1975, the Hawaii legislature enacted the Hawaii Endangered Species Act. The stated purpose of the Act was to "satisfy certain requirements of the federal 'Endangered Species Act of 1973'" in order "to qualify Hawaii for a cooperative agreement with the US Department of the Interior, making the State eligible for federal grant-in-aid funds and preclude federal pre-emption of Hawaii's authority in regulating endangered species."[78]

Five months later in *United States v. Helsley*,[79] the Ninth Circuit upheld the Airborne Hunting Act, a valid exercise of congressional power to regulate interstate commerce. The Court opined that the statute's purpose was to regulate game management:

We think the federal power to regulate the air space is as complete and as valid as the federal power, to the extent it rests upon the commerce clause, to regulate navigable waters.... congressional regulation is not thwarted by arguments that the incidental connection between commerce and the regulation is used merely as an expedient to justify the law. The power to regulate commerce is plenary. ... It is established that Congress may choose the commerce clause as the means [of] access to interstate goods, or that a transaction which is essentially local may be regulated when it, taken together with all similar incidents, has a cumulative effect on interstate commerce, or that Congress may find that a class of activities affects interstate commerce and thus regulate or prohibit all such activities without the necessity of demonstrating that the particular transaction in question has an impact which is more than local. ...[80]

Geer, which had been called into serious question by recent Supreme Court decisions, was finally overruled last Term in *Hughes v. Oklahoma* (1979). Even prior to Hughes, the Supreme Court made clear that "the states' control over wildlife is not exclusive and absolute in the face of federal regulation." A state's control over its resources, including wildlife, does not prohibit the proper exercise of federal power under provisions such as the commerce clause.[81]

These two 1979 cases demonstrate that federal courts would sustain federal authority to regulate wildlife under the Commerce or Property Clauses, unrestrained by the state-ownership doctrine.[82]

In 1982, a federal court decision in *Tangier Sound Waterman's Association v. Douglas*[83] forensically examined state wildlife authority and preemption precedents *Corfield* (1823), *Waddell* (1842), *McCready* (1876), *Geer* (1896), *Missouri v. Holland* (1920), *Foster-Fountain* (1928), *Takahashi* (1948), *Toomer* (1948), *Douglas* (1977), *Baldwin* (1978), and *Hughes* (1979).[84] The

Court addressed the concept of state jurisdictional authority over resident wildlife based on the "ownership" doctrine, which the Court said was not "devoid of meaning or force . . . and by no means absolute" under the Privileges and Immunities Clause or the Commerce Clause of the Constitution.[85] The Court held that state authority can override constitutional limitations within the limits of its police power to protect natural resources with special interests to its citizens:

> Under modern analysis, the question is simply whether the State has exercised its police power in conformity with the federal laws and Constitution. . . . In sum, the dilution of the ownership theory has been such that in the Court's analysis of a statutory scheme, "ownership" of a natural resource is but one factor that the Court must consider in determining whether a State has exercised its police power in conformity with federal laws and the Constitution. "[In *Douglas Seacoast*] in referring to . . . and characterizing [the 'ownership' or title language of Corfield, McCready, and Geer]" as no more than a 19th-century legal fiction, "the Court pointed out that the language nevertheless expressed the importance to its people that a State have power to preserve and regulate the exploitation of an important resource." The fact that the State's control over wildlife is not exclusive and absolute in the face of federal regulation and certain federally protected interests does not compel the conclusion that it is meaningless in their absence. [*Baldwin v. Fish and Game Commission of Montana.*] The crucial distinction which the Court drew was whether the proscribed or circumscribed activity involved a person's "commercial livelihood." . . . As stated by Blackmun, "(e)lk hunting by nonresidents in Montana is a recreation and a sport. . . . It is not a means to the nonresident's livelihood."[86]

Quoting Justice Burger's concurring opinion in *Baldwin*, the judge noted that "*McCready v. Virginia* made it clear that the Privileges and Immunities Clause does not prevent a State from preferring its own citizens in granting public access to natural resources in which they have a special interest."[87] This was the same holding in the 1823 *Corfield v. Coryell* case.[88] The Court held that state authority can override constitutional limitations within the limits of its police power to protect natural resources with special interests to its citizens.

Conversely, a year later, the Supreme Court denied the North Dakota governor's aberrant attempt to invoke a hostile state law. The governor had attempted to revoke the federal government's property right to acquire waterfowl-production area easements using Duck Stamp revenues.[89] The Court's ruling was based on federal property rights in easements used to sustain migratory waterfowl, an important national interest. Nine years earlier, the Eighth Circuit had ordered restoration of drainage ditches in migratory waterfowl production areas in North Dakota that had been intentionally drained and partially filled.[90]

Employing judicial restraint and strict construction, the Supreme Court in 1985[91] reaffirmed earlier Supremacy Clause cases[92] that had sustained congressional preemption of state laws when statutory language was clear, express, manifest, leaving no room for doubt of Congress's intent, or could "be inferred . . . where the federal interest is so dominate that the federal system will be assumed to preclude enforcement of state laws on the same subject."[93] "The Supreme Court has repeatedly explained that in determining whether (and to what extent) federal law preempts state law, the *purpose* [intent] of Congress is the 'ultimate touchstone' of its statutory analysis."[94]

This 1985 *Hillsborough* case decided by the Burger Court was later characterized during the Rehnquist Court by Justice Sandra Day O'Connor in *Gregory v. Ashcraft* as the Court's "preemption jurisprudence." In that later case, Justice O'Connor stated that "preemption will be found where there is a 'clear and manifest *purpose* to displace state law' or 'if it intends to pre-empt the historic powers of the States.'"[95] The preemption jurisprudence Justice O'Connor was referring to, which was later called the "plain statement rule," reads as follows:

> It is a familiar and well-established principle that the Supremacy Clause invalidates state laws that "interfere with, or are contrary to," federal law. Under the Supremacy Clause, federal law may supersede state law in several different ways. First, when acting within constitutional limits, Congress is empowered to pre-empt state law by so stating in express terms. In the absence of express pre-emptive language, Congress' intent to pre-empt all state law in a particular area may be inferred where the scheme of federal regulation is sufficiently comprehensive to make reasonable the inference that Congress "left no room" for supplementary state regulation. Pre-emption of a whole field also will be inferred where the field is one in which "the federal interest is so dominant that the federal system will be assumed to preclude enforcement of state laws on the same subject."[96]
>
> We have held repeatedly that state laws can be pre-empted by federal regulations as well as by federal statutes. Also, for the purposes of the Supremacy Clause, the constitutionality of local ordinances is analyzed in the same way as that of statewide laws.[97]
>
> The question whether the regulation of an entire field has been reserved by the Federal Government is, essentially, a question of ascertaining the intent underlying the federal scheme. . . .[98]
>
> Where . . . the field that Congress is said to have pre-empted has been traditionally occupied by the States "we start with the assumption that the historic police powers of the States were not to be superseded by the Federal Act unless that was the clear and manifest purpose of Congress.'" (deference to state regu-

lation of safety under the dormant Commerce Clause). . . . Of course, the same principles apply where, as here, the field is said to have been pre-empted by an agency, acting pursuant to congressional delegation. . . .[99]

We are even more reluctant to infer pre-emption from the comprehensiveness of regulations than from the comprehensiveness of statutes. As a result of their specialized functions, agencies normally deal with problems in far more detail than does Congress. To infer pre-emption whenever an agency deals with a problem comprehensively is virtually tantamount to saying that whenever a federal agency decides to step into a field, its regulations will be exclusive. Such a rule, of course, would be inconsistent with the federal-state balance embodied in our Supremacy Clause jurisprudence.[100]

"This plain statement rule," according to O'Connor, "is nothing more than an acknowledgement that the States retain substantial sovereign powers under our constitutional scheme, powers with which Congress does not readily interfere."[101]

Cumulatively, the Burger Court's preemption cases over its seventeen-year history enhanced state authority where traditional uses of police power were involved.[102] The Court exercised judicial restraint and refined the doctrine of *presumption against preemption*, permitting states to regulate where Congress had not exercised its power.[103] One of the Court's touchstones of judicial restraint in applying preemption was to look for a clear, unequivocal, and manifest expression of congressional intent to override state authority before exercising the power of preemption.[104] That was Burger's signature legacy in federal preemption law developed throughout his seventeen years on the Supreme Court, starting with *Tennessee Valley Authority v. Hill*. In *Goldstein v. California* (1973), the Court marked a reemergence of the presumption against preemption and a state-directed view of federalism. The Court's foundational policy was to maintain a balance of federalism and not restrain the legitimate exercise of federal power.[105]

Embracing the concept of cooperative federalism, the Court exhibited a cooperative problem-solving approach in its opinions.[106] Curtailing Congress's Commerce Clause power for the first time in forty years on a case-by-case basis,[107] the Burger Court developed a distinct construct of the integrity of the states within the federal framework without reliance on the reserved powers of the state doctrine or the principle of the enumerated powers of the federal government.[108] But two critics, echoing others who were more restrained, state that the Burger Court's opinions were "themeless . . . ambivalent . . . inconstant . . . lacking direction . . . [and] take on an ad hoc, unprincipled quality, seemingly bereft of any consistent doctrinal basis . . . this doctrinal inconsistency merely manifest[ed] the Court's vacillating perspective on federalism . . . [so that] the Burger Court gave America results, not principles."[109]

SUMMARY

The Burger Court was defined by a period of *judicial restraint*. With the passing of the landmark Endangered Species Act in 1973, which expanded the reach of the federal government into wildlife conservation, Congress tasked the federal government with implementing through a cooperative model of federalism the national mandate to safeguard the nation's valuable wildlife. This creation of a *regulatory floor*—not a ceiling—left room for cooperative federalism. Notably, the Court during this period reviewed more than twelve wildlife preemption cases. The consequence of these decisions—ranging from the first decision in *Tennessee Valley Authority v. Hill* (1978), shortly followed by *Hughes v. Oklahoma* (1979)—was (1) the expansion of the federal government's regulatory reach into wildlife conservation under the Endangered Species Act while (2) preserving the presumption-against-preemption framework that would allow states to regulate above the floor created by Congress, provided that congressional intent could be ascertained through strict constructionism. In attempting to strike a federalism balance, the Burger Court ended up rendering inconsistent, unprincipled decisions at the intersection of federalism, preemption, and wildlife authority. Thus, while the core of state "ownership" of wildlife was undoubtedly a fiction by now, questions at the doctrinal margins about preemption and federalism remained indeterminate.

NOTES

1. *Tennessee Valley Authority v. Hill*, 437 U.S. 153, (1978).
2. Moreover, the Ninth Circuit Court of Appeals decided a relevant wildlife case in November 1979.
3. Michael J. Graetz and Linda Greenhouse, *The Burger Court and the Rise of the Judicial Right* (New York: Simon and Schuster, 2016). Also see Drahozal, *Supremacy Clause*; and see Miller, "Burger Court's View," 581.
4. From Alan B. Morrison, review of *The Burger Court and the Rise of the Judicial Right*, by Michael Graetz and Linda Greenhouse, *Journal of Legal Education* 66, no. 3 (2017): 667, https://jle.aals.org/cgi/viewcontent.cgi?article=1508&context=home.
5. Hoffer, Hoffer, and Hull, *Supreme Court*, 407.
6. Young, "Making Federalism Doctrine," 1733, 1752.
7. Justin Driver, "Just How Rightward Leaning Was the Burger Supreme Court?" *Washington Post*, June 17, 2016, https://www.washingtonpost.com/opinions/just-how-rightward-leaning-was-the-burger-supreme-court/2016/06/17/4c722b8e-2b65-11e6-9de3-6e6e7a14000c_story.html.
8. Hoffer, Hoffer, and Hull, *Supreme Court*, 369–78; "Burger Court," Wikipedia, last modified March 24, 2021, https://en.wikipedia.org/wiki/Burger_Court.

During Burger's first year as chief justice, the US District Court for the Southern District of New York upheld two New York statues prohibiting the sale of articles made of alligator or crocodile hides, though the animals were not listed as threatened or endangered under the Endangered Species Act. The statues, the Court found, did not interfere with the treaty or commerce powers of Congress. New York could exercise its broad police powers solely for aesthetic purposes. See generally *Palladio v. Diamond*, 321 F.Supp. 630 (1970).

9. 441 U.S. 322, 335 (1979).
10. 426 U.S. 529 (1976).
11. Kleppe, 426 U.S. at 541, 543, 546.

One of the first cases to test the power of the Property Clause to protect public lands was *United States v. Grimaud*, 220 U.S. 506 (1911). See also *Concessions Co. v. Morris*, 186 P. 655, 658–60 (Wash. 1919), discussing *Fort Leavenworth R. Co. v. Lowe*, 114 U.S. 525 (1885).

12. These were *Organized Fishermen of Florida v. Andrus*, 488 F.Supp. 1351 (S.D. Fla. 1980); and *Organized Fishermen of Florida v. Hodel*, 775 F.2d 1544 (11th Cir. 1985). And also see *United States v. Midwest Oil Co.*, 236 U.S. 459, 483 (1915) (upholding the president's decision to withdraw land to preserve oil reserves); and *Light v. United States*, 220 U.S. 523, 536 (1911) ("The United States can prohibit absolutely or fix the terms on which its property may be used").

In *Organized Fishermen of Florida v. Hodel*, the Court found that Florida law provided no vested property right for commercial fishing in a national park. In *Organized Fishermen of Florida* (488 F. Supp. at 1355) the Court refused to enjoin enforcement of federal regulations restricting fishing in a national park given Congress's "complete power" over public lands, which "necessarily includes the power to regulate and protect the wildlife living there" (herein citing Kleppe, 426 U.S. at 540–41).

See also *Minnesota v. Block*, 660 F.2d 1240, 1249 (8th Cir. 1981) ("Congress' power must extend to regulation of conduct on or off the public land that would threaten the designated purpose of federal lands."); and see *United States v. Brown*, 552 F.2d 817, 822 (8th Cir. 1977) (stating that "congressional power over federal lands . . . include[s] the authority to regulate activities on non-federal public waters in order to protect wildlife and visitors on the [public] lands").

See also *Stupak-Thrall v. United States*, 89 F.3d 1269, 1269, 1272 (6th Cir. 1996) (en banc; an equally divided court affirmed the district court's decision—that the federal government could regulate private activities occurring on the surface of a lake even if the surface was private property); *Organized Fisherman of Florida*, 775 F.2d at 1549 (upholding federal restrictions on fishing on waters within Everglades National Park, some of which were presumably under state jurisdiction); *United States v. Lindsey*, 595 F.2d 5, 6 (9th Cir. 1979) (stating that the Property Clause "grants to the United States power to regulate conduct on non-federal land when reasonably necessary to protect adjacent federal property or navigable waters"); and *Grand Lake Estates Homeowners Ass'n v. Veneman*, 340 F.Supp. 2d 1162, 1167–69 (D. Colo. 2004) (holding that the US Forest Service could require special-use permits on docks and marinas on the association's land if doing so was reasonably necessary to protect the environment and water quality of Arapaho National Recreation Area).

13. *Organized Fishermen of Florida*, 488 F. Supp. at 1355 (internal citations omitted).

For a complete, in-depth study of the state/federal preemption issue of state authority on federal lands, see the following "dueling" law review articles: Nie, Barnes, Haber, et al., "Fish and Wildlife Management"; and Kisonak, "Fish and Wildlife Management."

14. *Douglas v. Seacoast Products, Inc.*, 431 U.S. 265 (1977).

15. *Douglas*, 431 U.S. at 284 (internal citations omitted; italics added).

In 1977, the Federal District Court for the Central District of California sustained the right of Los Angeles to not prepare an environmental impact statement or evaluate deep-ocean dumping of sludge so long as there existed a practical land disposal method to dispose of the sludge. See *Pacific Legal Foundation v. Quarles*, 440 F.Supp. 316 (C.D. Cal. 1977).

But the federal district court for Alaska that same year enjoined the State of Alaska from authorizing wolf hunting to protect the arctic caribou herd on federal lands under authority of the Property Clause of the Constitution. See *State of Alaska v. Andrus*, 429 F.Supp. 958 (D. Alaska 1977).

Three years later, the Ninth Circuit Court of Appeals affirmed the Alaska District Court's finding that distribution of revenues from oil and gas leases on federal wildlife refuges to the state and Kenai Peninsula Borough did not include revenues from land reserved for refuges based on the clear intent of Congress expressed in legislative history. See *Kenai Peninsula Borough v. State of Alaska*, 612 F.2d 1210 (9th Cir. 1980).

16. *Baldwin v. Fish and Game Commission of Montana*, 436 U.S. 371 (1978).

17. *Baldwin*, 436 U.S. at 386.

18. *Baldwin*, 436 U.S. at 384–86 (internal citations omitted; emphasis added).

19. *Baldwin*, 436 U.S. at 392 (J. Burger, concurring; internal citations omitted; emphasis added).

20. *Baldwin*, 436 U.S. at 405 (J. Brennan, dissenting) (emphasis original).

21. Tangier Sound Waterman's Association at 1307 n12, n18 (internal citations omitted).

22. See Bean and Rowland, *Evolution of National Wildlife Law*, 31–32.

23. US Congress, *Endangered Species Act of 1973*, Pub. L. No. 93–205, 87 Stat. 884 (1973), https://www.govinfo.gov/content/pkg/STATUTE-87/pdf/STATUTE-87-Pg884.pdf.

24. Even President Richard Nixon criticized the earlier acts, asserting that "even the most recent act to protect endangered species, which dates from 1969, simply does not provide the kind of management tools needed to act early enough to save a vanishing species." Richard Nixon, "Statement on Transmitting a Special Message to the Congress Outlining the 1972 Environmental Program," read in the Family Theater for sound and film recording, February 8, 1972, archived at https://www.presidency.ucsb.edu/documents/statement-transmitting-special-message-the-congress-outlining-the-1972-environmental.

25. *Endangered Species Act of 1973*, 93rd Cong., *Congressional Record* 119, pt. 35 (1973): 669–70. And see John Copeland Nagle, "The Original Role of the States in

the Endangered Species Act," *Idaho Law Review* 53, no. 2 (2017): 385, 388, https://digitalcommons.law.uidaho.edu/cgi/viewcontent.cgi?article=1017&context=idaho-law-review.

26. Nagle, "Original Role," 391.

27. Nagle, "Original Role," 404–406; J. B. Ruhl, "Cooperative Federalism and the Endangered Species Act: A Comparative Assessment and Call for Change," in *The Endangered Species Act and Federalism: Effective Conservation through Greater State Commitment*, ed. Barton H. Thompson Jr. and Kaush Arha (New York: Routledge, 2011), 35, 36; Robert L. Fischman and Jaelith Hall-Rivera, "A Lesson for Conservation from Pollution Control Law: Cooperative Federalism for Recovery under the Endangered Species Act," *Columbia Journal of Environmental Law* 27 (2002): 45–172, https://www.repository.law.indiana.edu/cgi/viewcontent.cgi?article=1228&context=facpub; Fischman, "Cooperative Federalism"; Fischman, "Predictions and Prescriptions"; and Jean O. Melious, "Enforcing the Endangered Species Act against the States," *William and Mary Environmental Law* 25, no. 3 (2001): 605, https://scholarship.law.wm.edu/cgi/viewcontent.cgi?article=1213&context=wmelpr.

28. Nagle, "Original Role," 390.

29. (16 U.S.C. § 1535(f). And see Nie, Barnes, Haber, et al., "Fish and Wildlife Management," 848; Nagle, "Original Role," 415.

30. Find this at US House of Representatives, *Endangered Species Act of 1973*, Sec. 2(a)(4)(A-G).

For a well-researched, in-depth article on the Treaties and Commerce Clause cases supporting the ESA, see Omar N. White, "The Endangered Species Act's Precarious Perch: A Constitutional Analysis under the Commerce Clause and the Treaty Power," *Ecology Law Quarterly* 27, no. 3 (2000): 215–56, https://scholarship.law.unc.edu/cgi/viewcontent.cgi?article=3910&context=nclr. Also see John P. Dwyer, "The Commerce Clause and the Limits of Congressional Authority to Regulate the Environment," *Environmental Law Reporter* 25, no. 8 (2000): 10421, 10424–42, https://elr.info/sites/default/files/articles/25.10421.htm; and see Belanger and Kinnane, *Managing American Wildlife*, 133–41, 177, 217–18.

31. Nie, Barnes, Haber, et al., "Fish and Wildlife Management," 826, n. 173.

Safari Club International v. Jewell (960 F.Supp. 2d 17, 67–68 [D.D.C. 2013]) notes that conserving species within their ecosystems is one purpose of the ESA, "but other purposes are 'to provide a program for the conservation of such endangered species and threatened species, and to take such steps as may be appropriate to achieve the purposes of the treaties and conventions set forth in subsection (a)[,]' including the CITES" (alteration in original).

32. ESA's drafters were concerned by the "incalculable" value of the genetic heritage that might be lost absent federal regulation. See US House of Representatives, Committee on Merchant Marine and Fisheries, report no. 93-412, submitted July 27, 1973, to accompany H.R. 37, 93rd Cong., 1st sess., the Endangered Species Act of 1973, report text archived at https://nctc.fws.gov/courses/csp/csp3116/resources/ESA_Section_7_Legislative_History/Part_1_pages_140-179.pdf.

With regard to a precursor to ESA, one Senate report observed that, "From a pragmatic point of view, the protection of an endangered species of wildlife with some commercial value may permit the regeneration of that species to a level where controlled exploitation of that species can be resumed." The report continued:

> In such a case, businessmen may profit from the trading and marketing of that species for an indefinite number of years, where otherwise it would have been completely eliminated from commercial channels in a very brief span of time. *Potentially more important, however, is the fact that with each species we eliminate, we reduce the [genetic] pool . . . available for use by man in future years. Since each living species and subspecies has developed in a unique way to adapt itself to the difficulty of living in the world's environment, as a species is lost, its distinctive gene material, which may subsequently prove invaluable to mankind in improving domestic animals or increasing resistance to disease or environmental contaminant, is also irretrievably lost.*

US Senate, Committee on Commerce, report no. 91-526, submitted November 6, 1969, to accompany H.R. 11363, 91st Cong., 1st sess., *An Act to Prevent the Importation of Endangered Species of Fish or Wildlife into the United States; to Prevent the Interstate Shipment of Reptiles, Amphibians, and Other Wildlife Taken Contrary to State Law; and for Other Purposes*, p. 3, text archived at https://books.google.com/books?id=i17ldYCd50AC; emphasis added.

See also *GDF Realty Investments, Ltd. v. Norton*, 326 F.3d 622 (5th Cir. 2003).

33. Roderick F. Nash, *The Rights of Nature: A History of Environmental Ethics* (Madison: The University of Wisconsin Press, 1989), 175; and statement of Bob Graham, in US Senate, *Endangered Species Act Amendments of 1993: Hearings on S. 921 before the Subcommittee on Clean Water, Fisheries, and Wildlife of the Committee on Environment and Public Works*, US Senate, 103rd Cong. (1994), https://www.congress.gov/bill/103rd-congress/senate-bill/921?s=1&r=2.

34. Senator Stevens's remarks recorded in US Congress, Senate, *Endangered Species Act of 1973*, S. 1983, 93rd Cong. vol. 119, part 20, *Congressional Record*, 769, July 24, 1973; see especially section 6, starting at p. 25695, text archived at https://www.govinfo.gov/content/pkg/GPO-CRECB-1973-pt20/pdf/GPO-CRECB-1973-pt20-3-2.pdf.

35. "Protecting Endangered Species," editorial, *Washington Post*, June 26, 1973, A22.

36. Interestingly enough, one of the giants in developing American game policy in the early nineteenth century was George Bird Grinnell, who strongly supported the national Migratory Bird Treaty Act because, left to local government, "it was almost a complete failure by the states." G. B. Grinnell to Aldo Leopold, January 8, 1923, archived as microfilm, box 33, folder 165, reel 38U, of the George Bird Grinnell Papers, Sterling Memorial Library, Yale University Library, https://archives.yale.edu/repositories/12/top_containers/141894?&filter_fields[]=child_container_u_sstr&filter_values[]=folder+165.

Aldo Leopold and Grinnell would both have agreed with a national approach to the extinction crisis. "I am personally convinced that the Federal Government must put pressure on the States to secure more rapid improvement of their game departments and game policy," Leopold once wrote. "Experience indicates that if we simply wait for them to come around, we will wait too long. The greatest leverage for exerting such pressure is Federal control. I am strictly against Federal control wherever it can be avoided but I am strong for it as a lever to bring the States around." Aldo Leopold to Barrington Moore, July 24, 1923, archived as microfilm, box 25, folder 106, reel 42U, in the George Bird Grinnell Papers, Sterling Memorial Library, Yale University Library.

37. Petersen, "Congress and Charismatic Megafauna," 463, 477.

38. Association of Fish and Wildlife Agencies, *Wildlife Management Authority: The State Agencies' Perspective; Findings from the AFWA President's Task Force on States Authorities* (Washington, DC: Association of Fish and Wildlife Agencies, February 2014), p. 4, text archived at https://wyoleg.gov/InterimCommittee/2015/SFR-0929APPENDIXB.pdf.

39. See Yaffee, *Prohibitive Policy*, 48. And also see Nagle, "Original Role," 393.

40. *Tennessee Valley Authority v. Hill*, 437 U.S. 153 (1978).

41. *Tennessee Valley Authority*, 437 U.S. at 154.

42. The issue of Section 7 consultation had come up earlier, before the Fifth Circuit in 1975 in the case of the *National Wildlife Federation v. Coleman* (529 F.2d 359 [5th Cir. 1976]). The court's opinion was contradictory, in that it said that Section 7 was an absolute prohibition on agency actions that directly or indirectly jeopardized protected species, but also that the final decision on proceeding with an agency action rested with the agency itself. Two years later the Supreme Court would resolve the contradiction in *Hill*.

43. Hill, 437 U.S. at 176, 180, 184 (emphasis added; internal citations omitted).

44. Ruhl, "Endangered Species Act's Fall," 487, 489–90, 492.

45. Ruhl, "Endangered Species Act's Fall," 490, 532.

46. These cases are, in order, 504 U.S. 555 (1992); 515 U.S. 687 (1995); 520 U.S. 154 (1997); and 551 U.S. 644 (2007).

47. Ruhl, "Endangered Species Act's Fall," 509, 511, 524.

48. Ruhl, "Endangered Species Act's Fall," 517.

49. Ruhl, "Endangered Species Act's Fall," 517.

50. Ruhl, "Endangered Species Act's Fall," 528–32.

51. Ruhl, "Endangered Species Act's Fall," 528, 532.

52. *Babbitt v. Sweet Home Chapter of Communities for a Great Oregon*, 515 U.S. at 714, 735–36.

53. Robert W. Adler, "The Supreme Court and Ecosystems: Environmental Science in Environmental Law," *Vermont Law Review* 27, no. 2 (2003): 249, 362. And also see Ruhl, "Endangered Species Act's Fall," 514, 522.

54. *Hughes v. Oklahoma*, 441 U.S. 322 (1979). And see *Geer v. Connecticut*, 161 U.S. 519 (1896).

55. *Martin v. Waddell's Lessee*, 41 U.S. 367 (1842).

56. 94 U.S. 391 (1876).

57. Belanger and Kinnane, *Managing American Wildlife*, 12–13, 42, 54–55, 101–106, 127–44, 162, 165.

58. Concurrent with this frustration were similar issues over enforcement of the Clean Water Act's wetlands protection program.

59. In order, these cases are *Hunt v. United States*, 278 U.S. 96 (1928); *Foster-Fountain Packing Company v. Haydel*, 278 U.S. 1 (1928); *Chalk v. United States*, 114 F. 2nd 207 (4th Cir. 1940); *Takahashi v. Fish and Game Commission*, 334 U.S. 410 (1948); *Toomer v. Witsell*, 334 U.S. 385 (1948); *Kleppe v. New Mexico*, 426 U.S. 529 (1976); *Douglas v. Seacoast Products, Inc.*, 431 U.S. 265 (1977); and *Baldwin v. Fish and Game Commission of Montana*, 436 U.S. 371 (1978).

60. Bean and Rowland, *Evolution of National Wildlife Law*, 34.
61. Hughes, 441 U.S. at 325.
62. Hughes, 441 U.S. at 328.
63. Hughes, 441 U.S. at 329.
64. Hughes, 441 U.S. at 332–33.
65. Hughes, 441 U.S. at 334–35.
66. Hughes, 441 U.S. at 335–36.
67. Hughes, 441 U.S. at 336.
68. Hughes, 441 U.S. at 337.
69. Hughes, 441 U.S. at 339 (J. Rehnquist, dissenting; internal citations omitted).
70. Hughes, 441 U.S. at 341–42 (J. Rehnquist, dissenting; internal citations omitted).
71. Hughes, 441 U.S. at 342 (J. Rehnquist, dissenting; internal citations omitted).
72. Hughes, 441 U.S. at 340 n. 3 (J. Rehnquist, dissenting; internal citations omitted).
73. *Palila v. Hawaii Department of Land and Natural Resources*, 471 F.Supp. 985, 995 (D. Haw. 1979).
74. *Palila*, 471 F.Supp. at 994–95.
75. *Palila*, 471 F.Supp. at 995.
76. *Palila*, 471 F.Supp. at 997 (internal citations omitted).
77. *Palila*, 471 F.Supp. at 998 (internal citations omitted).
78. *Palila*, 471 F.Supp. at 998 (internal citations omitted).

A second "Palila" case followed nine years later, comprised of virtually identical facts, and the court again held that uncontrolled animals placed in the wild forests of Hawaii for recreational sport hunting that destroyed the critical habitat of the palila bird, a listed species under ESA, violated the "take" provisions of Section 9 of the ESA. See *Palila v. Hawaii Department of Land and Natural Resources*, 852 F.2d 1106 (9th Cir. 1988).

79. 615 F.2d 784 (9th Cir. 1979).
80. Helsley, 615 F.2d at 786–87 (internal citations omitted).
81. Helsley, 615 F.2d at 788 (internal citations omitted).
82. Bean and Rowland, *Evolution of National Wildlife Law*, 24–25.

A similar logic was followed by the Ninth Circuit Court of Appeals when it preempted a California state statute exempting from prosecution trade in elephant ivory under a valid federal permit based on the ESA's authority under the Commerce Clause. See also *Man Hing Ivory v. Deukmejian*, 702 F.2d 760 (9th Cir. 1983).

On November 27, 1979, the Supreme Court decided another wildlife law case involving violations of the 1940 Bald Eagle Protection Act—an extension of the Migratory Bird Treaty Act—and of the Endangered Species Act of 1973. The decision did not raise a question of state sovereignty or preemption. Rather, it addressed the question as to whether both statutes violated Fifth Amendment property rights in banning the right to sell, barter, or exchange eagle feathers held prior to enactment of the statutes. Justice William Brennan, with Chief Justice Burger concurring in the opinion, was explicit in the Court's ruling.

Brennan quoted the Court's 1908 finding in *New York ex rel. Silz v. Hesterberg* (211 U.S. 31), that "the legislature . . . is authorized to pass measures for the protection of the people . . . in the exercise of the police power, and is itself the judge of the necessity or expediency of the means adopted." Brennan continued:

> Furthermore, Congress could not have been unaware that a traditional legislative tool for enforcing conservation policy was a flat proscription on the sale of wildlife, without regard to the legality of the taking. . . . Other conservation legislation enacted by Congress has employed the enforcement technique of forbidding the sale of protected wildlife without respect to the lawfulness of the taking. The Eagle Protection Act is a notable example. The more recent Endangered Species Act of 1973, as originally framed, prohibited the sale of products or parts of endangered species, without an exception for those products legally held for commercial purposes at the time of the Act's passage. . . . And when Congress has meant to exempt lawfully taken items from the retroactive application of statutory prohibitions, it has taken care to do so explicitly.

Andrus v. Allard, 444 U.S. 51, 60–62 (1979) (internal citation omitted).

83. 541 F. Supp. 1287 (E.D. Va. 1982).

84. These cases are *Corfield v. Coryell*, 6 Fed. Cas. 546, No. 3230 (C.C.E.D. Pa. 1823); *Martin v. Waddell's Lessee*, 41 U.S. 367 (1842); *McCready v. Virginia*, 94 U.S. 391 (1876); *Geer v. Connecticut*, 161 U.S. 519 (1896); *State of Missouri v. Holland*, 252 U.S. 416 (1920); *Foster-Fountain Packing Company v. Haydel*, 278 U.S. 1 (1928); *Takahashi v. Fish and Game Commission*, 334 U.S. 410 (1948); *Toomer v. Witsell*, 334 U.S. 385 (1948); *Douglas v. Seacoast Products, Inc.*, 431 U.S. 265 (1977); *Baldwin v. Fish and Game Commission of Montana*, 436 U.S. 371 (1978); and *Hughes v. Oklahoma*, 441 U.S. 322 (1979).

85. *Tangier*, 541 F. Supp. at 1294–95.

86. *Tangier*, 541 F. Supp. at 1293–98 (quoting *Baldwin*, 436 U.S. at 386; internal citations omitted).

87. *Tangier*, 541 F. Supp. at 1299 n. 12.

88. 6 Fed. Cas. 546, no. 3,230 (C.C.E.D.Pa. 1823).

89. *North Dakota v. United States*, 460 U.S. 300 (1983).

90. *United States v. Albrecht*, 496 F.2d 906 (8th Cir. 1974).

91. Hillsborough County, Fla. v. Automated Medical Laboratories, Inc., 471 U.S. 707 (1985).

92. See, for example, *United States v. Grimaud*, 220 U.S. 506 (1911); and *Jones v. Rath Packing Co.*, 430 U.S. 519 (1977).

In the *Jones* case, Justice Marshall, quoting from a 1947 case, stated the following:

> We start with the assumption that the historic police powers of the States were not to be superseded by the Federal Act unless that was the clear and manifest purpose of Congress *Rice v. Santa Fe Elevator Corp.* (1947). This assumption provides assurances that "the federal-state balance," *United States v. Bass* (1971), will not be disturbed unintentionally

by Congress or unnecessarily by the courts. But when Congress has "unmistakably . . . ordained," *Florida Lime & Avocado Growers, Inc. v. Paul* (1963), that its enactments alone are to regulate a part of commerce, state laws regulating that aspect of commerce must fall. This result is compelled whether Congress's command is explicitly stated in the statute's language or implicitly contained in its structure and purpose. *City of Burbank v. Lockheed Air Terminal Inc. (1973)*; *Rice v. Santa Fe Elevator Corp.* (1947).

Jones, 430 U.S. at 525 (internal citations omitted).
  93. Hillsborough County, Fla., 471 U.S. at 712.
  The Court has also referenced this as a cannon of construction referred to as the *presumption against preemption*, which directs that federal law should not be read to preempt state law "unless that was the clear and manifest purpose of Congress." Sykes and Vanatko, *Federal Preemption*, 3, quoting *Rice v. Santa Fe Elevator Corp.*, 331 U.S. 218, 230 (1947).
  94. Sykes and Vanatko, *Federal Preemption*, 3 emphasis added, quoting *Wyeth v. Levine*, 555 U.S. 555, 565 (2009), itself quoting *Retail Clerks v. Schermerhorn*, 375 U.S. 96, 103 (1963).
  95. *Gregory v. Ashcroft*, 501 U.S. 452, 478 (1991) (J. O'Connor, concurring in part; quoting Hillsborough County, Fla., 471 U.S. at 715; emphasis original).
  Justice O'Connor didn't reference the threshold case on congressional intent in an early New Deal court, *Mintz v. Baldwin* (289 U.S. 346 [1933]), which had built on this principle in *Reid v. People of State of Colorado* (187 U.S. 137 [1902]).
  96. Hillsborough County, Fla., 471 U.S. at 712–13 (internal citations omitted).
  97. Hillsborough County, Fla., 471 U.S. at 713 (internal citations omitted).
  98. Hillsborough County, Fla., 471 U.S. at 714.
  99. Hillsborough County, Fla., 471 U.S. at 715–16 (internal citations omitted).
  100. Hillsborough County, Fla., 471 U.S. at 717 (internal citations omitted).
  101. O'Brien, "Rehnquist Court," 16–17.
  102. Miller, "Burger Court's View," 581; and Bratton, "Preemption Doctrine," 649.
  103. Bratton, "Preemption Doctrine," 643.
  104. Bratton, "Preemption Doctrine," 643.
  105. Martin, "Burger Court," 1251.
  106. Miller, "Burger Court's View," 577, 580; and Bratton, "Preemption Doctrine," 643.
  107. As indicated, a clear emergence of state-directed presumption against preemption, embodying the principal of cooperative federalism, occurred in two early 1973 cases: *Goldstein v. California* (412 U.S. 546 [1973]) and *New York State Department of Social Services v. Dublino* (413 U.S. 405 [1973]), which switched the burden of proof to the federal government.
  These cases follow earlier cases—*Kewanee Oil Co. v. Bicron* (416 U.S. 470 [1974]) and *Hines v. Davidowitz* (312 U.S. 52 [1941]), from FDR's "second" New Deal court, which "redefined the judicial function in preemption cases . . . notwithstanding the absence of clear Congressional intent to occupy the field or actual conflict, when the nature of the federal regulation called for exclusive operation. . . . Hines led to a reformulation of the preemption doctrine and the principles of federalism that undergird it. A scheme fundamentally irreconcilable with the state-directed model of the [early]

1930s decisions emerged as a competing approach . . . between two conflicting frameworks [that] resulted in considerable doctrinal confusion and variability."

Quotation from Bratton, "Preemption Doctrine," 630–32, 637, 642–46. See also Gardbaum, "Breadth versus Depth," 70.

108. Miller, "Burger Court's View," 577.

109. Albert W. Alschuler, "Failed Pragmatism: Reflections on the Burger Court Commentaries," *Harvard Law Review* 100, no. 6 (1986): 1436, 1437, 1448; and Bratton, "Preemption Doctrine," 624, 626.

Bratton cited one case of note decided by the Burger Court in its last twenty months (1985) that had signaled the Court's further recognition of the evolving structure of federalism. The early twentieth century had witnessed the erosion of dual federalism as the Court's attempt to draw determinate boundaries between separate spheres of government collapsed amid the integration of federal and state laws and as regulations struggled to keep up with the progress of the Industrial Revolution. Hence a regime of concurrent powers or concurrent jurisdiction evolved that scholar Edward S. Corwin terms "cooperative federalism." In 1976 the Burger Court struggled to define this evolution and defend state autonomy in a tortured opinion in *National League of Cities v. Usery* (426 U.S. 833 [1976]). Nine years later, the Court reversed itself, overruling the earlier decision in the classic case of *Garcia v. San Antonio Transit Authority* (469 U.S. 528 [1985]).

In *Garcia*, the court left the autonomy of the states up to the solicitude of the national political process and the restraints the system provides for state participation in the federal government through this congressional delegation, rather than dictate a "sacred province of state autonomy" defined by hard political boundaries patrolled by the court. This shift was based on James Madison's older federalist theory that the loyalty of citizens runs first to the states that touch the daily lives of its citizens through government services they provide and beneficial regulations. Citizens are the wellspring of popular support. The *Rice* principal, requiring that the clear and manifest intent of Congress be expressed, protects state autonomy by notice to state congressional delegates of an intent to preempt state authority that then operationalizes the procedural safeguards of federalism. See *Garcia* at 550; and Young, "Ordinary Diet of the Law," 261–65, 320–24.

However, this approach is extremely controversial. See John F. Manning, "Federalism and the Generality Problem in Constitutional Interpretation," *Harvard Law Review* 122, no. 8 (2009): 2003, https://harvardlawreview.org/wp-content/uploads/pdfs/vol_122_manning.pdf; and see Young, "Making Federalism Doctrine," 1733, 1836–40.

13

The Rehnquist Court: A Continued Swing toward Conservative Federalism and Preemption, 1986–2005

The Rehnquist Court produced almost twenty years of federalism and preemption jurisprudence. It saw the arrival of the New Federalism movement, which sought to reinvigorate a federalism doctrine that sharply limited the power of the federal government, leaving more power reserved to the states under the Tenth Amendment. It produced a number of cases—from *United States v. Lopez* (1995) and *United States v. Morrison* (2000) to *New York v. United States* (1992) and *Printz v. United States* (1997)[1]—hinting at the arrival of a new, "state-centric" federalism doctrine that would be consistent through a number of cases and controversies. However, the Rehnquist Court was ultimately unable to draw a clear, bright line of rules governing the evolving federalism balance: because of the complex, integrated nature of new policy areas—such as pharmaceuticals, medical devices, and intellectual property—the power between federal and state governments became more *concurrent*, despite the Rehnquist Court's efforts to keep power *separate*. Overall, the rapid, ever-changing nature of the federalism dynamic prevented the Court from articulating a clear, consistent, and cognizable preemption doctrine.

REHNQUIST: THE MAN AND THE JUDGE

In 1972, at age forty-seven, William Rehnquist was appointed associate justice by President Richard Nixon, becoming the one-hundredth justice of the Supreme Court. He became chief justice in 1986, elevated by President Ronald Reagan. In all, Rehnquist served thirty-three years, one of the longest tenures on the Court. Rehnquist was a native of Milwaukee, Wisconsin, born October 1, 1924, and he died on September 3, 2005. He served three years in the US Army (1943–1946); went to college on the G.I. Bill at Stanford University, where he was elected into Phi Beta Kappa. He completed a master's program at Harvard University and graduated first in his class from Stanford University Law School in 1952—the same class as future Supreme Court justice Sandra Day O'Connor. After law school, Rehnquist clerked for Supreme Court Justice Robert A. Jackson in 1952 and 1953. After practicing law for several years in Phoenix, Arizona, Rehnquist became chief advisor first to 1964 presidential nominee Senator Barry Goldwater (R-AZ) then to Attorney General John Mitchell (under President Nixon, 1969–1971).[2] Rehnquist's more memorable moments included presiding over the US Senate during the 1998 impeachment trial of President William Jefferson Clinton, then in 2000 deciding that George W. Bush had won an electoral college majority in the presidential election over Vice President Al Gore, halting a recount that had been ordered by the Florida Supreme Court.

A hallmark of Rehnquist's management of the Supreme Court was his unparalleled organizational skills. Oral arguments were tightly controlled. The justices decided cases in private business-like conferences, and opinions were promptly assigned and delivered following his exacting standards of punctuality. He was a pragmatic realist with a judicious, restrained temperament, believing in a milder strain of certain conservative core values; he stayed in touch with national and world affairs and broad cultural shifts but refused to take sides in the culture wars.[3] Devoutly private, he was unpretentious and unassuming, avoiding the sin of pride. This gave him the ability to bring his ideologically discordant justices together to form a majority consensus on many difficult cases. In Justice Rehnquist's *New York Times* obituary of September 4, 2005, the lead paragraph described his unwavering commitment to "an enhanced role for the states within the federal system, which the court accomplished under his leadership by overturning dozens of federal laws that sought to project federal authority into what the Supreme Court majority viewed as the domain of the states . . . Among his most important opinions were those that set limits on the meaning of the Constitution's due process guarantee, declining to expand the boundaries of due process in a way that would create new rights or encroach on state power."[4]

Rehnquist was a decidedly conservative Republican who reflected the Reagan administration's conservative agenda, including a smaller federal government, radical deregulation, and New Federalism policies: "In the absence of the clear constitutional or statutory, the presumption of sovereignty should rest with the individual states."[5] He was a populist who ardently opposed the excesses of federal, state, and local authority. He told the *New York Times Magazine* in 1985, "I'm a strong believer in pluralism. Don't concentrate all the power in one place . . . you don't want all the power in the Government as opposed to the people. You don't want all the power in the Federal Government as opposed to the states."[6] Considered a lawyer's lawyer for his intellect, photographic memory of Supreme Court decisions, and encyclopedic knowledge of constitutional law, Rehnquist did not legislate from the bench like Earl Warren, and neither was he a rigid originalist. Rather, he followed a pragmatic conservative tradition in constitutional construction. He believed judges should not impose their personal views on the law or stray beyond the framers' intent by reading broad meaning into the Constitution.[7] He saw himself as an "apostle of judicial restraint."[8]

Rehnquist's philosophy of state-centered federalism was reflected in his view of the role of government and the rights of individuals. In his 1948 master's thesis written at Stanford, he wrote, "the highest end which the state can serve is to serve no end at all, but merely exist as a means for the individuals within it to realize their own ends."[9] He reaffirmed the Warren Court's decision in *Miranda v. Arizona*,[10] albeit with exceptions.[11]

He vigorously dissented in *Roe v. Wade*,[12] arguing in favor of traditionally historic state power on issues of abortion and individual rights and liberties. He lambasted the majority for ruling that a woman had a constitutional right to an abortion, thus overruling a majority of state laws prohibiting abortion. He was joined in his dissent by Justice White.[13] "The fact that a majority of the States . . . have had restrictions on abortions for at least a century is a strong indication . . . the asserted right to an abortion is not 'so rooted in the traditions and conscience of our people as to be ranked as [a] fundamental' [right as asserted by the majority]."[14]

In a dissent in a case over federal job quotas, his view on the rights of an individual and discrimination were sharply expressed: "There is perhaps no device more destructive to the nation of equality than the *numerus clausus*—the quota. Whether described as 'benign discrimination' or 'affirmative action,' the racial quota is nonetheless a creator of castes, a two-edged sword that must demean one in order to prefer another . . . the Court has sown the wind. Later courts will face the impossible task of reaping the whirlwind."[15]

REHNQUIST ON FEDERALISM AND PREEMPTION

The constitutional separation of state and federal authority and how to address preemption was a recurrent theme the justices continued to wrestle with throughout Rehnquist's thirty-three years on the Supreme Court. Was a clear statement required of the Congress's intention to preempt, or was the Court to make a presumption? Generally the courts have followed the *Rice* doctrine, requiring a clear and manifest congressional statement. For example, in 1992 in *Cipollone v. Liggett Group, Inc.*, the majority opinion by Justice Stevens leaned into a clear statement rule applying the *Rice* presumption in construing a statute's express preemption provisions. "The principles of federalism and respect for state sovereignty that underlie the Court's reluctance to find preemption where Congress has not spoken directly to the issue apply with equal force where Congress has spoken, though ambiguously," Justice Blackmun wrote in a concurring opinion. "In such cases, the question is not whether Congress intended to preempt state regulation, but to what extent. We do not, absent unambiguous evidence, infer a scope of preemption beyond that which clearly is mandated by Congress' language."[16]

Justice Antonin Scalia, favoring a general preemption rule, said in his dissent, "Under the Supremacy Clause, our job is to interpret Congress's decrees of pre-emption neither narrowly nor broadly, but in accordance with their apparent meaning. . . . Though we generally 'assume that the historic police powers of the States [are] not to be superseded by a . . . Federal Act unless that [is] the clear and manifest purpose of Congress,' we have traditionally not thought to require express statutory text."[17]

In the 1997 *Printz v. United States* decision,[18] the preemption principles of the Rehnquist Court's vision were artfully articulated by Justice Scalia, who discussed at length the history of federal-state relations. This helps us understand the Court's approach to defining the reach, limits, and application of the Commerce Clause:

> Residual state sovereignty was implicit . . . in the Constitution's conferral upon Congress of not all governmental powers, but only discrete, enumerated ones, Art. I, § 8, which implication was rendered express by the Tenth Amendment's assertion that "[t]he powers not delegated to the United States by the Constitution, nor prohibited by it to the States, are reserved to the States respectively, or to the people."
>
> The Framers rejected the concept of a central government that would act upon and through the States, and instead designed a system in which the State and Federal Governments would exercise concurrent authority over the people—who were, in Hamilton's words, "the only proper objects of government," The Federalist No. 15, at 109. We have set forth the historical record in more detail elsewhere . . . It suffices to repeat the conclusion: "the Framers explicitly chose a Constitution that confers upon Congress the power to regulate individuals, not States." The great innovation of this design was that "our citizens would have two political capacities, one state and one federal, each protected from incursion by the other"—"a legal system unprecedented in form and design, establishing two orders of government, each with its own direct relationship, its own privity, its own set of mutual rights and obligations to the people who sustain it and are governed by it." The Constitution thus contemplates that a State's government will represent and remain accountable to its own citizens.

This separation of the two spheres is one of the Constitution's structural protections of liberty. "Just as the separation and independence of the coordinate branches of the Federal Government serve to prevent the accumulation of excessive power in any one branch, a healthy balance of power between the States and the Federal Government will reduce the risk of tyranny and abuse from either front." To quote Madison once again:

"In the compound republic of America, the power surrendered by the people is first divided between two distinct governments, and then the portion allotted to each subdivided among distinct and separate departments. Hence a double security arises to the rights of the people. The different governments will control each other, at the same time that each will be controlled by itself." The Federalist No. 51, at 323.[19]

The courts have generally followed the *Rice* presumption principle requiring a clear and manifest statement of congressional intent as a rule of statutory construction.[20] The Rehnquist Court's philosophical view of protecting the value of state authority reverberated through its rulings. In one of the Rehnquist Court's last preemption decisions, *Bates v. Dow Agrosciences, LLC*, the Court's opinion stated "that in choosing between 'plausible alternative reading[s]' of a federal statute, we have a duty to accept the reading that disfavors preemption.'"[21] In an MSNBC interview, one constitutional law professor said Rehnquist "really does—along with [Justice Sandra Day] O'Connor—have a certain contempt for Congress. He wants to protect vulnerable states against a rampaging Congress. He is viscerally committed to the goodness of the states."[22]

THE STATE-CENTERED FEDERALISM REVOLUTION OF 1995: *LOPEZ* AND *MORRISON*

Late in his term, Rehnquist led a state-centered federalism revolution in 1995.[23] It was the first nullification since the New Deal of a congressional act exceeding congressional authority under the Commerce Clause—as decided in *United States v. Lopez*.[24] Moreover, in reinforcing state-sovereignty decisions, questioning the scope of Congress's enumerated powers, Rehnquist invalidated substantial portions of the 1994 Violence Against Women Act in the case of *United States v. Morrison*.[25] The *Morrison* case, like *Lopez*, was based on congressional excess of authority under the Commerce Clause.[26] The *Lopez* and *Morrison* opinions reestablished the principle that the Commerce Clause has judicially enforceable outer limits, and the decisions became the canon of the modern preemption doctrine. This was following a similar nullification decision in 1976 of a federal regulation that put federal regulatory authority on the defensive. In *National League of Cities v. Usery*, Rehnquist's majority opinion invalidated a federal law extending the federal wage and maximum-hours provision to state and local government employees. He wrote, "This exercise of congressional authority does not comport with the federal system of government embodied in the Constitution."[27]

Justice David Souter, however, disagreed with the majority in the *Morrison* case on the central issue of the state's freedom to make its own regulatory choices. Based on the Court's previous forays into enforcing federalism and the doctrinal disarray that resulted, Justice Souter warned that the Court's renewed attempt to enforce federalism raised a "portent of incoherence." He argued that doctrinal incoherence works to undermine the Court's legitimacy. Moreover, Justice Souter said, rigid subject matter categories or fixed and exclusive spheres of state and federal regulatory authority become unstable over time, as the troubled history of dual federalism has demonstrated.[28]

These three referenced cases represent a zenith in Rehnquist's unique jurisprudence on the Commerce Clause, limiting the expansive scope that had been created during the New Deal era. In the late 1930s, recognizing the great changes that had occurred in the way business was being conducted in the United States,[29] several cases decided by the "new" Supreme Court after 1937 ushered in an era of expansive Commerce Clause jurisprudence[30] that collectively defined the outer limits of its application: *N.L.R.B. v. Jones & Laughlin Steel Corp.* (1937), *United States v. Darby* (1941), and *Wickard v. Filburn* (1942).[31] These New Deal cases gave Congress greater authority and latitude in legislating many areas under the Commerce Clause. In the *Lopez* case, the Rehnquist Court stated that the greater authority recognized in the late 1930s is not without effective bounds where it intrudes into areas of traditional state regulation: "to preserve a distinction between what is truly national and what is truly local ... we must inquire whether the exercise of national power seeks to intrude upon an area of traditional state concern."[32]

Lopez laid out a three-point formula for measuring whether a specific activity was "commerce" constitutionally governed by the Commerce Clause that became the standard for all federal courts to follow:

> *Jones & Laughlin Steel*, *Darby*, and *Wickard* ushered in an era of Commerce Clause jurisprudence that greatly expanded the previously defined authority of Congress under that Clause. In part, this was a recognition of the great changes that had occurred in the way business was carried on in this country. Enterprises that had once been local or at most regional in nature had become national in scope. But the doctrinal change also reflected a view that earlier Commerce Clause cases artificially had constrained the authority of Congress to regulate interstate commerce.

... We have identified three broad categories of activity that Congress may regulate under its commerce power. *First*, Congress may regulate the use of the channels of interstate commerce. "'[T]he authority of Congress to keep the channels of interstate commerce free from immoral and injurious uses has been frequently sustained, and is no longer open to question.'"

Second, Congress is empowered to regulate and protect the instrumentalities of interstate commerce, or persons or things in interstate commerce, even though the threat may come only from intrastate activities.

Finally, Congress' commerce authority includes the power to regulate those activities having a substantial relation to interstate commerce, *i.e.* those activities that substantially affect interstate commerce.

Within this final category, admittedly, our case law has not been clear whether an activity must "affect" or "substantially affect" interstate commerce in order to be within Congress' power to regulate it under the Commerce Clause ... (the Court has never declared that "Congress may use a relatively trivial impact on commerce as an excuse for broad general regulation of state or private activities"). We conclude, consistent with the great weight of our case law, that the proper test requires an analysis of whether the regulated activity "substantially affects" interstate commerce.[33]

The *Morrison* case, which followed five years after *Lopez*, created a "presumption of constitutionality" and established a standard that the Court "invalidate a congressional enactment only upon a *plain showing* the Congress has exceeded its constitutional bounds."[34] This case went to the third standard set out in *Lopez*; that is, did the activity in question "substantially affect" interstate commerce? The Rehnquist Court addressed the issue of the outer limits of Congress's authority under the Commerce Clause against the sovereignty of the states' rights compass. In *Morrison* the Justices wrote,

> In *Jones & Laughlin Steel*, the Court warned that the scope of the interstate commerce power 'must be considered in the light of our dual system of government and may not be extended so as to embrace effects upon interstate commerce so indirect and remote that to embrace them, in view of our complex society, would effectually obliterate the distinction between what is national and what is local and create a completely centralized government. . . .[35]
>
> Were the Federal Government to take over the regulation of entire areas of traditional state concern, areas having nothing to do with the regulation of commercial activities, the boundaries between the spheres of federal and state authority would blur.
>
> *Lopez's* review of Commerce Clause case law demonstrates that in those cases where we have sustained federal regulation of intrastate activity based upon the activity's substantial effects on interstate commerce, the activity in question has been some sort of economic endeavor.

The regulation and punishment of intrastate violence that is not directed at the instrumentalities, channels, or goods involved in interstate commerce has always been the province of the States.[36]

And in *Gibbs v. Babbitt* they wrote,

> *Lopez* and *Morrison* properly emphasize that we must carefully evaluate legislation in light of our federal system of government. "The Constitution requires a distinction between what is truly national and what is truly local." *Morrison*, 529 U.S. at 599. We must particularly scrutinize regulated activity that "falls within an area of the law where States historically have been sovereign and countenance of the asserted federal power would blur the boundaries between the spheres of federal and state authority."[37]

REAL ESTATE DEVELOPMENT AND THE ENDANGERED SPECIES ACT

Protection of endangered species was at issue in three real estate–development cases, and each engaged the three standards of the *Lopez* test, measuring the reach of the Commerce Clause. In *National Ass'n of Home Builders v. Babbitt*,[38] the issue under discussion was a proposal to build a $470 million hospital and a power plant and to expand an adjacent interstate highway intersection. The Court determined that the "take" of a single endangered species—the Delhi Sands flower-loving fly—could be "aggregated" with the "take" of other species to create a "substantial" effect on interstate commerce. "The *de minimis* character of the individual instances arising under [the ESA] is of no consequence.... The [overall] effect of the loss of biodiversity on interstate commerce" was "substantial."[39] This was *Lopez*'s second test.

In *GDF Realty Investments, Ltd. v. Norton*, the Court held that the take provision in Section 9 of the Endangered Species Act is "economic in nature ... the interdependence of species compels the conclusion that regulated takes under ESA do affect interstate commerce.... The ESA is an economic regulatory scheme."[40] In this case, the economic activity was to build a shopping center, a Walmart, office buildings, and a subdivision. "A close reading of Lopez ... provides two recognized and historically rooted means of congressional regulation under the commerce power: (1) whether the activity is 'any sort of economic enterprise, however broadly one might define those terms'; or (2) whether the activity exists as 'an essential part of a larger regulation of economic activity, in which the regulatory scheme could be undercut unless the intrastate activity were regulated.'"[41]

The case of *Rancho Viejo v. Norton* involved a 202-acre, 208-unit housing development that would destroy the habitat of the endangered Arroyo southwestern toad, an economic enterprise the Court determined would have a substantial effect on interstate commerce. The Court stated that while the ESA does not constitute a general regulation on land use,[42] Congress had enacted the law out of a moral imperative to protect biodiversity and thereby established a presumption of constitutionality—*Lopez*'s first and second test.[43] The preservation of endangered species is historically a federal function. "The ESA represents a national response to a specific problem of 'truly national concern.'"[44] Rather than impeding on local land or wildlife and natural-resource management—areas traditionally of state concern—this authority is shared with the federal government when it exercises one of its enumerated constitutional powers. "It's clear from our laws and precedent that federal regulation of endangered wildlife does not trench impermissibly upon state powers."[45]

Protection of intrastate species is an integral part of the comprehensive ESA program that regulates "activities" having a substantial impact on interstate commerce. However, the regulation must be an appropriate means of attaining a legitimate end and part of a larger regulatory scheme properly governing interstate commerce—the third *Lopez* test. Preventing extinction of species is vital to the survival of the ecosystems on which they are dependent. Starting with *Tennessee Valley Authority v. Hill* in 1978, the federal courts have recognized that the Endangered Species Act is a comprehensive scheme to preserve the nation's genetic heritage and its incalculable inherent value.[46] For the reader to grasp the court's rationale, following are statements from three federal courts that summarize their collective view of how commercial and economic activity, endangered species, and the Commerce Clause all are interrelated. First, in *New York v. United States*:

> As interstate commerce has become ubiquitous, activities once considered purely local have come to have effects on the national economy, and have accordingly come within the scope of Congress' commerce power.[47]

And from *Gibbs v. Babbitt*:

> It is within the power of Congress to regulate the coexistence of commercial activity and endangered wildlife in our nation and to manage the interdependence of endangered animals and plants in large ecosystems.... Congress could find that conservation of endangered species and economic growth are mutually reinforcing. It is simply not beyond the power of Congress to conclude that a healthy environment actually boosts industry by allowing commercial development of our natural resources.

Congress has long been involved in the regulation of scarce and vital natural resources. The full payoff of conservation in the form of tourism, research, and trade may not be foreseeable. Yet it is reasonable for Congress to decide that conservation of species will one day produce a substantial commercial benefit to this country and that failure to preserve a species will result in permanent, though unascertainable, commercial loss.

Extinction, after all, is irreversible. If a species becomes extinct, we are left to speculate forever on what we might have learned or what we may have realized. If we conserve the species, it will be available for the study and benefit of future generations. In any event, it is for Congress to choose between inaction and preservation, not for the courts.[48]

And this last passage, still from *Gibbs*:

Given the interconnectedness of species and ecosystems, it is reasonable to conclude that the extinction of one species affects others and their ecosystems and that the protection of a purely intrastate species . . . will therefore substantially affect land and objects that are involved in interstate commerce.

The Supreme Court recently reiterated that "although States have important interests in regulating wildlife and natural resources within their borders, this authority is shared with the Federal Government when the Federal Government exercises one of its enumerated constitutional powers."

It is as threatening to federalism for courts to erode the historic national role over scarce resource conservation as it is for Congress to usurp traditional state prerogatives in such areas as education and domestic relations. Courts seeking to enforce the structural constraints of federalism must respect the balance on both sides.[49]

A SUMMARY OF WILDLIFE-PROTECTION CASES IN THE REHNQUIST COURT

During the years of the Rehnquist Court, the judiciary decided a series of cases addressing federal preemption of state authority over wildlife and natural resources. These cases are summarized as follows, chronologically organized for ease of reference (three of which were discussed earlier)[50]:

1986   Washington State Department of Fisheries v. FERC, 801 F.2d 1516 (9th Cir. 1986). Permits issued by the Federal Energy Regulatory Commission for hydroelectric projects without addressing environmental concerns violated the Fish and Wildlife Act and Federal Power Act.

1987 California Coastal Commission v. Granite Rock Co., 480 U.S. 572 (1987). State permits did not violate five related federal land-management acts because there was no conflict with the five laws, no congressional intent to occupy the regulatory field, nor legislative history of such intent.

1988 Christy v. Hodel, 857 F.2d 1324 (9th Cir. 1988). The Endangered Species Act did not deprive owners of wildlife killed by grizzly bears from Fifth Amendment constitutional due process or equal-protection rights. The secretary of the interior was within the limits of congressional authority to promulgate regulations promoting the conservation of threatened species.

Palila v. Hawaii Department of Land and Natural Resources, 852 F.2d 1106 (9th Cir. 1988). The destruction of critical habitat by state-owned feral wildlife was a violation of the Endangered Species Act.

1992 United States v. Glenn-Colusa Irrigation District, 788 F. Supp. 1126 (E.D. Cal. 1992). State water regulation with lower protection standards for salmon is preempted by the Endangered Species Act.

Swan View Coalition v. Turner, Inc., 824 F. Supp. 923 (D. Mont. 1992). The ESA definition of *taking* includes harm and significant habitat modification, which preempted lesser restrictive provisions of Montana law on grizzly bear and wolves.

1994 Clajon Production Corp. v. Petera, 854 F. Supp. 843 (D. Wyo. 1994). State hunting regulations were sustained on the constitutional grounds of the Commerce and Privileges and Immunities Clauses.

1995 United States v. Guthrie, 50 F.3d 936 (11th Cir. 1995). The state constitution was upheld in prosecution of a Lacey Act violation; the listing of species under the Endangered Species Act was neither arbitrary nor capricious.

Crow Tribe of Indians v. Repsis, 73 F.3d 982 (10th Cir. 1995). The state's broad trustee and police power over wildlife on private, state, or federal lands was upheld. 1868 Treaty rights were temporary and repealed when the state was admitted into the Union.

Babbitt v. Sweet Home Chapter of Communities for a Greater Oregon, 515 U.S. 687 (1995). The ESA's definition of *harm* includes "significant habitat modifications or degradation that kills or injures wildlife" both on private and public land; the definition was expanded based on clear legislative history.

1996 United States v. Romano, 929 F. Supp. 502 (D. Mass. 1996). A Lacey Act violation was upheld based on an interstate transaction, notwithstanding that the violation was intrastate.

United States v. Lundquist, 932 F. Supp. 1237 (D. Or. 1996). Bald and Golden Eagle Protection Act was valid within congressional authority under the Commerce Clause. The sale of eagle feathers to tourists for souvenirs is a form of economic activity within the reach of the Commerce Clause and therefore a violation of the act.

United States v. Bramble, 103 F.3d 1475 (9th Cir. 1996). The same holding as in *Lundquist* was made, based on the reach of the Commerce Clause and on *State of Missouri v. Holland* (252 U.S. 416 [1920]) which had held that the Migratory Bird Treaty Act is constitutional.

1997 Strahan v. Coxe, 127 F.3d 155 (1st Cir. 1997). Massachusetts permits issued for commercial lobster fishing are preempted by the ESA, due to injury and death caused to whales getting caught in equipment lines.

Bennett v. Spear, 520 U.S. 154 (1997). An economic impact is required in ESA biological opinions.

1998 Fund for Animals v. Clark, 27 F. Supp.2d 8 (D. D.C. 1998). The US Forest Service, the US Fish and Wildlife Service, the National Park Service, and State of Wyoming violated the National Environmental Policy Act when failing to do an environmental assessment prior to initiating an elk and bison winter-feeding program as part of an annual harvest program to thin the population of bison.

1999 Minnesota v. Mille Lacs Band of Chippewa Indians, 526 U.S. 172 (1999). 1893 treaty rights were found to be reconcilable with state sovereignty over natural resources. However, traditional state control over wildlife is shared with the federal government and is circumscribed by federal regulatory powers when the government exercises one of its enumerated constitutional powers.

2000 Loggerhead Turtle v. Volusia County, Florida, 92 F. Supp.2d 1296 (M.D. Fla. 2000). The ESA preempts state or local regulations that conflict with it. However, the ESA cannot compel or preclude the adoption of local regulations.

Gibbs v. Babbitt, 214 F.3d Supp. 483 (4th Cir. 2000). The preservation of endangered species has historically been a federal function and not an exclusive or primary state one. The conservation of scarce natural resources is a well-recognized area of federal regulations and flows from the Commerce Clause on commercial and economic activity.

2001 Solid Waste Agency of Northern Cook Cty. v. U.S. Army Corp. of Engineers, 531 U.S. 159 (2001). The Army Corps of Engineers exceeded its authority under the Clean Water Act and encroached on primary and traditional states' rights over land and water uses. Congressional intent must be clear when it potentially encroaches on traditional state powers.

2002 National Audubon Society v. Davis, 307 F.3d 835 (9th Cir. 2002). The ESA preempts state regulations that conflict, interfere with, or are contrary to the ESA. There are three standards applied to judge when a federal law preempts state law: express, implied, or actual conflict when compliance with both federal and state law or regulations is a physical possibility.

Wyoming v. United States, 279 F.3d 1214 (10th Cir. 2002). The Tenth Amendment did not reserve to the state an unrestricted right to manage wildlife on public lands. The National Wildlife Refuge System Improvement Act preempts state management when the two actually conflict or when the state regulations are an obstacle to the objectives of the federal government.

2005 Gonzales v. Raich, 545 U.S. 1 (2005). The Court held that the federal government has the power to prosecute those who grow marijuana for private medical use within the state of California notwithstanding the authority of a 1996 state law. The Supreme Court reasoned that even home consumption has a substantial effect on the supply and demand for the commodity nationwide. The Rehnquist and O'Connor dissent argued (per *Lopez* and *Morrison*) that the Constitution gives the federal government limited powers, not vast "police powers" over activities within each state.[51]

The principle of cooperative federalism developed during the New Deal Era recognizes that both federal and state governments can share authority in regulating the same activities. However, federal overreach that violates the sovereignty of the states and the Tenth Amendment occurs when the federal government compels a state to enact or administer a federal regulatory program. The Constitution confers upon Congress the power to regulate individuals, not states. It lacks the power to compel states to require or prohibit administering acts of Congress. The Constitution enables the federal government to preempt state regulatory control that is contrary to federal authority, using their enumerated constitutional powers, such as the Commerce Clause. Financial incentives to states are often tied to regulations of the federal government to encourage states to adopt and participate in a program. But when a state is conscripted or commandeered and compelled to enforce a regulation, a violation of the Tenth Amendment has occurred, and the principles of sovereignty, the bedrock of federalism, become unbalanced.

Two successive cases followed a common Tenth Amendment thread in the Rehnquist Court, each holding that to conscript or commandeer a state—forcing it to adopt federal laws and enact supporting state regulations—is a violation of the Tenth Amendment. Each case was based on the authority of the Commerce Clause, the Necessary and Proper Clause, or the Spending Clause. In both instances, the federal laws or parts thereof were nullified: *New York v. United States* and *Printz v. United States*.⁵² These two cases followed the precedents set in *Hodel v. Virginia Surface Mining & Reclamation Ass'n* and *FERC v. Mississippi*.⁵³

Conversely, in the 1987 case of *South Dakota v. Dole*, Rehnquist upheld Congress's 5 percent reduction of funds to states not complying with the national twenty-one-year-old drinking age required by state law. That requirement was a condition attached to the federal highway bill, which funded national highway infrastructure projects in all the states.⁵⁴

The last Rehnquist case addressing a Tenth Amendment violation was decided in 2000, when the Court unanimously upheld a federal law in *Reno v. Condon*.⁵⁵ Following are excerpts from two prominent Rehnquist Court cases that described the Court's jurisprudence on the subjects of commandeering, the Tenth Amendment, and the balance of federalism vis-à-vis Congress's limits on preemption. First, two excerpts from *New York v. United States* (1992):

> As an initial matter, Congress may not simply "commandee[r] the legislative processes of the States by directly compelling them to enact and enforce a federal regulatory program" . . . We observed that "this Court never has sanctioned explicitly a federal command to the States to promulgate and enforce laws and regulations."

> The Court has been explicit about this distinction. "Both the States and the United States existed before the Constitution. The people, through that instrument, established a more perfect union by substituting a national government, acting, with ample power, directly upon the citizens, instead of the Confederate government, which acted with powers, greatly restricted, only upon the States. "[U]nder our federal system, the States possess sovereignty concurrent with that of the Federal Government."⁵⁶

> In the end, the [1787 Constitutional] Convention opted for a Constitution in which Congress would exercise its legislative authority directly over individuals rather than over States. . . . In providing for a stronger central government, therefore, the Framers explicitly chose a Constitution that confers upon Congress the power to regulate individuals, not States. As we have seen, the Court has consistently respected this choice. We have always understood that even where Congress has the authority under the Constitution to pass laws requiring or prohibiting certain acts, it lacks the power directly to compel the States to require or prohibit those acts . . .

The allocation of power contained in the Commerce Clause, for example, authorizes Congress to regulate interstate commerce directly; it does not authorize Congress to regulate state governments' regulation of interstate commerce . . . where Congress has the authority to regulate private activity under the Commerce Clause, we have recognized Congress' power to offer States the choice of regulating that activity according to federal standards or having state law pre-empted by federal regulation . . .[57]

And from *Reno v. Condon*:

This arrangement, which has been termed "a program of cooperative federalism" . . . is replicated in numerous federal statutory schemes. These include the Clean Water Act . . . (Clean Water Act "anticipates a partnership between the States and the Federal Government, animated by a shared objective"). . . . Whatever the outer limits of that sovereignty may be, one thing is clear: The Federal Government may not compel the States to enact or administer a federal regulatory program . . . the Constitution enables the Federal Government to pre-empt state regulation contrary to federal interests, and it permits the Federal Government to hold out incentives to the States as a means of encouraging them to adopt suggested regulatory schemes. It does not, however, authorize Congress simply to direct the States to provide for the disposal of the radioactive waste generated within their borders.[58]

REHNQUIST IN RETROSPECT: THE DIGITAL AGE MUDDLES THE COURT'S DIRECTION

Rehnquist's thirty-three years on the Supreme Court (1972–2005) spans the period of enactment, regulatory development, and application of the Endangered Species Act. It also spans a period of extraordinary technological advancement in the United States that forced more state and federal legislation and regulations comprehensively addressing the explosive growth in the following areas: pharmaceutical and drugs; medical devices; health, safety, product labeling, insecticides, and pollution; energy and environmental matters; heavy industry; telecommunications; automobile safety; agriculture; immigration; airline, rail, and trucking; transportation and infrastructure; developing technology and intellectual property; banking and financial issues; federal arbitration; labor and employment;the Employee Retirement Income Security Act of 1974 and pensions; and transboundary challenges.[59]

Before this explosion of an ever-increasing industrialized society, states had exercised their police power through statutes, regulations, and common law to combat the multifarious problems presented by rapid growth. This diversity of judicial subjects caused the preemption doctrine to become balkanized into a multitiered system of jurisprudence: statutory, obstacle, express, implied, impossibility, tort, frustration of purpose, occupation of the field, and conflict preemption.[60] Hence, while today only 7 percent of the federal civil docket is made up of preemption cases,[61] 75 percent of all preemption cases fall into the many multitiered subjects itemized above.[62]

The Rehnquist Court's early opinions cut across ideological lines and developed no clear preemption doctrine that could address new congressional statutes and separate subject areas presented by emerging diverse technological and commercial fields and products.[63] In close cases like *Lorillard* and *Grier*, the Rehnquist Court liberals (Justices Stevens, Souter, Ginsburg, and Breyer) favored state regulatory autonomy and authority, while the conservatives (Justices Rehnquist, O'Connor, Scalia, Kennedy, and Thomas) insisted on limiting national, federal power.[64] In the classic federalism cases like *Lopez* and *Seminole Tribe*, there remained a static division between the two ideological groups.[65] This results from the perception that preemption is deregulatory in its impact. Conservatives favor it, and the liberals oppose it.[66] As a rigid textualist, Justice Scalia generally sided with the conservatives. In the opinion of Professor Ernest A. Young, the Rehnquist Court's most important contributions were along the lines of Federalism's nationalist dimensions, notwithstanding "the absence of any corresponding move to loosen federalism-based constraints on state authority."[67]

The Rehnquist Court opinions "oscillate[d] between a law of federalism, which would suggest a restrictive view of preemption, and an aversion to state interference with federal programs."[68] The Court was expected to be solicitous of states' rights based on the 1976 ruling in *National League of Cities v. Usery*,[69] the Reagan administration's New Federalism rhetoric throughout the 1980s, and their commitment to deregulation.[70] In the early Rehnquist Court, preemption was less likely,[71] except in the areas of civil rights and liberties. The Court ultimately failed to vigorously enforce the Tenth Amendment, imposing only limited barriers to Congress's power over the states,[72] as in *New York v. United States*.[73] As one writer near the end of Rehnquist's term dismissively opined, "The Court appears to have abandoned altogether the project of reinvigorating the Tenth Amendment."[74] Another scholar wrote, "After four more appointments by Reagan and George Bush, the Court appeared poised to reverse prior rulings on federal preemption. Reagan appointed Antonin Scalia in 1986 and Anthony Kennedy in 1987; Bush named David Souter in 1990 and Clarence Thomas in 1991."[75] Thereafter, another generational liberal shift began after 1993 and 1994, when Ruth Bader Ginsburg and Stephen Breyer joined the Court (the "second" Rehnquist Court), replacing Justices White and Blackmun. The Court's composition didn't change for eleven years thereafter, and the Court's view became pro-preemption.[76]

For example, following a preemption construct developed in the previous Burger Court, in *Gregory v. Ashcroft* the Rehnquist Court stated that when a federal statute would "upset the usual constitutional balance of federal and state powers, [Congress] must make its intention to do so 'unmistakably clear in the language of the statute.'"[77] But later the same year, in *Chisom v. Roemer*[78] the plain-statement rule laid down in *Ashcroft*[79] was confusingly rendered dicta by both the majority and dissenters without any uniform deference accorded precedent. This demonstrates the Rehnquist Court's inability to develop a coherent theory on preemption[80] and its defense of federalism or to revive the constitutional theory of dual sovereignty abandoned during the New Deal in 1937.

Congress recognized the Court's frustration in determining congressional intent on preemption. In 1995, Congress added a provision in the Legislative Accountability and Reform Act designed to strengthen the partnership between the federal government and state, local, and tribal governments:

> (e) *Preemption Clarification and Information*—When a committee of authorization of the Senate or the House of Representatives reports a bill or joint resolution of public character, the committee report accompanying the bill or joint resolution shall contain, if relevant to the bill or joint resolution, an explicit statement on the extent to which the bill or joint resolution is intended to preempt any State, local or tribal law, and, if so, an explanation to the effect of such preemption.[81]

The provision requires that every federal bill contain an explicit statement of the extent to which it would preempt local law and the effect of such preemption. The provision had little to no effect.

CAN THE NATIONAL POLITICAL PROCESS PROTECT FEDERALISM AND STATE SOVEREIGNTY?

The Rehnquist opinions would at times suggest the Court would rather not struggle with an implied preemption question but rather leave it to the states' elected representatives in Congress and the national political process for preservation of the states' interests.[82] At other times, Rehnquist's Commerce Clause cases suggested a complete disregard for the relevant jurisprudence,[83] thus leaving commerce conflict resolution to the questionable national political process. See, for example, the Court's opinion in *Garcia*:

> With rare exceptions, like the guarantee, in Article IV, § 3, of state territorial integrity, the Constitution does not carve out express elements of state sovereignty

that Congress may not employ its delegated powers to displace.... The power of the Federal Government is a "power to be respected" as well, and the fact that the States remain sovereign as to all powers not vested in Congress or denied them by the Constitution offers no guidance about where the frontier between state and federal power lies. In short, we have no license to employ freestanding conceptions of state sovereignty when measuring congressional authority under the Commerce Clause.

Apart from the limitation on federal authority inherent in the delegated nature of Congress' Article I powers, the principal means chosen by the Framers to ensure the role of the States in the federal system lies in the structure of the Federal Government itself. It is no novelty to observe that the composition of the Federal Government was designed in large part to protect the States from overreaching by Congress. The Framers thus gave the States a role in the selection both of the Executive and the Legislative Branches of the Federal Government. The States were vested with indirect influence over the House of Representatives and the Presidency by their control of electoral qualifications and their role in Presidential elections. U.S. Const., Art. I, § 2, and Art. II, § 1. They were given more direct influence in the Senate, where each State received equal representation and each Senator was to be selected by the legislature of his State. Art. I, § 3.

In short, the Framers chose to rely on a federal system in which special restraints on federal power over the States inhered principally in the workings of the National Government itself, rather than in discrete limitations on the objects of federal authority. State sovereign interests, then, are more properly protected by procedural safeguards inherent in the structure of the federal system than by judicially created limitations on federal power.

We are convinced that the fundamental limitation that the constitutional scheme imposes on the Commerce Clause to protect the "States as States" is one of process rather than one of result. Any substantive restraint on the exercise of Commerce Clause powers must find its justification in the procedural nature of this basic limitation, and it must be tailored to compensate for possible failings in the national political process rather than to dictate a "sacred province of state autonomy.[84]

This deference to the national political process persisted as a recurrent theme in a number of Rehnquist Court opinions in which the justices defined the concept of federalism.[85] However, Justice O'Connor found the national political process an untrustworthy safeguard for federalism.[86]

At one time in our history, the view that the structure of the Federal Government sufficed to protect the States might have had a somewhat more practical, although not a more logical, basis.... Not only is the premise of this view... the task of safeguarding the role of the states in the federal system and protecting the fundamental values of federalism [through the political process and separation of powers] clearly at odds with the proliferation of national legislation over the past 30 years, but "a variety of structural and political changes occurring in this century have combined to make Congress particularly *insensitive* to state and local values.[87]

REHNQUIST'S CONTINUED STRUGGLE WITH THE PREEMPTION DOCTRINE: MUDDLING ALONG!

The Court's mixed performance reflects its incremental case-by-case decision-making. It further highlights both the political priorities of four successive presidents over nineteen years who appointed associate justices to the bench, and also the lack of commitment to federalism's defense by most of the associate justices on the Rehnquist Court, except Justices O'Connor and Rehnquist.[88] One hundred eleven preemption cases were decided during Rehnquist's nineteen years as chief justice, half of which were unanimous decisions.[89] In one seven-year period alone, the court struck down thirty federal laws—a higher rate than any other court in US history.[90]

Professor Ernest A. Young has developed a scholarly perspective that perhaps explains why the Rehnquist Court struggled with the preemption doctrine over its long history:

> The *Rice* presumption [against preemption] rests not on the implied repeals canon but rather on the evolving structure of our federalism. The presumption, along with the Court's other federalism-based "clear statement" rules, developed ... for a reason: The Founders' initial institutional strategy for limiting national power and preserving state autonomy had failed. That strategy relied on the specific enumeration of national powers in Article I of the Constitution and the Tenth Amendment's corresponding reservation of all other powers to the states. ... This dual federalist regime ultimately collapsed as a result of the Court's difficulty in drawing determinate boundaries to cabin terms like "commerce among the several states" and "necessary and proper," as well as due to increasing pressure for national regulation in response to industrialization and economic crisis. Notwithstanding the Rehnquist Court's effort to retain *some* limits on the Commerce Power, the principle of enumerated powers now offers relatively little constraint on national action. The expanding scope of potential federal regulatory authority in the mid-twentieth century transformed our federalism from a regime of separate spheres to one of concurrent powers.[91]

At the very heart of federalism are statutory preemption and the constitutional balance of concurrent powers shared by the separate spheres of state and federal government. Inconsistent preemption decisions arise from different particulars and varying statutory regimes, and, hence, no unified preemption doctrine can emerge.[92] Every citizen is directly impacted.[93] "Preemption cases implicate a number of cross-cutting ideological and methodological conflicts on the Court."[94] Professor Ernest A. Young has concluded they are multidimensional and heterogeneous, with many novel issues presented by technology under untested statutes. To deal with the onslaught of complex preemption challenges posed by the diversity of subjects facing the Supreme Court, Justice Breyer in 2000 offered this cautionary opinion in lieu of a standing preemption principle:

> [In] pre-emption analysis, the Court has said [we] must "respect" the "separate spher[e]" of state "authority. . . . In so stating, the Court has recognized the practical importance of preserving local independence, at retail, i.e., by applying pre-emption analysis with care, statute by statute, line by line, in order to determine how best to reconcile a federal statute's language and purpose with federalism's need to preserve state autonomy. Indeed, in today's world, filled with legal complexity, the true test of federalist principle may lie, not in the occasional constitutional effort to trim Congress' commerce power at its edges . . . but rather in those many statutory cases where courts interpret the mass of technical detail that is the ordinary diet of the law."[95]

State laws and regulations frequently following federal grants-in-aid programs have become so interwoven and integrated into federal law that they have become interstitial, and Justice Breyer's surgical line-by-line analysis in the above quotation necessarily follows.[96]

If the reader has found this chapter difficult to follow, know that the author has been seriously challenged to articulate the Rehnquist Court's position on preemption within the federalist context (and the next chapter on the Roberts Court). Others have shared the same frustration.

Preemption jurisprudence in both the Rehnquist and Roberts Courts has hence been called a "muddle" by both a leading practitioner and a legal scholar.[97] Conversely, other scholars note "that in creating the 'delicate allocation of management jurisdiction in federal land law,' the Congress has been extremely solicitous of state sensibilities, and the main legislative theory [of Congress] seems to be on the order of 'let's just muddle through as best we can and let the courts handle the hard cases.'"[98] One law review article surveyed preemption over the twentieth century within the context of the political structure of federalism safeguards in contemporary constitutional law[99] and footnoted another scholar as follows: "Preemption doctrine . . . has evolved over the last century from one based on an assumption of congressional legislative exclusivity and almost certain preemption of state regulations to a doctrine, in the mid-part of the century, based on a search for congressional intent to preempt so that state laws, particularly those based on historical police powers, were not needlessly displaced."[100]

One keen overseer of the federal court's struggle to maintain a balance in federalism utilizing the *Rice* doctrine on preemption makes the following observation: "Given that many post–New Deal constitutional options for protecting federalism have been foreclosed,

> the [*Rice*] presumption against preemption may be the last best hope for preserving a meaningful measure of state autonomy in our constitutional system. . . . The more that the Justices see preemption cases as not simply disputes about the scope of federal and state regulation under specific regulatory statutes, but rather as raising fundamental questions of federalism, the more likely they are to transcend the current divide between proponents and opponents of regulation. Their ability to do so will be, in Justice Breyer's phrase, "the true test of federalist principle."[101]

SUMMARY

The Rehnquist Court sought to revive the long-standing, deeply entrenched principle of dual sovereignty under the New Federalism philosophy, first exposed during the New Deal Era after 1937, and reemerging during the Reagan presidency. With landmark cases such as *United States v. Lopez* (1995) and *United States v. Morrison* (2000) supplying new doctrinal limitations on the Commerce Clause (for the first time since 1937) and the Court correspondingly buttressing its anticommandeering doctrine in *New York v. United States* (1992) and *Printz v. United States* (1997), the future for a vibrant devolution movement seemed to have a real prospect for success. However, despite the national message around the centrality of state power and its relation with the Tenth Amendment—and a few moments in the Court's history hinting at a New Federalism doctrine—the Court ultimately struggled to develop a *consistent* preemption doctrine reflecting the essence of its federalism ethos.

With new policy subject areas emerging into the vortex of federal lawmaking—such as pharmaceuticals and drugs, medical devices, and intellectual property—the Rehnquist Court was unable to develop a clear preemption doctrine. For example, the *multifarious* preemption categories—from statutory and obstacle to express and implied, to name a few—reflected the complex and evolving nature of lawmaking. Thus, lines could not be neatly drawn according to the precepts of New Federalism. Overall, the Rehnquist Court's struggle to define the general federalism balance would create "muddled" confusion over the precise contours of wildlife preemption.

NOTES

1. *United States v. Lopez*, 514 U.S. 549 (1995); *United States v. Morrison*, 529 U.S. 598 (2000); *New York v. United States*, 505 U.S. 144 (1992); and *Printz v. United States*, 521 U.S. 898 (1997).
2. Herman J. Obermayer, *Rehnquist: A Personal Portrait of the Distinguished Chief Justice of the United States* (New York: Simon and Schuster, 2009), 24–26.
3. Jeffrey Rosen, "Rehnquist the Great?" *The Atlantic*, April 2005. https://www.theatlantic.com/magazine/archive/2005/04/rehnquist-the-great/303820/.
4. Linda Greenhouse, "Obituary: William H. Rehnquist, Chief Justice of the Supreme Court, Is Dead at 80," *New York Times*, September 4, 2005, https://www.nytimes.com/2005/09/04/politics/william-h-rehnquist-chief-justice-of-supreme-court-is-dead-at-80.html.
5. Quoting Ronald Reagan, Executive Order 12612: Federalism, 52 Fed. Reg. 41685, October 26, 1987, archived at https://www.archives.gov/federal-register/codification/executive-order/12612.html.
6. Rosen, "Rehnquist the Great?" 6, 10.
7. "William Rehnquist," Wikipedia, last modified September 18, 2021, https://en.wikipedia.org/wiki/William_Rehnquist.
8. Evan Thomas, "Reagan's Mr. Right," *Time Magazine*, June 30, 1986, http://content.time.com/time/subscriber/article/0,33009,961645,00.html.
9. Greenhouse, "Obituary: William H. Rehnquist."
10. *Miranda v. Arizona*, 384 U.S 436 (1966).
11. See *Roe v. Wade*, 410 U.S. 113 (1973).
12. *Roe*, 410 U.S. 113.

In a later abortion case, Rehnquist also dissented. See *Stenberg v. Carhart*, 530 U.S. 914 (2000).

13. Rosen, "Rehnquist the Great?" 1673.
14. *Roe*, 410 U.S. at 174 (J. Rehnquist, dissenting).
15. *United Steelworkers of America, AFL-CIO v. Weber*, 443 U.S. 193, 254–55 (1979) (J. Rehnquist, dissenting) (emphasis original).
16. *Cipollone v. Liggett Group, Inc.*, 505 U.S. 504, 533, 544–45 (1992) (J. Blackmun, concurring).
17. *Cipollone*, 505 U.S. at 544–45. (J. Scalia, concurring in part and dissenting in part; internal citations omitted).
18. 521 U.S. 898 (1997).
19. *Printz*, 521 U.S. at 919–22 (internal citations omitted).
20. William N. Eskridge Jr. and Philip P. Frickey, "Quasi-constitutional Law: Clear Statement Rules as Constitutional Lawmaking," *Vanderbilt Law Review* 45 (1992): 593, 607, https://digitalcommons.law.yale.edu/cgi/viewcontent.cgi?referer=https://www.google.com/&httpsredir=1&article=4814&context=fss_papers; and Young, "'Ordinary Diet,'" 274.
21. *Bates v. Dow Agrosciences LLC*, 544 U.S. 431, 449 (2005), as quoted in Young, "'Ordinary Diet,'" 274.

22. Sanford Levinson, constitutional law professor at the University of Texas Law School, as interviewed by Tom Curry, "Chief Justice Shaped High Court Conservatism," *NBC News*, September 3, 2005, https://www.nbcnews.com/id/wbna5304454.

23. Erwin Chemerinsky, "Keynote Address: Rehnquist Court's Federalism Revolution," *Willamette Law Review* 41, no. 5 (2005): 827–46, https://scholarship.law.duke.edu/cgi/viewcontent.cgi?article=2132&context=faculty_scholarship.

24. 514 U.S. 549 (1995). And see O'Brien, "Rehnquist Court and Federal Preemption," 16; White, "The Endangered Species Act's Precarious Perch," 215, 236.

25. 529 U.S. 598 (2000).

26. See Chemerinsky, "Keynote Address," .

27. *National League of Cities v. Usery*, 426 U.S. 833, 852 (1976).

The 1976 *National League of Cities* decision was later overturned in 1985 by *Garcia v. San Antonio Transit Authority* (469 U.S. 528 [1985]). The court held "The Constitution divests the states of 'their original powers,' and that federalism is a political structure in which states' interests, for better or worse, are represented in the national political process. . . . Following the 1976 NLC decision, the Tenth Amendment was referenced in 42 cases, 13 after Rehnquist because Chief Justice . . . i.e. 20% of all decisions mentioning the Tenth Amendment in the court's history." O'Brien, "Rehnquist Court and Federal Preemption," 18.

28. Morrison, 529 U.S. at 647 (J. Souter, dissenting).

29. Morrison, 529 U.S. at 556.

30. Lopez, 514 U.S. 549, 556–57 (1995); and Morrison, 529 U.S. at 608.

31. *N.L.R.B. v. Jones & Laughlin Steel Corp.*, 301 U.S. 1 (1937); *United States v. Darby*, 312 U.S. 100 (1941); *Wickard v. Filburn*, 317 U.S. 111 (1942).

32. *Lopez*, 514 U.S. at 580 (J. Kennedy, concurring).

33. *Lopez*, 514 U.S. at 555–59 (citations omitted; emphasis original).

34. *Morrison*, 529 U.S. at 608 (emphasis added). And also see Lopez, 514 U.S. at 568, 577–78.

35. *Morrison*, 529 U.S. at 608.

36. *Morrison*, 529 U.S. at 612–16 (citations omitted).

37. *Gibbs v. Babbitt*, 214 F.3d 483, 499 (4th Cir. 2000).

38. 130 F.3d 1041 (D.C. Cir. 1997); and *Nat Ass'n of Home Builders of the US v. Babbitt*, 949 F.Supp.1 (D.D.C. 1996).

39. *Babbitt*, 949 F.Supp.1, at 1047; repeated in *GDF Realty Investments, Ltd. v. Norton*, 326 F.3rd 622, 630 (5th Cir. 2003).

40. *GDF Realty Investments*, 326 F.3rd at 640.

The endangered species here involved six species of subterranean invertebrates that live in caves, the golden-cheeked warbler, and the black-capped vireo.

41. GDF Realty Investments, 326 F.3rd at 644 n. 9.

42. *Rancho Viejo v. Norton*, 323 F.3d 1062, 1078 (D.C. Cir. 2003).

43. *Rancho Viejo*, 323 F.3d at 1074, 1078.

44. *Rancho Viejo*, 323 F.3d at 1078–79 (citing *Morrison*, 529 U.S. at 617–18).

45. *Rancho Viejo*, 323 F.3d at 1079 (quoting *Gibbs v. Babbitt*, 214 F.3d 483, 500–501 [4th Cir. 2000]).

46. *Rancho Viejo*, 323 F.3d at 644 (J. Dennis, concurring).

47. *New York v. United States*, 505 U.S. 144, 158 (1992).
48. *Gibbs*, 214 F.3d at 496.
49. *Gibbs*, 214 F.3d at 497, 499, 505.
50. While Rehnquist was an associate justice in 1981, Secretary of the Interior James Watt moved control of the Arctic National Wildlife Refuge from the Fish and Wildlife Service to the United States Geological Survey. The Court held that Watt had exceeded his statutory authority and thereby invalidated his action. *Trustees for Alaska v. Watt*, 524 F.Supp. 1303 (D. Alaska 1981).
51. *Watt*, 524 F. Supp. at 42–43 (J. O'Connor, dissenting).
52. *New York v. United States*, 505 U.S. 144 (1992); *Printz v. United States*, 521 U.S. 898 (1997).
53. *Hodel v. Virginia Surface Mining & Reclamation Ass'n*, 452 U.S. 264 (1981); *FERC v. Mississippi*, 456 U.S. 742 (1982).
54. *South Dakota v. Dole*, 483 U.S. 203 (1987).
55. 528 U.S.141 (2000).
56. *New York v. United States*, 505 U.S. 144, 158, 161–64 (1992) (emphasis omitted; internal citations omitted).
57. *New York*, 505 U.S. 166–67.
58. *Reno v. Condon*, 528 U.S. 141 (2000).
59. Sandra Zellmer, "Preemption By Stealth," *Houston Law Review*, 45, no. 5 (2009): 1659, 1673–1702, https://houstonlawreview.org/article/4433-preemption-by-stealth.
60. Bratton, "Preemption Doctrine," 623–51.
For a discussion of all the various types of preemption, see also Greve, Klick, Petrino, and Sevilla, "Preemption in the Rehnquist and Roberts Courts," and related chapters. Note also Stephen A. Gardbaum, "New Evidence on the Pressumption against Preemption," 1604, 1609.
61. Greve, Klick, Petrino, and Sevilla, "Preemption in the Rehnquist and Roberts Courts," 8.
62. See appendix 2 for more graphic detail on preemption history.
63. O'Brien, "Rehnquist Court and Federal Preemption," 17.
64. *Lorillard Tobacco Co. v. Reilly*, 533 U.S. 525 (2001); *Grier v. American Honda Motor Co., Inc.*, 529 U.S. 861 (2000).
65. *United States v. Lopez*, 514 U.S. 549 (1995); *Seminole Tribe of Fla. v. Florida*, 517 U.S. 44 (1996).
66. Young, "Federal Preemption and State Autonomy," 263.
67. Young, "Federal Preemption and State Autonomy," 249.
68. Zellmer, "Preemption By Stealth," 1670.
69. 426 U.S. 833 (1976).
70. O'Brien, "Rehnquist Court and Federal Preemption," 15.
71. Zellmer, "Preemption By Stealth," 1662.
72. Zellmer, "Preemption By Stealth," 1662. See also O'Brien, "Rehnquist Court and Federal Preemption," 15.
73. 505 U.S. 144 (1992).
74. O'Brien, "Rehnquist Court and Federal Preemption," 20.

75. O'Brien, "Rehnquist Court and Federal Preemption," 16.

76. Greve, Klick, Petrino, and Sevilla, "Preemption in the Rehnquist and Roberts Courts," 26.

77. *Gregory v. Ashcroft*, 501 U.S. 452, 460 (1991), quoting Atascadero State Hospital v. Scanlon, 473 U.S. 243, 242 (1985).

78. 501 U.S. 380 (1991).

79. See Ashcroft, 501 U.S. at 460–61.

80. *Chisom* was not an isolated case in which the court disregarded, distinguished, or dismissed its rules for clear statements of Congressional preemption. See, e.g., *Rust v. Sullivan*, 500 U.S. 173 (1991), in which the Rehnquist Court did not apply its plain-statement rule but asserted another rule that when confronted with ambiguous congressional legislation, the Court would defer to the executive branch's interpretation of the statute. But, in *Presley v. Etowah County Commission*, 502 U.S. 491 (1992), the Court rejected both the Bush administration's reliance on *Rust* in support of its interpretation of the Voting Rights Act, and the administration's view of the act. See also *Tafflin v. Levitt*, 493 U.S. 455 (1990) (creating a clear-statement rule on the basis of the Supremacy Clause that federal regulatory schemes are enforceable in state and federal courts).

O'Brien, "Rehnquist Court and Federal Preemption," 25, n40.

81. US Congress, *Unfunded Mandates Reform Act of 1995*, Pub. L. No. 104–4, 109 Stat. 48, section 423(e) (1995), https://www.congress.gov/104/plaws/publ4/PLAW-104publ4.pdf.

82. O'Brien, "Rehnquist Court and Federal Preemption," 18, 19, 26, 29.

83. O'Brien, "Rehnquist Court and Federal Preemption," 20, 26–29.

84. *Garcia v. San Antonio Transit Authority*, 469 U.S. 528, 550–53 (1985) (internal citations omitted).

85. Young, "'Ordinary Diet,'" 279.

86. See *New York v. United States*, 505 U.S. 144 (1992); *Garcia*, 469 U.S. at 565–66 nn. 7–9 (J. Powell, dissenting); O'Brien, "Rehnquist Court and Federal Preemption," 19; Young, "'Ordinary Diet,'" 279, 320–21.

87. Garcia, 469 U.S. at 555 n. 9.

For a good discussion of the pros and cons of relying on the political safeguards of federalism, see Young, "Federal Preemption and State Autonomy," 253–54.

88. O'Brien, "Rehnquist Court and Federal Preemption," 17, 25, 26, 30, 31.

89. Greve, Klick, Petrino, and Sevilla, "Preemption in the Rehnquist and Roberts Courts," 10, 33.

Another law review article said in the 105 preemption cases analyzed, no clear antiregulatory sentiment was found. Zellmer, "Preemption By Stealth," 1670, n44.

90. Rosen, "Rehnquist the Great?" Also see appendix 2.

91. Young, "'Ordinary Diet,'" 320, 321. See also Young, "Federal Preemption and State Autonomy," 249–76.

92. Young, "Federal Preemption and State Autonomy," 261.

93. See generally Zellmer, "Preemption By Stealth," 1660–1723; Greve, Klick, Petrino, and Sevilla, "Preemption in the Rehnquist and Roberts Courts," 3, 8–9, 15–17; and Young, "'Ordinary Diet,'" 254–55, 262–63, 306.

The Supreme Court's annual calendar interpreting a range of diverse statutory and regulatory regimes has shrunk proportionally as the Court struggles to manage the litigation and conflict that the new laws and integrated regulations have created across diverse subject matters and industries. For example, from 1986 to 2005 the Rehnquist Court issued 2,079 opinions—or an average of 109 per term. The Roberts Court, in its first fifteen terms (2005–2020), issued 1,169 opinions, or 78 per term. The regular Court term runs from September to May annually. US Supreme Court, "Opinions," SupremeCourt.gov, accessed February 7, 2021, https://www.supremecourt.gov/opinions/opinions.aspx.

94. Young, "'Ordinary Diet,'" 253, 342.

95. *Egelhoff v. Egelhoff*, 532 U.S. 141, 160 (2001) (J. Breyer, dissenting; internal citations omitted).

96. Weiser, "Towards a Constitutional Architecture."

As one scholar characterized the dilemma of the complexities of interwoven integration that is forcing case-by-case and area-specific decision making:

> Modern regulatory programs put in place across a variety of fields ranging from nearly all environmental programs to telecommunications regulation to health care-and those now on the drawing board, ranging from insurance regulation to tobacco regulation—all embrace a unified federal structure that includes a role for state implementation. Significantly, these programs neither leave state authority unconstrained within its domain, as would a dual federalism program, nor displace such authority entirely with a unitary federal program, as would a preemptive federalism. Preemptive federalism, like dual federalism, views the federal government and the states as two separate spheres, but instead of leaving room for state regulation, it preempts all state authority and supplants it with a unitary federal regime. By crafting a middle ground solution between the extremes of dual federalism and preemptive federalism, Congress continues to outstrip existing constitutional rhetoric, which envisions a separation that does not exist in practice.

Weiser, "Towards a Constitutional Architecture."

97. Young, "Puzzling Persistence of Dual Federalism," 255; and Epstein and Greve, "Introduction: Preemption in Context," 2.

98. George Cameron Coggins and Michael E. Ward, "The Law of Wildlife Management on the Federal Public Lands," *Oregon Law Review* 60, nos. 1–2 (1981): 59, 84–85.

99. Young, "'Ordinary Diet,'" 269.

100. Quoting Davis, "Unmasking the Presumption in Favor of Preemption," 971.

101. Young, "'Ordinary Diet,'" 344.

14

The Roberts Court and the Development of Area-Specific Jurisprudence, 2005–2022

The confusing, *muddled* nature of the Supreme Court's preemption doctrine continued with the Roberts Court. Indeed, the modern Supreme Court does *not* review as many preemption cases as the Rehnquist Court did. However, because of the modern advances in science and technology in the Information Age, the Court continues to use a balkanized, *area-specific* approach when reviewing preemption cases in regulatory areas, such as banking and finance, pharmaceuticals, medical devices, and intellectual property. The Roberts Court displays a cautious, piecemeal approach to developing precedent, and two notable environmental cases—*Weyerhaeuser v. U.S. Fish and Wildlife Service* (2018) and *Cottonwood Environmental Law Center v. U.S. Forest Service* (9th Cir. 2015)—highlight these ideas as applied to wildlife.[1]

ROBERTS: THE MAN AND THE COURT

John G. Roberts Jr. was appointed chief justice by President George W. Bush and assumed office on September 29, 2005, at age fifty. Prior to that, he was a judge on the US Court of Appeals for the District of Columbia Circuit, following his role as principal deputy solicitor general of the United States. He was primarily raised in the Midwest, attended an academically rigorous Catholic boarding school, and graduated from Harvard College *summa cum laude* and Phi Beta Kappa. He graduated from Harvard Law School *magna cum laude* and served as managing editor of the *Harvard Law Review*. Thereafter he clerked for Justice William Rehnquist at the Supreme Court in the 1980–1981 term.[2]

The "first" Roberts Court (2005–2017), prior to the Trump administration's appointment of Justices Neil Gorsuch, Brett Kavanaugh, and Amy Coney Barrett, leaned toward propreemption, following in the ideological wake of the "second" Rehnquist Court. However, the second Roberts Court with the Trump appointments hardened as a conservative voting bloc, decidedly business-friendly and propreemption.[3] Moreover, "lawyerly preemption questions have assumed a distinctly ideological flavor . . . [preemption cases are more] likely to be contested . . . [because of] sharper and better lawyering on all sides . . . the failure of Congress to update old statutes . . . and the partial substitution of litigation for federal rulemaking as a principal means of industry regulation has been some of the issues."[4] An in-depth statistical analysis completed in 2016 reveals that Republican-appointed federal judges are three times more likely than Democratic judges to vote for preemption, especially in highly contested cases.[5] The Roberts Court preemption decisions clearly reflect this pattern. The 2016 statistical analysis of the Roberts Court from its inception in 2005, however, reflects only twenty-eight preemption cases over its first eleven years, versus the 108 cases for the Rehnquist Court.[6] (See Appendix 2) Republicans' inherent preference is to view federal preemption as generally deregulatory,[7] following in the wake of President Reagan's radical deregulation campaign, New Federalism. A number of renowned academic scholars have concluded that since 1976 the courts have trended toward protecting business interests, especially when aligned with the government's position in environmental cases.[8] This has been especially true of the Roberts Court.[9]

THE INFORMATION AGE BALKANIZES THE PREEMPTION DOCTRINE AND THREATENS THE 1947 *RICE* PRESUMPTION AGAINST PREEMPTION

As observed at the end of the last chapter, scholars have called both the Rehnquist and Roberts treatments of preemption a "muddle." The Information Age has fractured preemption jurisprudence into multiple area-specific regulatory spheres, and the doctrinal *Rice* standard has either been ignored or frequently misapplied. This has added further confusion to the presumption principle already balkanized into express versus implied preemption, obstacle versus impossibility, conflict preemption, tort, and frustration-of-purpose preemption.[10] This evolution from the latter part of the 1900s to today has frustrated our understanding of this area of the law, with layer upon layer of complex factual and legal considerations confusing the brightest reader. It's clearly muddled the Supreme Court's decisions, as the following will demonstrate, articulated without apology.

The Information Age could be said to have originated with the creation of IBM's first electronic computing machine in 1944, followed by the creation of the System/360 mainframe in 1964, IBM's first personal computer or "PC" in 1981, Texas Instruments in 1951, Sperry Univac's integrated circuit microchip in 1958, Ross Perot's Electronic Data System in 1962, Microsoft in 1975, Apple in 1976, Dell in 1984, and the growth of Silicon Valley. These, and the development of intellectual-property law and jurisprudence are all a reflection of society's need for high-speed computer support, data collection, and storage. The Information Age has generated massive, diverse, and complex litigation that has reached the Supreme Court and led to the creation of new preemption jurisprudence for a variety of area-specific factual patterns. This has further confused preemption jurisprudence, which was balkanized into eight to ten separate categorical distinctions (express versus implied, or obstacle versus impossibility, and so on).[11] Balkanization and fracturing of preemption jurisprudence into area-specific categories has undermined the effect of *Rice* and, thus, presents a threat to state autonomy.[12] Moreover, the *Rice* presumption was "a normative canon of statutory construction rather than a descriptive canon designed to get at what Congress actually intended. It's a legitimate way of giving effect to underenforced constitutional principles, and a political and procedural check on national power."[13]

In a denser and more complex federal regulatory environment, the present danger to a balance of federalism comes from the overexpansion of federal authority at the expense of state autonomy.[14] "Since the New Deal Court in 1937, overlapping state and federal regulations has become a norm for many, if not most, subjects."[15] The doctrine grounded in the Supremacy Clause, the functional heart of the Court's federalism doctrine, is supposed to manage the areas of overlapping authority. But as the number of areas of concurrent state and federal jurisdiction increased following the New Deal, courts struggled to apply the doctrine.[16] The preemption doctrine became a substitute for the old constitutional architecture of dual federalism, which could not address the concurrent jurisdictions of the states and federal government. "Preemption and its corollaries must now serve as substitutes—a presumption against preemption in lieu of enumerated powers constraints, implied preemption in lieu of exclusive federal jurisdiction."[17]

In response to the onslaught of technology and the proliferation of balkanized economic sectors, the Roberts Court appears to have developed a series of different sector-specific preemption jurisprudences tailored to economic and regulatory spheres, such as banking and securities, pharmaceutical, medical devices, Medicare, telecommunications, automotive, and so on. Prominent Washington appellate attorney Steffen N. Johnson observes, "One thread that seems to run through the [Roberts preemption] cases is a common-sense, non-formalistic approach to analyzing the purposes of Congress and the practical effects of state law."[18] Of the Court's trend in preemption jurisprudence, constitutional scholar William Eskridge concludes, "The larger project of preemption jurisprudence is to develop area-specific precepts for calibrating the state-federal balance."[19]

Professor Ernest A. Young concludes the following regarding his concern about the development of area-specific jurisprudence to resolve federal-state preemption cases:

> To some extent, area-specific doctrine is inevitable. Preemption stems from Congress's intent, which varies from statute to statute, and as the Court decides a series of cases under a particular statute, the Court will likely develop an area-specific picture of Congress's intent under that statute.... My own view, however, is that preemption questions are too critical to the overall balance of our federalism to leave them as matters of "ordinary" statutory construction, unconnected to the broader themes of national power and state autonomy.
>
> Our constitutional system has always left much, if not most, of the institutional architecture of federalism to be worked out through ordinary legislation; hence, federal statutes, administrative regulations, institutional practices, and judge-made doctrines play a greater role in defining the balance of state and federal power than do the entrenched provisions of the canonical constitution.... The enumerated limits of Congress's powers now play an extremely limited role in preserving the federal balance, and preemption has become the central question of our federalism. It is critical to approach preemption questions in ways that cohere with the broader concerns of constitutional federalism doctrine.... Indeed, the contemporary danger to our federal balance comes from the overexpansion of federal authority at the expense of state autonomy.[20]

ROBERTS CONTINUES TO MUDDLE ALONG ON PREEMPTION

The 1947 *Rice v. Santa Fe Elevator Corp.*[21] standard of presumption against preemption is being selectively applied (or ignored) by the Roberts Court, depending on the regulatory field being analyzed.[22] The Roberts Court has flip-flopped in its application of the *Rice* doctrine in many area-specific cases.[23] "The Justices evidently consider themselves bound to specific statutory interpretations in prior preemption opinions in which they concurred, but they often seem to treat discussions of interpretive methodology in those prior cases as dictum."[24] In a 2010 case upholding an Arizona law against express preemption from a federal statute, without invoking the "*Rice* doctrine per se, Chief Justice Roberts' opinion insisted that '[o]ur precedents establish that a high threshold must be met if a state law is to be preempted for conflicting with the purpose of a federal Act.'"[25] Hence, the role of statutory construction rather than purely constitutional interpretations has increased.[26] It is yet to be determined if the Roberts Court with three new conservative Republican associate justices appointed by President Trump will tend to favor broad preemption of state law. *Rice* remains the standard "as a rule of statutory construction—that is, a tool for interpreting the legal import of ambiguous statutory language" to preserve meaningful state autonomy, especially where historic police power is involved—but its scope and applicability have become controversial and inconsistent under Roberts.[27]

For example, the Roberts Court has struggled to apply the *Rice* rule to impossibility, obstacle, conflict, tort, and frustration-of-purpose preemption cases, all of which developed throughout the twentieth century as the preemption doctrine became balkanized and more confused.[28] However, in an express preemption case in 2008, the Court found a Maine statute prohibiting false advertising was not preempted by the federal Cigarette Labeling and Advertising Act. Justice Stevens's opinion incorporated the language of the *Rice* rule "that the historic police powers of the state [are] not to be superseded by [federal] law unless that was the clear and manifest purpose of Congress."[29] A year later, moreover, the Roberts Court said *Rice* remains the "cornerstone of our preemption jurisprudence."[30] Yet in a 2011 case involving a drug vaccine for children, the Court suggested that the *Rice* rule wasn't applicable in implied-preemption situations.[31] In *Bruesewitz* the justices dueled over the statutory construction of the applicable federal law and whether they were analyzing express or implied preemption.[32] The majority opinion by Justice Scalia concluded that the state claim based on common tort law was preempted by federal law, never mentioning *Rice*.[33]

The Roberts Court's vacillation over the *Rice* preemption doctrine is reflected in a survey of twenty-seven major preemption cases between 2007 and 2020. The *Rice* doctrine was referenced in only six cases,[34] three of which held that state actions were not preempted. In three others, federal law preempted state action. *Rice* was quoted in the dissents in four other cases,[35] two preempted state action, and two did not. The progeny of *Rice*—namely, *Wyeth v. Levine*—was referenced six times in majority opinions[36] and one time in dissents.[37] Again in the six cases, the Court was split three and three between state actions prevailing and preempted, and no reference was made to either *Rice*, *Wyeth*, or similar holdings in ten separate cases.[38] In summary, in sixteen of these cases, the Roberts Court found that state actions had not been preempted by federal law or regulations, and in eleven cases they found that they had been preempted. Reflective of the Roberts Court's selective use of *Rice*, not one of the above referenced cases cited the *Rice* case, notwithstanding their use of the *Rice* doctrine and *Rice*'s recent progeny, such as *Lopez, Morrison, Raich, GDF Realty, NAHB,* and *Printz*.

Notwithstanding the confusion these opinions have created,[39] a leading legal scholar on preemption is of the opinion "that the legitimacy, strength, and scope of a presumption against preemption remains a live issue."[40] "Even though the Justices are beginning to develop broadly principled frameworks [and unified treatment] for deciding preemption cases, the different methodological commitments held by individual Justices have thus far prevented the Court from coalescing around a single theory."[41] Nor is it likely that such a unified theory can ever be developed. Given that statutory regimes follow the changing character of Congress and successive presidential administrations, and considering the rapid technological advances and cartelization of the economy, with new business and organizational models emerging, and private actors arbitraging the regulatory boundaries, each requires a different preemption regime.[42]

WEYERHAEUSER AND *COTTONWOOD*: AGENCY OVERREACH?

Among the leading natural resource cases heard recently by the Supreme Court, *Weyerhaeuser v. U.S. Fish and Wildlife Service*[43] is notable for its unanimous decision and opinion by Chief Justice Roberts. The case considered whether the US Fish and Wildlife Service could designate an unoccupied area of 1,544 acres (never used historically) as critical habitat for future occupancy by the endangered dusky gopher frog. The Supreme Court preempted and struck down the FWS's decision, refusing to give deference to the agency's expert biological analysis underlying its habitat designation; deference had been accorded by the Fifth Circuit, following the *Chevron* deference doctrine. Moreover, the Supreme Court took note that FWS's estimate of $34 million in damages may be flawed, and on remand to the Fifth Circuit ordered a cost-benefit analysis. Moreover, it is noteworthy that the plaintiff, Weyerhaeuser Corp., the nation's largest timber company, held the rights to the timber on the 1,544 acres designated as critical habitat by the FWS and that the Roberts Court traditionally favors large-business interests.

The other notable federal natural resource case during the Roberts Court's 2015 term emanated from the Ninth Circuit: *Cottonwood Environmental Law Center v. U.S. Forest Service*.[44] The Forest Service initially closed a forest land-management plan during which it had completed a Section 7 consultation with the FWS regarding the Canada lynx. Later that year, the FWS listed the Canada lynx as endangered. The Ninth Circuit held that the Forest Service, as required by Section 7 of the ESA, had failed to reinitiate consultation with the FWS *after* the FWS had designated the Canada lynx as an endangered species. The Ninth Circuit ordered duplicative work wasting taxpayer dollars without benefit to the Canada lynx. The Court's decision so outraged Congress that it immediately enacted a law permanently reversing the Ninth Circuit's order and any similar cases.[45]

Notwithstanding the Ninth Circuit's rebuke from Congress, the opinion of both the majority and minority in *Cottonwood* paid tribute to the holding in *Tennessee Valley Association v. Hill*, written by Justice Burger in 1978, each quoting the operative language: "Congress has spoken in the plainest words, making it abundantly clear that the balance has been struck in favor of affording endangered species the highest of priorities. . . . In Congress's view, projects that jeopardized the continued existence of endangered species threatened incalculable harm: accordingly, it decided that the balance of hardships and the public interest tip heavily in favor of endangered species."[46]

Apart from the US Supreme Court, Federal District Courts and Courts of Appeals have addressed several natural resource issues of note. The Roberts Court has only considered the *Weyerhaeuser* and *Cottonwood* cases in the wildlife management context.[47] Like the Roberts Court, the lower courts have shown deference to precedent with four cases preempting state authority. Seven of these cases held that a state law or action was not preempted by a federal statute, as the courts leaned heavily into state authority.[48] The remaining cases,[49] plus two other cases of note, while preempting state authority, were careful to distinguish the states' broad historic police powers over their resident wildlife, so far as its exercise is not incompatible with or restrained by federal law.[50]

The Roberts Court has been consistent in its few state wildlife authority cases recognizing the traditional role of the state's sovereign jurisdiction, except for endangered species, which fall under federal jurisdiction. The court looks to the historic police powers of the state as the basis for their traditional and sovereign role of managing their wildlife, within which states had occupied originally as colonies well over a century before the adoption of the US Constitution in 1787 and the creation of a national federalist government. This reflects Chief Justice Roberts's temperament of adherence to precedent. Given that wildlife authority has traditionally and historically been a provenance of state jurisdiction, states can find comfort in the federal courts' and Chief Justice Roberts' predilection.

SUMMARY

The preemption doctrine continues on its unpredictable path. Indeed, the continued "balkanization" of the preemption doctrine into several discrete, *area-specific* categories has produced increasing doctrinal confusion over *when, how*, and to *what extent* federal power preempts state authority, especially in the context of wildlife. However, while the Roberts Court has inconsistently (and sometimes even incorrectly) applied the *Rice* presumption against preemption canon of statutory interpretation, the cases have been sharply limited (i.e., twenty-eight over the first eleven years) in proportion to the high number of preemption cases (i.e., 108) reviewed by the Rehnquist Court. In large measure, the Roberts Court has been more circumspect in its overall calibration of the state-federal balance in the general context of preemption. Thus the use of area-specific rules more clearly reflects the Roberts Court's general jurisprudence in producing the small, incremental development of precedent. Overall, while the case-by-case method to preemption contrasts markedly with the broad, ambitious approach from the Rehnquist Court, the Roberts Court has nonetheless been unpredictable in its doctrinal application. Because of the Court's area-specific rules in preemption cases, the future balance of state-federal authority will be intensely debated, discussed, and decided. And yet the looming question remains: What *exactly* will the future of preemption hold?

NOTES

1. *Weyerhaeuser v. U.S. Fish and Wildlife Service*, 139 S. Ct. 361 (2019); *Cottonwood Environmental Law Center v. U.S. Forest Service*, 789 F.3d 1075 (9th Cir. 2015).
2. "John Roberts," Wikipedia, last modified September 20, 2021, https://en.wikipedia.org/wiki/John_Roberts.
3. Young, "'Ordinary Diet of the Law,'" 3, 10, 17, 25, 27.
4. Greve, Klick, Petrino, and Sevilla, "Preemption in the Rehnquist and Roberts Courts," 31–32.
5. Greve, Klick, Petrino, and Sevilla, "Preemption in the Rehnquist and Roberts Courts," 5n17.
6. Greve, Klick, Petrino, and Sevilla, "Preemption in the Rehnquist and Roberts Courts," 8.

See appendix 2 for a graphic survey of preemption cases decided by the US Supreme Court.

7. Greve, Klick, Petrino, and Sevilla, "Preemption in the Rehnquist and Roberts Courts," 342.

8. Ruhl, "The Endangered Species Act's Fall," 522–23; Richard E. Levy and Robert L. Glicksman, "Judicial Activism and Restraint in the Supreme Court's Environmental Law Decisions," *Vanderbilt Law Review* 42, no. 2 (1989): 421–22, https://scholarship.law.vanderbilt.edu/cgi/viewcontent.cgi?article=2559&context=vlr; and Richard J. Lazarus, "Thirty Years of Environmental Protection Law in the Supreme Court: Fifth Annual Lloyd K. Garrison Lecture on Environmental Law," *Pace Environmental Law Review* 17, no. 1 (1999): 12, https://digitalcommons.pace.edu/cgi/viewcontent.cgi?article=1276&context=pelr.

9. See Jonathan H. Adler, "Business, the Environment, and the Roberts Court: A Preliminary Assessment," *Santa Clara Law Review* 49, no. 4 (2009): 943–78, https://digitalcommons.law.scu.edu/lawreview/vol49/iss4/2/; Stephen M. Johnson, "The Roberts Court and the Environment," *Boston College Environmental Affairs Law Review* 37, no. 2 (2010): 317–63, https://lawdigitalcommons.bc.edu/cgi/viewcontent.cgi?article=1053&context=ealr; and Peter M. Manus, "Five against the Environment," *New England Law Review* 44, no. 2 (2010): 221–48.

10. For a detailed explanation of each type of preemption, see Bratton, "Preemption Doctrine," 623, and see the references in footnote 657 therein.

11. See generally Young, "'Ordinary Diet of the Law'"; and Greve, Klick, Petrino, and Sevilla, "Preemption in the Rehnquist and Roberts Courts."

12. Young, "Federal Preemption and State Autonomy," 262.

13. Young, "Federal Preemption and State Autonomy," 265.

14. Young, "Federal Preemption and State Autonomy," 258 nn. 20, 323.

15. Robert Schapiro, "From Dualism to Polyphony," in *Preemption Choice: The Theory, Law and Reality of Federalism's Core Question*, ed. William W. Buzbee (Cambridge: Cambridge University Press, 2009), 33, 41.

16. Greve, Klick, Petrino, and Sevilla, "Preemption in the Rehnquist and Roberts Courts," 254.

17. Epstein and Greve, "Introduction: Preemption in Context," 21.

18. Steffen N. Johnson, "The Roberts Court and Preemption Decisions," *The National Law Journal Supreme Court Brief*, August 7, 2013, https://www.winston.com/images/content/3/9/v2/39411/005081305-Winston.pdf.

19. William N. Eskridge Jr., "Vetogates, Chevron, Preemption," *Notre Dame Law Review* 83, no. 1441 (2008): 1441, 1445.

20. Young, "'Ordinary Diet of the Law,'" 253, 306.

21. 331 U.S. 218 (1947).

22. Young, "'Ordinary Diet of the Law,'" 334; see also Johnson, "The Roberts Court and Preemption Decisions."

23. Young, "'Ordinary Diet of the Law,'" 334.

24. Young, "'Ordinary Diet of the Law,'" 334.

25. Young, "'Ordinary Diet of the Law,'" 328 (quoting Chamber of Commerce v. Whiting, 563 U.S. 582, 607 (2011).

26. Christopher Shortell, "The End of the Federalism Five? Statutory Interpretation and the Roberts Court," *Publius* 42, no. 3 (2012): 516.

27. Shortell, "The End of the Federalism Five?", 265–83, 274, 323; Young, "'Ordinary Diet of the Law,'" 307–10.

28. Young, "'Ordinary Diet of the Law,'" 274–78.
29. *Altria Group, Inc. v. Good*, 555 U.S. 70, 77 (2008) (quoting *Rice v. Santa Fe Elevator Corp.*, 331 U.S. at 230.
30. *Wyeth v. Levine*, 555 U.S. 555, 565 (2009).
31. *Bruesewitz v. Wyeth LLC*, 562 U.S. 223 (2011).
32. 562 U.S. 223 (2011).
33. Young, "'Ordinary Diet of the Law,'" 292–97.
34. *Hillman v. Maretta*, 569 U.S. 483 (2013); *Arizona v. Inter Tribal Council of Arizona, Inc.*, 570 U.S. 1 (2013); *Arizona v. United States*, 567 U.S. 387 (2012); *Wyeth v. Levine; Cuomo v. Clearing House Association*, 557 U.S. 519 (2009); Altria Group, 555 U.S. 70 (2008).
35. *Mutual Pharmaceutical Co. v. Bartlett*, 570 U.S. 472 (2013); *PLIVA v. Mensing*, 564 U.S. 604 (2011); Bruesewitz, 562 U.S. 223 (2011).
36. *Virginia Uranium, Inc. v. Warren*, 139 S. Ct. 1894 (2019); *Oneok v. Learjet*, 575 U.S. 373 (2015); *American Trucking Associations v. City of Los Angeles*, 569 U.S. 641 (2013); *Williamson v. Mazda Motor of America*, 562 U.S. 323 (2011); *AT&T Mobility v. Concepcion*, 563 U.S. 333 (2011); PLIVA, 564 U.S. 604 (2011).
37. PLIVA, 564 U.S. 604 (2011)
38. *Rutledge v. Pharmaceutical Care Mgmt. Ass'n.*, 140 S. Ct. 812 (2020); *Utah Native Plant Society v. U.S. Forest Service*, 923 F.3d 860 (10th Cir. 2019); *Weyerhaeuser v. U.S. Fish and Wildlife Service*, 139 S. Ct. 361 (2019); *Northwest Inc. v. Ginsberg*, 572 U.S. 273 (2014); *Dan's City Used Cars v. Pelkey*, 569 U.S. 215 (2013); *WOS v. E.M.A*, 568 U.S. 627 (2013); *Tarrant Regional Water District v. Herrmann*, 569 U.S. 614 (2013); *National Meat Association v. Harris*, 565 U.S. 452 (2012); *National Federation of Independent Business v. Sebelius*, 567 U.S. 519 (2012); *Massachusetts v. EPA*, 549 U.S. 497 (2007).
39. During the 2010 court term, Justice Clarence Thomas said, "the court's reliance on the [*Rice*] presumption against preemption has waned in the express preemption context" because the presumption results in "artificially narrow construction[s]" of preemption provisions that "distort the statutory text." *Altria Group, Inc. v. Good*, at 98, 101 (J. Thomas, dissenting), as quoted in Young, "'Ordinary Diet of the Law,'" 277.
40. Young, "'Ordinary Diet of the Law,'" 278.
41. Young, "'Ordinary Diet of the Law,'" 255, 256.
42. Epstein and Greve, "Introduction: Preemption in Context," 19–20. See also Scott, "Federalism and Financial Regulation," 139–65; and Young, "Federal Preemption and State Autonomy," 261.
43. Weyerhaeuser, 139 S. Ct. 361 (2019).
44. 789 F.3d 1075 (9th Cir. 2015).
45. US Congress, *Consolidated Appropriations Act*, 2018, Pub. L. No. 115–141, 132 Stat. 348 (2018), https://www.congress.gov/115/plaws/publ141/PLAW-115publ141.pdf.
46. Cottonwood, 789 F.3d at 1091, 1093.
47. While not a preemption case per se, indirectly the Roberts Court did decide such a case in *Herrera v. Wyoming* (139 S. Ct. 1686 [2019]). A member of the

Crow tribe was convicted of poaching an elk out of season, and in a national forest. Herrera argued that a 1868 treaty gave the Crow tribe the perpetual right to hunt in that national forest. The State of Wyoming argued that the Wyoming Statehood Act extinguished those treaty rights and that they had authority over the natural resources within their state. The Court held that the Crow treaty rights survived. Hence, indirectly Wyoming's authority was preempted by the treaty, which was not directly at issue in the case.

48. *Fednav Ltd. v. Chester*, 547 F.3d 607 (6th Cir. 2008); *Safari Club International v. Jewell*, 960 F. Supp.2d 17 (D.C. Cir 2013); *Bohmker v. Oregon*, 903 F.3d 1029 (9th Cir 2018); *Art and Antique Dealers League of America v. Beggos*, 394 F. Supp.3d 447 (S.D.N.Y. 2019); *Center for Biological Diversity v. Bernhardt*, 946 F.3d 553 (9th Cir 2019); *Utah Native Plant Society v. U.S. Forest Service*, 923 F.3d 860 (10th Cir. 2019); *Virginia Uranium, Inc. v. Warren*, 139 S. Ct. 1894 (2019).

49. *Gonzales v. Raich*, 545 U.S. 1 (2005); *UFO Chuting of Hawaii v. Smith*, 508 F.3d 1189 (9th Cir 2007); *Defenders of Wildlife v. Salazar*, 651 F. 3d 112 (D.C. Cir 2011); *PETPO v. U.S. Fish and Wildlife Service*, 852 F. 3d 990 (10th Cir 2017).

For a contextual appreciation of the federal courts' leanings on preemption, two other preemption nonwildlife cases of note are *National Federation of Independent Business v. Sebelius* (567 U.S. 519 [2012]) and *United States v. Arizona* (119 F. Supp 3d 955 [D. Az 2014]).

50. Utah Native Plant Society, 923 F.3d 860 (10th Cir. 2019).

15

The Future of Federal Preemption of State Authority over Wildlife and the Presumption Against Preemption Doctrine in Wildlife Cases

There is a specific analytic frame for determining preemption in wildlife authority cases and preserving the delicate arrangement of federalism. Core *threshold* questions of constitutional law range from enumerated powers to the scope of traditional and historical functions. Federal wildlife regulation must be examined through the prism of the Commerce Clause, as well as the Property Clause if federal land is involved, in order to establish a firm and holistic foundation for predicting the future of wildlife preemption cases.

THE ANALYSIS FOR DETERMINING PREEMPTION IN WILDLIFE AUTHORITY AND PRESERVING FEDERALISM

From the deep reservoir of federal law dating back to the first Supreme Court in 1789, an abundance of jurisprudence on "preemption" has developed, managing the conflict between federal and state laws. Only a small percentage of preemption cases have been related to wildlife. However, from all the diverse conflict cases in many subject areas, substantive principles of preemption jurisprudence have been developed that apply to federal and state laws governing the control and management of wildlife and natural resource management. But as Professor Young notes, "the court's record of activism on behalf of the states as against national power is neither impressive nor durable. Although the court has been a nationalizing force in our history far more often than it has befriended the states, it has occasionally acted to check national power."[1] Speaking for the majority, Judge Wilkinson of the Fourth Circuit Court of Appeals said, "It is as threatening to federalism for courts to erode the historic national role over scarce resource conservation as it is for Congress to usurp traditional state prerogatives in such areas as education and domestic relations. Courts seeking to enforce the structural constraints of federalism must respect the balance on both sides."[2]

The analysis of federalism in wildlife management starts with a recognition that the US Constitution organized two separate but sovereign spheres of government:

> Though on the surface the idea may seem counterintuitive, it was the insight of the Framers that freedom was enhanced by the creation of two governments, not one. In the compound republic of America, the power surrendered by the people is first divided between two distinct governments, and then the portion allotted to each subdivided among distinct and separate departments. Hence a double security arises to the rights of the people. The different governments will control each other, at the same time that each will be controlled by itself.[3]

> Each State in the Union is sovereign as to all the powers reserved. It must necessarily be so, because the United States have no claim to any authority but such as the States have surrendered to them.[4]

The first principle of preserving federalism is to ask the obvious questions: Does the federal government have the authority to act where the states have acted? Is there an actual conflict between state and federal laws, or can the two separate laws—one federal, one state—function concurrently? Next, has each sovereign sphere stayed within its constitutional powers? For Congress and the federal government, those powers are specifically enumerated by the Constitution. Wildlife law conflict analysis has fallen within one of the following enumerated provisions of the Constitution: Supremacy Clause, Commerce Clause, Property Clause, Necessary and Proper Clause, Tax Clause, Treaty Clause, Spending Clause, and the Tenth Amendment. If the disputed action of Congress exceeds the bounds of one of these provisions, it is void, and state law prevails. Conversely, if a state government has regulated less strictly than has the federal government, then the state law or regulation will be declared null and void.[5]

In determining if an act of Congress falls within one of its enumerated powers, a principal question is whether the subject matter is one *traditionally and historically* occupied by the state: "[We] must carefully evaluate legislation in light of our federal system of government. 'The Constitution requires a distinction between what is truly national and what is truly local.' We must particularly scrutinize regulated activity that 'falls within an area of the law where States historically have been sovereign and countenance of the asserted federal power would blur the boundaries between the spheres of federal and state authority.'"[6]

If that answer is unclear, then the Court searches for which sovereign power has *predominantly* regulated the subject's field or occupied it historically. This search starts with a presumption against preemption based on the Supremacy Clause.[7] "The *Rice* presumption becomes an interpretive default rule—a 'thumb on the scale' representing the value of state autonomy . . . it is the tie-breaker."[8] "When the text of a preemption clause is susceptible of more than one plausible reading, courts ordinarily accept the reading that disfavors preemption."[9]

The third principle in preserving federalism asks whether or not Congress was clear and manifest in its intent to preempt state authority. Congress's enactment may be invalidated upon a plain showing that it has exceeded its constitutional bounds.[10] If congressional intent was not clearly expressed, was it implied? Does the conflict present an irreconcilable impossibility for both state and federal law to govern concurrently and therefore require federal preemption?

> [W]e start with the assumption that the historic police powers of the States were not to be superseded by the Federal Act unless that was a clear and manifest purpose of Congress. . . . Or the Act of Congress may touch a field in which the federal interest is so dominant that the federal system will be assumed to preclude enforcement of state laws on the same subject. . . . It is often a perplexing question whether Congress has precluded state action, or by the choice of selective regulatory measures has left the police power of the States undisturbed except as the state and federal regulations collide.[11]

The three general principles of preserving federalism as described provide the analytical framework used by the courts for evaluating preemption and federalism in the area of wildlife management. The analysis readily answers the question of which sovereign sphere of law prevails and preempts the other or whether they concurrently regulate together.

WILDLIFE AUTHORITY AND THE REACH OF THE COMMERCE CLAUSE

The majority of wildlife cases revolve around the reach of the Commerce Clause, which until 1937[12] was restrictively interpreted.

> Great changes had occurred in the way business was carried on in this country. Enterprises that had once been local or at most regional in nature had become national in scope. But the doctrinal change also reflected a view that earlier Commerce Clause cases artificially had constrained the authority of Congress to regulate interstate commerce. . . . In *Jones & Laughlin Steel*, the Court warned

that the scope of the interstate commerce power "must be considered in the light of our dual system of government and may not be extended so as to embrace effects upon interstate commerce so indirect and remote that to embrace them, in view of our complex society, would effectually obliterate the distinction between what is national and what is local and create a completely centralized government.[13]

The courts look initially for a commercial nexus and a plain showing of congressional intent.

[The] ESA is an economic regulatory scheme. . . . Moreover, ESA is "truly national" in scope. . . . ESA's protection of endangered species is economic in nature. As noted, ESA's drafters were concerned by the "incalculable" value of the genetic heritage that might be lost absent regulation.[14]

Given the existing economic and commercial activity involving [endangered species] and wildlife generally, Congress could find that conservation of endangered species and economic growth are mutually reinforcing. It is simply not beyond the power of Congress to conclude that a healthy environment actually boosts industry by allowing commercial development of our natural resources.[15]

[A] review of Commerce Clause case law demonstrates that in those cases where we have sustained federal regulation of intrastate activity based upon the activity's substantial effects on interstate commerce, the activity in question has been some sort of economic endeavor.[16]

It took until 1995 for the case of *United States v. Lopez* to provide three definitive criteria to measure the reach of the Commerce Clause: (1) Does the activity have a substantial effect on interstate commerce so that regulations are essential to protect it from burdens and obstructions, including the channels used for interstate commerce? (2) Does the activity in question threaten instrumentalities of interstate commerce, including persons or things, even if they come from intrastate activity? (3) Does the activity have a substantial relationship to interstate commerce?[17] Since 1995, these three questions have become doctrinal in the application of the Commerce Clause to questionable activities. As to which federal entities can preempt state law, federal administrative-agency regulations exercising authority delegated by Congress can preempt state law, as can the president via executive order, with the federal courts being the final arbiter on judicial review of both state and federal challenges.[18]

The key contemporary cases—the majority of which involve wildlife issues—that collectively constitute the fortress of state authority limiting federal preemption as all discussed herein include the following: *Toomer v. Witsell, Kleppe v. New Mexico, Douglas v. Seacoast Products, Baldwin v.*

Montana, Foster-Fountain Packing v. Haydel, Hughes v. Oklahoma, Organized Fisherman of Florida v. Hodel, Tangier Sound Watermen's Association v. Douglas (see for a historically forensic analysis of state authority cases), *Defenders of Wildlife v. Andrus, Palila v. Hawaii, Gregory v. Ashcroft*, which reinforced the *Rice v. Santa Fe Elevator* presumption against preemption, *Medtronics, Inc. v. Lohr, Printz v. United States, United States v. Lopez, United States v. Morrison, California Coastal Commission v. Granite Rock Co., NAHB v. Babbitt, Rancho Viejo v. Norton, GDF Realty v. Norton, Utah Native Plant Society v. U.S. Fish and Wildlife Service, Gibbs v. Babbitt, Wyoming v. United States, Reno v. Condon, Federal Maritime Commission v. South Carolina State Ports Authority, Alden v. Maine, Seminole Tribe v. Florida,* and, of course, the Fish and Wildlife Coordination Act of 1934.[19]

WILDLIFE AUTHORITY ON FEDERAL LANDS AND THE PROPERTY CLAUSE

Wildlife conflicts relating to endangered species on lands publicly owned by the federal government have governance standards for wildlife management based on the Constitution and federal court decisions.[20] Endangered species have historically been the domain of the federal government.[21] The language of *Tennessee Valley Authority v. Hill* in 1978 could not have made it any clearer:

> [The Congress in 1966 declared] the preservation of endangered species a national policy.
>
> Examination of the language, history, and structure of the legislation under review here indicates beyond doubt that Congress intended endangered species to be afforded the highest of priorities. . . . The Endangered Species Act of 1973 represented the most comprehensive legislation for the preservation of endangered species ever enacted by any nation. . . . Congress has spoken in the plainest of words, making it abundantly clear that the balance has been struck in favor of affording endangered species the highest of priorities thereby adopting a policy which it described as "institutionalized caution."[22]

The respective federal courts of appeal have rigorously followed the precedent laid down by Chief Justice Burger in *Hill*. The Fourth Circuit Court of Appeals in 2000 said that "The preservation of endangered species is historically a federal function."[23]

In 2003, the D.C. Court of Appeals following the *Gibbs* cases stated,

> The protection of endangered species cannot fairly be described as a power "which the Founders denied the National Government and reposed in the

States." Rather, "the preservation of endangered species is historically a federal function" ... and invalidating this application of the ESA "would call into question the historic power of the federal government to preserve scarce resources in one locality for the future benefit of all Americans." We therefore agree ... that to sustain challenges of this nature "would require courts to move abruptly from preserving traditional state roles to dismantling historic federal ones."

"[A]lthough States have important interest in regulating wildlife and natural resources within their borders, this authority is shared with the Federal Government when the Federal Government exercises one of its enumerated constitutional powers." Moreover, while "states and localities possess broad regulatory and zoning authority over land within their jurisdictions, ... [i]t is well established ... that Congress can regulate even private land use for environmental and wildlife conservation." Tracing a hundred-year history of congressional involvement in natural resource conservation, "it is clear from our laws and precedent that federal regulation of endangered wildlife does not trench impermissibly upon state powers."[24]

The Fourth Circuit in its 2000 opinion further stated,

[It] does not invade traditional state concerns—it is simply one small part of an ongoing federal effort to preserve the scarcest natural resources for future generations. ... Given the history of federal regulation over wildlife and related environmental concerns, it is hard to imagine how this anti-taking regulation trespasses impermissibly upon traditional state functions—either control over wildlife or local land use. *Lopez* and *Morrison* properly caution that States should receive judicial protection from unconstitutional federal encroachments on state matters. *Yet endangered wildlife regulation has not been an exclusive or primary state function.*

The conservation of scarce natural resources is an appropriate and well-recognized area of federal regulation. The federal government has been involved in a variety of conservation efforts since the beginning of this century. In 1900, Congress passed the Lacey Act, which provided penalties for the taking of wildlife in violation of state laws. The Migratory Bird Treaty Act of 1918 forbade all takings of numerous bird species and explicitly preempted state laws. Furthermore, Congress has regulated wildlife on nonfederal property through numerous statutes, including the Bald Eagle Protection Act of 1940, which prohibits, inter alia, the taking, possession, selling, or exporting of bald eagles or any of their parts. Similarly, the Marine Mammal Protection Act of 1972 regulates the taking of marine mammals and restricts the importing of marine mammals and their products through an elaborate system of permits. The Magnuson Fishery Conservation and Management Act of 1976 provides national standards for fishery conservation and management along with an elaborate system of enforcement.

Post-Lopez cases addressing wildlife conservation statutes uphold the exercise of agency power over private land use in order to conserve endangered species. ... In sum, it is clear from our laws and precedent that federal regulation of endangered wildlife does not trench impermissibly upon state powers. Rather, the federal government possesses a historic interest in such regulation—an interest that has repeatedly been recognized by the federal courts. . . . '[P]rotection of endangered species is not a matter that can be handled in the absence of coherent national and international policies: the results of a series of unconnected and disorganized policies and programs by various states might well be confusion compounded.' . . . If the federal government cannot regulate the taking of an endangered or threatened species on private land, its conservation and preservation efforts would be limited to only federal lands. A ruling to this effect would place in peril the entire federal regulatory scheme for wildlife and natural resource conservation.[25]

In 1997 the D.C. Court of Appeals who addressed the Commerce Clause connection to wildlife:

The federal courts repeatedly concluded that congressional efforts at protecting endangered and migratory species are constitutional under the Commerce Clause. See *Andrus v. Allard* (discussing the Migratory Bird Treaty Act and noting that the "assumption that the national commerce power does not reach migratory wildlife is clearly flawed"); *Leslie Salt Co. v. United States*. ("The commerce clause power . . . is broad enough to extend [federal] jurisdiction to local waters which may provide habitat to migratory birds and endangered species.") ("Congress does have power under the Commerce Clause to regulate wildlife and endangered species."); see also *Hughes v. Oklahoma*, (holding that state regulations of intrastate wildlife are within [reach of] dormant Commerce Clause).[26]

Wildlife management on federal lands of wildlife *not* classified as endangered species or on land *not* classified as critical habitat has been the provenance of state authority, except when the federal government has found it necessary to intercede under the Property Clause of the Constitution. "Although States have important interests in regulating wildlife and natural resources within their borders, this authority is shared with the Federal Government when the Federal Government exercises one of its enumerated constitutional powers, such as treaty making [or to protect federal lands]."[27]

Each federal natural resource and land management agency has in its organic act or enabling legislation—either in a savings clause or by express language—a preemption of state authority in areas the federal agency regulates. They all establish engagement points for state and local governments to participate in the wildlife management and land use planning processes, but the entire process is conditioned on federal primacy. These agency laws include the following: the 1897 Organic Act establishing national forests; the Multiple Use Sustained Yield Act of 1960 (MUSYA); the National Forest

Service Management Act of 1976 (NFMA); the 2012 Forest Service Planning Rule; the 2005 Forest Service Cooperation in Wildlife Management Regulation; the 1916 Organic Act creating the National Park Service; the National Park Service 2006 Management Policy; that 1976 Federal Land Policy and Management Act (FLPMA—considered Bureau of Land Management's Organic Act); areas of critical environmental concern created by FLPMA; the Bureau of Land Management (BLM) 2008 Special Status Species Management Policy designated in the BLM Management Manual; the National Landscape Conservation System administered by the BLM, roughly 4.1 million acres; and roughly 9.5 million acres of national monuments, codified in the Omnibus Public Land Management Act of 2009; the Wilderness Act of 1964; and the Alaska National Interest Land Conservation Act of 1980 (ANILCA).[28]

Beyond established jurisprudence regarding the control of wildlife on federal lands, a major block of congressional enactments concerning federalism falls under the US Constitution's Treaty Clause, which provides that the president

> "shall have the Power . . . to make Treaties, provided two thirds of the Senators present concur." In recognition of the international nature of wildlife conservation, the United States has entered into several landmark wildlife treaties within the past century, which Congress has implemented through domestic legislation. With respect to the management of wildlife on federal lands, the most notable of these include the Migratory Bird Treaty of 1918 and the Convention on International Trade in Endangered Species of Wild Fauna and Flora (CITES), [*and the Endangered Species Act of 1973*]. Other international provisions include the Agreement on the Conservation of Polar Bears, the Pacific Salmon Treaty, the Northwest Atlantic Fisheries Treaty, the Migratory Bird and Game Mammal Treaty with Mexico, and the International Convention for the Regulation of Whaling." These treaties are implemented through the Marine Mammal Protection Act, the Magnuson-Stevens Fishery Conservation and Management Act, the Whaling Convention Act, and other pieces of domestic legislation.[29]

On the subject of preempting state law, in a 1928 case[30] the Supreme Court held that the federal government had the right to manage wildlife on its public lands, notwithstanding New Mexico state law. Again, in 1932 a similar ruling preempting North Carolina law gave the federal government control over wildlife in a national forest.[31] In the 1976 case of *Kleppe v. New Mexico*, addressing overpopulating wild horses and burros on federal land, the Supreme Court provided an overview of the reach of the Constitution's Property Clause on public land:

While the furthest reaches of the power granted by the Property Clause have not yet been definitively resolved, we have repeatedly observed that "(t)he power over the public land thus entrusted to Congress is without limitations. . . . The decided cases have supported this expansive reading. . . . And even over public land within the States, "(t)he general government doubtless has a power over its own property analogous to the police power of the several states, and the extent to which it may go in the exercise of such power is measured by the exigencies of the particular case" . . . In short, Congress exercises the powers both of a proprietor and of a legislature over the public domain. . . . Although the Property Clause does not authorize "an exercise of a general control over public policy in a State," it does permit "an exercise of the complete power which Congress has over particular public property entrusted to it." In our view, the "complete power" that Congress has over public lands necessarily includes the power to regulate and protect the wildlife living there. . . .[32]

Absent consent or cession a State undoubtedly retains jurisdiction over federal lands within its territory, but Congress equally surely retains the power to enact legislation respecting those lands pursuant the Property Clause. . . . And when Congress so acts, the federal legislation necessarily overrides conflicting state laws under the Supremacy Clause. As we said in *Camfield v. United States*, in response to a somewhat different claim: "A different rule would place the public domain of the United States completely at the mercy of state legislation." . . . The Federal Government does not assert exclusive jurisdiction over the public lands in New Mexico, and the State is free to enforce its criminal and civil laws on those lands. But where those state laws conflict with the Wild Free-roaming Horses and Burros Act, or with other legislation passed pursuant to the Property Clause, the law is clear: The state laws must recede. . . .[33]

Unquestionably the States have broad trustee and police powers over wild animals within their jurisdictions. . . . But, those powers exist only "in so far as (their) exercise may be not incompatible with, or restrained by, the rights conveyed to the federal government by the constitution." "No doubt it is true that as between a State and its inhabitants the State may regulate the killing and sale of (wildlife), but it does not follow that its authority is exclusive of paramount powers. . . . We hold today that the Property Clause also gives Congress the power to protect wildlife on the public lands, state law notwithstanding.[34]

The more recent 2002 case of *Wyoming v. United States* clearly states that the Tenth Amendment did not reserve to the states an unrestricted right to manage wildlife on public lands. States retain the authority to regulate the harvest of wildlife, set seasons and bag limits, and generally control game on federal lands absent conflict with the plenary powers of the national government. There has not been a manifest "federal interest" in regulating wildlife since the beginning of the Republic, and, indeed, wildlife management is a field "which the States have traditionally occupied."[35]

Historically, States have possessed "broad trustee and police powers over the . . . wildlife within their borders, including . . . wildlife found on Federal lands within a State." But those powers are not constitutionally based. The Property Clause of the United States Constitution delegates to Congress (thus the Tenth Amendment does not reserve to the States) "the Power to dispose of and make all needful Rules and Regulations respecting the Territory or other Property belonging to the United States." Of course, the Property Clause alone does not withdraw federal land within a State from the jurisdiction of the State. ("The Property Clause itself does not automatically conflict with all state regulation of federal land."). "[F]or many purposes a State has civil and criminal jurisdiction over lands within its limits belonging to the United States." The Property Clause simply empowers Congress to exercise jurisdiction over federal land within a State if Congress so chooses. . . .[36]

Notably, Congress' power in this regard is "plenary." State jurisdiction over federal land "does not extend to any matter that is not consistent with full power in the United States to protect its lands, to control their use and to prescribe in what manner others may acquire rights in them." If Congress so chooses, federal legislation, together with the policies and objectives encompassed therein, necessarily override and preempt conflicting state laws, policies, and objectives under the Constitution's Supremacy Clause ("'A different rule would place the public domain of the United States completely at the mercy of [the State])'" In view of the foregoing, we believe the point painfully apparent that the Tenth Amendment does not reserve to the State of Wyoming the right to manage wildlife on the national elk range regardless of the circumstances.[37]

In 2017 Professor Martin Nie and five coauthors published an extensive review of federal wildlife authority on public lands, thoroughly addressing this issue.[38] The article, however, brought serious rebuke by Lane Kisonak,[39] counsel for the Association of Fish and Wildlife Agencies.

To assert that state agencies and AFWA "fundamental[ly] misunderstand[]" the federal dimensions of wildlife management is to ignore the ambiguities in federal case law that feed this very debate. . . Nie et al., by glossing over ambiguities in federal case law and disregarding the exigencies for informal state-federal collaboration, seeks to advance a misunderstanding not only of wildlife conservation but also of federal and state relations in general, and state regulatory organizations' role within that framework. Moreover, Nie et al. have unnecessarily exaggerated its perception of conflict, becoming self-fulfilling to a sympathetic audience, without advancing the important conservation measures needed to sustain fish and wildlife populations on the landscape.[40]

SUMMARY

The future of federal preemption of state authority over wildlife will largely hinge on how the new Supreme Court will interpret the scope of federal power under the Constitution. Operating under the historical assumption that both states and the federal government retain legitimate, dual sovereignty over wildlife affairs, the Supreme Court will have to wrestle with three primary questions: *First*, does the federal government have the constitutional authority to act where the states have acted? *Second*, has each sovereign government acted pursuant to its vested constitutional powers? *Third*, was Congress clear and manifest in its intent to preempt state authority? Most importantly, when the question of authority is ambiguous, the *Rice* principle—presumption against preemption—controls the analysis, tipping the scales in favor of state sovereignty over traditional areas of police powers. Indeed, while the federal government will likely continue to *predominantly* regulate the domain over endangered species—as it has been authorized to do so since the Endangered Species Act of 1973—the broader regulation of wildlife will likely continue to be shared *concurrently* with states. Accordingly, the Supreme Court's answers to these pressing and unique questions will guide the future of the preemption and federalism doctrines.

NOTES

1. Young, "Making Federalism Doctrine," 1753 (quoting Vicki C. Jackson, "Narratives of Federalism: Of Continuities and Comparative Constitutional Experience," *Duke Law Journal* 51, no. 1 (2001): 223, 280, https://scholarship.law.duke.edu/cgi/viewcontent.cgi?article=1126&context=dlj).
2. *Gibbs v. Babbitt*, 214 F.3d 483, 505 (4th Cir. 2000).
3. *GDF Realty Investments, Ltd. v. Norton*, 326 F.3rd 622, 628 (5th Cir. 2003).
4. *United States v. Lopez*, 514 U.S. 549, 585 (1995).
5. Young, "'Ordinary Diet of the Law,'" 342.

For preemption of a state law less protective than the Endangered Species Act, see *United States v. Glenn-Colusa Irrigation District*, 788 F. Supp 1126, 1134 (E.D. Cal. 1992).

6. Babbitt, 214 F.3d at 499 (citations omitted).
7. See *Building & Construction Trades Council v. Associated Builders & Contractors*, 507 U.S. 218, 224 (1993) ("We are reluctant to infer preemption"); Maryland v. Louisiana, 451 U.S. 725, 746 (1981) ("Consideration under the Supremacy Clause starts with the basic assumption that Congress did not intend to displace state law"); and Young, "'Ordinary Diet of the Law,'" 332, n. 417.
8. Young, "'Ordinary Diet of the Law,'" 271, 274–75.

9. The *Altria Group, Inc. v. Good*, 555 U.S. 70, 77 (2008) (quoting *Bates v. Dow Agrosciences* LLC, 544 U.S. 431, 449 [2005]).

And see Young, "'Ordinary Diet of the Law,'" 276: It should be noted that in the 2008 Altria Group case "the court rejected a strong push from propreemption *amicus curiae* [friends of the court] to eliminate the presumption [against preemption] in express preemption cases." This is a clear indication that the Roberts Court in its early years considered the *Rice* principle doctrinal jurisprudence.

10. Morrison, 529 U.S. 598, 607 (2000).

11. *Rice v. Santa Fe Elevator Corp.*, 331 U.S. 218, 231 (1947) (citations omitted). See also *School Board of Avoyelles Parish v. United States*, 647 F. 3d 570, 582 (5th Cir. 2011).

12. See *N.L.R.B. v. Jones & Laughlin Steel Corp.*, 301 U.S. 1, 37 (1937).

13. *Lopez*, 514 U.S. at 556.

14. *GDF Realty*, 326 F.3rd at 639–40.

15. *Babbitt*, 214 F.3d 483, (4th Cir. 2000).

16. *Morrison*, 529 U.S. at 611 (citations omitted).

17. See *Lopez*, 514 U.S. at 558–59.

18. Young, "'Ordinary Diet of the Law,'" 278–81.

19. *Toomer v. Witsell*, 334 U.S. 385 (1948); *Kleppe v. New Mexico*, 426 U.S. 529 (1976); *Douglas v. Seacoast Products, Inc.*, 431 U.S. 265 (1977); *Baldwin v. Fish and Game Commission of Montana*, 436 U.S. 371 (1978); *Foster-Fountain Packing Company v. Haydel*, 278 U.S. 1 (1928); *Hughes v. Oklahoma*, 441 U.S. 322 (1979); *Organized Fishermen of Florida v. Hodel*, 775 F.2d 1544 (11th Cir. 1985); *Tangier Sound Waterman's Association v. Douglas*, 541 F. Supp. 1287 (E.D. Va. 1982) (see for a historically forensic analysis of state authority cases); *Defenders of Wildlife v. Andrus*, 627 F.2d 1238 (D.C. Cir. 1980); Palila; *Gregory v. Ashcroft*, 501 U.S. 452 (1991) (which reinforced the *Rice v. Santa Fe Elevator* presumption against preemption); *Medtronic, Inc. v. Lohr*, 518 U.S. 470, 485 (1996); *Printz v. United States*, 521 U.S. 898 (1997); *United States v. Lopez*, 514 U.S. 549 (1995); *United States v. Morrison*, 529 U.S. 598 (2000); *California Coastal Commission v. Granite Rock Co.*, 480 U.S. 572 (1987); *Babbitt; Rancho Viejo v. Norton*, 323 F.3d 1062 (D.C. Cir. 2003); *GDF Realty Investments, Ltd. v. Norton*, 326 F.3rd 622 (5th Cir. 2003); *Utah Native Plant Society v. U.S. Forest Service*, 923 F.3d 860 (10th Cir. 2019); *Gibbs v. Babbitt*, 214 F.3d 483 (4th Cir. 2000); *Wyoming v. United States*, 279 F.3d 1214 (10th Cir. 2002); *Reno v. Condon*, 528 U.S.141 (2000); *Federal Maritime Comm'n v. South Carolina Ports Authority*, 535 U.S. 743 (2002); *Alden v. Maine*, 527 U.S. 706 (1999); *Seminole Tribe of Fla. v. Florida*, 517 U.S. 44 (1996); and US Congress, *Fish and Wildlife Coordination Act*, Pub. L. No. 73–121, 48 Stat. 401 (1934), codified as amended at 16 U.S.C. §§ 661–67, https://www.govinfo.gov/content/pkg/USCODE-2013-title16/html/USCODE-2013-title16-chap5A.htm.

20. See *Defenders of Wildlife v. Andrus*, 627 F.2d 1238, 1248–50 (D.C. Cir. 1980): this decision holds that the Department of the Interior's decision to not halt a state program of culling wolves on federal land was not a major federal action under the National Environmental Policy Act because, "far from attempting to alter the traditional division of authority over wildlife management, FLPMA broadly and explicitly

reaffirms it" and a state agency required to seek federal approval for such a program "can hardly be said to have 'responsibility and authority' for its own affairs").

See also *Utah Native Plant Society v. U.S. Forest Service*, 923 F. 3d 860, 870 (10th Cir. 2019): this decision holds that state agencies "retain[] a measure of sovereignty over wildlife management within the national forest [system] . . . absent federal law to the contrary."

21. White, "Endangered Species Act's Precarious Perch," 250–51; Fischman, "Predictions and Prescriptions," 454–66.

22. *Tennessee Valley Authority v. Hill*, 437 U.S. 153, 174, 175, 180, 194 (1978). This language has been cited in 6,852 cases and appellate appeals as of January 1, 2021.

23. *Babbitt*, 214 F.3d at 505.

24. *Rancho Viejo v. Norton*, 323 F.3d 1062, 1079–80 (D.C. Cir. 2003) (internal citations omitted).

25. *Babbitt*, 214 F.3d at 500–502, 504 (internal citations omitted; emphasis added).

26. *National Ass'n of Home Builders v. Babbitt*, 130 F.3d 1041, n15 (D.C. Cir. 1997).

27. *Minnesota v. Mille Lacs Band of Chippewa Indians*, 526 U.S. 172, 204 (1999) (internal citations omitted).

28. For an exhaustive review of each of these laws, see Nie et al., "Fish and Wildlife Management," 838–96.

29. From Nie et al., "Fish and Wildlife Management," 825–26 (internal citations omitted).

30. *Hunt v. United States*, 278 U.S. 96 (1928).

31. *Chalk v. United States*, 114 F. 2d 207 (4th Cir. 1940).

32. *Kleppe v. New Mexico*, 426 U.S. 529, 539–541 (1976).

33. *Kleppe*, 426 U.S. at 543 (internal citations omitted).

34. *Kleppe*, 426 U.S. at 545–46.

35. Kisonak, "Fish and Wildlife Management," 957.

36. *Wyoming v. United States*, 279 F. 3d 1214, 1226–1227, 1230–31 (2002) (internal citations omitted).

37. *Wyoming*, 279 F. 3d at 1226–27 (internal citations omitted).

See also Nie et. al., "Fish and Wildlife Management," 898 ("Federal agencies most often defer to the states when it comes to regulating the harvest of fish and wildlife on federal lands. Congress has shown no interest in usurping this traditional role of the states.")

38. Nie et al., "Fish and Wildlife Management," 797.

39. Kisonak, "Fish and Wildlife Management," 935.

40. Kisonak, "Fish and Wildlife Management," 938, 971.

16

State and Federal Cooperation and Coordination under the Endangered Species Act: Past and Present

In order to access where US wildlife policy is heading, it is necessary to consider the historical and present relationship over wildlife regulation between state and federal authorities. Section 6 of the Endangered Species Act of 1973 and its implementation by agency regulations and policies did not support state agencies but instead contributed to the growing concentration of federal power. A viable path forward can be found by looking back to the past—to the Migratory Bird Treaty of 1918—which serves as a model of cooperative federalism in wildlife.

THE PAST: SECTION 6, CONGRESSIONAL INTENT, AND AGENCY AUTHORITY

A concern central to Section 6 of the Endangered Species Act is the congressional mandate that the federal government coordinate and cooperate with the states to protect endangered species and their critical habitats. During the congressional debate on the ESA, Senator Ted Stevens (R-AK) described Section 6 as "the major backbone" of the act. The floor manager, Senator John Tunney (D-CA), called Section 6 "the most important section of the ESA."[1] The Wildlife Society, in a technical review further described the congressional intent behind Section 6 of the 1973 ESA, writing, "When the ESA was passed in 1973, Congress stated, 'the successful development of an endangered species program will ultimately depend upon a good working arrangement between the Federal agencies, which have broad policy perspective and authority, and the State agencies, which have the physical facilities and the personnel to see that State and Federal endangered species policies are properly executed.' Section 6 requires the Services to cooperate to the maximum extent practicable with the states in carrying out the program authorized by the ESA."[2]

By 1975, the US Fish and Wildlife Service issued the first regulations to administer the ESA, which totaled thirty pages, and a policy manual followed.[3] Within these were the protocol for the administration of Section 6 and the standards for grant funding thereunder.[4] Policy guidance for day-to-day operations are managed by a Joint Federal/State Task Force for ESA Policy, established in 2011 to maintain smooth administration of the ESA and resolve disputes.[5] The Joint Federal/State Task Force on Federal Aid Assistance Policy (JTF), established in 2002, monitors the annual distribution of funds under the Federal Aid to Wildlife Restoration Fund (P-R, D-J).[6] Sometimes, the process can become contentious, resulting in tension with the states, which is addressed by one of the two task forces.

One example of this is the creation of a habitat conservation plan (HCP) for an endangered species. HCPs are frequently negotiated by the FWS and a private-sector land developer to include *nonlisted species* while ignoring the states who read about it later in the Federal Register. The legality of an HCP for a nonlisted species is highly questionable. Yet it occurs because of the weight and "asserted" authority of the federal government, the courts, and the nonprofit intervenors who litigate endlessly. The states bitterly complain that it's all about the "sue and settle" gambit, run by a very few zealously litigious "environmental" groups.

Admittedly, with federal funding comes bureaucratic paperwork compliance. However, the ESA paperwork imposed on the states has become so exponentially burdensome that states selectively juggle federal programs, use their own state funds in lieu of federal funds, or simply ignore federal programs and funding so as to avoid the bureaucratic compliance and paperwork burden. For example, when restoring certain types of habitat on private land, a state agency using its own funding can complete a project in a matter of weeks. To utilize federal funding, on the other hand, paperwork and approvals required by FWS can take months or years, and willing landowners often end up walking away. Compliance with federal paperwork obligations is now a Faustian bargain: either a state protects its autonomy, or gives it up in exchange for federal funding that the state may need desperately if it is to comply with ESA statutory requirements managed by the FWS.[7]

Other dynamics are involved in understanding tensions on federalism in the administration of the ESA. From the start, in the 1970s, when the FWS was mandated to administer the ESA, federal primacy and supremacy created a top-down management style that the FWS adopted. In the opinion of many state directors—especially in the West—back then it showed a lack of trust and respect toward the states. The federal government had a near monopoly on trained professional biologists and money. They wrote the regulations with a top-down-enforcement mentality. The states were technically unprepared and understaffed when forced into the ESA program because of their critical need for funding, contrary to the belief of Congress in 1973. The states' technical and administrative supports simply couldn't maintain their position within the federalism framework. Resentment and tensions became systemic from the beginning, and federal officials were characterized as having "a combat mentality," stretching their authority far beyond Congress's intent. Moreover, states fought the listing of species because the heavy burden of species recovery fell on them, not the FWS; conversely, it was the job of the FWS to list species after extensive fieldwork, data collection, and a scientific biological opinion. So the federal management system from the start was unbalanced and burdened by inherent countervailing forces and underlying tensions. The failure of Congress to fully fund the cost of compliance with their ESA mandate and keep pace with increased demands by larger sociocultural and socioeconomic issues driving species loss has further added to the dysfunctional dynamic and tensions.

In February 2014 the Association of Fish and Wildlife Agencies issued "Wildlife Management Authority: The State Agencies' Perspective," a report in which they summarized their perspective on the working relationship with the FWS:

State wildlife agency leadership harbors growing concern about the increasingly strained relationship between state wildlife agencies and their federal partner. . . . State agency directors occasionally see the ESA as a vehicle for federal overreach, or of inappropriate reallocation of states' wildlife management duties into federal hands. . . . Some states also perceive that bureaucratic rigidity is replacing those aspects of the ESA that Congress drafted with well-intended rigor. These states believe this bureaucratic rigidity sometimes impedes wildlife conservation. . . . It is cooperative federalism, rather than an overly centralized national approach to government, that synchronizes the combined resources of the states, federal government and the private sector, that allows them to deliver their mutual energy to "conservation action on the ground."[8]

The Department of the Interior had issued three policy statements on the principles of federal-state wildlife federalism. In part, the 1983 policy states,

Federal authority exists for specified purposes while State authority regarding fish and resident wildlife remains the comprehensive backdrop applicable in the absence of specific, overriding Federal Law.

The Policy goes further than these fundamental principles of federalism, however, by stating that it is intended "to reaffirm the basic role of the States in fish and resident wildlife management, especially where States have primary authority and responsibility, and to foster improved conservation of fish and wildlife." In other sections, the Policy recognizes that "[s]tate jurisdiction remains concurrent with Federal authority, and asserts that, in passing FLPMA, Congress "recognized and reaffirmed the primary authority and responsibility of the States for management of fish and resident wildlife on such lands."[9]

In 1994, a policy statement was issued by the Department of Interior regarding the role of state fish and wildlife agencies in implementing the ESA; in 2016 a substantially revised statement was issued to recognize a suite of conservation tools that hadn't been available in 1994. The 2016 statement reads as follows:

States possess broad trustee and police powers over fish, wildlife and plants and their habitats within their borders. Unless preempted by Federal authority, States possess primary authority and responsibility for protection and management of fish, wildlife and plants and their habitats within their borders. Unless preempted by Federal authority. The updated policy . . . reaffirms the commitment for engagement and collaboration between the Services and State fish and wildlife agencies on many aspects of ESA implementation. . . . The revised policy reflects a renewed commitment by the Services and State fish and wildlife agencies to work together in conserving America's imperiled wildlife.[10]

In 2018, the 1983 policy was reaffirmed and strengthened as follows:

In 1983, the Department codified in the United States Code of Federal Regulations, 43 C.F.R. Part 24, establishing a policy that Federal authority exists for specified purposes while State authority regarding fish and resident wildlife remains the comprehensive backdrop applicable in the absence of specific, overriding Federal law. This 35-year-old rule is more relevant today than ever.

Therefore, I reaffirm the authority of the States to exercise their broad trustee and police powers as stewards of the Nation's fish and wildlife species on public lands and waters under the jurisdiction of the Department. Each of us must recognize the fundamental role of the States in fish and wildlife management, especially where States have primary authority and responsibility, foster improved conservation of fish and wildlife, and encourage a good neighbor policy with the States.

The 50 State governments have extensive capacities and competencies to exercise their responsibilities to serve as trustees for fish and wildlife species resident in the respective States. These capacities and competencies are grounded in State constitutional and statutory laws, as well as an extensive body of administrative rules that collectively form a comprehensive legal underpinning to ensure that State governments effectively function as trustees of fish and wildlife resources with broad police powers to enforce those laws and regulations.

The States' fundamental responsibility for fish and wildlife management includes responsibility for appropriate regulation of public use and enjoyment of fish and wildlife species. The Department recognizes States as the first-line authorities for fish and wildlife management and hereby expresses its commitment to defer to the States in this regard except as otherwise required by Federal law.[11]

Notwithstanding those formal policy statements recognizing state wildlife authority mandating cooperation with states, federal primacy continues to prevail, upsetting the balance of federalism.

The Wildlife Society makes specific recommendations toward strengthening the cooperative working relationship between the states and federal government in administering the ESA. "The Section 6 cooperative agreement provisions should be redesigned to function as a true partnership agreement requiring close collaboration and coordination between and among the states and the Services," they write. "The Section 6 agreement can be the vehicle to identify the respective roles of the states and federal agencies. It should provide the flexibility to allow states that so choose to assume the lead for prelisting conservation, recovery planning and implementation oversight, SHA and HCP administration, and post-delisting monitoring."[12]

Hope beckons with generational changes—and the Conservation Without Conflict initiative, next discussed.[13]

COOPERATIVE FEDERALISM TODAY: HOPE FOR THE FUTURE?

Over the last fifty years, as state conservation programs have slowly matured and began being funded with qualified state biologists on board, the playing field has been dramatically leveled between federal and state interests. Lane Kisonak, counsel for the Association of Fish and Wildlife Agencies, authored a law review article in 2020 that characterizes today's contemporary state/federal dichotomy succinctly:

The decentralized structures of federal agencies including FWS—with regional offices encouraging attention to the priorities of state agencies rather than adversarial or competitive activity—often counterbalance the force of preemption. Indeed, interagency collaboration on a wide variety of fish and wildlife management issues is the norm, not the exception. For example, biologists from FWS serve on technical committees convened by state fish and wildlife agencies, and FWS routinely invites state fish and wildlife agency biologists to participate in conservation planning on federal lands or for federal trust species (e.g., endangered species and migratory wildlife) or both.

In addition, the rapid professionalization of state agencies in many fields since the mid-20th century has also increased the benefits of cooperation in setting and implementing policy. As Heather Gerken puts it, "[s]tates and localities don't shield people from national norms, but constitute sites for constructing those norms." Indeed, some courts have begun to conceive of situations where states may merit deference to their interpretations of statute. Even if deference of this sort is unlikely to become a pervasive fixture of federal doctrine, as a mediating principle it may be useful outside the courtroom. In wildlife conservation, looking at "the specific ways that Congress utilizes state implementers" would require an honest accounting for legislative findings and statements of jurisdiction like the savings clauses in the NWRSAA [National Wildlife Refuge System Administration Act], FLPMA, and the Wilderness Act.[14]

David Willms—point man for Wyoming governor Matt Mead in his role as chairman of the Western Governors' Conference—pushed for ESA reform back in 2018. In testimony before the Senate Committee on Environment and Public Works on July 10, 2018, Willms laid out in detail the expectations of the states based on the 1973 act's prescribed plan of concurrent jurisdiction, with primary jurisdiction on nonlisted species. Willms outlined the states' role in endangered-species administration based on their qualified personnel and biologists, internal and field resources, technical databases, and history of species recovery throughout the twentieth century on both sides of the ESA. He detailed the competence in species-recovery techniques learned over the last forty years working with the federal government in ESA recovery, and urged Congress to give states the latitude to exercise their professional expertise, too long underrated by the federal government.

The eight directors of the regional offices of the FWS all have different personalities and perspectives on how endangered species should be administered. Hence, the relationship with the states varies by region and individual temperament. Moreover, there is a divide at the Mississippi River. Eastern states seem to traditionally have had more congenial relationships with the FWS than have Western states. Western states appear to view the ESA as a land use control vehicle and "federalization" of their resident wildlife.[15] One seasoned observer characterizes Alaska's struggle with the FWS as still fighting for statehood.

The 2019 initiative Conservation Without Conflict was inspired by two FWS regional directors—Wendi Weber and Cindy Dohner. The program was funded by the Wildlife Management Institute in 2020 and now has a full time executive director. This program promises to influence the human dimension of the administration of the ESA, which inevitably will cause positive change as the old guard retires and younger generations more sensitized to conflict resolution move into leadership roles and supplant old cultural attitudes. A much more cooperative and enlightened relationship between the states and federal government has refreshingly begun to develop within recent years.

SUMMARY

The gap between federal and state wildlife authority continues to grow. Specifically, Section 6 of the Endangered Species Act of 1973—which mandates that the federal government *cooperate* with states on protecting endangered species and their habitats, considered the "backbone" of the act—has failed to fully meet the expectations of the states in cooperation and coordination with the FWS. The states complain that the federal government's power has expanded and that state authority has diminished. However, history furnishes a successful blueprint that can be used for the future: The Migratory Bird Treaty Act of 1918 established a framework for *concurrent* regulation. Federal policymakers today could bring states into the fold and give them more room to exercise their local expertise and professionalism, respecting the long historical tradition of states exercising power in wildlife affairs. Accordingly, the *future* model for federalism can take wisdom from its rich *past*.

NOTES

1. As recounted in Petersen, "Congress and Charismatic Megafauna," 478.

2. Robert P. Davison, William P. Burger, Henry Campa III, Paul J. Conry, Kenneth D. Elowe, Gary Frazer, Dorothy C. Mason, Donald E. Moore III, and Robert D. Nelson, "Practical Solutions to Improve the Effectiveness of the Endangered Species Act for Wildlife Conservation," ed. Krista E. M. Galley, Wildlife Society Technical Review 05-1, (The Wildlife Society, Bethesda, MD, December 2005), 10, https://wildlife.org/wp-content/uploads/2014/05/ESA05-11.pdf.

3. US Fish and Wildlife Service Service manual, chap. 521, "FW 4: Endangered Species," Division of Federal Aid, October 10, 2001. https://www.fws.gov/policy/521fw4.pdf.

4. US Government, "Applications for Financial Assistance," *Federal Register* 40, no. 197 (October 9, 1975): 47509, https://www.govinfo.gov/content/pkg/FR-1975-10-09/pdf/FR-1975-10-09.pdf.

5. See, for example, US House of Representatives, *The Endangered Species Act: How Litigation Is Costing Jobs and Impeding True Recovery Efforts: Oversight Hearing Before the Committee on Natural Resources, United States House of Representatives*, 112th Cong., 92 (2011), https://www.govinfo.gov/content/pkg/CHRG-112hhrg71642/html/CHRG-112hhrg71642.htm (statement of Eric Schwab).

6. US Fish and Wildlife Service and International Association of Fish and Wildlife Agencies, "Charter for a Joint Federal/State Task Force on Federal Aid Policy,"

September 5, 2002, https://www.fws.gov/wsfrprograms/subpages/policy/files/charter.pdf.

7. The author interviewed a large number of active and retired state wildlife directors across the country on the condition of anonymity.

8. Association of Fish and Wildlife Agencies, *Wildlife Management Authority*, 2, 4, 8.

9. Nie et al., "Fish and Wildlife Management," 876.

10. National Archives of the United States, "Department of the Interior Fish and Wildlife Policy; State-Federal Relationships," *Federal Registry* 48, no. 54 (March 18, 1983): 11642, https://www.govinfo.gov/content/pkg/FR-1983-03-18/pdf/FR-1983-03-18.pdf.

11. Ryan Zinke, "State Fish and Wildlife Authority on Department of the Interior Lands and Water," memorandum to Heads of Bureaus and Offices (Washington, DC: United States Department of the Interior, September 10, 2018), https://www.peer.org/wp-content/uploads/attachments/9_11_18_Zinke_memo.pdf.

This memorandum was issued on behalf of the Association of Fish and Wildlife Agencies at the request of its general counsel, M. Carol Bambery. Since it was not subject to the rulemaking requirements of the Administrative Procedure Act (US Congress, 5 U.S.C. § 553 [2012] https://www.archives.gov/federal-register/laws/administrative-procedure/553.html), it does not carry the force of law. See *Christensen v. Harris County*, 529 U.S. 576, 587 (2000).

12. Davison et al., "Practical Solutions," 11.

13. A perfect example of concurrent jurisdiction for the ESA to follow is the model of the Migratory Bird Treaty Act (MBTA) of 1918. When the legislation was first being discussed, there was serious conflict with the states, and the act was constitutionally challenged by the State of Missouri before the US Supreme Court. However, once its legality was accepted and the supremacy and primacy of the federal government established in 1920, the states worked with the federal government to cooperatively implement the MBTA. Today it is managed by having the four primary flyways (Atlantic, Mississippi, Central, and Pacific), each separately administered by a Flyway Council comprised of top officials from the respective state, federal, provincial, and territorial governments within that flyway. Moreover, the federal government has a Federal Council for the Conservation of Migratory Birds, consisting of some seventeen relevant departments that manage all the federal partners. The MBTA Flyaway Council administration is a perfect model for the ESA that would address the states' concerns for inclusion in ESA management.

14. Kisonak, "Fish and Wildlife Management," 964–65.

And also see Gillian E. Metzger, "Administrative Law as the New Federalism," *Duke Law Journal* 57, no. 7 (2008): 2023–109, https://scholarship.law.duke.edu/cgi/viewcontent.cgi?article=1370&context=dlj. See generally Nie et.al., "Fish and Wildlife Management," 847–48; Abbe R. Gluck, "Intrastatutory Federalism and Statutory Interpretation: State Implementation of Federal Law in Health Reform and Beyond," *Yale Law Journal* 121 (2011): 534, 552, n. 169 at 564, https://docs.google.com/viewerng/viewer?url=https://www.yalelawjournal.org/pdf/1032_qcrpe69v.pdf; and Heather K. Gerken, "Federalism 3.0," *California Law Review* 105

(2017): 1695, 1714, https://29qish11qx5q2k5d7b491joo-wpengine.netdna-ssl.com/wp-content/uploads/2018/01/Gerken-34-formatted.pdf.

15. Nagle, "The Original Role of the States," 387. And see Association of Fish and Wildlife Agencies, *Wildlife Management Authority*, 2, 4, 8.

17

The Three Biggest Threats Undermining Federalism and State Wildlife-Management Authority

Wildlife management must confront the three *most* dangerous threats undermining federalism and the robust enforcement of state wildlife authority: *First*, the exponential growth and pervasiveness of federal agency actions in rulemaking and regulations that can occasionally result in overreach; *second*, the grants-in-aid to states with unreasonable conditions attached; *third*, insufficient federal funding to support the administration and regulatory enforcement of the Endangered Species Act and its operative provisions—the most concerning of the three threats. Specifically, this chapter examines the first two threats, with a particular focus on *Chevron* and *Auer* deference, as well as "conditional" preemption through federal conditions attached to spending federal funding.[1]

THE AUTHORITY OF FEDERAL AGENCIES, THEIR REGULATORY POWERS, AND PREDILECTION

One of the greatest threats to maintaining balance in the federalist structure comes from the decisions of multiple federal agencies in adopting binding rules, regulations, secretarial orders, policies, guidance, and advisory memoranda. The first US administrative agency was founded in 1789, created to provide pensions for wounded Revolutionary War soldiers. The Department of the Treasury and the Post Office were created that same year, followed by the Department of State, War, and Navy. Within each major epoch in US history, federal agencies have been created. The industrial expansion driven by railroads and the push Westward before and after the Civil War brought the Department of Interior (1849); the Department of Agriculture and the General

Land Office (1862), which later became the Bureau of Land Management; the Division of Economic Ornithology and Mammalogy within the Department of Agriculture (1862), thence the Division of Entomology (1896), which became the Bureau of Biological Survey and later the Fish and Wildlife Service; and the Interstate Commerce Commission in 1887. The Industrial Revolution and the Progressive Era ushered in the Bureau of Immigration and Naturalization (1906); the Federal Reserve System and the Department of Labor, both in 1913; and the Federal Trade Commission in 1914, along with major antitrust enforcement by the Department of Justice. Prohibition dramatically expanded the Treasury Department.

The New Deal Era led to the creation of huge federal-relief programs and bureaucracies to address unemployment, housing, pensions, health care, banking, and agriculture. World War II brought massive urban and suburban expansion and intercity urban renewal projects, which became catalysts for public demand for stringent environmental, consumer protection, and safety laws. Each of these in turn led to new federal agencies, including those addressing welfare and housing for the poor and national health care programs, the Environmental Protection Agency, the Department of Housing and Urban Development, Department of Health and Human Services, and the Council on Environmental Quality.

During the 1800s a clear separation between state and federal powers meant each provided their own sources of revenue to support their separate governmental functions—a period of *dual federalism*. However, as the growth and complexity of the nation's affairs increasingly threatened this separation by the early 1900s, *concurrent federalism* and jurisdictions replaced dual federalism. Concurrent federalism later transitioned into *cooperative federalism*.[2]

On two occasions, the Supreme Court attempted to define for the agencies their role under the Administrative Procedure Act.[3] While the Constitution presupposes clear distinctions between legislative, executive, and judicial functions, it offers little guidance for the judicially enforceable separation of powers. The Constitution was designed to achieve balance among the three branches of government at the federal level. Justice Sandra Day O'Connor even recognized in *New York v. United States* that "The Constitution has never been understood to confer upon Congress the ability to require states to govern according to Congress's instructions."[4] When overlap occurs—notwithstanding their judicial review function established by *Marbury v. Madison*[5]—the Supreme Court does not referee conflict very well. Conflict is negotiated in the political, not the judicial, arena.

Today the number of agencies varies, depending on the source of information queried: The Federal Register agency list reports 440, but their online index separately lists 272; the Administrative Conference of the United States lists 115 agencies; the United States Government Manual says 316; USA. gov's tally is 443; and FOIA.gov reports 252 agencies.[6]

Franklin Delano Roosevelt, decrying administrative tyranny, called the administrative state the fourth branch of government. The result was congressional enactment the Administrative Procedure Act (APA) in 1946, devised to rein in agency conduct after a detailed ten-year study by the attorney general revealed dysfunction. The law was also meant to control agency expansion and ensure accessibility, accountability, consistency, efficiency, and fairness in governance.[7] Its performance has been mixed, which explains why in 1980 Ronald Reagan's presidential campaign pledge was "deregulation."

According to the record, when Congress considered and enacted the Endangered Species Act in 1972 and 1973, their intent was that Section 6 mandate coordination and cooperation between the federal and state governments. This section of the law has variously been referred to as "the major backbone" and "the most important section of the ESA."[8] ESA regulations and policy manuals were written by the US Fish and Wildlife Service, with federal primacy and supremacy imbedded in them, which created a top-down management style. The original 1975 ESA regulations were thirty pages; today they are five thousand pages. Congressional oversight has been mixed—except during the Reagan administration, when ESA enforcement was virtually suspended by Interior Secretary James Watt, with very negative results to wildlife conservation.[9]

Congress's legislative power cannot constitutionally be channeled through the executive branch. Yet Congress hides its legislative power within the policymaking discretion of the executive branch and controls it through appropriations:

> Under the justification that it can exact laws "necessary and proper for carrying into execution" its constitutional powers . . . the net result is that agencies are able to ram through sweeping regulations of society that never would pass Congress. Members of Congress can claim credit for the benefits, while escaping accountability [for bad results or] for the costs . . . and the people's ability to control the government through the ballot box is significantly diluted . . . Executive agencies add 60,000 pages of new regulations every year, vastly more than the volume of new laws passed by Congress.[10]

The agency decisions and regulations create pervasive problems with less obvious solutions. Federal agencies without clear congressional mandate interfere with state police powers that protect their citizens. Yet federalists and major corporations argue that preemption provides uniformity and is a safeguard against inconsistent state actions.[11]

Congress, through the power of the purse, can manipulate federal agencies and their policies and rulemaking and can disclaim responsibility for their actions and results.[12] Therein lies the problem: The intertwined federal and state laws and regulations, enhanced by federal grants to carry out the conditions that accompany the grants, have become so interstitial that all sense of sovereign separateness is lost. Moreover, agencies can be captured wholesale through citizen lawsuits or by industry influence and the revolving door of "professional expertise" appointees from the regulated industry. The Supreme Court's acclaimed 1984 *Chevron v. NRDC* decision and its progeny, *Auer v. Robbins*, embraced an extreme form of judicial deference to the executive branch agencies' interpretations of federal law.[13] The Court has yet to grasp that this deference to these agencies stealthily increases the invisible power of both the agencies and Congress in our increasingly complex society with ever-expanding technology—as noted by the Court in *Mistretta v. United States*.[14] The Court has acknowledged that Congress simply cannot do its job absent the ability to delegate power under broad general directives, which suggests a failure of judicial review. This is why Justice Sandra Day O'Connor was so outspoken regarding the Supreme Court's deference to the political process most notably in *Gregory v. Ashcroft*.[15]

Thomas Jefferson's 1821 admonition on the judiciary rings as true today for executive agencies as it did then:

> The germ of dissolution of our federal government is in the constitution of the federal Judiciary [or federal agencies] . . . working like gravity by night and by day, gaining a little to-day & a little tomorrow, and advancing its noiseless step like a thief, over the field of jurisdiction, until all shall be usurped from the states, & the government of all be consolidated into one . . . [and] shall be drawn to Washington as the center of all power, it will render powerless the checks provided of one government on another . . . [and] if the states look with apathy on this silent descent of their government into the gulph which is to swallow all, we have only to weep over the human character . . . incapable of self-government.[16]

FEDERAL GRANTS-IN-AID AND CONDITIONAL PREEMPTION: THE TROJAN HORSE IN WILDLIFE AUTHORITY AND FEDERALISM

Mandated federal funding and discretionary appropriated grants-in-aid for wildlife all have conditions attached for acceptance of the funding, as do many new laws and regulations. There are penalties for failure to accept the conditions. These conditions frequently abrogate state sovereignty and violate the balance of federalism. Moreover, the real threat to state sovereignty

Figure 17.1. Thomas Jefferson (1743–1826), oil painting by Rembrandt Peale, 1800. *Source*: White House Collection/White House Historical Association.

and autonomy beyond the prescribed financial penalties is the threat that the federal government will implement new programs and regulations on their own. If states cannot or will not do so, the federal government reserves the right to implement the program themselves. In the context of cooperative federalism, this bureaucratic assault has been referred to as "coercive federalism." It is a constitutionally flawed doctrine wherein the federal government gives states conditional "permission" to accept funding and implement federal law. Some scholars have confusingly referred to this as "*conditional preemption*" or alternatively "coercive preemption."[17]

Through the conditions attached as precedent to spending, the federal government confiscates state authority. As professor Thomas Merrill has documented, "The environmental revolution of the 1970s was achieved primarily through conditional spending and conditional regulation, rather than by direct congressional mandates, which obscured the momentous nature of the shift in the allocation of power. The federal piper made the states dance to its tune."[18] This creates a subtle distinction between commandeering versus coercion, which the Supreme Court has struggled with in several notable cases.[19]

Yet paradoxically the ESA could be made stronger, with more on-the-ground conservation achieved, if more funding were provided by both the states and federal government's administrative agency, the US Fish and Wildlife Service. But therein lies the main problem: Congress issued an absolute mandate in 1973, declaring that all endangered species must be protected and conserved—and, the Supreme Court added, at "whatever the cost." Then Congress failed to follow through and fund the costs of complying with their own mandate. This is the ESA's Achilles' heel.

Conditional funding has been perverse in most federal government programs—notably in the air-quality standards in the Clean Air Act and in the 2010 Affordable Care Act's health-care reform.[20] Mario Loyola has been particularly outspoken on federal-funding conditions abrogating state sovereignty at the outer limits of Congress's Commerce Clause immunity:

> The arrangement contemplated in the Clean Air Act is typical. The U.S. Environmental Protection Agency (EPA) says to each state, "We'll give you permission to implement our regulations yourself, so long as you design your State Implementation Plan according to our specifications. Otherwise we will pre-empt your regulation and impose our own Federal Implementation Plan." Because the business community is increasingly terrified of the EPA (with good reason), states usually jump at the chance to implement the regulations themselves, even at their own expense. The fiction of "voluntary" state acceptance is even more tenuous here than in the conditional grants context, because the state gets a bad deal no matter what choice it makes—hardly the paradigm of an arms' length contract freely entered into.[21]

During the last fifty years, state and federal laws have become interstitial. The Court held in one notable case of great significance for state sovereignty that states couldn't be threatened with the loss of their existing Medicare funds just because they refused to comply with the Medicaid expansion conditions required by the Affordable Care Act. It had been a "gun to the head," commandeering and coercion, pure and simple. Moreover, for the first time ever, the Court concluded that a federal law exceeded its Spending Clause authority because it was coercive.[22] However, in two cases the Supreme

Court has twice concluded that state receipt of a federal grant requires that the state comply with the conditions of the grant, even where compliance conflicts with state law.[23] Professor Robert L. Fischman has written a very descriptive article on how the federal government maintains close control of state wildlife management and limits state discretion through the distribution of its funding, which he classifies as an example of cooperative federalism.[24]

As early as 1938, distinguished legal historian Edward S. Corwin[25] addressed the state-dependency problems created by laws requiring that federally generated funds be shared with the states and how this strengthens national power at the expense of state authority. "When two cooperate, it is the stronger member of the combination who calls the tune."[26] However, this cost sharing began as early as 1911, during the Progressive Era, with congressional funding subsidizing forest protection and reforestation, education in agricultural, vocational rehabilitation, and highway construction, all on a cost-sharing basis with the states, pursuant to regulations established by Congress.[27]

The total grants-in-aid expenditures by the federal government for all projects in 1915 amounted to $6 million; in 1930, that had grown to $109 million; in 1931, it was $198 million; and in 1932, it had grown to a staggering $234 million.[28] Professor Corwin asserts that "'grants-in-aid' tends to break down state initiative and devitalize state policies." And, he continues, "'Cooperative Federalism' spells farther aggrandizement of national power . . . Cooperative Federalism has been to date, a short expression for a constantly increasing concentration of power at Washington in the instigation and supervision of local policies."[29] It moreover embodies the talisman of preemption when grants-in-aid are involved.[30]

Professor Joseph Zimmerman concludes that Congress directly influences the nature of services provided by states and local governments through the many conditions it attaches to federal grants-in-aid to the states. Zimmerman also argues that this subsidization—beginning as early as 1911—actually ended the period of dual federalism, which had dated back to the early Taney Court, after 1836.[31] Professor William Anderson contrasts 1789 and 1942. "*Then* (before 1788)," he writes, "state grants *to* the Congress of the United States [were] for defense and debt purposes. *Now* grants-in-aid *by* the national government to the states [are] in increasing amounts and with steadily tightening national controls over state action."[32] This dependent relationship derails the energy to achieve real boots-on-the-ground conservation and turns into turf building, defensive isolationism, and siloing. Ongoing federal oversight by the FWS's Federal Aid Coordinator for Pittman-Robertson, Dingell-Johnson funds, and the ESA Wildlife and Sport Fish Restoration Chief all remain to ensure compliance with the law and regulations and to ensure the required performance assurances by the states. It is a source of tension that puts pressure on wildlife management and enforcement of the Endangered Species Act.[33]

SUMMARY

The nature of federalism and state wildlife authority are under direct constitutional attack. With the rise of the modern administrative state, the nature and scope of federal power has been aggregated in the so-called "fourth branch" of government. Crucially, the vision of judicial review that Chief Justice John Marshall articulated in *Marbury v. Madison*—"to say what the law is"—has been abrogated by federal courts applying the *Chevron* and *Auer* deference doctrines. Indeed, while the *vertical* separation of powers scheme has been altogether transformed by the modern administrative state, the rapid and accelerated use of agency regulations and rulemaking has also fundamentally upended the *horizontal* relationship between states and the federal government, with more power being lodged in Washington. In addition, federal grants-in-aid to states influence the structure of the wildlife federalism relationship. Thus, because the federal government may flexibly establish *national* policies through its appending power under the Constitution, states will continue to be subordinated to the federal power exercised from the halls of Congress. And it will happen under the constitutional guise of "cooperation."

NOTES

1. *Chevron U.S.A., Inc. v. Natural Resources Defense Council, Inc.*, 467 U.S. 837 (1984); *Auer v. Robbins*, 519 U.S. 452 (1997).

The third threat, lack of funding—the major challenge underlying the future of endangered species—will be discussed in chapter 18.

2. Corwin, "Passing of Dual Federalism," 18; Kincaid, "From Dual to Coercive Federalism," 29; Corwin, "Passing of Dual Federalism," 4.

See also Epstein and Greve, "Conclusion: Preemption Doctrine and Its Limits," 309 (discussing the evolution of ideological thought). This trend led to the slow absorption of state authority by the federal government. See Gardbaum, "Breadth versus Depth," 72.

3. *Universal Camera Corp. v. NLRB*, 340 U.S. 474 (1951); and *SEC v. Chenery Corp.*, 332 U.S. 194 (1947).

4. In *New York v. United States*, 505 U.S. 144, (1992).

5. *Marbury v. Madison*, 5 U.S. 137 (1803).

6. Clyde Wayne Crews Jr., "How Many Federal Agencies Exist? We Can't Drain the Swamp Until We Know," Forbes.com, July 5, 2017, https://www.forbes.com

/sites/waynecrews/2017/07/05/how-many-federal-agencies-exist-we-cant-drain-the-swamp-until-we-know/?sh=67fd69021aa2; and "Administrative Agency; History of Administrative Agency," Law Library: American Law and Legal Information, accessed June 17, 2021, https://law.jrank.org/pages/4061/Administrative-Agency-History-Administrative-Agency.html.

7. Franklin D. Roosevelt, message from the president of the United States to the Congress, January 12, 1937, in *The President's Committee on Administrative Management: Report of the President's Committee on Administrative Management* (Washington, DC: US Government Printing Office, 1937), iii–v, text viewable at https://www.presidency.ucsb.edu/documents/message-congress-recommending-reorganization-the-executive-branch.

8. Montrie, *Myth of Silent Spring*, 62–98.

9. Congress swiftly rebuked Watt and the administration by amending the ESA in 1982.

10. Loyola, "Federal-State Crack Up."

This transfer of power to the agencies is really one of default. Representatives and senators in Congress are so preoccupied with getting reelected that they can't leave it to their young staff, who are inexperienced, overworked, and too immature to navigate complex legislative matters requiring institutional memory and knowledge.

11. Young, "Federal Preemption and State Autonomy," 267; Epstein and Greve, "Introduction: Preemption in Context," 1.

12. John P. Dwyer, "The Role of State Law in an Era of Federal Preemption: Lessons from Environmental Regulation," *Law and Contemporary Problems (Duke University)* 40, no. 3 (1997): 219.

13. *Chevron U.S.A., Inc. v. Natural Resources Defense Council, Inc.*, 467 U.S. 837 (1984); *Auer v. Robbins*, 519 U.S. 452 (1997).

14. 488 U.S. 361 (1989).

15. 501 U.S. 452 (1991).

16. US National Archives, "From Thomas Jefferson to C. Hammond."

17. Loyola, "Federal-State Crack Up."

18. Thomas W. Merrill, "Preemption in Environmental Law: Formalism, Federalism Theory, and Default Rules," in *Federal Preemption: States' Powers, National Interests*, ed. Richard A. Epstein and Michael S. Greve (Washington, DC: AEI Press, 2007), 176.

Also see Bruce Ackerman, Donald Elliott, and John Millian, "Toward a Theory of Statutory Evolution: The Federalization of Environmental Law," *The Journal of Law, Economics, and Organization* 1, no. 2 (1985): 313; and Richard B. Stewart, "Pyramids of Sacrifice? Problems of Federalism in Mandating State Implementation of National Environmental Policy," *Yale Law Journal* 86, no. 6 (1977): 1196, https://digitalcommons.law.yale.edu/cgi/viewcontent.cgi?article=6427&context=ylj.

19. *Hodel v. Virginia Surface Mining & Reclamation Ass'n*, 452 U.S. 264 (1981); *New York v. United States*, 505 U.S. 144 (1992); and *Printz v. United States*, 521 U.S. 898 (1997).

20. "See for example, Clean Air Act, 42 USC § 7401 et seq (regulating air emissions by, in part, establishing 'National Ambient Air Quality Standards' for every

state and requiring participating states to develop and enforce state implementation plans to reach those standards); Patient Protection and Affordable Care Act, Pub. L. No. 111–148, 124 Stat 119 (2010), to be codified in scattered sections of 26, 42 USC) (using federal and state regulators to address health care reform)." US Congress, *Equal Employment Opportunity Act of 1972*, Pub. L. No. 92–261, 86 Stat 103 (1972), https://www.govinfo.gov/content/pkg/STATUTE-86/pdf/STATUTE-86-Pg103.pdf, codified as amended at 42 USC § 2000e(a) (extending Title VII of the 1964 Civil Rights Act to cover state governments).

The Voting Rights Act preempts state authority to draw congressional districts in certain circumstances. And although the national health-care law permits certain waivers in order to allow state policy experimentation, it also supplants state regulatory authority in innumerable ways. The Court has interpreted the Federal Arbitration Act and the National Bank Act as broadly preempting state law, while construing the regime governing new medical drugs as leaving an important role for state tort regulation. Young, "'Ordinary Diet of the Law,'" 318, nn. 348, 341, n. 467.

21. Loyola, "Federal-State Crack Up."

Also see Young, "'Ordinary Diet of the Law,'" 320; Smith, *Conservation Constitution*, 3–4, 8–9; Daniel Carpenter, *The Forging of Bureaucratic Autonomy* (Princeton: Princeton University Press, 2001), 4, 16–17.

22. *NFIB v. Sebelius*, 567 U.S. 519, 588 (2012).

For an analysis of environmental regulations compromised by federal funding, see Dwyer, "Role of State Law," 203, 208.

23. *King v. Smith*, 392 U.S. 309, 333–34 (1968); and *Rosado v. Wyman*, 397 U.S. 397, 422–23 (1970).

24. Fischman, "Predictions and Prescriptions for the Endangered Species Act," 461–66.

25. See Corwin, *Court Over Constitution*.

The Supreme Court even took notice of the massive federal-aid programs during the later part of twentieth century:

> The effectiveness of the federal political process in preserving the States' interests is apparent even today in the course of federal legislation. On the one hand, the States have been able to direct a substantial proportion of federal revenues into their own treasuries in the form of general and program-specific grants in aid. The federal role in assisting state and local governments is a longstanding one; Congress provided federal land grants to finance state governments from the beginning of the Republic, and direct cash grants were awarded as early as 1887 under the Hatch Act. In the past quarter-century alone, federal grants to States and localities have grown from $7 billion to $96 billion. As a result, federal grants now account for about one-fifth of state and local government expenditures. The States have obtained federal funding for such services as police and fire protection, education, public health and hospitals, parks and recreation, and sanitation. Moreover, at the same time that the States have exercised their influence to obtain federal support, they have been able to exempt themselves from a wide variety of obligations imposed by Congress under the Commerce Clause. For example, the Federal Power Act, the National Labor Relations Act, the Labor-Management Reporting and Disclosure Act, the Occu-

pational Safety and Health Act, the Employee Retirement Income Security Act, and the Sherman Act all contain express or implied exemptions for States and their subdivisions.

Garcia v. San Antonio Metropolitan Transit Authority, 469 U.S. 528, 553–54 (1985).

26. Corwin, *Court Over Constitution*, 21.

27. Corwin, "Passing of Dual Federalism," 20; see also Corwin, *Court Over Constitution*.

28. Wooddy, *Growth of the Federal Government*, 552.

29. Corwin, "Passing of Dual Federalism," 20–21.

30. Bratton, "Preemption Doctrine: Shifting Perspectives on Federalism and the Burger Court," 623, 643; and *New York State Department of Social Services v. Dublino*, 413 U.S. 405 (1973).

31. Joseph F. Zimmerman, "National-State Relations: Cooperative Federalism in the Twentieth Century," *Publius* 31, no. 2 (2001): 15, 20, 28.

32. William Anderson, "Federalism—Then and Now," *State Government* 16 (1943): 107–12, emphasis and parentheticals original.

33. The issue of federal assistance grants and their illusory advantages and hidden dangers is far beyond the scope of this chapter or book. Called by legal and constitutional scholar Mario Loyola the "Trojan horse of cooperative federalism" because it is not readily discernible or easy to see, these federal grants implicitly carry within a "conditional preemption" because the money is conditioned on complying with accompanying federal regulations and direction in applying the funds, diminishing the state's autonomy. If spent inconsistently with the accompanying federal regulations or standards, there are penalties. The Clean Air Act, Highway Act and the Affordable Care Act are notable examples. See Loyola, "Federal-State Crack-Up."

Congress and federal agencies cross the constitutional line when they fail to distinguish between encouragement and coercion. See *New York v. United States*, 505 U.S. 144 (1992); and see *Printz v. United States*. As it applies directly to states, their residents pay federal income and estate taxes. If states refuse grants-in-aid-because of the conditions attached, their federal taxes are simply transferred to other states, and they lose the benefits. For more on this subject, read the writings of attorney and scholar Michael S. Greve, *The Upside-Down Constitution* (Cambridge: Harvard University Press, 2012), and his other writings. Also read Epstein and Greve, *Federal Preemption*, or read the works of Mario Loyola, who publishes in *The Atlantic*, *The American Interest*, and *National Review*. See also Samuel P. Hays, *Beauty, Health, and Permanence: Environmental Politics in the United States, 1955–1985* (Cambridge: Cambridge University Press, 1987), 443–48.

18

Funding Endangered Species Conservation: The Achilles Heel

The problem created by insufficient federal funding for wildlife conservation is the most significant impediment to realizing the full potential of the Endangered Species Act. Because of the federal government's persistent *under*funding of wildlife conservation, the ESA's promise has *not* been fully realized. However, increases in annual funding of $1.4 billion, which would be allocated to states, would greatly enhance the act's full potential and promise. Thus the Recovering America's Wildlife Act (RAWA) offers a *preventative* model for wildlife conservation that would protect twelve thousand at-risk wildlife from extinction while facilitating true cooperation between state and federal wildlife authorities. RAWA awaits approval by the Congress.

* * *

Funding is the biggest problem of federalism's balance with the ESA. This poses a grave danger to state sovereignty in wildlife management. Increasing federal funding for the states has been the leading recommendation of both federal and state administrators for improving both federalism and performance under the Endangered Species Act.[1] Congress established a national policy in 1973 to stem the loss of biodiversity by preserving endangered species and declared the job a historical federal function.[2] Yet the 1973 ESA legislation imposed the burden of conserving endangered species, once listed, on the states wherein the wildlife was located, reserving to the federal government—through the US Fish and Wildlife Service—the task of listing threatened or endangered species after extensive scientific research. The 100th Congress in 1988 amended the original 1973 ESA and stated that there *shall* be deposited into the Cooperative Endangered Species Conservation Fund annually appropriated funds equal to 5 percent of the Federal Aid to Wildlife Restoration Fund (under the Pittman-Robertson and Dingell-Johnson Acts) for Section 6 endangered species conservation work.[3] In fiscal year 2021, the Pittman-Robertson, Dingell-Johnson fund distributed $1,093,154,901. Five percent of that equals $54,657,745. Congress, however, appropriated only $23,702,000 to the Cooperative Endangered Species Conservation Fund for Section 6 expenses in the same fiscal year. Pursuant to the 1988 amendment, Congress shorted the transfer by $30,955,745.[4] Congress has failed to fulfill and honor their own directive.

Regardless of which dictionary one consults, *preemption*'s several synonyms include "appropriation."[5] This is precisely what Congress has done by underfunding the Endangered Species Act and failing to recognize the increasing number of endangered species caused by the ever-increasing US population and their expansion into wildlife habitat. Since 1973, the US population has grown by 57 percent.[6] Demands for food, cars, and vital materials to live, work, and recreate and provision of housing, retail facilities, offices, factories, and jobs has caused land fragmentation, thus reducing natural habitat for all species. Congress created a national policy in 1973 to preserve all endangered species, at whatever the cost,[7] but then failed to provide sufficient funds to carry out the policy. That is an abdication of congressional responsibility and the worst type of preemption Congress can suffer upon the states and the FWS. If adequate funding had been appropriated, many of the problems discussed in the last chapter would be mitigated, and tensions between the states and FWS would be abated.

Funding for the states was never commensurate with the workload imposed on them to conserve listed species with recovery programs. There was an initial appropriation in the 1973 act of $10 million for grants-in-aid to the states, increasing each year thereafter by $3 million through fiscal year 1977. By contrast, Congress appropriated $4 million for the FWS to operate the program in fiscal year 1974, increasing to $10 million by fiscal year 1976, and $5.5 million through fiscal year 1976 to the Commerce Department for the National Marine Fisheries Service, but with no money for grants-in-aid to the states commensurate with their obligations.[8]

Notwithstanding annual increases thereafter, Congress failed to keep pace with the demands that the law imposed on the states. Congress's failure to properly fund the grants-in-aid needed by the states has led to disastrous consequences as the rate of species extinctions continues to grow exponentially. Following is an example of this dilemma drawn from the 2005 The Wildlife Society technical report. "State fish and wildlife agencies," they write, "are not being provided adequate and stable funding from the Section 6 Cooperative Endangered Species Conservation Fund to fulfill state roles in the conservation of endangered and threatened species. For instance, in fiscal year 1977, there were 194 US species listed under the ESA, and $4,300,000 was appropriated for state grants under Section 6. By the end of 2002, there were 1,263 listed US species—more than 6 times the number in 1977, yet the $7,520,000 provided that year had only about one-third as much buying power as the funds provided in 1977."[9]

In two different 1977 congressional budget hearings on the ESA appropriations, Lynn Greenwalt, director of the US Fish and Wildlife Service, sounded the alarm:

> The Endangered Species Act does not mandate that the program be solely a Federal responsibility. The Act contains a strong Federal commitment for close coordination and cooperation with State conservation agencies. Indeed, we in the Department of Interior, and in particular, we in the Fish and Wildlife Service, cannot accomplish the goals of the Act alone.
>
> State conservation agencies have the expertise and manpower essential for carrying out a program of the magnitude and complexity of the Endangered Species Act. In addition, many States have had programs to protect endangered species for decades and their continued work is essential if the purpose of the Act are to be achieved.[10]

Greenwalt concluded, "the wisdom of that language becomes more apparent with the passage of time. We in the Fish and Wildlife Service cannot accomplish the goals of the act alone."[11]

In their own report on the matter, the joint House and Senate Committee of Conference stated:

> It should be noted that the successful development of the endangered species program will ultimately depend upon a good working arrangement between the Federal agencies, which have broad policy perspectives and authority, and the State agencies, which have the physical facilities and the personnel to see that State and Federal endangered species policies are properly executed. The grant program authorized by this legislation is essential to an adequate program. Since the Federal Government is directing new, innovative and perhaps expensive programs, it seems only fair that it should also bear a significant portion of their costs.[12]

In the 1977 congressional budget hearings on ESA appropriations in both the House and Senate, John S. Gottschalk, executive vice president of the International Association of Fish and Wildlife Agencies (now known as AFWA), testified that only seventeen states were participating in the ESA, managing thirty-two endangered species and receiving grants-in-aid.[13] Gottschalk bluntly described the states' position on initiating ESA participation in the respective states. "The States are understandably reluctant to commit scarce manpower and funds for a planning effort that may not materialize because of a shortage of Federal funds at the Federal level," he told the House.

> No State is going to stick its neck out in terms of trying to get more people and put more money into the planning effort if there is no visible hope in getting any funds. . . .
> The way the law stands now, a State must agree in advance that they will enact or have enacted laws that protect any species which any Secretary of Interior may at any time in the future declare to be endangered.
> As professionals, the State and wildlife managers might be willing to grit their teeth and go along with giving this kind of blank check to some future Secretary of the Interior, but most legislators are somewhat reluctant to do that. Therefore, we still have a number of States which have not qualified themselves under the terms of the Federal act to participate under Section 6.
> Originally, the idea was if we had this kind of constraint on the States, it would force them into a position to protecting all endangered species. In fact, as you can see, it is not working out that way. Some States are simply not going to commit themselves to the future – to follow the future actions of some Secretary of Interior.[14]

And to the Senate, Gottschalk stated:

> It is practically scandalous . . . to go out to the States and ask them to participate in a program that doesn't even have any money at all showing. . . . It is no secret that some of the States have been somewhat unhappy with the way the endangered species program has been handled. To put it somewhat commonly, they are a bit miffed. They don't even want to talk to the Fish and Wildlife Service because they feel they have been preempted, that they had adequate programs going and suddenly their authority to deal with these species has been taken away from them, in some cases without what you might call due process. They are not consulted to the extent they would like to have been, so there is a little problem of communication existing here in some circumstances.[15]

Jack Gehringer, deputy director of the National Marine Fisheries Service, charged with enforcement of the Marine Mammal Protection Act, testified that NMFS had never been appropriated grant-in-aid funds for states under the ESA—which state of affairs Gottschalk found "scandalous."[16] In fiscal year 1978, Gehringer estimated immediate funding needs for the coastal states to be a total of $1,301,000, with the federal funding portion being $867,500.[17] Just one example of the funding disparity: Four states have borne the burden of managing grizzly bear recovery, an early iconic species listed as endangered and living in five separate ecosystems. According to the Interagency Grizzly Bear Committee Report of January 2016, Wyoming spent

$3.9 million on recovery for fiscal years 2014 and 2015 combined; the federal contribution for that period was $96,000. Montana spent $1.5 million, with a federal contribution of $285,000. The State of Washington's costs equaled the federal contribution, and Idaho spent $202,000 against a federal contribution of $146,000.[18]

The funding that Congress appropriates specifically for all endangered-species work has been relatively stable. In fiscal year 2019, the appropriated amount was $251.8 million. In fiscal year 2020, it was $266 million. In fiscal year 2021, it was $269.7 million—all of this for the Fish and Wildlife Service to implement all the various Endangered Species Act programs and oversee 1,235 listed species. Apart from this, state fish and wildlife agencies receive an annual apportionment from the FWS through the State and Tribal Wildlife Grants program to address species of greatest conservation need, identified in federally approved State Wildlife Action Plans. This program provides funding to conserve candidate, listed, threatened, and endangered species. However, the funding is primarily intended to keep species from falling through the cracks by supporting proactive conservation of fish and wildlife that are declining but are not yet to the point where federal ESA listing is warranted. Funding is also provided to tribes for species of cultural and traditional importance through competitive grants. The budget for fiscal year 2021 appropriated for this program about $72.4 million.

To be clear, these appropriated funds are separate from funding under the Pittman-Robertson, Dingell-Johnson excise tax fund, which is allocated to states to supplement their general wildlife-management program budgets.[19] In fiscal year 2020, that program distributed $971,552,178 to the states; since 1937, the program has distributed $22.9 billion to the states. However, as the next section will demonstrate, $1.3 billion per year is needed if Congress would honor the mandate they issued in 1973 to protect and conserve *all* of America's endangered species and their habitats. That is the most critical of all the issues confronting the Endangered Species Act.

HOPE FOR THE FUTURE: RECOVERING AMERICA'S WILDLIFE ACT

The funds required for endangered-species recovery and programs to address species at risk of extinction are estimated at $1.3 billion per year of *dedicated* rather than *appropriated* funding. Congress can change appropriated funding at will or defund it entirely. This $1.3 billion figure was developed by the Association of Fish and Wildlife Agencies' Blue Ribbon Panel in 2016 when its research determined that each state on average needed $26 million ($1.3 billion collectively above their 25 percent contribution) and $97.5 million for the tribes (a combined total of $1,397,500,000) in funding annually for at-risk species of greatest conservation need, covering twelve thousand species.[20]

Recovering America's Wildlife Act (RAWA) is a program to start protecting these twelve thousand species *before* they become listed as threatened or endangered. To stabilize and recover endangered species, a variety of programs have been developed similar to the many prelisting programs used to stabilize and recover the greater sage grouse, the lesser prairie chicken, the dunes sagebrush lizard, and the New England cottontail. These programs are conceptually similar to the Affordable Care Act (known colloquially as Obamacare), which is a preventive medicine program designed to stabilize and address the population's critical illnesses before patients end up in the emergency room and intensive care—a poignant parallel with the Section 6 program, meant to aid threatened and endangered species headed for extinction. If RAWA is enacted, Section 6 and the Pittman-Robertson, Dingell-Johnson program would continue.

The bipartisan Recovering America's Wildlife Act was first introduced in the House of Representatives in 2017 and the Senate in 2018, and passed the House in 2020. In 2021, the legislation was reintroduced, cosponsored in the House by Representatives Debbie Dingell (D-MI), Jeff Fortenberry (R-NE), and eight others (H.R. 2773), and in the Senate by Senators Roy Blunt (R-MO) and Martin Heinrich (D-NM) (S. 2372). The updated bill would provide about $1.4 billion in dedicated funding for the states and $97.5 million for the tribal nations. Hearings were held in both chambers in 2021, and the legislation now awaits passage. Funding remains the predominate threat to realization of the ESA's full potential and the need for federalism's balance in managing all wildlife—both threatened and nonthreatened.

SUMMARY

A question remains: *Will federalism be able to withstand its modern challenges?* Indeed, while the rise of the administrative state and conditional preemption pose threats to state sovereignty in wildlife affairs, the final threat that could put a nail in the American conservation coffin will continue to be insufficient federal funding to protect endangered species. According to state and federal administrators, the Endangered Species Act and its promise for conservation will be *fully* realized with more federal funding—specifically, $1.4 billion per year. Thus, the recent introduction in the House and Senate of the Recovering America's Wildlife Act would also proactively safeguard twelve thousand species at risk, thereby reducing their prospect of extinction. This *dedicated* funding to the states could rebalance federalism, thereby allowing state wildlife authorities to implement the promise of conservation with fresh policy solutions to complex problems that could not be anticipated by the Congress or Washington bureaucrats. Overall, with increased funding, states can return to a more reliable place of governing influence—one that allows them to cooperatively meet new challenges with the federal government, which has harnessed resources to be *distributed to states* to conquer the greatest needs ever experienced in American wildlife conservation.

NOTES

1. Fischman, "Predictions and Prescriptions," 471–75.
2. *Tennessee Valley Authority v. Hill*, 437 U.S. 153, 174, 175, 180, 194 (1978).
3. US Congress, *Endangered Species Act Amendments of 1988*, § 1005, Pub. L. No. 100–478, 102 Stat. 2306, 2308 (1988), https://www.govinfo.gov/content/pkg/STATUTE-102/pdf/STATUTE-102-Pg2306.pdf.
4. US Congress, *Consolidated Appropriations Act, 2021*, Public Law No. 116-260, _ Stat. _, 116 H.R. 133 (2021): 300, https://www.congress.gov/116/bills/hr133/BILLS-116hr133enr.pdf.

In fiscal year 2021, $19,638,000 were also transferred for Section 6 expenses from the Land and Water Conservation Fund.

5. See, for example, Merriam-Webster.com, s.v. "preemption," accessed September 23, 2021, https://www.merriam-webster.com/dictionary/preemption.
6. When the ESA was enacted in 1973, the nation's population was 211.9 million. In 2021 it was 332.7 million—a 57 percent increase. US Census Bureau, Population Division, "National Intercensal Tables: 1900–1990; 1973," Census.gov, October 1, 2004, excel file with data downloadable from https://www.census.gov/data/tables/time-series/demo/popest/pre-1980-national.html; and US Census Bureau, "U.S. and World Population Clock," Census.gov, accessed September 23 2021, https://www.census.gov/popclock/.
7. Hill, 437 U.S. at 174, 175, 176, 180.
8. When the ESA was created in 1973, the regulatory and administrative functions were separated into two separate agencies. The FWS was responsible for terrestrial, avian, and freshwater species, while jurisdiction over marine and anadromous species were the responsibility of the Commerce Department's National Marine Fisheries Service.
9. Davison et al., "Practical Solutions," 10.
10. US Senate, *Authorizations for the Endangered Species Act and for Three Wildlife Refuges: Hearing before the Subcommittee on Resource Protection of the Committee on Environment and Public Works*, 95th Cong., 1st sess., on S. 1237 and S. 1316 (1977): 25, archived at https://babel.hathitrust.org/cgi/pt?id=mdp.39015078591297&view=1up&seq=1.

Also see US House of Representatives, *Fish and Wildlife Miscellaneous, Part 1: Hearing on H.R. 4741 before the Subcommittee on Fisheries and Wildlife Conserva-*

tion and the Environment, Committee on Merchant Marine and Fisheries, 95th Cong. (1977) (statement of Lynn Greenwalt).

11. US Senate, *Authorizations for the Endangered Species Act*.

12. US House of Representatives, Committee on Conference, Endangered Species Act of 1973, report to accompany S. 1983, H.R. Rep. No. 93-740 (1973), 26.

13. US House of Representatives, Committee on Conference, Endangered Species Act of 1973, report, 114.

14. US House of Representatives, Committee on Conference, Endangered Species Act of 1973, report, 115, 116.

15. US Senate, *Authorizations for the Endangered Species Act*, 52, 54.

16. US Senate, *Authorizations for the Endangered Species Act*, 56–57.

17. US Senate, *Authorizations for the Endangered Species Act*, 48.

18. Interagency Grizzly Bear Committee, Expenditure Report, fiscal year 2014–2015 (January 2016), 21, 23, 25, 27.

19. Confusingly, there is also a small fund of $11 million spent annually called the MultiState Conservation Grant Program, a subsection of the Pittman-Robertson Wildlife Restoration Program. This funds—on a competitive basis—grants primarily for research, multistate education, and hunter reactivation, recruitment, and retention programs. Association of Fish and Wildlife Agencies, "Multistate Conservation Grant Program Overview," FishWildlife.org, accessed February 9, 2021, https://www.fishwildlife.org/afwa-informs/multi-state-conservation-grants-program.

20. Blue Ribbon Panel on Sustaining America's Diverse Fish and Wildlife Resources, "The Future of America's Fish and Wildlife: A 21st Century Vision for Investing in and Connecting People to Nature," March 2016, https://www.fishwildlife.org/application/files/8215/1382/2408/Blue_Ribbon_Panel_Report2.pdf.

Conclusion

America has come a long way in the four centuries since the establishment of the first colonies in the early 1600s. The Pilgrims' and the founders' objective was to create a society of free people based on natural laws and beholden to the principles of colonial (state) sovereignty, justice, freedom of speech and assembly, limited government, and democratic governance. The federalist government that the founders created was the first of its kind in the world, a model of democratic republicanism. The federalist system survives yet today, albeit badly tattered by the pressures of economic, technological, and industrial growth and the demands of its citizens for care and feeding from birth to the grave—that is, social security, health care, disability and unemployment compensation, and so on.

Nature and wildlife remain primary today among the nation's many treasures in our abundant land and provide the virtues of solace, stability, social interconnectedness, and personal strength and morality as a common thread that binds the people together. This love of nature and wildlife also creates a common bond among a cadre of men and women in both the public and private sectors dedicated to protecting the common good by protecting our natural heritage. Conservatives and liberals, saints and sinners, abound in our multifarious society, and they do so in the wildlife management community as well. The political and ideological battles between our wildlife professionals are not personal but an issue of contesting belief systems and ideals. These public servants face a national crisis, the character of which remains concealed from the nation gripped by it—that of ideological polarization, ignorance of history, and lack of understanding of how we got into an ideological battle to begin with.

The purpose of this book is to provide a history of how the United States' growth and development, together with societal demand for government services and programs, has led to the ideological gridlock blocking efforts to protect nature and wildlife. With that understanding, hopefully we can return to rediscover that common bond, our desire to preserve and protect the wildlife and nature we all love so dearly. We are all stewards of the planet. It is ours to protect or destroy. We have a choice. On his deathbed, hero of James Fenimore Cooper's *Leatherstocking Tale*, Natty Bumppo, lamented, "How much has the beauty of the wilderness been deformed in two short lives." The same can be said today. The Eden that the Pilgrims discovered no longer exists, and we can't re-create it; it is a mythical concept. But we can conserve what we have if we work together, bound by our commonalities.

Three prominent threats continue to undermine the Endangered Species Act and state sovereignty over wildlife management: (1) federal agency actions in rulemaking and regulations that can result in overreach, (2) grants-in-aid to states where unreasonable conditions are attached, and (3) a lack of federal funding to support administration of the Endangered Species Act—the biggest threat of all. Admittedly, human challenges underlie the application and enforcement of wildlife law at all levels. The ESA unfortunately has built into it inherent administrative and enforcement conflicts between the states and federal government. These same conflicts are embedded in the federal-state relationship established by the US Constitution and have been repeatedly reflected in over 235 years of governance of wildlife management. "While the law is clear, the politics of wildlife management is not. The jurisdictional imbroglio is more political than legal."[1] That political imbroglio extends, moreover, to a Congress that refuses to honor funding the very mandate they established in 1973: to protect and preserve our endangered species and their habitats, regardless of cost!

The conflicts are controllable if we restrain both the federal bureaucracy and the states' demands, and give each other more space to resolve our differences. One of the greatest dangers to state sovereignty in wildlife administration and management is the growth of federal agency power, which is aggravated by the states' demands and conflicting regulatory agendas. That threat is precisely what President Franklin D. Roosevelt alluded to decrying administrative tyranny when he called federal agencies the fourth branch of government.[2] And it is what President Ronald Reagan meant when he said "Government is not the solution to our problems; government is the problem."[3] President Jefferson's eloquent description of the slow erosion of constitutional authority applies equally well today to the evolution of federal-agency preemption of state authority and to the states' competing regulatory agendas over wildlife and nature as a silent trend that few recognize, but that has been the state of affairs for well over the last century and a half.[4]

The Wildlife Society is our most distinguished group of wildlife professionals monitoring, critiquing, and guiding wildlife science and its application. In their 2005 technical review of the ESA—*Improving the Effectiveness of the Endangered Species Act for Wildlife*—they made the following observations that remain as true today as when they were first published:

> The ESA is a fundamentally sound and successful mechanism to prevent species extinctions and conserve biological diversity. Its effectiveness in recovering species has been constrained largely by funding levels that have not kept pace with increased demands and by larger sociocultural and socioeconomic issues that drive species loss.
>
> The Section 6 Cooperative Endangered Species Conservation Fund should be restored to its original intended purpose of providing adequate and stable funding to state fish and wildlife agencies to fulfill state responsibilities under the ESA.
>
> Amounts deposited to the Cooperative Endangered Species Conservation Fund [the mandatory 5 percent from P-R, D-J] should be made available to the states without further appropriation to make it possible for state fish and wildlife agencies to assume the lead for prelisting conservation, recovery planning and implementation oversight, SHA and HCP administration, and post-delisting monitoring.
>
> If the ESA is to remain effective, sufficient resources for its implementation need to be provided by the US government.[5]

Let us not forget President Jefferson's 1821 admonition: "The germ of dissolution of our federal government is in the constitution of the federal Judiciary . . . over the field of jurisdiction, until all shall be usurped from the states, & the government of all be consolidated into one . . . [and] shall be drawn to Washington as the center of all power, it will render powerless the checks provided of one government on another . . . [and] if the states look with apathy on this silent descent of their government into the gulph which is to swallow all, we have only to weep over the human character . . . incapable of self-government."[6]

NOTES

1. Coggins and Ward, "Law of Wildlife Management," 84.
2. Franklin D. Roosevelt, message, iii–v.
3. Ronald Reagan, Inaugural Address to the Nation, January 20, 1986. http://www.reaganfoundation.org/ronald-reagan/reagan-quotes-speeches/inauguraladdress-2/.

4. For a contemporary look at similar perverse elements that are eroding our federalist system of democracy, read Victor Davis Hanson, *The Dying Citizen: How Progressive Elites, Tribalism, and Globalization Are Destroying the Idea of America* (New York: Basic Books, 2021); Anne Applebaum, *Twilight of Democracy: The Seductive Lure of Authoritarianism* (New York: Doubleday, 2020); Steven Levitsky and Daniel Ziblatt, *How Democracies Die* (New York: Crown Publishing, 2018); Randy E. Barnett, *Our Republican Constitution: Securing the Liberty and Sovereignty of We the People* (New York: Harper Collins Publishers, 2016); Randy E. Barnett, *The Structure of Liberty: Justice and the Rule of Law* (Oxford: Oxford University Press, 1998); Presser, *Recapturing the Constitution*; and Wendell Berry, *The Unsettling of America: Culture and Agriculture* (San Francisco: Sierra Club Books, 1977).

5. Davison, et al., "Practical Solutions," 1, 11.

6. US National Archives, "From Thomas Jefferson to C. Hammond, August 18, 1821."

Acknowledgments

This book started initially as part of the outline for a PhD dissertation at the Institute for Environmental History in the Department of History at the University of St. Andrews in Scotland. My gifted faculty advisor, Dr. John F. M. Clark, exercised remarkable patience instructing this senior attorney without any academic background in history on how to write in a historiographic style. To Dr. Clark I am deeply indebted for the education he gave me in historical research sources, techniques, and historiography. I hope I've lived up to his expectations. From there this research evolved further as a chapter in a book to be released next year celebrating the fiftieth anniversary of the Endangered Species Act—*The Codex of the Endangered Species Act, Volume I: The Last 50 Years*. The chapter grew much too large for that book; thus the decision to publish it as a stand-alone book.

During my research and writing journey, several guardian angels appeared who became invaluable in assisting me. I thank them in alphabetical order: Timothy L. Harker, former assistant general counsel and advisor to William Ruckelshaus at EPA in the early 1970s. Tim is quite knowledgeable in constitutional law and federalism and gifted in his literary skills. Hence he not only educated me in federalism but also proofread the manuscript draft twice and was an invaluable guide in enabling me to get the book written and organized in a style and content for the popular reader. My colleague Dr. John F. Organ was likewise involved. John is a forty-plus-year veteran of public service in wildlife conservation with the US Fish and Wildlife Service and US Geological Survey and has served as Chief of the Wildlife and Sport Fish Restoration Program in the Northeast and as Chief of the Cooperative Wildlife Research Units Program, a forty unit PhD-level program housed in forty universities across the country. John proofread parts of the manuscript to ensure the accuracy of the history of conservation and that its key milestones and environmental policies were properly characterized and recognized; that the influence of the early Marshall and Taney Supreme Court doctrines were properly treated; and that the working relationships between the state and federal wildlife professionals after 1973 were characterized appropriately as the Endangered Species Act was implemented. Dr. Organ knows as much about the legal history of conservation as he does its biology, ideology, policies, and popular development periods. He has a wealth of knowledge and is a blessing to our country in his past and continuing public service.

Next I thank my senior associate, research assistant, and colleague, Christopher E. Segal, who joined me twelve years ago out of Georgetown Law School. I call him "Yoda," because he is invaluable in his depth of research skills, follow-up, diligence, intuitive sense of what's important in evaluating a topic, prioritization thereof, etc. In manuscript preparation, editing, fact-checking, and attention to accuracy and detail, he is outstanding. This book couldn't have been written without the combined efforts of the individuals described herein.

My executive assistant, Janice Shoyooee, is the daily hero in deciphering legions of handwritten material; anticipating my unrelenting need for perfection, information, and facts; locating lost files; and scrambling to stay ahead of me and keep my schedule organized.

Bonnie Baier keeps the home fires burning, patiently tolerating my exhausting schedule and publishing deadlines.

Thanks to two third-year law student interns at Indiana University's School of Law who edited the footnotes and helped with the chapter introductions and summaries: Charles Rice and Michael Froedge will make terrific attorneys one day; watch for them in the future.

These people have all blessed my journey over the last two years of research and writing right through the COVID-19 pandemic.

Throughout the research and preparation of this book, a variety of people have furnished me with key information and data to fill in research gaps, for which I am indebted. In alphabetical order they are Dr. Ed Arnett, E. U. Curtis "Buff" Bohlen, James F. Bullock Jr., the late John D. Dingell Jr., Cindy Dohner, Robert Fischman, Carol Frampton, Gary Frazer, Lynn Greenwalt, Michael Greve, Dale Hall, Mark Humpert, Lane Kisonak, Ya-Wei (Jake) Li, Mario Loyola, James Lyons, Jen Mock Schaeffer, Dr. Gregory Schildwachter, the late Dr. Lee M. Talbot, Wendi Weber, Douglas P. Wheeler, and Dr. Steve Williams. Further to be recognized are a large number of state wildlife agency directors who spoke to me off the record on the condition of anonymity.

It had been sixty years since I took a constitutional law course; hence the need to read my way back into federalism, preemption, and constitutional law from the scholarship of many gifted professors who published books and law review articles on this subject. These became invaluable guides and educational sources. In alphabetical order, these scholars include Michael Bean, William W. Bratton, Dr. Alston Chase, George Cameron Coggins, William N. Eskridge Jr., Robert L. Fischman, Stephen Gardbaum, Michael Greve, Samuel P. Hays, Peter Hoffer, William Hoffer, Lane Kisonak, Richard J. Lazarus, Mario Loyola, Chad Montrie, John Copeland Nagle, Dr. John Organ, Shannon Petersen, Robert Post, Hal K. Rothman, J. D. Ruhl, Steven Lewis Yaffee, and Ernest A. Young. My apologies to those whom I have inadvertently omitted throughout these acknowledgments.

And my thanks go to the publishing house of Rowman & Littlefield Publishers, Inc., vice president and senior executive editor Jon Sisk, and president and CEO Jed Lyons for their continuing faith in my research and writing, and in thanks of their recognition of the importance of publishing this story.

Lowell E. Baier
Bethesda, Maryland
July 4, 2021

Appendix 1

Federal Environmental and Consumer-Protection Statutes and Agencies Established during the 1960's and 1970's Green Revolution

Table A1.1.

Year	Environmental Legislation	Consumer Protection Legislation
1963	Clean Air Act (amended 1965, 1966, 1969, 1970, 1977, 1990)	
	Federal Water Quality Control Act	
1964	The Wilderness Act	
	The Land and Water Conservation Fund Act	
1965	Water Quality Act of 1965	
	National Emissions Standards Act	
	Motor Vehicle Air Pollution Control Act	
	Solid Waste Disposal Act	
1966	Fur Seal Act	Motor Vehicle Safety Act
	Clean Water Restoration Act	Federal Cigarette Labeling and Advertising Act
	Endangered Species Act (amended 1969, 1973)	Child Protection Act of 1966
		Fair Packaging and Labeling Act of 1966
1967	Air Quality Act	Flammable Fabrics Act of 1967
		Wholesome Poultry Products Act of 1967
		Whole Meat Act of 1967
1968	National Trails System Act	Federal Consumer Credit Protection Act
	Wild and Scenic Rivers Act	Natural Gas Pipeline Safety Act of 1968
		Radiation Control Act of 1968

(continued)

Table A1.1. *(continued)*

Year	Environmental Legislation	Consumer Protection Legislation
1969		Child Protection and Safety Toy Act
		Coal Mine Health and Safety Act of 1969
		Fire Research and Safety Act of 1969
1970	National Environmental Policy Act (NEPA)	Fair Credit Reporting Act of 1970
	Environmental Quality Improvement Act	Lead-Based Paint Poisoning Prevention Act
	Environmental Protection Agency created (EPA)	Occupational Safety and Health Administration agency created (OSHA)
	Council for Environmental Quality (CEQ)	
1971	Wild Free-Roaming Horses and Burros Act	
1972	Marine Mammal Protection Act (MMPA)	Federal Insecticide, Fungicide, and Rodenticide Act
	Coastal Zone Management Act	Consumer Products Safety Commission created
	Federal Water Pollution Control Act Amendments of 1972 (Clean Water Act)	Noise Control Act
	Marine Protection, Research, and Sanctuaries Act of 1972 (Ocean Dumping Act)	
1973	Endangered Species Act (amended 1978, 1982, 1988)	
1974	National Reserves Management Act	Emergency Highway Energy Conservation Act
	The Safe Water Drinking Act	
	Forest and Rangeland Renewal Resources Planning Act of 1974	
1975	Energy Policy and Conservation Act	Magnuson-Moss Warranty Act
		Hazardous Materials Transportation Act
1976	National Forest Management Act (NFMA)	
	Federal Land Policy and Management Act (FLPMA)	
	Resource Conservation and Recovery Act	
	Toxic Substances Control Act	
	Magnuson-Stevens Fisheries Conservation and Management Act	

Year	Environmental Legislation	Consumer Protection Legislation
1977	Surface Mining Control and Reclamation Act	
	Department of Energy created	
	US Strategic Petroleum Reserve established	
1978		National Energy Conservation Policy Act
1980	Equal Access to Justice Act	Power Plant and Industrial Fuel Use Act of 1978
	Comprehensive Environmental Response, Compensation, and Liability Act (CERCLA)	Natural Gas Policy Act of 1978
	Alaska National Interest Lands Conservation Act	Public Utilities Regulatory Policies Act of 1978
	Fish and Wildlife Conservation Act	Energy Tax Act of 1978

Appendix 2

Graphs of Preemption Statues and US Supreme Court Cases

	Banking & Finance	Civil Rights	Commerce	Health & Safety	Natural Resources	Tax	Other	Total	Preemption Relief Statutes
Before 1900	0	7	15	4	1	3	0	30	3
1900–1909	0	0	7	5	2	0	0	14	1
1910–1919	1	0	16	3	1	0	1	22	1
1920–1929	2	0	12	3	0	0	0	17	3
1930–1939	8	0	21	2	0	2	0	33	4
1940–1949	1	0	9	3	2	0	1	16	3
1950–1959	3	1	10	6	3	2	2	27	4
1960–1969	5	7	9	23	3	0	0	47	2
1970–1979	15	10	31	32	9	6	5	108	5
1980–1989	13	6	35	26	6	5	9	100	7
1990–1991	2	2	11	6	0	3	1	25	1
Totals	50	33	176	113	27	21	19	439	34

Federal preemption and preemption-relief statutes, 1790–1991 (by date of enactment and purposes). *Source*: US Advisory Commission on Intergovernmental Relations, *Federal Statutory Preemption of State and Local Authority: History, Inventory, and Issues* (Washington, DC: ACIR, 1992), 9.

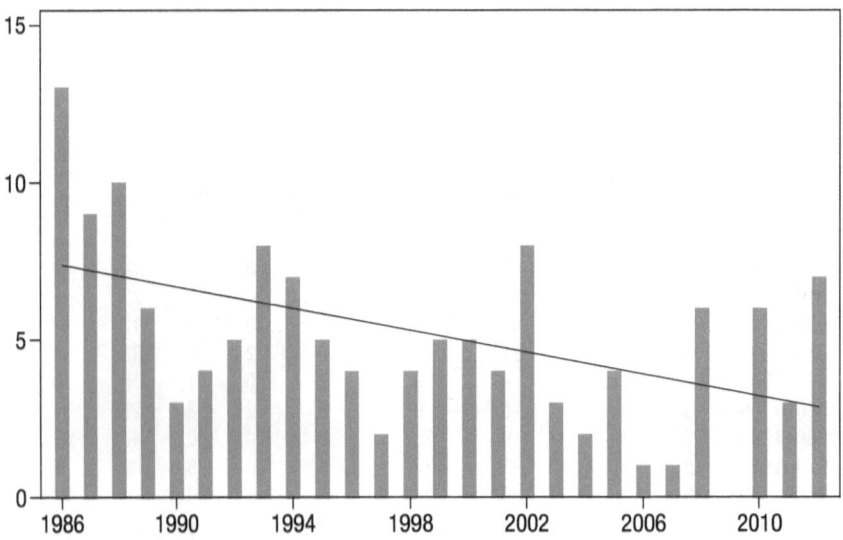

US Supreme Court preemption cases by term, 1986–2012. *Source*: Michael Greve et al., "Preemption in the Rehnquist and Roberts Courts: An Empirical Analysis," *Supreme Court Economic Review* 23 (2015): 360.

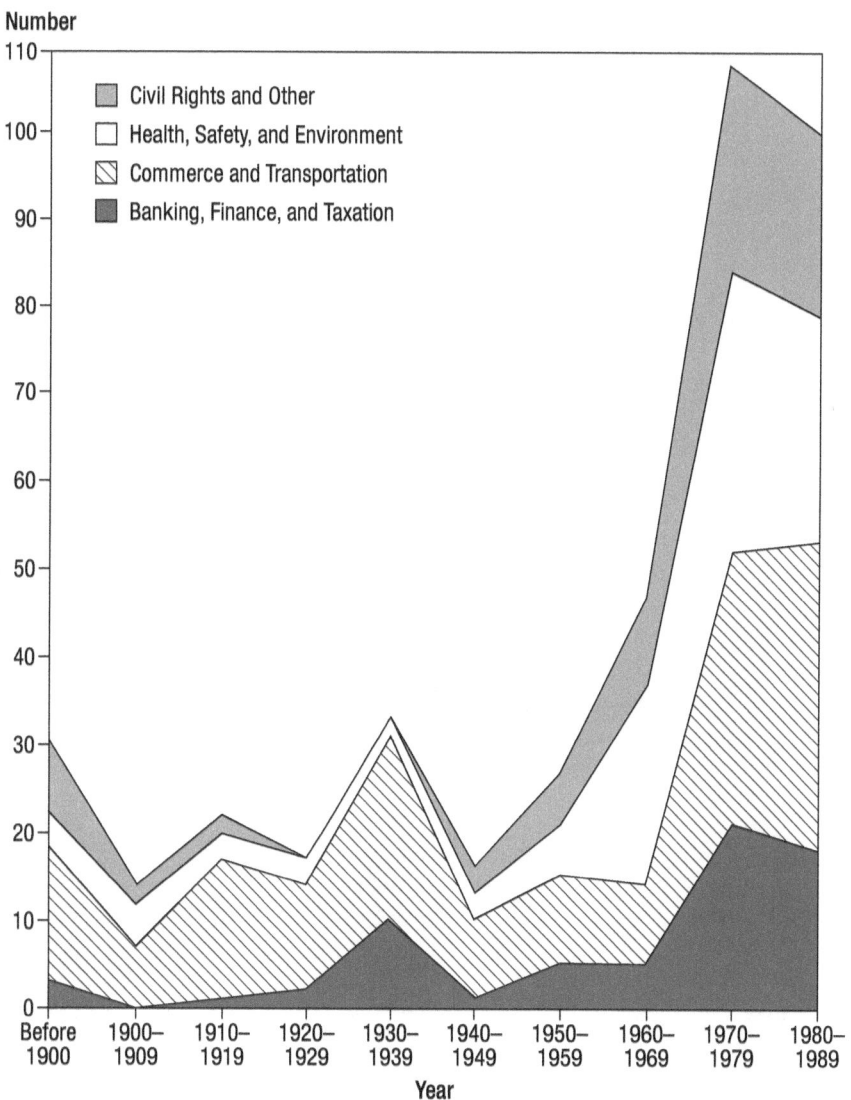

Number of federal preemption statutes enacted per decade, 1790–1989 (by date of enactment and purpose). *Source*: US Advisory Commission on Intergovernmental Relations, *Federal Statutory Preemption of State and Local Authority: History, Inventory, and Issues* (Washington, DC: ACIR, 1992), 8.

Bibliography

BOOKS

Applebaum, Anne. *Twilight of Democracy: The Seductive Lure of Authoritarianism*. New York: Doubleday, 2020.

Ambrose, Stephen E. *Nothing Like It in the World: The Men Who Built the Transcontinental Railroad, 1860–1897*. New York: Simon and Schuster, 2000.

Andrews, Richard N. L. *Managing the Environment: Managing Ourselves*. New Haven: Yale University Press, 1999.

Baier, Lowell E. *Inside the Equal Access to Justice Act: Environmental Litigation and the Crippling Battle over America's Lands, Endangered Species, and Critical Habitats*. Lanham, MD: Rowman & Littlefield, 2016.

———. *Records of North American Big Game*. 10th ed. Edited by Jack Reneau and Susan Reneau. The Boone and Crockett Club: A 106 Year Retrospective. Missoula: Boone and Crockett Club, 1993.

Bailey, James A., William Elder, and Ted D. McKinney. *Reading in Wildlife Conservation*. Washington, DC: The Wildlife Society, 1974.

Bailyn, Bernard. *The Origins of American Politics*. New York: Alfred A. Knopf, 1968.

Barber, William J. *From New Era to New Deal: Herbert Hoover, the Economists, and American Economic Policy, 1921–1933*. Cambridge: Cambridge University Press, 1988.

Barnett, Randy E. *Our Republican Constitution: Securing the Liberty and Sovereignty of We the People*. New York: HarperCollins, 2016.

———. *The Structure of Liberty: Justice and the Rule of Law*. Oxford: Oxford University Press, 1998.

Bean, Michael J., and Melanie J. Rowland. *The Evolution of National Wildlife Law*. 3rd ed. Westport, CT: Praeger, 1997.

Beard, Charles A. *An Economic Interpretation of the Constitution of the United States*. New York: The Macmillan Company, 1913.

Belanger, Dian Olson, and Adrian Kinnane. *Managing American Wildlife: A History of the International Association of Fish and Wildlife Agencies*. Rockville, MD: Montrose Press, 2002.

Berry, Wendell. *The Unsettling of America: Culture and Agriculture*. San Francisco: Sierra Club Books, 1977.

Brinkley, Douglas. *The Wilderness Warrior: Theodore Roosevelt and the Crusade for America, 1858–1919*. New York: Harper Perennial, 2010.

Broadwater, Jeff. *George Mason: Forgotten Founder*. Chapel Hill: The University of North Carolina Press, 2006.

Burnett, Edmund C. *The Continental Congress*. Westport, CT: Greenwood Publishing Group, 1975.

Carpenter, Daniel. *The Forging of Bureaucratic Autonomy*. Princeton: Princeton University Press, 2001.

Carson, Rachel. *Silent Spring*. Boston: Houghton Mifflin Company, 1962.

Chase, Alston. *In a Dark Wood: The Fight over Forests and the Rising Tyranny of Ecology*. New York: Houghton Mifflin Company, 1995.

———. *Playing God in Yellowstone: The Destruction of America's First National Park*. San Diego and New York: Harcourt Brace Jovanovich, 1987.

Commoner, Barry. *The Closing Circle: Nature, Man, and Technology*. New York: Alfred A. Knopf, 1971.

Cooper, Thomas, and George Harris. *The Institutes of Justinian*, 3rd ed. New York: J. S. Voorhies, 1852.

Corwin, Edward S. *Court over Constitution: A Study of Judicial Review as an Instrument of Popular Government*. Princeton: Princeton University Press, 1938.

Crane, Jeff. *The Environment in American History: Nature and the Formation of the United States*. New York: Routledge, 2015.

Divine, Robert A., ed. *The Johnson Years*. Lawrence: The University Press of Kansas, 1987.

Drahozal, Christopher R. *The Supremacy Clause: A Reference Guide to the United States Constitution*. Westwood, CT: Praeger, 2004.

DuPont, B. G. *E. I. DuPont De Nemours and Company: A History 1802–1902*. Boston and New York: Houghton Mifflin Company, 1920.

Epstein, Richard A., and Michael Greve, eds. *Federal Preemption: States' Powers, National Interests*. Washington, DC: AEI Press, 2007.

Fiege, Mark. *The Republic of Nature: An Environmental History of the United States*. Seattle: University of Washington Press, 2012.

Fisher, James, Noel Simon, and Jack Vincent. *Wildlife in Danger*. New York: Viking Press, 1969.

Flexner, Eleanor, and Ellen Fitzpatrick. *Century of Struggle: The Woman's Right Movement in the United States*. Cambridge: Harvard University Press, 1996.

Fogel, Robert W. *Railroads and American Economic Growth in Econometric History*. Baltimore and London: The Johns Hopkins University Press, 1964.

Freeman, Joshua B. *Behemoth: A History of the Factory and the Making of the Modern World*. New York: W. W. Norton and Company, 2018.

Frum, David. *How We Got Here: The 70's; The Decade That Brought You Modern Life (For Better or Worse)*. New York: Basic Books, 2000.

Gabrielson, Ira N. *Wildlife Refuges*. New York: The MacMillian Company, 1943.

Garner, Bryan A., ed. *Black's Law Dictionary*. 11th ed. Saint Paul, MN: Thomson Reuters, 2019.

Goble, Dale D., J. Michael Scott, and Frank W. Davis, eds. *The Endangered Species Act at Thirty*, vol. 2. Washington, DC: Island Press, 2006.

Goforth, W. Reid. *The Cooperative Fish and Wildlife Research Unit Program*. Reston, VA: US Geological Survey, 2006.

Gottlieb, Robert. *Forcing the Spring: The Transformation of the American Environmental Movement*. Washington, DC: Island Press, 1993.

Graetz, Michael J., and Linda Greenhouse. *The Burger Court and the Rise of the Judicial Right*. New York: Simon and Schuster, 2016.

Greve, Michael S. *The Upside-Down Constitution*. Cambridge: Harvard University Press, 2012.

Grinnell, George Bird, ed. *A Brief History of the Boone and Crockett Club*. New York: Forest and Stream Publishing Company, 1910.

———, ed. *Hunting at High Altitudes*. New York: Harper and Brothers, 1913.

Haeckel, Ernst. *Generelle Morphologie der Organismen*, 2 vols. Berlin: Reimer, 1866.

Hallock, Charles. *The Sportsman's Gazetteer and General Guide*. New York: Forest and Stream Publishing Company, 1872.

Hanson, Victor Davis. *The Dying Citizen: How Progressive Elites, Tribalism, and Globalization Are Destroying the Idea of America*. New York: Basic Books, 2021.

Harbaugh, William Henry. *Power and Responsibility: The Life and Times of Theodore Roosevelt*. New York: Farrar, Straus and Cudahy, 1961.

Hays, Samuel P. *Beauty, Health, and Permanence: Environmental Politics in the United States, 1955–1985*. Cambridge: Cambridge University Press, 1987.

———. *Conservation and the Gospel of Efficiency: The Progressive Conservation Movement, 1890–1920*. Cambridge: Harvard University Press, 1959.

———. *Explorations in Environmental History*. Pittsburgh: University of Pittsburgh Press, 1998.

———. *A History of Environmental Politics since 1945*. Pittsburgh: University of Pittsburgh Press, 2000.

Herring, George C. *From Colony to Superpower: U.S. Foreign Relations since 1776*. Oxford: Oxford University Press, 2008.

Hoffer, Peter Charles, Williamjames Hoffer, and N. E. H. Hull. *The Supreme Court: An Essential History*. Lawrence: University Press of Kansas, 2007.

Hornaday, William T. *Our Vanishing Wildlife: Its Extermination and Preservation*. New York: New York Zoological Society, 1913.

Hounshell, David A. *From the American System to Mass Production, 1800–1932: The Development of Manufacturing Technology in the United States*. Baltimore: The Johns Hopkins University Press, 1984.

Howe, Daniel Walker. *What Hath God Wrought: The Transformation of America, 1815–1848*. New York: Oxford University Press, 2009.

Interagency Grizzly Bear Committee. Expenditure Report. Fiscal year 2014–2015. January 2016.

Justinian I. *The Institutes of Justinian*, 3rd ed.. Notes by Thomas Cooper, translated by George Harris. New York: J. S. Voorhies, 1852.

Kennedy, David M. *Freedom from Fear: The American People in the Great Depression*. New York: Oxford University Press, 1999.

Koppes, Clayton R. *JPL and the American Space Program: A History of the Jet Propulsion Laboratory*. New Haven: Yale University Press, 1982.

Lear, Linda. *Rachel Carson: Witness for Nature*. New York: Houghton Mifflin, 1997.

Leopold, Aldo. *Game Management*. New York: Charles Scribner's Sons, 1933.

———. *Round River*. New York and Oxford: Oxford University Press, 1953.

———. *Sand County Almanac*. New York and Oxford: Oxford University Press, 1949.

Leuchtenburg, William E. *The Supreme Court Reborn: The Constitutional Revolution in the Age of Roosevelt*. New York: Oxford University Press, 1995.

Levitsky, Steven, and Daniel Ziblatt. *How Democracies Die*. New York: Crown, 2019.

Lutz, Donald S. *The Origins of American Constitutionalism*. Baton Rouge and London: Louisiana State University Press, 1986.

Madison, James, and George Mason. *The Bill of Rights: With Writings that Formed Its Foundation*. Bedford, MA: Applewood Books, 2008.

McGerr, Michael. *A Fierce Discontent: The Rise and Fall of the Progressive Movement in America, 1870–1920*. New York: Simon and Schuster, 2003.

McIntosh, R. P. *The Background of Ecology: Concept and Theory*. New York: Cambridge University Press, 1986.

McNeill, Ian. *An Encyclopedia of the History of Technology*. London: Routledge, 1990.

McPherson, James M. *Battle Cry for Freedom: The Civil War Era*. New York and Oxford: Oxford University Press, 1988.

Meine, Curt. *Aldo Leopold: His Life and Work*. Madison: The University of Wisconsin Press, 1988.

Merriner, James L. *Grafters and Goo Goos: Corruption and Reform in Chicago, 1833–2003*. Bristol, UK: Policy Press, Southern Illinois University Press, 2004.

Middlekauff, Robert. *The Glorious Cause*. New York: Oxford University Press, 1982.

Montesquieu, Charles Louis de Secondat, Baron of. *The Spirit of the Law (De l'esprit des loix)*. Translated by Thomas Nugent. London: Printed for J. Nourse and P. Vaillant, the Strand, 1750.

Montrie, Chad. *The Myth of Silent Spring: Rethinking the Origins of American Environmentalism*. Oakland: University of California Press, 2018.

———. *A People's History of Environmentalism in the United States*. New York: Continuum Press, 2011.

Mothershead, Harmon Ross. *The Swan Land and Cattle Company, Ltd*. Norman: University of Oklahoma Press, 1971.

Nash, Roderick F. *The Rights of Nature: A History of Environmental Ethics*. Madison: The University of Wisconsin Press, 1989.

Newton, Julianne Lutz. *Aldo Leopold's Odyssey*. Washington, DC: Island Press, 2006.

Obermayer, Herman J. *Rehnquist: A Personal Portrait of the Distinguished Chief Justice of the United States*. New York: Simon and Schuster, 2009.

Organ, John F., Valerius Geist, Shane P. Mahoney, S. Williams, P. R. Krausman, G. R. Batcheller, T. A. Decker, R. Carmichael, P. Nanjappa, R. Regan, R. A. Medellin, R. Cantu, R. E. McCabe, S. Craven, G. M. Vecellio, and D. J. Decker. *The North American Model of Wildlife Conservation*. The Wildlife Society and the Boone and Crockett Club Technical Review 12–04. Edited by Theodore H. Bookhout. Bethesda, MD: The Wildlife Society, 2012. https://perma.cc/68VB-FJ7F.

Palmer, T. S. *Chronology and Index of the More Important Events in American Game Protection, 1776–1911*. US Biological Survey bulletin no. 41. Washington, DC: Government Printing Office, 1912.

Patterson, James T. *Grand Expectations: The United States, 1945–1974*. New York: Oxford University Press, 1996.

———. *Restless Giant: The United States from Watergate to "Bush v. Gore"*. Oxford: Oxford University Press, 2005.

Pearce, William Martin. *The Matador Land and Cattle Company*. Norman: University of Oklahoma Press, 1964.

Petersen, Shannon. *Acting for Endangered Species*. Lawrence: University of Kansas Press, 2002.

———. "The Modern Ark: A History of the Endangered Species Act." PhD diss., University of Wisconsin–Madison, 2000.

Presser, Stephen B. *Recapturing the Constitution: Race, Religion, and Abortion Reconsidered*. Washington, DC: Regnery, 1994.

Reiger, John F. *American Sportsmen and the Origins of Conservation*. Corvallis: Oregon State University Press, 2001.

Riis, Jacob. *The Battle with the Slum*. New York: Macmillan Co., 1902.

———. *The Children of the Poor*. New York: Scribner's Sons, 1892.

———. *How the Other Half Lives: Studies among the Tenements of New York*. New York: Charles Scribner's Sons, 1890.

———. *The Making of an American*. New York: Macmillan, 1901.

———. *Out of Mulberry Street*. New York: The Century Co., 1898.

Rome, Adam. *The Bulldozer in the Countryside: Suburban Sprawl and the Rise of American Environmentalism*. Cambridge: Cambridge University Press, 2001.

Rothman, Hal K. *The Greening of a Nation? Environmentalism in the United States since 1945*. Fort Worth: Harcourt Brace College Publishers, 1998.

———. *Saving the Planet: The American Response to the Environment in the Twentieth Century*. Chicago: Ivan R. Dee Publishing, 2000.

Schlesinger, Arthur M. *The Politics of Upheaval: The Age of Roosevelt, 1935–1936*. New York: Houghton Mifflin Harcourt, 2003.

Schmeckebier, Laurence F. *The Bureau of Prohibition: Its History, Activities and Organization*. Washington, DC: Brookings Institution, 1929.

Sellers, Christopher C. *Crabgrass Crucible: Suburban Nature and the Rise of Environmentalism in Twentieth-Century America*. Chapel Hill: The University of North Carolina Press, 2012.

Sinclair, Upton. *The Flivver King*. Detroit: United Automobile Workers, 1937.

———. *The Jungle*. New York: Doubleday, Page and Co., 1906.

———. *King Coal: A Novel*. New York: Macmillan Co., 1917.

———. *Oil!* New York: Albert and Charles Boni, 1927.

Smith, Kimberly K. *The Conservation Constitution: The Conservation Movement and Constitutional Change, 1870–1930*. Lawrence: University Press of Kansas, 2019.

Souder, William. *On a Farther Shore: The Life and Legacy of Rachel Carson*. New York: Crown Publishers, 2012.

Stein, Bruce A., Naomi Edelson, Lauren Anderson, John J. Kanter, and Jodi. Stemler. *Reversing America's Wildlife Crisis: Securing the Future of our Fish and Wildlife*. Washington, DC: National Wildlife Federation, 2018. https://www.nwf.org/-/media/Documents/PDFs/NWF-Reports/2018/Reversing-Americas-Wildlife-Crisis_2018.ashx.

Stone, Richard D. *The Interstate Commerce Commission and the Railroad Industry: A History of Regulatory Policy*. New York: Praeger, 1991.

Sutter, Paul S. *Driven Wild: How the Fight against Automobiles Launched the Modern Wilderness Movement*. Seattle: University of Washington Press, 2002.

Sykes, Jay B., and Nicole Vanatko. "Federal Preemption: A Legal Primer." Congressional Research Service, Report No. R45825, July 23, 2019. https://sgp.fas.org/crs/misc/R45825.pdf.

Tarbell, Ida M. *The History of the Standard Oil Company*. New York: McClure, Phillips and Company, 1904.

Taylor, George R. *The Transportation Revolution, 1815–1860*. Economic History of the United States. Milton Park, Abingdon, Oxfordshire: Routledge, 1960.

Tober, James A. *Wildlife and the Public Interest: Nonprofit Organizations and Federal Wildlife Policy*. New York: Praeger Publishers, 1989.

Trefethen, John B. *An American Crusade for Wildlife*. New York: Winchester Press, 1975.

Turner, Frederick Jackson. *The Frontier in American History*. New York: Henry Holt and Company, 1920.

Wells, Christopher W. *Car Country: An Environmental History*. Seattle: University of Washington Press, 2012.

West, Elliott. *Theodore Roosevelt: Naturalist in the Arena*. Edited by Char Miller and Clay S. Jenkinson. Lincoln: University of Nebraska Press, 2020.

White, G. Edward. *The Constitution and the New Deal*. Cambridge: Harvard University Press, 2000.

White, Richard. *Railroaded: The Transcontinentals and the Making of Modern America*. New York: W. W. Norton and Company, 2011.

———. *The Republic for Which It Stands: The United States During Reconstruction and the Gilded Age, 1865–1896*. New York: Oxford University Press, 2019.

Wood, Gordon S. *The Creation of the American Republic, 1776–1787*. Chapel Hill: University of North Carolina Press, 1969.

———. *Empire of Liberty: A History of the Early Republic, 1789–1815.* Oxford: Oxford University Press, 2009.

Wooddy, Carroll Hill. *The Growth of the Federal Government, 1915–1932.* New York: McGraw-Hill, 1934.

Yaffee, Steven Lewis. *Prohibitive Policy: Implementing the Federal Endangered Species Act.* Cambridge: MIT Press, 1982.

JOURNAL ARTICLES AND BOOK CHAPTERS

Ackerman, Bruce, Donald Elliott, and John Millian. "Toward a Theory of Statutory Evolution: The Federalization of Environmental Law." *The Journal of Law, Economics, and Organization* 1, no. 2 (1985): 313–40.

Adler, Jonathan H. "Business, the Environment, and the Roberts Court: A Preliminary Assessment." *Santa Clara Law Review* 49, no. 4 (2009): 943–78. https://digital commons.law.scu.edu/lawreview/vol49/iss4/2/.

Adler, Robert W. "The Supreme Court and Ecosystems: Environmental Science in Environmental Law." *Vermont Law Review* 27, no. 2 (2003): 249–370.

Agar, Jon. "What Happened in the Sixties?" *The British Journal for the History of Science* 41, no. 4 (2008): 567–600.

Allen, Durward. "Report of the Committee on North American Wildlife Policy." *Wildlife Society Bulletin* 1, no. 2 (Summer 1973): 73–92.

Alschuler, Albert W. "Failed Pragmatism: Reflections on the Burger Court Commentaries." *Harvard Law Review* 100, no. 6 (1986): 1436–56.

Anderson, William. "Federalism, Then and Now." *State Government* 16 (1943): 107–12.

Blocher, Joseph. "Selling State Borders." *University of Pennsylvania Law Review* 162, no. 2 (2014): 241–305. https://scholarship.law.upenn.edu/cgi/viewcontent.cgi?article=1544&context=penn_law_review.

Bratton, William W. "Preemption Doctrine: Shifting Perspectives on Federalism and the Burger Court." *Columbia Law Review* 75, no. 3 (April, 1975): 623–54.

Chemerinsky, Erwin. "Keynote Address: Rehnquist Court's Federalism Revolution." *Willamette Law Review* 41, no. 5 (2005): 827–46. https://scholarship.law.duke.edu/cgi/viewcontent.cgi?article=2132&context=faculty_scholarship.

Coggins, George Cameron. "Federal Wildlife Law Achieves Adolescence: Developments in the 1970s." *Duke Law Journal* 27, no. 3 (1978): 753–817. https://scholarship.law.duke.edu/cgi/viewcontent.cgi?article=2668&context=dlj.

Coggins, George Cameron, and Michael E. Ward. "The Law of Wildlife Management on the Federal Public Lands." *Oregon Law Review* 60, nos. 1–2 (1981): 59–156.

Corwin, Edward S. "The Passing of Dual Federalism." *Virginia Law Review* 36, no. 1 (1950): 1–24.

Davies, Lincoln L. "Lessons for an Endangered Movement: What a Historical Juxtaposition of the Legal Response to Civil Rights and Environmentalism." *Environmental Law* 21, no. 2 (Spring 2001): 229–370.

Davis, Mary J. "Unmasking the Presumption in Favor of Preemption." *South Carolina Law Review* 53, no. 4 (2002): 963–1030.

Deveney, Patrick. "Title, Jus Publicum, and the Public Trust: An Historical Analysis." *Sea Grant Law Journal* 1 (1976): 13–82.

Dinh, Viet D. "Federal Displacement of State Law: The Nineteenth-Century View." In *Federal Preemption: States' Powers, National Interests*, edited by Richard A. Epstein and Michael S. Greve, 27–47. Washington, DC: AEI Press, 2007.

Donahue, Charles, Jr. "On Translating the 'Digest.'" Review of *The Digest of Justinian*, translated and edited by Theodore Mommsen, Paul Krueger, and Alan Watson. *Stanford Law Review* 39, no. 4 (1987): 1057–77.

Dwyer, John P. "The Commerce Clause and the Limits of Congressional Authority to Regulate the Environment." *Environmental Law Reporter* 25, no. 8 (2000): 10421–31. https://elr.info/sites/default/files/articles/25.10421.htm.

———. "The Role of State Law in an Era of Federal Preemption: Lessons from Environmental Regulation." *Law and Contemporary Problems (Duke University)* 40, no. 3 (1997): 203–30.

Epstein, Richard A. and Michael S. Greve. "Conclusion: Preemption Doctrine and Its Limits." In *Federal Preemption: States' Powers, National Interests*, edited by Richard A. Epstein and Michael S. Greve, 309–342. Washington, DC: AEI Press, 2007.

———. "Introduction: Preemption in Context." In *Federal Preemption: States' Powers, National Interests*, edited by Richard A. Epstein and Michael S. Greve, 1–24. Washington, DC: AEI Press, 2007.

Ernst, Julia L. "The Mayflower Compact: Celebrating Four Hundred Years of Influence on U.S. Democracy." *North Dakota Law Review* 95, no. 1 (2020): 1–135.

Eskridge, William N., Jr. "Vetogates, Chevron, Preemption." *Notre Dame Law Review* 83, no. 1441 (2008): 1441–94.

Eskridge, William N., Jr., and Philip P. Frickey. "Quasi-constitutional Law: Clear Statement Rules as Constitutional Lawmaking." *Vanderbilt Law Review* 45 (1992): 593–646. https://digitalcommons.law.yale.edu/cgi/viewcontent.cgi?referer=https://www.google.com/&httpsredir=1&article=4814&context=fss_papers.

Fischman, Robert L. "Cooperative Federalism and Natural Resource Law." *NYU Environmental Law Journal* 14, no. 1 (2005): 179–231.

———. "Predictions and Prescriptions for the Endangered Species Act." *Environmental Law* 34 (2004): 451–81. https://www.repository.law.indiana.edu/cgi/viewcontent.cgi?article=1224&context=facpub.

Fischman, Robert L., and Jaelith Hall-Rivera. "A Lesson for Conservation from Pollution Control Law: Cooperative Federalism for Recovery under the Endangered Species Act." *Columbia Journal of Environmental Law* 27 (2002): 45–172. https://www.repository.law.indiana.edu/cgi/viewcontent.cgi?article=1228&context=facpub.

Gardbaum, Stephen. "The Breadth versus the Depth of Congress's Commerce Power: The Curious History of Preemption During the Lochner Era." In *Federal Preemption: States' Powers, National Interests*, edited by Richard A. Epstein and Michael S. Greve, 48–78. Washington, DC: AEI Press, 2007.

———. "New Deal Constitutionalism and the Unshackling of the States." *University of Chicago Law Review* 483, no. 2 (1997): 483–566. https://chicagounbound.uchicago.edu/cgi/viewcontent.cgi?article=4956&context=uclrev.

———. "The Nature of Preemption." *Cornell Law Review* 79, no. 4 (1994): 767–815. https://core.ac.uk/download/pdf/216737946.pdf.

———. "New Evidence on the Presumption against Preemption: An Empirical Study of Congressional Responses to Supreme Court Preemption Decisions." *Harvard Law Review* 120, no. 6 (2007): 1604–26. https://harvardlawreview.org/wp-content/uploads/pdfs/new_evidence_on_the_presumption.pdf.

Gerken, Heather K. "Federalism 3.0." *California Law Review* 105 (2017): 1695–1723. https://29qish1lqx5q2k5d7b491joo-wpengine.netdna-ssl.com/wp-content/uploads/2018/01/Gerken-34-formatted.pdf.

Gluck, Abbe R. "Intrastatutory Federalism and Statutory Interpretation: State Implementation of Federal Law in Health Reform and Beyond." *Yale Law Journal* 121 (2011): 534–622. https://docs.google.com/viewerng/viewer?url=https://www.yalelawjournal.org/pdf/1032_qcrpe69v.pdf.

Greve, Michael, Jonathan Klick, Michael Petrino, and J. P. Sevilla. "Preemption in the Rehnquist and Roberts Courts: An Empirical Analysis." *Supreme Court Economic Review* 23 (2015): 353–92. https://www.journals.uchicago.edu/doi/pdf/10.1086/686541.

Horner, Susan M. "Embryo, Not Fossil: Breathing Life into Public Trust in Wildlife." *Land & Water Law Review* 35, no. 1 (2000): 23–53. https://scholarship.law.uwyo.edu/cgi/viewcontent.cgi?article=2127&context=land_water.

Hughes, Richard A. "Pro-justice Ethics, Water Scarcity, Human Rights." *Journal of Law & Religion* 25, no. 2 (2009–2010): 521–40.

Ingram, Helen, and Cy R. Oggins. "The Public Trust Doctrine and Community Values in Water." *Natural Resources Journal* 32, no. 3 (1992): 515–37. https://digitalrepository.unm.edu/cgi/viewcontent.cgi?article=1966&context=nrj.

Jackson, Vicki C. "Narratives of Federalism: Of Continuities and Comparative Constitutional Experience." *Duke Law Journal* 51, no. 1 (2001): 223–87. https://scholarship.law.duke.edu/cgi/viewcontent.cgi?article=1126&context=dlj.

Johnson, Stephen M. "The Roberts Court and the Environment." *Boston College Environmental Affairs Law Review* 37, no. 2 (2010): 317–63. https://lawdigitalcommons.bc.edu/cgi/viewcontent.cgi?article=1053&context=ealr.

Kincaid, John. "From Dual to Coercive Federalism in American Intergovernmental Relations." In *Globalization and Decentralization: Institutional Contexts, Policy Issues, and Intergovernmental Relations in Japan and the United States*, edited by Jong S. Jun and Deil S. Wright, 29–47. Washington, DC: Georgetown University Press, 1996.

Kisonak, Lane. "Fish and Wildlife Management on Federal Lands: The Authorities and Responsibilities of State Fish and Wildlife Agencies." *Environmental Law* 50, no. 4 (2021): 935–71.

Lazarus, Richard J. "Thirty Years of Environmental Protection Law in the Supreme Court: Fifth Annual Lloyd K. Garrison Lecture on Environmental Law." *Pace Environmental Law Review* 17, no. 1 (1999): 1–32. https://digitalcommons.pace.edu/cgi/viewcontent.cgi?article=1276&context=pelr.

Leuchtenburg, William E. "Charles Evans Hughes: The Center Holds." *North Carolina Law Review* 83, no. 5 (June 2005): 1187–1203. https://scholarship.law.unc.edu/cgi/viewcontent.cgi?referer=&httpsredir=1&article=4160&context=nclr.

Levy, Richard E., and Robert L. Glicksman. "Judicial Activism and Restraint in the Supreme Court's Environmental Law Decisions." *Vanderbilt Law Review* 42, no. 2 (1989): 343–431. https://scholarship.law.vanderbilt.edu/cgi/viewcontent.cgi?article=2559&context=vlr.

Lowry, Kelly. "Zoning the Water: Using the Public Trust Doctrine as a Basis for a Comprehensive Water-Use Plan in Coastal South Carolina." *South Carolina Environmental Law Journal* 5 (1996): 79–97.

Lutz, Donald S. "From Covenant to Constitution in American Political Thought." *Publius* 10, no. 4 (1980): 101–33.

Manning, John F. "Federalism and the Generality Problem in Constitutional Interpretation." *Harvard Law Review* 122, no. 8 (2009): 2003–69. https://harvardlawreview.org/wp-content/uploads/pdfs/vol_122_manning.pdf.

Manus, Peter M. "Five against the Environment." *New England Law Review* 44, no. 2 (2010): 221–48.

Martin, Elaine M. "Burger Court and Preemption Doctrine: Federalism in the Balance." *Notre Dame Law Review* 60, 10, no. 5 (1985): 1233–54. https://scholarship.law.nd.edu/cgi/viewcontent.cgi?article=2346&context=ndlr.

Martinez, Fernando Rey. "The Religious Character of the American Constitution: Puritanism and Constitutionalism in the United States." *Kansas Law Journal of Law and Public Policy* 12 (2002–2003): 459–92.

Mawdsley, Jonathan R., Robin O'Malley, and Dennis S. Ojima. "A Review of Climate-Change Adaptation Strategies for Wildlife Management and Biodiversity Conservation." *Conservation Biology* 23, no. 5 (2009): 1080–89. https://conbio.onlinelibrary.wiley.com/doi/epdf/10.1111/j.1523-1739.2009.01264.x.

Melious, Jean O. "Enforcing the Endangered Species Act against the States." *William and Mary Environmental Law* 25, no. 3 (2001): 605–74. https://scholarship.law.wm.edu/cgi/viewcontent.cgi?article=1213&context=wmelpr.

Merrill, Thomas W. "Preemption in Environmental Law: Formalism, Federalism Theory, and Default Rules." In *Federal Preemption: States' Powers, National Interests*, edited by Richard A. Epstein and Michael S. Greve, 166–93. Washington, DC: AEI Press, 2007.

Metzger, Gillian E. "Administrative Law as the New Federalism." *Duke Law Journal* 57, no. 7 (2008): 2023–109. https://scholarship.law.duke.edu/cgi/viewcontent.cgi?article=1370&context=dlj.

Miller, Louise Byer. "The Burger Court's View of Federalism." *Policy Studies Journal* 13, no. 3 (1985): 576–83.

Monaghan, Henry Paul. "The Burger Court and 'Our Federalism.'" *Law and Contemporary Problems* 43, no. 3 (1980): 39–50. https://scholarship.law.columbia.edu/cgi/viewcontent.cgi?article=1772&context=faculty_scholarship.

Morrison, Alan B. Review of *The Burger Court and the Rise of the Judicial Right*, by Michael Graetz and Linda Greenhouse. *Journal of Legal Education* 66, no. 3 (2017): 653–67. https://jle.aals.org/cgi/viewcontent.cgi?article=1508&context=home.

Nagle, John Copeland. "The Original Role of the States in the Endangered Species Act." *Idaho Law Review* 53, no. 2 (2017): 385–424. https://digitalcommons.law.uidaho.edu/cgi/viewcontent.cgi?article=1017&context=idaho-law-review.

Nie, Martin, Christopher Barns, Jonathan Haber, Julie Joly, Kenneth Pitt, and Sandra Zellmer. "Fish and Wildlife Management on Federal Lands: Debunking State Supremacy." *Environmental Law* 47, no. 4 (2017): 797–932.

O'Brien, David M. "Rehnquist Court and Federal Preemption: In Search of a Theory." *Publius* 23, no. 4 (Autumn 1993): 15–31.

Organ, John F. "Federal Aid in Wildlife and Fisheries Conservation." In *North American Wildlife Policy and Law*, edited by Bruce D. Leopold, Winifred B. Kessler, and James L. Cummins, 163–76. Missoula: Boone and Crockett Club, 2017.

Petersen, Shannon. "Bison to Blue Whales: Protecting Endangered Species before the Endangered Species Act of 1973." *Environs: Environmental Law and Policy Journal* 22, no. 2 (Spring 1999): 71–105. https://environs.law.ucdavis.edu/volumes/22/2/articles/petersen.pdf.

———. "Congress and Charismatic Megafauna: A Legislative History of the Endangered Species Act." *Environmental Law* 29, no. 2 (1999): 463–91.

Post, Robert. "Federalism, Positive Law, and the Emergence of the American Administrative State: Prohibition in the Taft Court Era." *William and Mary Law Review* 48, no. 1 (2006): 1–183. https://scholarship.law.wm.edu/cgi/viewcontent.cgi?article=1100&context=wmlr.

Ratcliffe, Donald. "The Right to Vote and the Rise of Democracy, 1787–1828." *Journal of the Early Republic* 33, no. 2 (Summer 2013): 219–54.

Ruhl, J. B. "Cooperative Federalism and the Endangered Species Act: A Comparative Assessment and Call for Change." In *The Endangered Species Act and Federalism: Effective Conservation through Greater State Commitment*, edited by Barton H. Thompson Jr. and Kaush Arha, 35–52. New York: Routledge, 2011.

———. "The Endangered Species Act's Fall from Grace in the Supreme Court." *Harvard Environmental Law Review* 36 (2012): 487–532. https://scholarship.law.vanderbilt.edu/cgi/viewcontent.cgi?article=1563&context=faculty-publications.

Sax, Joseph L. "The Public Trust Doctrine in Natural Resource Law: Effective Judicial Intervention." *Michigan Law Review* 68, no. 3 (1970): 471–566. https://repository.law.umich.edu/cgi/viewcontent.cgi?article=4782&context=mlr.

Schapiro, Robert. "From Dualism to Polyphony." In *Preemption Choice: The Theory, Law and Reality of Federalism's Core Question*, edited by William W. Buzbee, 33–53. Cambridge: Cambridge University Press, 2009.

Scott, Hal S. "Federalism and Financial Regulation." In *Federal Preemption: States' Powers, National Interests*, edited by Richard A. Epstein and Michael S. Greve, 139–65. Washington, DC: AEI Press, 2007.

Shortell, Christopher. "The End of the Federalism Five? Statutory Interpretation and the Roberts Court." *Publius* 42, no. 3 (2012): 516–37.

Starr, Kenneth W. "Preface." In *Federal Preemption: States' Powers, National Interests*, edited by Richard A. Epstein and Michael S. Greve, xi–xviii. Washington, DC: AEI Press, 2007.

Stewart, Richard B. "Pyramids of Sacrifice? Problems of Federalism in Mandating State Implementation of National Environmental Policy." *Yale Law Journal* 86, no. 6 (1977): 1196–1272. https://digitalcommons.law.yale.edu/cgi/viewcontent.cgi?article=6427&context=ylj.

Stoellinger, Temple. "Wildlife Issues Are Local—So Why Isn't ESA Implementation?" *Ecology Law Quarterly* 44, no. 3 (2017): 681–25. https://www.ecologylawquarterly.org/wp-content/uploads/2020/03/Wildlife-Issues-Are-Local—-So-Why-Isnt-ESA-Implementation.pdf.

Taylor, Dorceta E. "American Environmentalism: The Role of Race, Class and Gender in Shaping Activism, 1820–1995." *Environmentalism and Race, Gender, Class Issues* 5, no. 1 (1997): 16–62.

Weiser, Philip J. "Towards a Constitutional Architecture for Cooperative Federalism." *North Carolina Law Review* 79, no. 3 (2001): 663–720.

White, Omar N. "The Endangered Species Act's Precarious Perch: A Constitutional Analysis under the Commerce Clause and the Treaty Power." *Ecology Law Quarterly* 27, no. 3 (2000): 215–56. https://scholarship.law.unc.edu/cgi/viewcontent.cgi?article=3910&context=nclr.

Wilkinson, Charles. "The Headwaters of the Public Trust: Some Thoughts on the Source and Scope of the Traditional Doctrine." *Environmental Law* 19 (1989): 425–72.

Witte, John, Jr. "How to Govern a City on a Hill: The Early Puritan Contribution to American Constitutionalism." *Emory Law Journal* 39, no. 3 (1989): 41–64.

Wright, Deil S. "The Advisory Commission on Intergovernmental Relations: Unique Features and Policy Orientation." *Public Administration Review* 25, no. 3 (1965): 193–202.

Young, Ernest A. "Federal Preemption and State Autonomy." In *Federal Preemption: States' Powers, National Interests*, edited by Richard A. Epstein and Michael S. Greve, 249–76. Washington, DC: AEI Press, 2007.

———. "Making Federalism Doctrine: Fidelity, Institutional Competence, and Compensating Adjustments." *William and Mary Law Review* 46, no. 5 (2005): 1733–1855. https://scholarship.law.wm.edu/cgi/viewcontent.cgi?article=1296&context=wmlr.

———. "'The Ordinary Diet of the Law': The Presumption against Preemption in the Roberts Court." *Supreme Court Review* 2011, no. 1 (2012): 253–344. https://scholarship.law.duke.edu/cgi/viewcontent.cgi?article=5297&context=faculty_scholarship.

———. "The Puzzling Persistence of Dual Federalism: A Bad Idea, but Not Self-Defeating." In *Federalism and Subsidiarity*. Nomos LV, American Society for Political and Legal Philosophy, edited by James E. Fleming and Jacob T. Levy, 34–82. New York: New York University Press, 2014. https://scholarship.law.duke.edu/cgi/viewcontent.cgi?article=5365&context=faculty_scholarship.

Zellmer, Sandra. "Preemption by Stealth." *Houston Law Review* 45, no. 5 (2009): 1659–1735. https://houstonlawreview.org/article/4433-preemption-by-stealth.

Zimmerman, Joseph F. "National-State Relations: Cooperative Federalism in the Twentieth Century." *Publius* 31, no. 2 (Spring 2001): 15–30.

NEWSPAPER AND MAGAZINE ARTICLES

Bekoff, Marc. "Hats: The Deadly History of Who We Put On Our Heads." *Psychology Today*, January 11, 2020. https://www.psychologytoday.com/us/blog/animal-emotions/202001/hats-the-deadly-history-who-we-put-our-heads.

Chrisman-Campbell, Kimberly. "Fowl Intentions: Fashion, Activism, Conservation." *Ornament Magazine* 40, no. 4 (2018): 46–51. Available online at https://lsc-pagepro.mydigitalpublication.com/publication/?m=60607&i=598875&p=48&ver=html5.

Crews, Clyde Wayne, Jr. "How Many Federal Agencies Exist? We Can't Drain the Swamp Until We Know." Forbes.com, July 5, 2017. https://www.forbes.com/sites/waynecrews/2017/07/05/how-many-federal-agencies-exist-we-cant-drain-the-swamp-until-we-know/?sh=67fd69021aa2.

Curry, Tom. "Chief Justice Shaped High Court Conservatism." *NBC News*, September 3, 2005. https://www.nbcnews.com/id/wbna5304454.

Driver, Justin. "Just How Rightward Leaning Was the Burger Supreme Court?" *Washington Post*, June 17, 2016. https://www.washingtonpost.com/opinions/just-how-rightward-leaning-was-the-burger-supreme-court/2016/06/17/4c722b8e-2b65-11e6-9de3-6e6e7a14000c_story.html.

Greenhouse, Linda. "Obituary: William H. Rehnquist, Chief Justice of the Supreme Court, Is Dead at 80." *New York Times*, September 4, 2005. https://www.nytimes.com/2005/09/04/politics/william-h-rehnquist-chief-justice-of-supreme-court-is-dead-at-80.html.

Johnson, Steffen N. "The Roberts Court and Preemption Decisions." *The National Law Journal Supreme Court Brief*, August 7, 2013. https://www.winston.com/images/content/3/9/v2/39411/005081305-Winston.pdf.

Loyola, Mario. "Federal-State Crack Up." *The American Interest* 8, no. 3, December 12, 2012. https://www.the-american-interest.com/2012/12/12/the-federal-state-crack-up/.

New York Times. "Prohibition and Federal Judges." May 29, 1925, p. 16. https://timesmachine.nytimes.com/timesmachine/1925/05/29/104174646.html.

———. "Tragedy of the White Heron, Victim of Woman's Vanity." In "Alfred Henry Lewis on Literary Critics and Henry James." August 13, 1905, p. 4. https://timesmachine.nytimes.com/timesmachine/1905/08/13/issue.html.

Rosen, Jeffrey. "Rehnquist the Great?" *The Atlantic*, April 2005. https://www.theatlantic.com/magazine/archive/2005/04/rehnquist-the-great/303820/.

Serratore, Angela. "Keeping Feathers Off Hats—and on Birds." *Smithsonian Magazine*, May 15, 2018. https://www.smithsonianmag.com/history/migratory-bird-act-anniversary-keeping-feathers-off-hats-180969077/.

Souder, William. "How Two Women Ended the Deadly Feather Trade." *Smithsonian Magazine*, March 1, 2013. https://www.smithsonianmag.com/science-nature/how-two-women-ended-the-deadly-feather-trade-23187277/.

Tarbell, Ida M. "The History of the Standard Oil Company." *McClure's Magazine* 20, no. 2, December 1902, pp. 115–28. Online at https://archive.org/details/sim_new-mcclures-magazine_1902-12_20_2/mode/2up.

Thomas, Evan. "Reagan's Mr. Right." *Time Magazine*, June 30, 1986. http://content
.time.com/time/subscriber/article/0,33009,961645,00.html.
Washington Post. "Protecting Endangered Species." June 26, 1973, A22.

CASES

The Abby Dodge v. United States, 223 U.S. 166 (1912).
Ableman v. Booth, 62 U.S. 506 (1858).
Addyston Pipe & Steel Co. v. United States, 175 U.S. 211 (1899).
Alden v. Maine, 527 U.S. 706 (1999).
Altria Group, Inc. v. Good, 555 U.S. 70 (2008).
American Tobacco Co. v. United States, 221 U.S. 106 (1911).
American Trucking Associations v. City of Los Angeles, 569 U.S. 641 (2013).
Andrus v. Allard, 444 U.S. 51 (1979).
Arizona v. Inter Tribal Council of Arizona, Inc., 570 U.S. 1 (2013).
Arizona v. United States, 567 U.S. 387 (2012).
Arnold v. Mundy, 6 N.J.L. 1 (N.J. 1821).
Art and Antique Dealers League of America v. Beggos, 394 F.Supp.3d 447 (S.D.N.Y. 2019).
AT&T Mobility v. Concepcion, 563 U.S. 333 (2011).
Atascadero State Hospital v. Scanlon, 473 U.S. 234 (1985).
Auer v. Robbins, 519 U.S. 452 (1997).
Babbitt v. Sweet Home Chapter of Communities for a Great Oregon, 515 U.S. 687 (1995).
Baldwin v. Fish and Game Commission of Montana, 436 U.S. 371 (1978).
Bates v. Dow Agrosciences LLC, 544 U.S. 431 (2005).
Bennett v. Spear, 520 U.S. 154 (1997).
Bohmker v. Oregon, 903 F.3d 1029 (9th Cir 2018).
Brown v. Board of Education of Topeka, 347 U.S. 483 (1954).
Bruesewitz v. Wyeth LLC, 562 U.S. 223 (2011).
Building & Construction Trades Council v. Associated Builders & Contractors, 507 U.S. 218 (1993).
California Coastal Commission v. Granite Rock Co., 480 U.S. 572 (1987).
Carroll v. United States, 267 U.S. 132 (1925).
Carson v. Blazer, 2 Binn. 475 (Penn. 1807).
Center for Biological Diversity v. Bernhardt, 946 F.3d 553 (9th Cir 2019).
Chalk v. United States, 114 F.2nd 207 (4th Cir. 1940).
Chamber of Commerce v. Whiting, 563 U.S. 582 (2011).
Charleston & Western Carolina Ry v. Varnville Furniture Co., 237 U.S. 597 (1915).
Chevron U.S.A., Inc. v. Natural Resources Defense Council, Inc., 467 U.S. 837 (1984).
Chicago Board of Trade v. United States, 246 U.S. 231 (1918).
Chicago Rock Island & Pacific Railway Co. v. Hardwick Farmers Elevator Co., 226 U.S. 426 (1913).

Chisholm v. Georgia, 2 U.S. 419 (1793).
Chisom v. Roemer, 501 U.S. 380 (1991).
Christensen v. Harris County, 529 U.S. 576 (2000).
Christy v. Hodel, 857 F.2d 1324 (9th Cir. 1988).
Cipollone v. Liggett Group, Inc., 505 U.S. 504 (1992).
City of Montpelier v. Barnett, 2012 VT 32, 191 Vt. 441, 49 A.3d 120 (2012).
Clajon Production Corp. v. Petera, 854 F.Supp. 843 (D. Wyo. 1994).
Cloverleaf Butter Co. v. Patterson, 315 U.S. 148 (1942).
Concessions Co. v. Morris, 186 P. 655 (Wash. 1919).
Corfield v. Coryell, 6 Fed. Cas. 546, No. 3230 (C.C.E.D. Pa. 1823).
Cottonwood Environmental Law Center v. U.S. Forest Service, 789 F.3d 1075 (9th Cir. 2015).
Crow Tribe of Indians v. Repsis, 73 F.3d 982 (10th Cir. 1995).
Cuomo v. Clearing House Association, 557 U.S. 519 (2009).
Dan's City Used Cars v. Pelkey, 569 U.S. 215 (2013).
Defenders of Wildlife v. Andrus, 627 F.2d 1238 (D.C. Cir. 1980).
Defenders of Wildlife v. Salazar, 651 F.3d 112 (D.C. Cir 2011).
Dickson v. Uhlmann Grain Company, 288 U.S. 188 (1933).
Douglas v. Seacoast Products, Inc., 431 U.S. 265 (1977).
Dred Scott v. Sandford, 60 U.S. 393 (1856).
Egelhoff v. Egelhoff, 532 U.S. 141 (2001).
Erie R.R. Co. v. Tompkins, 304 U.S. 64 (1938).
Fairchild v. Kraemer, 11 App. Div. 2d 232, 204 N.Y.S. 2d 823 (1960).
Federal Maritime Comm'n v. South Carolina Ports Authority, 535 U.S. 743 (2002).
Fednav Ltd. v. Chester, 547 F.3d 607 (6th Cir. 2008).
FERC v. Mississippi, 456 U.S. 742 (1982).
Forestier v. Johnson, 164 Cal. 24127 (1912).
Fort Leavenworth R. Co. v. Lowe, 114 U.S. 525 (1885).
Foster-Fountain Packing Company v. Haydel, 278 U.S. 1 (1928).
Fund for Animals v. Clark, 27 F.Supp.2d 8 (D.D.C. 1998).
Gambino v. United States, 275 U.S. 310 (1927).
Garcia v. San Antonio Transit Authority, 469 U.S. 528 (1985).
GDF Realty Investments, Ltd. v. Norton, 326 F.3rd 622 (5th Cir. 2003).
Geer v. Connecticut, 161 U.S. 519 (1896).
Gibbons v. Ogden, 22 U.S. 1 (1824).
Gibbs v. Babbitt, 214 F.3d 483 (4th Cir. 2000).
Glass v. Goeckel, 703 N.W.2d 58 (Mich. 2005).
Goldstein v. California, 412 U.S. 546 (1973).
Gonzales v. Raich, 545 U.S. 1 (2005).
Gowanus Indus. Park, Inc. v. Amerada Hess Corp., No. 01-CV-0902 (ILG), 2003 WL 22076651 (S.D.N.Y. Sept. 5, 2003).
Grand Lake Estates Homeowners Ass'n v. Veneman, 340 F. Supp. 2d 1162 (D. Colo. 2004).
Gregory v. Ashcroft, 501 U.S. 452 (1991).
Grier v. American Honda Motor Co., Inc., 529 U.S. 861 (2000).

Hebert et al. v. Louisiana, 272 U.S. 312 (1926).
Herrera v. Wyoming, 139 S.Ct. 1686 (2019).
Hester v. United States, 265 U.S. 57 (1924).
Hillman v. Maretta, 569 U.S. 483 (2013).
Hillsborough County, Fla. v. Automated Medical Laboratories, Inc., 471 U.S. 707 (1985).
Hines v. Davidowitz, 312 U.S. 52 (1941).
Hodel v. Virginia Surface Mining & Reclamation Ass'n, 452 U.S. 264 (1981).
Hughes v. Oklahoma, 441 U.S. 322 (1979).
Hunt v. United States, 278 U.S. 96 (1928).
Hylton v. United States, 3 U.S. 171 (1796).
Illinois Central Railroad Co. v. Illinois, 146 U.S. 387 (1892).
James Everard's Breweries v. Day, 124 U.S. 545 (1924).
Jones v. Rath Packing Co., 430 U.S. 519 (1977).
Katz v. United States, 389 U.S. 347 (1967).
Kenai Peninsula Borough v. State of Alaska, 612 F.2d 1210 (1980).
Kewanee Oil Co. v. Bicron, 416 U.S. 470 (1974).
King v. Smith, 392 U.S. 309 (1968).
Kleppe v. New Mexico, 426 U.S. 529 (1976).
Lambert v. Yellowley, 272 U.S. 581 (1926).
Lawrence v. Clark County, 254 P.3d 606 (Nev. 2011).
Light v. United States, 220 U.S. 523 (1911).
Lochner v. New York, 198 U.S. 45 (1905).
Loggerhead Turtle v. Volusia County, Florida, 92 F. Supp.2d 1296 (M.D. Fla. 2000).
Lorillard Tobacco Co. v. Reilly, 533 U.S. 525 (2001).
Lujan v. Defenders of Wildlife, 504 U.S. 555 (1992).
Manchester v. Commonwealth of Massachusetts, 139 U.S. 240 (1891).
Man Hing Ivory v. Deukmejian, 702 F.2d 760 (9th Cir. 1983).
Marbury v. Madison, 5 U.S. 137 (1803).
Marks v. Whitney, 6 Cal.3d 251 (1971).
Martin v. Waddell's Lessee, 41 U.S. 367 (1842).
Maryland v. Louisiana, 451 U.S. 725 (1981).
Massachusetts v. EPA, 549 U.S. 497 (2007).
Matthews v. Bay Head Improvement Ass'n, 471 A.2d 355 (N.J. 1984).
McCready v. Virginia, 94 U.S. 391 (1876).
McCulloch v. Maryland, 17 U.S. 316 (1819).
Medtronic, Inc. v. Lohr, 518 U.S. 470, 485 (1996).
Minnesota v. Block, 660 F.2d 1240 (8th Cir. 1981).
Minnesota v. Mille Lacs Band of Chippewa Indians, 526 U.S. 172 (1999).
Mintz v. Baldwin, 289 U.S. 346 (1933).
Miranda v. Arizona, 384 U.S 436 (1966).
Missouri Pac. R.R. v. Stroud, 267 U.S. 404 (1925).
Mistretta v. United States, 488 U.S. 361 (1989).
Morgan v. Negodich et al., 40 La. Ann. 246 (La. 1887).
Mutual Pharmaceutical Co. v. Bartlett, 570 U.S. 472 (2013).

National Ass'n of Home Builders v. Babbitt, 130 F.3d 1041 (D.C. Cir. 1997).
Nat Ass'n of Home Builders of the US v. Babbitt, 949 F.Supp. 1 (D.D.C. 1996).
National Assn. of Home Builders v. Defenders of Wildlife, 551 U.S. 644 (2007).
National Audubon Society v. Davis, 307 F.3d 835 (9th Cir. 2002).
National Audubon Society v. Superior Court of Alpine County, 33 Cal. 3d 419, 658 P. 2d 709 (1983).
National Federation of Independent Business v. Sebelius, 567 U.S. 519 (2012).
National League of Cities v. Usery, 426 U.S. 833 (1976).
National Meat Association v. Harris, 565 U.S. 452 (2012).
National Wildlife Federation v. Coleman, 529 F.2d 359 (5th Cir. 1976).
New Mexico State Game Commission v. Udall, 410 F.2d 1197 (10th Cir. 1969).
New York Cent. R. Co. v. Winfield, 244 U.S. 147 (1917).
New York State Department of Social Services v. Dublino, 413 U.S. 405 (1973).
New York v. United States, 505 U.S. 144 (1992).
N.L.R.B. v. Jones & Laughlin Steel Corp., 301 U.S. 1 (1937).
North Dakota v. United States, 460 U.S. 300 (1983).
Northern Securities v. United States, 24 S.Ct. 436 (1904).
Northwest Inc. v. Ginsberg, 572 U.S. 273 (2014).
Olmstead v. United States, 277 U.S. 438 (1928).
Oneok v. Learjet, 575 U.S. 373 (2015).
Organized Fishermen of Florida v. Andrus, 488 F.Supp. 1351 (S.D. Fla. 1980).
Organized Fishermen of Florida v. Hodel, 775 F.2d 1544 (11th Cir. 1985).
Pacific Legal Foundation v. Quarles, 440 F.Supp. 316 (C.D. Cal. 1977).
Palila v. Hawaii Department of Land and Natural Resources, 471 F.Supp. 995 (D. Haw. 1979).
Palila v. Hawaii Department of Land and Natural Resources, 852 F.2d 1106 (9th Cir. 1988).
Palladio v. Diamond, 321 F.Supp. 630 (1970).
PETPO v. U.S. Fish and Wildlife Service, 852 F.3d 990 (10th Cir 2017).
Pierson v. Post, 3 Cai. R. 175 (N.Y. Sup. Ct. 1805).
Plessy v. Ferguson, 163 U.S. 537 (1896).
PLIVA v. Mensing, 564 U.S. 604 (2011).
Pollard's Lessee v. Hagen, 44 U.S. 212 (1845).
PPL Montana, LLC v. Montana, 565 U.S. 576 (2012).
Presley v. Etowah County Commission, 502 U.S. 491 (1992).
Printz v. United States, 521 U.S. 898 (1997).
Rancho Viejo v. Norton, 323 F.3d 1062 (D.C. Cir. 2003).
Reid v. People of State of Colorado, 187 U.S. 137 (1902).
Reno v. Condon, 528 U.S. 141 (2000).
Retail Clerks v. Schermerhorn, 375 U.S. 96 (1963).
Rettkowski v. Dep't of Ecology, 858 P.2d 232 (Wash. 1993).
Rice v. Santa Fe Elevator Corp., 331 U.S. 218 (1947).
Roe v. Wade, 410 U.S. 113 (1973).
Rosado v. Wyman, 397 U.S. 397 (1970).
Rupert v. United States, 181 F. 87 (8th Cir. 1910).

Rust v. Sullivan, 500 U.S. 173 (1991).
Rutledge v. Pharmaceutical Care Mgmt. Ass'n., 140 S.Ct. 812 (2020).
Safari Club International v. Jewell, 960 F.Supp.2d 17 (D.D.C. 2013).
Savage v. Jones, 225 U.S. 501 (1912).
School Board of Avoyelles Parish v. United States, 647 F.3d 570 (5th Cir. 2011).
SEC v. Chenery Corp., 332 U.S. 194 (1947).
Seminole Tribe of Fla. v. Florida, 517 U.S. 44 (1996).
Shively v. Bowlby et al. 152 U.S. 1 (1894).
Smith v. Maryland, 59 U.S. 71 (1855).
Solid Waste Agency of Northern Cook Cty. v. U.S. Army Corp. of Engineers, 531 U.S. 159 (2001).
South Carolina Highway Dep't v. Barnwell Bros., Inc., 303 U.S. 177 (1938).
South Dakota v. Dole, 483 U.S. 203 (1987).
Southern Ry. Co. v. Reid, 222 U.S. 424 (1912).
Standard Oil Co. of New Jersey v. United States, 221 U.S. 1 (1911).
State of Alaska v. Andrus, 429 F.Supp. 958 (D. Alaska 1977).
State of Missouri v. Holland, 252 U.S. 416 (1920).
State v. Sorensen, 436 N.W.2d 358 (Iowa 1989).
Stenberg v. Carhart, 530 U.S. 914 (2000).
Strahan v. Coxe, 127 F.3d 155 (1st Cir. 1997).
Stupak-Thrall v. United States, 89 F.3d 1269 (6th Cir. 1996).
Swan View Coalition v. Turner, Inc., 824 F.Supp. 923 (D. Mont. 1992).
Tafflin v. Levitt, 493 U.S. 455 (1990).
Takahashi v. Fish and Game Commission, 334 U.S. 410 (1948).
Tangier Sound Waterman's Association v. Douglas, 541 F.Supp. 1287 (E.D. Va. 1982).
*Tarrant Regional Water District v. Herrm*ann, 569 U.S. 614 (2013).
Tennessee Valley Authority v. Hill, 437 U.S. 153 (1978).
Thorpe v. Rutland and Burlington R.R., 27 Vt. 140 (1854).
Toomer v. Witsell, 334 U.S. 385 (1948).
Trustees for Alaska v. Watt, 524 F.Supp. 1303 (D. Alaska 1981).
Tumey v. Ohio, 273 U.S. 510 (1927).
UFO Chuting of Hawaii v. Smith, 508 F.3d 1189 (9th Cir 2007).
United States v. Albrecht, 496 F.2d 906 (8th Cir. 1974).
United States v. Arizona, 119 F. Supp.3d 955 (D. Az. 2014).
United States v. Bramble, 103 F.3d 1475 (9th Cir. 1996).
United States v. Brown, 552 F.2d 817 (8th Cir. 1977).
United States v. Darby, 312 U.S. 100 (1941).
United States v. E. C. Knight Co., 156 U.S. 1 (1895).
United States v. Glenn-Colusa Irrigation District, 788 F.Supp. 1126 (E.D. Cal. 1992).
United States v. Grimaud, 220 U.S. 506 (1911).
United States v. Guthrie, 50 F.3d 936 (11th Cir. 1995).
United States v. Helsley, 615 F.2d 784 (9th Cir. 1979).
United States v. Lanza, 260 U.S. 377 (1922).
United States v. Lee, 274 U.S. 559 (1927).

United States v. Lindsey, 595 F.2d 5 (9th Cir. 1979).
United States v. Lopez, 514 U.S. 549 (1995).
United States v. Lundquist, 932 F.Supp. 1237 (D. Or. 1996).
United States v. McCullagh, 221 F. 288 (D. Kan. 1915).
United States v. Midwest Oil Co., 236 U.S. 459, 483 (1915).
United States v. Morrison, 529 U.S. 598 (2000).
United States v. Romano, 929 F.Supp. 502 (D. Mass. 1996).
United States v. Shauver, 214 F. 154 (E.D. Ark 1914). Appeal dismissed 248 U.S. 594 (1919).
United States v. Trans-Missouri Freight Association, 166 U.S. 290 (1897).
United Steelworkers of America, AFL-CIO v. Weber, 443 U.S. 193 (1979).
Universal Camera Corp. v. NLRB, 340 U.S. 474 (1951).
Utah Native Plant Society v. U.S. Forest Service, 923 F.3d 860 (10th Cir. 2019).
Virginia Uranium, Inc. v. Warren, 139 S.Ct. 1894 (2019).
Ward v. Race Horse, 163 U.S. 504 (1896).
Ware v. Hylton, 3 U.S. 199 (1796).
Washington State Department of Fisheries v. FERC, 801 F.2d 1516 (9th Cir. 1986).
Weeks v. United States, 232 U.S. 383 (1913).
Weyerhaeuser v. U.S. Fish and Wildlife Service, 139 S.Ct. 361 (2019).
Wickard v. Filburn, 317 U.S. 111 (1942).
Wilbour v. Gallagher, 77 Wash. 2d 306, 462 P.2d 232 (1969).
Williamson v. Mazda Motor of America, 562 U.S. 323 (2011).
WOS v. E.M.A, 568 U.S. 627 (2013).
Wyeth v. Levine, 555 U.S. 555 (2009).
Wyoming v. United States, 279 F.3d 1214 (10th Cir. 2002).

LEGISLATIVE MATERIALS

US Advisory Commission on Intergovernmental Relations. *Federal Statutory Preemption of State and Local Authority: History, Inventory, and Issues*. Washington, DC: ACIR, 1992.

US Congress. *Administrative Procedure Act*, 5 U.S.C. § 553 (2012). Archived at https://www.archives.gov/federal-register/laws/administrative-procedure/553.html.

———. Clean Air Act Amendments of 1970, Pub. L. No. 91–604, 84 Stat. 1705 (1970). https://www.govinfo.gov/content/pkg/STATUTE-84/pdf/STATUTE-84-Pg1676.pdf.

———. *Consolidated Appropriations Act, 2021*, Public Law No. 116-260, _ Stat. _, 116 H.R. 133 (2021). https://www.congress.gov/116/bills/hr133/BILLS-116hr133enr.pdf.

———. Endangered Species Act of 1973, Pub. L. No. 93–205, 87 Stat. 884 (1973). https://www.govinfo.gov/content/pkg/STATUTE-87/pdf/STATUTE-87-Pg884.pdf.

———. *Endangered Species Act* Amendments of 1988, Pub. L. No. 100–478, 102 Stat. 2306 (1988). https://www.govinfo.gov/content/pkg/STATUTE-102/pdf/STATUTE-102-Pg2306.pdf.

———. *Endangered Species Act of 1973*, Pub. L. No. 93–205, 87 Stat. 884 (1973). https://www.govinfo.gov/content/pkg/STATUTE-87/pdf/STATUTE-87-Pg884.pdf.

———. *Equal Employment Opportunity Act of 1972*, Pub. L. No. 92–261, 86 Stat 103 (1972). https://www.govinfo.gov/content/pkg/STATUTE-86/pdf/STATUTE-86-Pg103.pdf.

———. U.S.C. 669–69(i) (1937). https://www.ssa.gov/OP_Home/comp2/F075-412.html.

———. *Federal Water Pollution Control Act* Amendments of 1972, Pub. L. No. 92–500, 86 Stat. 816 (1972). https://www.govinfo.gov/content/pkg/STATUTE-86/pdf/STATUTE-86-Pg816.pdf.

———. *Fish and Wildlife Coordination Act*, Pub. L. No. 73–121, 48 Stat. 401 (1934). Codified as amended at 16 U.S.C. §§ 661–67, https://www.govinfo.gov/content/pkg/USCODE-2013-title16/html/USCODE-2013-title16-chap5A.htm.

———. *Fish and Wildlife Programs Improvement and National Wildlife Refuge System Centennial Act of 2000*, Pub. L. No. 106–408, 114 Stat. 1763 (2000). https://uscode.house.gov/statutes/pl/106/408.pdf.

———. *Interstate Commerce Act of 1887*, Pub. L. No. 49–104, 24 Stat. 379 (1887). https://www.ourdocuments.gov/print_friendly.php?flash=true&page=transcript&doc=49.

———. *Lacey Act*, 31 Stat. 187, 16 U.S.C. §§ 3371–78 (1900). https://www.fws.gov/le/pdffiles/Lacey.pdf.

———. *Marine Mammal Protection Act of 1972*, Pub. L. No. 92–522, 85 Stat. 1027 (1972). https://www.fws.gov/international/pdf/legislation-marine-mammal-protection-act.pdf.

———. *Migratory Bird Hunting and Conservation Stamp Act*, Pub. L. No. 73–124, 48 Stat. 451 (1934).

———. *Migratory Bird Treaty Act*, Pub. L. No. 65–186, 40 Stat. 755 (1918). https://www.fws.gov/laws/lawsdigest/migtrea.html.

———. *National Bison Legacy Act*, Pub. L. No. 114–152, 130 Stat. 373 (2016). https://www.govinfo.gov/content/pkg/PLAW-114publ152/pdf/PLAW-114publ152.pdf.

———. *National Environmental Policy Act of 1969*, Pub. L. No. 91–190, 83 Stat. 852 (1970). https://www.govinfo.gov/content/pkg/STATUTE-83/pdf/STATUTE-83-Pg852.pdf.

———. *Noise Control Act of 1972*, Pub. L. No. 92–574, 86 Stat. 1234 (1972). https://www.govinfo.gov/content/pkg/STATUTE-86/pdf/STATUTE-86-Pg1234.pdf.

———. *North American Wetlands Conservation Act*, Pub. L. No. 101–233, 103 Stat. 1968 (1989). https://www.govinfo.gov/content/pkg/STATUTE-103/pdf/STATUTE-103-Pg1968.pdf.

———. *Patient Protection and Affordable Care Act*, Pub. L. No 111–148, 124 Stat 119 (2010). https://www.congress.gov/111/plaws/publ148/PLAW-111publ148.pdf.

———. Senate. *Endangered Species Act of 1973*, S. 1983, 93rd Cong. vol. 119, part 20, *Congressional Record*, 769, July 24, 1973. Text archived at https://www.govinfo.gov/content/pkg/GPO-CRECB-1973-pt20/pdf/GPO-CRECB-1973-pt20-3-2.pdf.

———. *Unfunded Mandates Reform Act of 1995*, Pub. L. No. 104–4, 109 Stat. 48 (1995). https://www.congress.gov/104/plaws/publ4/PLAW-104publ4.pdf.

———. *Weeks-McLean Act*, Pub. L. No. 62–430, Chap. 145, 37 Stat. 828 (1913).

US Continental Congress. Articles of Confederation and Perpetual Union between the states of New-Hampshire, Massachusetts-Bay, Rhode-Island and Providence Plantations, Connecticut, New-York, New-Jersey, Pennsylvania, Delaware, Maryland, Virginia, North-Carolina, South-Carolina and Georgia. Article XIII. Printed Lancaster, Pennsylvania, 1777. Reproduced at https://www.loc.gov/resource/bdsdcc.n001001/?sp=9&st=text.

US Constitution. Text archived at https://www.senate.gov/civics/constitution_item/constitution.htm.

US House of Representatives. Committee on Conference. Endangered Species Act of 1973, Report to accompany S. 1983. H.R. Rep. No. 93-740 (1973).

———. Committee on Commerce. Endangered Species: Report to Accompany H.R. 11363. S. Rep. No. 91-5263 (1969).

———. Committee on Merchant Marine and Fisheries. Report No. 93-412, submitted July 27, 1973, to accompany H.R. 37, 93rd Cong., 1st sess., the Endangered Species Act of 1973. Report text archived at https://nctc.fws.gov/courses/csp/csp3116/resources/ESA_Section_7_Legislative_History/Part_1_pages_140-179.pdf.

———. Endangered Species Conservation Act, H.R. 37 (1973). https://www.congress.gov/bill/93rd-congress/house-bill/37.

———. *The Endangered Species Act: How Litigation Is Costing Jobs and Impeding True Recovery Efforts: Oversight Hearing Before the Committee on Natural Resources*, 112th Cong. (2011). https://www.govinfo.gov/content/pkg/CHRG-112hhrg71642/html/CHRG-112hhrg71642.htm.

———. *Fish and Wildlife Miscellaneous, Part 1: Hearing on H.R. 4741 before the Subcommittee on Fisheries and Wildlife Conservation and the Environment, Committee on Merchant Marine and Fisheries*, 95th Cong. (1977).

US Senate. *Authorizations for the Endangered Species Act and for Three Wildlife Refuges: Hearing before the Subcommittee on Resource Protection of the Committee on Environment and Public Works*. 95th Cong., 1st sess., on S. 1237 and S. 1316 (1977). Archived at https://babel.hathitrust.org/cgi/pt?id=mdp.39015078591297&view=1up&seq=1.

———. Committee on Commerce. Report No. 91-526, submitted November 6, 1969, to accompany H.R. 11363, 91st Cong., 1st sess., An Act to Prevent the Importation of Endangered Species of Fish or Wildlife into the United States; to Prevent the Interstate Shipment of Reptiles, Amphibians, and Other Wildlife Taken Contrary to State Law; and for Other Purposes. Text archived at https://books.google.com/books?id=i17ldYCd50AC.

———. *Endangered Species Act Amendments of 1993: Hearings on S. 921 before the Subcommittee on Clean Water, Fisheries, and Wildlife of the Committee on Environment and Public Works*, 103rd Congress (1994). https://www.congress.gov/bill/103rd-congress/senate-bill/921?s=1&r=2.

OTHER SOURCES

Association of Fish and Wildlife Agencies. "Multistate Conservation Grant Program Overview." FishWildlife.org, accessed February 9, 2021. https://www.fishwildlife.org/afwa-informs/multi-state-conservation-grants-program.

———. *Wildlife Management Authority: The State Agencies' Perspective; Findings from the AFWA President's Task Force on States Authorities*. Washington, DC: Association of Fish and Wildlife Agencies, February 2014. Archived at https://wyoleg.gov/InterimCommittee/2015/SFR-0929APPENDIXB.pdf.

Blue Ribbon Panel on Sustaining America's Diverse Fish and Wildlife Resources. "The Future of America's Fish and Wildlife: A 21st Century Vision for Investing in and Connecting People to Nature." March 2016. https://www.fishwildlife.org/application/files/8215/1382/2408/Blue_Ribbon_Panel_Report2.pdf.

Boone and Crockett Club Records. Boone and Crockett Club Game Preservation Committee Policy Report of 1912. Archived in box 85, folder 4, 1909–1929, Mansfield Library Special Collections, University of Montana, Missoula, Montana. Searchable at http://archiveswest.orbiscascade.org/ark:/80444/xv46765.

Britannica.com. "Second Industrial Revolution." Accessed February 4, 2021. https://www.britannica.com/topic/Second-Industrial-Revolution.

Bureau of Alcohol, Tobacco, Firearms and Explosives. "ATF's Legacy of Diversity." ATF.gov, last reviewed September 22, 2016. https://www.atf.gov/our-history/atfs-legacy-diversity.

———. "Fallen Prohibition Agents." ATF.gov, accessed February 4, 2021. https://www.atf.gov/our-history/fallen-agents.

Concord Museum. "The Shot Heard Round the World: April 19, 1775." Concord Museum.org, accessed May 10, 2020. https://concordmuseum.org/online-exhibition/the-shot-heard-round-the-world-april-19-1775.

Davison, Robert P., William P. Burger, Henry Campa III, Paul J. Conry, Kenneth D. Elowe, Gary Frazer, Dorothy C. Mason, Donald E. Moore III, and Robert D. Nelson. "Practical Solutions to Improve the Effectiveness of the Endangered Species Act for Wildlife Conservation." Edited by Krista E. M. Galley. Wildlife Society Technical Review 05–1, The Wildlife Society, Bethesda, MD, December 2005. https://wildlife.org/wp-content/uploads/2014/05/ESA05-11.pdf.

Editors of the Encyclopedia Britannica. "Battles of Lexington and Concord." Britannica.com, accessed May 10, 2020. https://www.britannica.com/event/Battles-of-Lexington-and-Concord.

General Court of the Colony of New Plymouth. Pilgrim Code of Law. Promulgated November 15, 1636. Archived at https://teachingamericanhistory.org/library/document/pilgrim-code-of-law.

Grinnell, George Bird. Aldo Leopold to Barrington Moore, July 24, 1923. Archived as microfilm, box 25, folder 106, reel 42U, in the George Bird Grinnell Papers, Sterling Memorial Library, Yale University Library.

———. Barrington Moore to Dr. George Bird Grinnell, August 3, 1920. Archived as microfilm, reel 39U, box 25, folder 106, of the George Bird Grinnell Papers, Sterling Memorial Library, Yale University Library.

―――. G. B. Grinnell to Aldo Leopold, January 8, 1923. Archived as microfilm, box 33, folder 165, reel 38U, of the George Bird Grinnell Papers, Sterling Memorial Library, Yale University Library. https://archives.yale.edu/repositories/12/top_containers/141894?&filter_fields[]=child_container_u_sstr&filter_values[]=folder+165.

―――. G. B. Grinnell to John F. Lacey, February 25, 1903. Archived as microfilm in box 7, folder 12, of the George Bird Grinnell Papers, Sterling Memorial Library, Yale University Library. https://archives.yale.edu/repositories/12/top_containers/141868.

―――. G. B. Grinnell to Luther North, December 23, 1903. Archived as microfilm in reel 9U, box 8, folder 13, of the George Bird Grinnell Papers, Sterling Memorial Library, Yale University Library. https://archives.yale.edu/repositories/12/top_containers/141869.

―――. G. B. Grinnell to Mark Sullivan, August 23, 1900. Archived as microfilm, reel 7U, box 6, folder 11, of the George Bird Grinnell Papers, Sterling Memorial Library, Yale University Library. https://archives.yale.edu/repositories/12/top_containers/207138.

―――. Henry C. Wallace to George Bird Grinnell, February 18, 1924. Archived as microfilm in reel 40U, box 39, folder 133, of the George Bird Grinnell Papers, Sterling Memorial Library, Yale University Library. https://archives.yale.edu/repositories/12/archival_objects/1248823.

Independence Hall Association. "American History: From Pre-Columbian to the New Millennium." USHistory.org, accessed June 16, 2021. https://www.ushistory.org/us/index.asp.

―――. "2a. The Colonial Experience." USHistory.org, accessed June 15, 2021. https://www.ushistory.org/gov/2a.asp.

Internal Revenue Service. "Historical Highlights of the IRS." IRS.gov, updated December 18, 2020. https://www.irs.gov/newsroom/historical-highlights-of-the-irs.

Lacey, John F. Statement made at 56th Congress, 1st sess. Congressional Record H.4871–72, vol. 33, pt. 9. 1900.

Land of the Brave. "Colonial America." Accessed February 3, 2021. https://www.landofthebrave.info/.

Law Library: American Law and Legal Information. "Administrative Agency; History of Administrative Agency." Accessed June 17, 2021. https://law.jrank.org/pages/4061/Administrative-Agency-History-Administrative-Agency.html.

Library of Congress. "Constitution Annotated." Congress.gov, accessed June 24, 2021. Searchable at https://constitution.congress.gov/.

MacDonald, James. "Appointment as Commander in Chief." MountVernon.org, accessed February 3, 2021. https://www.mountvernon.org/library/digitalhistory/digital-encyclopedia/article/appointment-as-commander-in-chief/.

Madison, James. "The Same Subject Continued: The Union as a Safeguard against Domestic Faction and Insurrection." *The Federalist Papers*, no. 10, November 23, 1787. Archived at https://guides.loc.gov/federalist-papers/text-1-10#s-lg-box-wrapper-25493273.

———. "The Structure of the Government Must Furnish the Proper Checks and Balances Between the Different Departments." *The Federalist Papers*, no. 51, February 8, 1788. Archived at https://guides.loc.gov/federalist-papers/text-51-60#s-lg-box-wrapper-25493427.

Merriam-Webster.com. S.v. "preemption." Accessed September 23, 2021. https://www.merriam-webster.com/dictionary/preemption.

National Archives of the United States. "Department of the Interior Fish and Wildlife Policy; State-Federal Relationships." *Federal Registry* 48, no. 54 (March 18, 1983): 11642. https://www.govinfo.gov/content/pkg/FR-1983-03-18/pdf/FR-1983-03-18.pdf.

National Park Service. "Quick History of the National Park Service." NPS.gov, last modified May 14, 2018. https://www.nps.gov/articles/quick-nps-history.htm.

Nixon, Richard. "Statement on Transmitting a Special Message to the Congress Outlining the 1972 Environmental Program." Read in the Family Theater for sound and film recording, February 8, 1972. Archived at https://www.presidency.ucsb.edu/documents/statement-transmitting-special-message-the-congress-outlining-the-1972-environmental.

Organ, John F., Robert M. Muth, Jan E. Dizard, Scot J. Williamson, and Thomas A. Decker. "Fair Chase and Humane Treatment: Balancing the Ethics of Hunting and Trapping." Presentation made at the 63rd North American Wildlife and Natural Resources Conference, Orlando, Florida, March 20–24, 1998.

Pruitt, Sarah. "How the Mayflower Compact Laid a Foundation for American Democracy." History.com, accessed September 10, 2021. https://www.history.com/news/mayflower-compact-colonial-america-plymouth.

Reagan, Ronald. Executive Order 12612: Federalism. 52 Fed. Reg. 41685. October 26, 1987. Archived at https://www.archives.gov/federal-register/codification/executive-order/12612.html.

Reagan, Ronald. "Inaugural Address to the Nation." January 20, 1981. http://www.reaganfoundation.org/ronald-reagan/reagan-quotes-speeches/inaugural-address-2/.

Revolutionary War. "13 Colonies." Last modified March 4, 2020. https://www.revolutionary-war.net/13-colonies/.

Roosevelt, Franklin D. Message from the president of the United States to the Congress, January 12, 1937. In *The President's Committee on Administrative Management: Report of the President's Committee on Administrative Management*, iii–v. Washington, DC: US Government Printing Office, 1937. Text viewable at https://www.presidency.ucsb.edu/documents/message-congress-recommending-reorganization-the-executive-branch.

Salesforce. "Learn about the Fourth Industrial Revolution." Accessed July 26, 2020. https://trailhead.salesforce.com/en/content/learn/trails/4th-industrial-revolution.

Teaford, Jon C. S.v. "Good Government Movements." *The Encyclopedia of Chicago*, accessed May 10, 2001. http://www.encyclopedia.chicagohistory.org/pages/527.html.

US Census Bureau. "Following the Frontier Line, 1790 to 1890." Census.gov, September 6, 2012. https://www.census.gov/dataviz/visualizations/001/.

———. "Pop Culture: 1800." History. Last modified December 17, 2020. https://www.census.gov/history/www/through_the_decades/fast_facts/1800_fast_facts.html.

———. "Pop Culture: 1850." History. Last modified December 17, 2020. https://www.census.gov/history/www/through_the_decades/fast_facts/1850_fast_facts.html.

———. Population Division. "National Intercensal Tables: 1900–1990; 1973." Census.gov, October 1, 2004. Excel file with data downloadable from https://www.census.gov/data/tables/time-series/demo/popest/pre-1980-national.html.

———. *Statistical Abstract of the United States: 1900*. Washington, DC: US Government Printing Office, 1901. Downloadable at https://www.census.gov/library/publications/1901/compendia/statab/23ed.html.

———. *Statistical Abstract of the United States: 1920*. Washington, DC: US Government Printing Office, 1921. Downloadable at https://www.census.gov/library/publications/1920/compendia/statab/23ed.html.

———. "U.S. and World Population Clock." Census.gov, accessed September 23 2021. https://www.census.gov/popclock/.

US Department of Agriculture. Forest Service. "Our History." FS.USDA.gov, accessed September 16, 2021. https://www.fs.usda.gov/learn/our-history.

US Fish and Wildlife Service. "About the U.S. Fish and Wildlife Service." FWS.gov. Last modified February 12, 2021. https://www.fws.gov/help/about_us.html.

———. "1952 through 2021 Sport Fish Restoration Apportionments." Wildlife and Sport Fish Restoration Program, last modified February 24, 2021. Downloadable from https://www.fws.gov/wsfrprograms/subpages/grantprograms/sfr/sfr_funding.htm.

———. "1939 through 2021 Wildlife Restoration Apportionments (Includes Hunter Ed)." Wildlife and Sport Fish Restoration Program, last modified February 24, 2021. Downloadable from https://www.fws.gov/wsfrprograms/subpages/grantprograms/wr/wr_funding.htm.

———. "Pelican Island: History." FWS.gov, last modified October 14, 2015. https://www.fws.gov/refuge/pelican_island/about/history.html.

———. Service manual, chapter 521, "FW 4: Endangered Species." Division of Federal Aid. October 10, 2001. https://www.fws.gov/policy/521fw4.pdf.

US Fish and Wildlife Service and International Association of Fish and Wildlife Agencies. "Charter for a Joint Federal/State Task Force on Federal Aid Policy." September 5, 2002. https://www.fws.gov/wsfrprograms/subpages/policy/files/charter.pdf.

US Government. "Applications for Financial Assistance." *Federal Register* 40, no. 197 (October 9, 1975): 47509. https://www.govinfo.gov/content/pkg/FR-1975-10-09/pdf/FR-1975-10-09.pdf.

US House of Representatives. "1st to 9th Congresses (1789–1807)." House.gov, accessed February 3, 2021. https://history.house.gov/Institution/Session-Dates/1-9/.

US National Archives. "From Thomas Jefferson to C. Hammond, 18 August 1821." *Founders Online*, Archives.gov, accessed September 10 2021. https://founders.archives.gov/documents/Jefferson/98-01-02-2260.

US Statutes at Large. Vol. 27, Proclamation No. 39, Stat. 1052 (1892). https://memory.loc.gov/cgi-bin/ampage?collId=amrvl&fileName=vl153//amrvlv1153.db&recNum=0&itemLink=r?ammem/AMALL:@field(NUMBER+@band(amrvl+vl153))&linkText=0.

US Supreme Court. "Opinions." SupremeCourt.gov, accessed February 7, 2021. https://www.supremecourt.gov/opinions/opinions.aspx.

Wallenfeldt, Jeff. "Timeline of the American Revolution." Britannica.com, accessed April 14, 2020. https://www.britannica.com/list/timeline-of-the-american-revolution.

Wikipedia. "American Revolutionary War." Last modified September 22, 2021. https://en.wikipedia.org/wiki/American_Revolutionary_War.

———. "Bureau of Prohibition." Last modified September 1, 2021. https://en.wikipedia.org/wiki/Bureau_of_Prohibition.

———. "Burger Court." Last modified March 24, 2021. https://en.wikipedia.org/wiki/Burger_Court.

———. "Colonial Government in the Thirteen Colonies." Last modified July 24, 2021. https://en.wikipedia.org/wiki/Colonial_government_in_the_Thirteen_Colonies.

———. "Ecology." Last modified September 20, 2021. https://en.wikipedia.org/wiki/Ecology.

———. "First Continental Congress." Last modified July 28, 2021. https://en.wikipedia.org/wiki/First_Continental_Congress.

———. "History of Rail Transportation in the United States." Last modified June 18, 2021. https://en.wikipedia.org/wiki/History_of_rail_transportation_in_the_United_States.

———. "Industrial Revolution in the United States." Last modified May 30 2021. https://en.wikipedia.org/wiki/Industrial_Revolution_in_the_United_States.

———. "Interstate Commerce Commission." Last modified September 2, 2021. https://en.wikipedia.org/wiki/Interstate_Commerce_Commission.

———. "John Roberts." Last modified September 20, 2021. https://en.wikipedia.org/wiki/John_Roberts.

———. "New Nationalism (Theodore Roosevelt)." Last modified September 2, 2021. https://en.wikipedia.org/wiki/New_Nationalism_(Theodore_Roosevelt).

———. "Second Continental Congress." Last modified July 3, 2021. https://en.wikipedia.org/wiki/Second_Continental_Congress.

———. "Second Industrial Revolution." Last modified August 28, 2021. https://en.wikipedia.org/wiki/Second_Industrial_Revolution.

———. "William Rehnquist." Last modified September 18, 2021. https://en.wikipedia.org/wiki/William_Rehnquist.

Winthrop, John. Sermon, New England, 1630. As transcribed by the *American Yawp Reader* in "John Winthrop Dreams of a City on a Hill, 1630." Text at https://www.americanyawp.com/reader/colliding-cultures/john-winthrop-dreams-of-a-city-on-a-hill-1630/.

Zinke, Ryan. "State Fish and Wildlife Authority on Department of the Interior Lands and Water." Memorandum to Heads of Bureaus and Offices, Washington, DC: United States Department of the Interior, September 10, 2018. https://www.peer.org/wp-content/uploads/attachments/9_11_18_Zinke_memo.pdf.

Index

Abelman v. Booth, 24
abortion, xxiii, 133–34, 164
Adams, John, 15
Addams, Jane, 66
Adler, Robert, 143
Administrative Conference of the United States, 222–23
Administrative Procedure Act of 1946, 63, 222–23
administrative state, xxiii, 63, 67–68, 75–76, 79–84, 90, 223, 228, 237
admiralty law, 4, 17
Afognak Island, Alaska, 43n22
Agreement on the Conservation of Polar Bears, 206
Agricultural Adjustment Act of 1933, 88, 93
agriculture, xvii, 23, 34–35, 42n22, 88, 99, 101–2, 140, 143, 176, 222, 227
Airborne Hunting Act, 148
airlines, 80, 176
air quality. *See* pollution
Alaska, 43n22, 217
Alaska National Interest Land Conservation Act of 1980, 205–6
alcohol, 66, 73n66, 75–84, 97
Alden v. Maine, 202–3
Allen, Durward, 103

American Civil War, 22–23, 33–34, 58, 73n66, 83, 125
American Federation of Labor, 72n53
American Game Policy of 1930, 102–3, 105, 107
American Revolutionary War, 1, 3–4, 7–8, 11–12n13, 12n14, 14, 16, 26–27, 221; see also Treaty of Paris (1783)
American Tobacco, 65
Anderson, William, 106, 227
Andrews, Richard, 97
animal health, 62
Anthracite Coal Strike, 72n53
Anti-Federalists, 1–2, 5–6, 8–9
Anti-Saloon League, 76
antitrust legislation, 57, 139. *See also* Clayton Antitrust Act of 1914; Mann-Elkins Act of 1910; Sherman Antitrust Act of 1890
Appeal to Reason, 73n63
Arapaho National Recreation Area, 153
Articles of Confederation, 4–5, 7–8, 144
A Sand County Almanac, 101
assembly lines, 57–58, 66, 98
Association of Fish and Wildlife Agencies, 95n29, 140, 208, 214,

216–17, 234; Blue Ribbon Panel, 236–37
Athenian law, 38
Auer v. Robbins, 221, 224, 228
automobiles, 78, 82, 121–22, 125–26, 176, 190, 233

Babbitt v. Sweet Home Chapter of Communities for a Great Oregon, 142–43, 172
Bacon, Francis, 101
Bald and Golden Eagle Protection Act, 158–59n82, 173, 204
Bald Eagle Protection Act of 1940. *See* Bald and Golden Eagle Protection Act
Baldwin v. Fish and Game Commission of Montana, 135–37, 144, 144, 146, 148–49, 202–3
Baltimore and Ohio Railroad, 22
Bank of the United States, First, 22
banks, 34, 64, 80, 88, 91, 176, 188, 190, 222; failures, 88; state-chartered, 22, 27
Barrett, Amy Coney, 189
Bates v. Dow Agrosciences, LLC, 166
Beard, Charles, 37
Beard, Mary, 37
Bennett v. Spear, 142
Bill of Rights. *See* United States Constitution, Bill of Rights
biodiversity, xxiii, 103, 127, 139, 169–70
biologists, 51, 104, 214, 216–17
birds, xvii, 25, 38, 44–45, 48–49, 52, 55n21, 103, 105, 139, 146, 204–5, 219n13. *See also* wildlife
bison. *See* buffalo
Bituminous Coal Conservation Act of 1935, 88
Black, Hugo, 122–23
Black Lives Matter, 132n37
Blackmun, Harry, 135–36, 149, 165, 177
Blackstone, William, 38

Black Tuesday, 87–88
Blunt, Roy, 237
Boone and Crockett Club, 99, 108n3
Brandeis, Louis, 49, 61, 83–84
Brennan, William J., Jr., 136, 144–46, 158–59n82
Breyer, Stephen, 177, 181–82
Brown v. Board of Education, 125, 127
Bruesewitz v. Wyeth, 192
Bryan, William Jennings, 59
buffalo, 44–47, 53n7, 173
bureaucracy, xxii, 57, 67–68, 75–82, 214, 242
Bureau of Alcohol, Tobacco and Firearms, 78
Bureau of Alcohol, Tobacco, Firearms, and Explosives, 78
Bureau of Biological Survey. *See* United States Fish and Wildlife Service
Bureau of Immigration and Naturalization, 222
Bureau of Industrial Alcohol, 78
Bureau of Internal Revenue. *See* Internal Revenue Service
Bureau of Land Management, 205–6, 221–22; 2008 Special Status Species Management Policy, 205–6
Bureau of Narcotics, 78
Bureau of Prohibition, 73–74n67, 77–78
The Burger Court, 120, 128–29, 132n39, 133–34, 150–52, 161n109
The Burger Court and the Rise of the Judicial Right, 133
Burger, Warren, 133–36, 141, 146, 149, 151, 158–59n82, 194, 203
Bush, George H. W., 177
Bush, George W., 163, 188
Butler, Pierce, 61, 88–89

California Coastal Commission v. Granite Rock Co., 172, 202–3
Camfield v. United States, 207
Canada, 35, 48–49, 79
cancel culture, 132n37
capitalism, 58

Carnegie, Andrew, 58
Carson, Rachel, 125, 127, 130n18
Catt, Carrie Chapman, 67
Cattle Contagious Diseases Act, 62
Center for Biological Diversity, 126
Chalk v. United States, 92, 144
Charlemagne, 37
Charter of the Forest, 24–25
Chase, Alston, 127
Chevron U.S.A., Inc. v. Natural Resources Defense Council, Inc., 193, 221, 224, 228
Chicago, Illinois, 34–35, 39, 66
Chicago, Rock Island & Pacific Railway Co. v. Hardwick Farmers Elevator Co., 61, 68
child labor, 65–66
Chisholm v. Georgia, 15
Chisom v. Roemer, 178
Christy v. Hodel, 172
Chronology and Index of the More Important Events in American Game Protection, 1776–1911, 42n22
Cigarette Labeling and Advertising Act, 192
Cipollone v. Liggett Group, Inc., 164–65
CITES. See Convention on International Trade in Endangered Species of Wild Fauna and Flora (CITES) (1973)
cities. *See* urbanization
citizen lawsuits, 142, 224
Civil Aeronautics Board, 80
civil disobedience, 126
civil liberties, 115, 125, 127–28, 177
civil rights, 91, 133–34, 177
Civil Rights Act of 1866, 33–34
Civil Rights Act of 1870, 90
Civil Rights Act of 1871, 33–34, 90
Civil Rights Act of 1964, xviii
civil rights movement, 125–27
Civil War. *See* American Civil War
Clajon Production Corp. v. Petera, 172
Clayton Antitrust Act of 1914, 64, 69

Clean Air Act of 1970, 103, 114n54, 126, 142, 226, 229n20, 231n33
Clean Water Act of 1972, 103, 126, 137, 142, 173, 176
climate change, 111–12
Clinton, William Jefferson, 163
clothing, 22, 44
Cloverleaf Butter Co. v. Patterson, 117
Cold War, 120
Colonial America, xxi, 2–4, 7–9, 26, 194
commandeering, 79, 81, 83, 174–76, 182, 222, 226, 231n33
Commentaries on the Laws of England, 38
commissioner of internal revenue, 73n66, 73–74n67
common law, 26, 176
computers, 190
concurrent authority, xviii, xxi, 61–63, 68, 75, 79, 81, 83–84, 116, 161n109, 162, 165, 175, 180, 190, 200, 201, 209, 215, 217–18, 219n13
concurrent jurisdiction. *See* concurrent authority
conflict of laws, 1, 17, 39, 61–62, 68, 134, 160–61n107, 172–74, 176–77, 189, 192, 199–201, 207–8, 226–227
Congress. *See* United States Congress
congressional intent, xxii, 61–63, 116–18, 150, 152, 166, 172–73, 178, 190, 192, 201, 209, 217.
See also Endangered Species Act of 1973, congressional intent
conservation biology, 126–27
Conservation Without Conflict, 216–18
Constitution. *See* United States Constitution
Constitutional Convention of 1787, 5–8, 14–15, 144, 175
consumer protection, 126, 222
Continental Army, 7
Continental Congress, First, 12n15
Continental Congress, Second, 4, 8, 12n15, 14, 23

286 Index

Convention Between the United Kingdom and the United States for the Protection of Migratory Birds in Canada and the United States (1916), 206

Convention Between the United States of America and the United Mexican States for the Protection of Migratory Birds and Game Mammals (1972), 206

Convention on International Trade in Endangered Species of Wild Fauna and Flora (CITES) (1973), 103, 138, 206

Cooperative Wildlife Research Units, 102, 104

Cooper, James Fenimore, 242

Copyright Act, 90

Corfield v. Coryell, 17–19, 24, 26, 136, 148–49

Corwin, Edwin S., 24, 39, 105, 161n109, 227

cost-sharing, 105–6, 227

cost-benefit analysis, 142–43, 193

cost-effectiveness, 142–43

cotton, 22, 27, 35

Cottonwood Environmental Law Center v. U.S. Forest Service, 188, 193–94

Council on Environmental Quality, 222

criminal law, 115, 133–34

Crow Tribe of Indians v. Repsis, 172

culture wars, 163

currency, 4, 34

dams, 98

Darwin, Charles, 35, 98, 101

Declaration of Independence. *See* United States Declaration of Independence

Defenders of Wildlife v. Andrus, 202–203

Democratic Party, 23, 66, 189

deregulation, 91, 177, 189, 223

Dingell, Debbie, 237

Dingell, John D., Jr., 137

Dingell-Johnson Act, 105, 111–13n42, 227–28, 232–33, 236–37, 243

Dinh, Viet, 60

disease. *See* health

Dobzhansky, Theodosuis, 131n28

Dohner, Cindy, 217

Douglas v. Seacoast Products, Inc., 136, 144–46, 148–49, 202–3

Douglas, William O., 117

Dred Scott v. Sandford, 23

drinking age, 175

dual sovereignty. *See* federalism, dual

Duck Stamp. *See* Migratory Bird Hunting Stamp Act

Ducks Unlimited, 55n21

due process, xxiii, 4, 33, 163

du Pont, Éleuthère Irénée, 22

The Dust Bowl, 88

Earth Day, 126

easements, 24, 27, 149

Eastern United States, 21–22, 35, 50, 217

Ecological Society of America, 99

ecology, 35, 96, 98–100, 103, 107, 126–27, 129, 143

ecosystems, 101, 103, 126–27, 138, 143; carrying capacity, 99–100

Edison, Thomas, 58

education, xxiii, 96, 105, 107, 125, 171, 199–200, 227, 230n25, 239n19

eighteenth century, xxiii, 42n22, 58, 127

Eisenhower administration, 120, 122

Eisenhower, Dwight D., 127

electricity, 58, 65, 169; hydroelectric, 98, 171

elk, 45, 173, 197–98n46

Ellsworth, Oliver, 15

Employee Retirement Income Security Act of 1974, 113–14n46, 176, 230n25

endangered species, xxii, 2, 65, 203–5. *See also* Endangered Species Act of 1966; Endangered Species Act of

1969; Endangered Species Act of 1973
Endangered Species Act of 1966, 137–38
Endangered Species Act of 1969, 137–38
Endangered Species Act of 1973, xviii, xxiii, 17, 103, 106, 126, 133, 137–44, 147–48, 152, 158–59n82, 169–70, 172–74, 176, 202–4, 209, 212–18, 242–43; amendments, 143, 232–33; biological opinions, 173; candidate species, 112n43, 236; congressional intent, 137–41, 147, 155n31, 155–56n32, 203, 212–14, 223, 226, 234; Cooperative Endangered Species Conservation Fund, 232–33, 243; critical habitat, 147, 172, 193; economic impact analysis, 173; funding, xxii–xxiii, 140, 214, 221, 226, 232–36, 242; habitat conservation plans, 213, 216, 243; harm, 172; post-delisting monitoring, 216, 243; recovery, 214, 217, 232, 237; regulations, 213–14, 223; safe harbor agreements, 216, 243; Section 6, 110n28, 139, 148, 212–16, 218, 223, 233–35, 237, 243; Section 7, 110n28, 140–41, 152n32, 193–94; Section 9, 147, 169; take, 147, 169, 172
energy crisis, 125–26
England, 2–3, 25–26, 58
English Crown, 1–4, 7, 26–27, 38
Environmental Defense Fund, 126
environmental disasters, 125
environmental groups: litigation, 126, 129, 130–31n21; membership, 126
environmental litigation, 126, 129, 130–31n21, 142–43, 213
environmental movement, 121–22, 126, 130n18, 137, 140, 222, 226
Environmental Protection Agency, 67, 222, 226
Epstein, Richard, 60, 90, 119n17

Erie Canal, 21, 35
Eskridge, William, 191
ethnology, 126
eugenics, 132n37
Europe, 120
evidence, admissibility, 83
executive privilege, 133–34
executive orders, 202
extinction, 45–49, 51, 98–99, 103, 170–71, 237

factories. *See* assembly lines
Fair Labor Standards Act of 1938, 62
farms. *See* agriculture
feathers. *See* birds; millinery
federal agencies, xxiii, 51–52, 57, 141, 144, 205–6, 212–13, 221–24, 228; overreach, 63, 75, 81, 140, 214, 221, 242; regulatory capture, 224
federal aid coordinators, 112n42, 227–28
Federal Aid Highway Act, 114n54, 231n33
Federal Aid to Wildlife Restoration Fund, 213, 232–33
Federal Arbitration Act, 230n20
Federal Bureau of Investigation, 77–78
Federal Deposit Insurance Corporation, 80
Federal Employer Liability Act of 1906, 72n53
Federal Employer Liability Act of 1908, 72n53
Federal Energy Regulatory Commission, 171
federal government, size, 80
federal grants. *See* grants
federalism: coercive, xxi, 91; 225; cooperative, xviii, xxi, 52, 57, 62, 68, 83, 87, 91, 93, 106–7, 116, 137, 151, 161n109, 174, 212, 222, 225, 227; dual, xviii, xxi, 8, 21, 23–24, 27–28, 33, 39–40, 44, 52, 57, 59, 61, 68, 81–82, 90–91, 93, 106, 161n109, 167, 178, 180, 190, 209, 222, 227

The Federalist Papers, 1–2, 8, 14–15, 165–66
Federalists, 1–2, 6, 8–9, 15–16, 19, 23, 27
federal judiciary, 16, 78–79, 224. See also United States Courts of Appeals; United States District Courts; United States Supreme Court
Federal Land Policy and Management Act of 1976, 205–6, 215, 217; areas of critical environmental concern, 205–6
Federal Lottery Act, 72n53
Federal Maritime Commission v. South Carolina State Ports Authority, 202–3
Federal Power Act, 113–14n46, 171, 230n25
Federal Power Commission, 65
Federal Preemption: State Powers, Natural Interests, 60
Federal Register, 213, 222
Federal Reserve System, 64, 88, 222
Federal Trade Commission, 64, 69, 222
FERC v. Mississippi, 175
Field, Stephen J., 39, 145
Fischman, Robert L., 227
fish, 37, 43n22, 103, 172. See also wildlife
Fish and Wildlife Coordination Act of 1934, 102–3, 107, 171, 202–3
Fish and Wildlife Service. See United States Fish and Wildlife Service
fishing: commercial, 24–25, 43n22, 173; recreational, 24–26, 92, 105
Fisk, Jim, 58
Florida Supreme Court, 163
flyway councils, 55n21, 219n13
food supply. See wildlife, as food source
Ford, Henry, 73n63
Forest and Stream, 53n5
Forest Reserve Act of 1891, 43n22
forest reserves. See national forests
Forest Service. See United States Forest Service

Fortenberry, Jeff, 237
Foster-Fountain Packing Co. v. Haydel, 43n24, 96, 101, 107, 124, 136, 144–45, 148, 202–3
Founding Fathers of the United States, xxi, 8–9, 14, 18, 51–52, 116–17, 144, 164–65, 175, 179, 200
Frankfurter, Felix, 37, 40, 101, 124
Frazier-Lemke Act, 88
freedom of speech, 4, 115, 241
freedom of the press, 115
free market, 58, 60
Friends of the Earth, 126
frontier, 50
The Fuller Court, 41–42n18, 48, 88
Fuller, Melville W., 48
Fulton, Robert, 22
Fund for Animals v. Clark, 173

Gambino v. United States, 83–84
Game Management, 101
game refuges, 51, 99–100, 107
Garcia v. San Antonio Transit Authority, 161n109, 178–79, 184n27
Gardbaum, Stephen, 60, 62, 116
GDF Realty Investments, Ltd. v. Norton, 169, 192–93, 202–3
Geer v. Connecticut, 33, 37–40, 44, 48, 100–101, 136, 143–46, 148–49
Gehringer, Jack, 235
General Land Office. See Bureau of Land Management
General Mining Law of 1872, 98
Gerken, Heather, 217
Gibbons v. Ogden, 16–17, 19, 26, 146
Gibbs v. Babbitt, 169–71, 173, 202–4
Gilded Age, 39, 57–58, 138
Ginsburg, Ruth Bader, 177
Gold Rush of 1849, 21
gold standard, 125–26
Goldstein v. California, 151
Goldwater, Barry, 163
Gompers, Samuel, 72n53
Gonzales v. Raich, 174, 192–93

Good Government Guys Movement
  (Goo Goo Guys), 97
Goodyear, Charles, 22
Gore, Albert, Jr., 163
Gorsuch, Neil, 189
Gottschalk, John S., 234
Gould, Jay, 58
Graham, Bob, 139
Granger movement, 72n53
Grant, Madison, 46–47
grants, 34, 106–107, 113–14n46, 148, 181, 213, 227–28, 230n25, 233, 236; conditions on, xxii, 62, 90, 106–7, 114n54, 221, 224–28, 231n33, 242
Grant, Ulysses S., 43n22, 47
Great Depression, 70n10, 87–89, 91, 93, 104, 121
Great Lakes, 21, 35, 39
Greenwalt, Lynn, 234
Gregory v. Ashcraft, 150, 178, 202–3, 224
Greve, Michael, 60, 90, 119n17
Grier v. American Honda Motor Co., Inc., 177
Grinnell, George Bird, 46–47, 52, 53n5, 53n7, 96–98, 108n3, 156–57n36
grizzly bear, 137, 172, 235

habeas corpus, 4, 17
habitat, 25, 101–2, 139, 147, 233; fragmentation, 42n22, 233; restoration, 55n21, 103
habitat conservation plans. *See* Endangered Species Act of 1973, habitat conservation plans
Haeckel, Ernst, 98, 101
Hall v. De Cuir, 146
Hamilton, Alexander, 1–2, 27, 165
Harlan, John Marshall, 60, 145
Harrison Narcotics Tax Act of 1914, 78
Harrison, William Henry, 43n22
Hawaii Department of Land and Natural Resources, 147
Hays, Samuel P., 96–97, 125

health, xxiii, 9, 19, 58, 66–67, 98–99, 142, 222, 241; Health Insurance Act (1996), 91; Patient Protection and Affordable Care Act (Obamacare), 114n54, 226, 229–30n20, 231n33, 237
Heinrich, Martin, 237
Henry III, 25
Hepburn Act, 61
Herrera v. Wyoming, 197–98n46
Hester v. United States, 82–83
highways, 105, 121–22, 169, 175, 227
Hillsborough County, Fla. v. Automated Medical Laboratories, Inc., 150–51
Hines v. Davidowitz, 63, 116–17, 160–61n107
Hodel v. Virginia Surface Mining & Reclamation Ass'n, 175
Holmes, Oliver Wendell, 49, 52, 60–61, 122–23, 136, 145
Homeland Security Act of 2002, 78
Homestead Act of 1862, 35–36, 40
Homestead Strike, 72n53
Hoover, Herbert, 70n10, 88
Hornaday, William T., 46–47, 53n5
hospitals, 169, 230n25
housing, 66, 97, 222, 233
How the Other Half Lives: Studies among the Tenements of New York, 72n61
Hudson Bay Company, 35
Hughes, Charles Evans, 88, 115
The Hughes Court, 89, 91–92, 115–16
Hughes v. Oklahoma, 134, 143–44, 147–48, 152, 202–3, 205
Hull House, 66
hunting, xxiii, 37–38, 92, 101–2, 105, 172, 239n19; bag limits, 45, 48–49, 92, 99, 207; licenses, 92, 103, 105, 113n42, 135; market, xvii, 37–38, 42n22, 44–48, 52, 55n21, 99; recreational, 25, 137, 147, 149; seasons, 45, 48–49, 92, 99, 207
Hunt v. United States, 144
Huxley, Julian, 131n28

illegal drugs, 66, 174
Illinois Central Railroad Co. v. Illinois, 33, 39–40
immigrants, 48, 66, 68, 122, 176
Improving the Effectiveness of the Endangered Species Act for Wildlife, 243
In a Dark Wood: The Fight over Forests and the Rising Tyranny of Ecology, 127
Indians. *See* native Americans
Industrial Revolution, xxi, 57–59, 66, 68, 97, 161n109, 222; first, 7, 21–22, 27, 58; second, 33–34, 40, 50
industrial waste, 98, 103, 176
industry, 21–24, 176, 241
Information Age, 188–91
integration, racial, 125, 128–29
intellectual property, 162, 176, 182, 188, 190
Internal Revenue Service, 67, 73–74n67, 76; Alcohol Tax Unit, 78; Narcotics Division, 77; Prohibition Unit, 77–78, 83; Technical Division, 77
International Convention for the Regulation of Whaling, 206
interstate commerce, xvii, xxiii, 4, 17, 23, 34, 39, 48, 61, 65, 90, 101, 107, 124, 135–36, 139, 144–48, 167–71, 176, 201–2; definition, 17, 101, 107, 167–68
Interstate Commerce Act of 1887, xviii, 64–65
Interstate Commerce Commission, 34, 64–65, 69, 221–22
Interstate Commerce Railroad Association, 64–65
invasive species, 99, 111–12

Jackson, Andrew, 21, 23, 27
Jackson, Robert A., 163
James Everard's Breweries v. Day, 82, 84
Jay, John, 1–2, 15
Jefferson, Thomas, 16, 22, 224, 242–43

Johnson, Lyndon B.: Great Society, 66
Johnson, Steffen N., 190–91
Joint Federal/State Task Force for ESA Policy, 213
Joint Federal/State Task Force on Federal Assistance Policy, 213
Jones v. Rath Packing Co., 159–60n92
judicial restraint, 128, 134, 150–52, 164
judicial review. *See* United States Constitution, judicial review
Judiciary Act of 1837, 23
The Jungle, 67–68
jus publicum, 25–26
Justinian, 25

Kaibab National Forest, 92
Kaibab Plateau, 100
Kavanaugh, Brett, 189
Kenai Peninsula Borough v. State of Alaska, 154n15
Kennedy, Anthony, 177
Kennedy, David M., 88
Kennedy, John F., 125; New Frontier, 66
Kent State massacre, 125–26
Kidd v. Pearson, 146
King, Martin Luther, Jr., 125–26
Kisonak, Lane, 208, 216–17
Kleppe v. New Mexico, 94n28, 134–36, 144, 202–3, 206
Koppes, Clayton R., 97
Korean War, 120

labor law, 58, 60, 65–66, 167, 176
Labor-Management Reporting and Disclosure Act, 113–14n46, 230n25
labor relations, 23, 91
labor unions, 72n53
Lacey Act of 1900, xvii, xxiii, 44, 48–49, 42, 65, 138, 144, 172, 204
Lacey, John, 48
Lambert v. Yellowley, 82, 84
land-grant colleges and universities, 36, 104
landscape conservation, 127

land use regulation, 142, 170
Leatherstocking Tale, 242
Legislative Accountability and Reform Act of 1995, 178
Leopold, Aldo, 98, 100–102, 126, 156–57n36; land ethic, 101
Linnaeus, Carolus, 98, 101
Lochner era, 57, 60, 62–63, 68
Lochner v. New York, 60
Loggerhead Turtle v. Volusia County, Florida, 173
Lorillard Tobacco Co. v. Reilly, 177
Louisiana Department of Conservation, 100
Lovejoy, Tom, 127
Loyola, Mario, 226, 231n33
Lujan v. Defenders of Wildlife, 142

Madison, James, 1–2, 5, 8, 161n109, 166
Magna Carta, 24–25, 38
Magnuson–Stevens Fishery Conservation and Management Act, 204, 206
manifest destiny, 21
Mann-Elkins Act of 1910, 64, 69
manufacturing, 22–23, 58
Marbury v. Madison, 14–16, 18–19, 222, 228
Marine Mammal Protection Act of 1972, 126, 204, 206, 235
maritime commerce, 17, 24–25
The Marshall Court, 15–18, 21, 27
Marshall, John, xvii, 5, 14–16, 18–19, 26, 228
Marshall Plan, 120
Marshall, Thurgood, 134–36, 159–60n92
Marsh, George Perkins, 35, 98, 101
Marsh, Othniel Charles, 35
Martin v. Waddell's Lessee, 17, 21, 24, 26, 28, 33–34, 37, 40, 52, 143, 148
Massachusetts, 3, 8–9
Massachusetts Bay Association, 3

Massachusetts Bay Colony charter of 1629, 3
Mason, George, 5
Matador Land and Cattle Company, 35
Mayflower, xxi, 3, 7
Mayflower Compact, 1, 3, 18
Mayr, Ernst, 131n28
McCready v. Virginia, 33–34, 37–38, 40, 123–24, 136, 143, 148–49
McCulloch v. Maryland, 16, 19
McPherson, James, 34
McReynolds, James, 88–89
Mead, Matt, 217
Meat Inspection Act, 67, 73n63
media, 22, 27, 64, 66–67, 125
Medicaid, 226
medical devices, 162, 176, 182, 188, 190
medical drugs. *See* pharmaceuticals
Medicare, 190, 226
Medtronics, Inc. v. Lohr, 202–3
Merrill, Thomas, 60, 226
Mexico, 48–49, 79
middle class, 76
Midwestern United States, 34–35, 88
migration corridors, 42n22
Migratory Bird Conservation Act fund, 105
Migratory Bird Conservation Act of 1929, 54n11
Migratory Bird Hunting Stamp Act of 1934 (Duck Stamp Act), 103, 149
migratory birds. *See* birds
migratory bird treaties. *See* Convention Between the United Kingdom and the United States for the Protection of Migratory Birds in Canada and the United States (1916), Convention Between the United States of America and the United Mexican States for the Protection of Migratory Birds and Game Mammals (1972)
Migratory Bird Treaty Act of 1918, xviii, xxiii, 17, 29n23, 44, 48–49, 52,

65, 105, 137–38, 144–45, 147, 158–59n82, 173, 204, 212, 218, 219n13
millinery, 45, 48
Minnesota v. Mille Lacs Band of Chippewa Indians, 173
Mintz v. Baldwin, 57, 62–63, 68, 116, 118
Miranda v. Arizona, 164
Mississippi River, 22, 36, 217
Missouri v. Holland, 49, 52, 123, 136, 145, 148, 173, 219n13
Mistretta v. United States, 224
Mitchell, John, 163
monopolies, 38–39, 48, 51, 57, 63–65, 69, 138–39
Montana, 135, 236
Montesquieu (Charles-Louis de Secondat, Baron de La Brède et de Montesquieu), 18
Moore, Barrington, 99
Morgan, John Pierpont, 58
Morgan v. Negodich et al., 31n35
Morrill Act of 1862, 36, 40
MSNBC, 166
muckraking, 64–65, 73n63
Multiple Use Sustained Yield Act of 1960, 205–6
Municipal Bankruptcy Act, 88

Napoleonic Code, 38
Nash, Roderick, 139
National American Woman Suffrage Association, 67
National Association of Home Builders v. Babbitt, 169, 192–93, 202–3
National Association of Home Builders v. Defenders of Wildlife, 142
National Audubon Society, 126
National Audubon Society v. Davis, 174
National Bank Act, 230n20
National Bison Legacy Act, 53n8
National Environmental Policy Act of 1969, 126, 130n21, 173, 210–11n20
National Forest Management Act of 1976, 205–6

national forests, 43n22, 49, 51, 99–100, 107, 197–98n46; land management plans, 193–94
National Industrial Recovery Act of 1933, 88, 93
National Labor Relations Act of 1935, 113–14n46, 230n25
National Labor Relations Board, 80
National Landscape Conservation System, 205–6
National League of Cities v. Usery, 166–67, 177
National Marine Fisheries Service, 212–13, 233, 235, 238n8
national monuments, 51, 205–6
national parks, 49, 51, 99–100, 107, 121–22
National Park Service, 56n28, 121–22, 173; Management Policy (2006), 205–6; Organic Act (1916), 205–6
National Prohibition Act of 1919, 77, 83
National Wildlife Federation, 126
National Wildlife Federation v. Coleman, 157n42
National Wildlife Refuges, 49, 103
National Wildlife Refuge System Administration Act of 1966, 217
National Wildlife Refuge System Improvement Act of 1997, 174
National Woman's Party, 67
native Americans, 7–8, 47, 178, 236–37; treaty rights, 172, 173, 197–98n46. *See also* Tribal Wildlife Grants
naturalists, 51, 98
natural law, 37–38, 241
natural resources, 21, 24, 28, 37, 40
Natural Resources Defense Council, 126
navigable waters, 4–5, 21–22, 24–26, 43n22
Neo-Darwinism, 131n28
New Deal, 61, 66, 91, 178, 182, 190
The New Deal Court, xxi, 63, 89–91, 93
New Deal era, 60–61, 166–67, 174, 222
New Federalism movement, 162–63, 177, 182, 189

newspapers. *See* media
New York Central Railroad Company v. Winfield, 61
New York City, 21–22, 34, 66, 97
New York Minimum Wage Law, 88
The New York Times, 163
New York v. United States, 162, 170, 175–77, 182, 222
Nie, Martin, 208
nineteenth century, xvii, xxiii, 33, 39–40, 42n22, 51, 61, 127, 222
Nixon, Richard, 134, 137, 162–63
N.L.R.B. v. Jones & Laughlin Steel Corp., 167–68, 201–2
Noise Control Act of 1972, 126
nonviolence, 126
North American Waterfowl Management Plan, 55n21
North American Wetlands Conservation Act of 1989, 55n21
North American Wetlands Conservation Fund, 105
North American Wildlife Policy (1973), 103
North Dakota, 149–50
Northern Securities v. United States, 65
Northeastern United States, 34–35
Northwest Atlantic Fisheries Treaty, 206

Occupational Safety and Health Act of 1970, 113–14n46, 230n25
Occupational Safety and Health Administration, 67
O'Connor, Sandra Day, 150–51, 163, 166, 174, 177, 179–80, 222, 224
Office of the US Commissioner of Fish and Fisheries, 43n22
Olmstead v. United States, 82–84
Omnibus Public Land Management Act of 2009, 205–6
open fields doctrine, 82
Organized Fisherman of Florida v. Hodel, 153n12, 202–3
organized labor, 58, 115

Osborn, Fairfield, 46–47
"Our Federalism", 132n39
Our Vanishing Wildlife, 53n5

Pacific Railroad Act of 1862, 34
Pacific Salmon Treaty, 206
Palila v. Hawaii Department of Land and Natural Resources (1979), 94n28, 147, 202–3
Palila v. Hawaii Department of Land and Natural Resources (1988), 158n78, 172
Palmer, T. S., 42n22
papermaking, 21, 58
Patent Act, 90
Paul, Alice, 67
Peckham, Rufus W., 60
Pelican Island, 49
pensions, 176, 222
People for the Ethical Treatment of Animals, 126
Perot, Ross, 190
Petersen, Shannon, 42–43n22, 109n14, 130n18, 130–31n21, 131–32n30
pharmaceuticals, 162, 176, 182, 188, 190, 192, 230n20
Philadelphia, Pennsylvania, 4–5, 8
Pilgrim Code of Law of 1636, 3, 10–11n6
Pilgrims, xxi, 241–42
Pinchot, Gifford, 46–47, 96–98
Pisgah National Forest, 92
Pittman-Robertson Act of 1937, 96, 102, 104–7, 111–13n42, 227–28, 232–33, 236–37, 239n19, 243
Plessy v. Ferguson, 132n37
police powers, 17, 21, 23, 27, 39–40, 48, 60, 66–67, 75–75, 81–82, 88, 116–17, 133, 136, 145–46, 149, 151, 165, 172, 174, 176, 192, 194, 201, 207–9, 215
pollution, 24–25, 43n22, 66–67, 90–91, 97–98, 107, 120–21, 142, 176
Postal Service, 4
Post, Robert, 83

Powell, Lewis F., Jr., 141
predator control, 99–102
predator-prey relationships, 99–100
preemption: coercive, 225; conditional, 114n54, 221; express, 62–63, 68, 141, 150–51, 159–60n92, 164–66, 174, 176–77, 182, 189–90, 201, 230n25; implied, 63, 116, 174, 176–78, 182, 189–90, 201, 230n25; presumption against, 57, 62–63, 68, 92, 115–18, 134, 151–52, 164–66, 180, 182, 189–93, 195, 201–3, 209
Printz v. United States, 162, 165–66, 175, 182, 192–93, 202–3
prisons, 78–79
private property, xviii, 2, 18, 23–24, 38, 60, 63, 138, 140, 143, 145, 153n12, 172, 204–5, 213
Progressive Era, 44, 51, 57–60, 63, 65–68, 75, 80, 93, 96–107, 138–39, 227
Progressive movement, 40, 51–52, 57, 68, 72n53, 96–107, 129
Prohibition, 61, 68, 75–84, 90, 222; enforcement, 78–81, 84. *See also* Bureau of Prohibition; Internal Revenue Service, Prohibition Unit; National Prohibition Act of 1919; temperance movement; Woman's Christian Temperance Union
protests, 126, 132n37, 140
public health, 58, 66, 68, 97, 115, 176, 230n25
public lands, 21, 24, 36, 39–40, 43n22, 51, 92, 97, 134, 138, 153n12, 172, 174, 199, 203–8
public trust doctrine, 17, 21, 24–28, 33–34, 37–40, 43n22, 143, 215; in England, 25–26, 31n39; in the Roman Empire, 25–26; state public trust doctrine, 34
public welfare, 9, 19, 66–67, 97, 115, 139, 142
public works, 97

Pure Food and Drug Act of 1906, xviii, 61, 67, 72n53, 73n63
Puritans, 3

quotas, racial, 164

race riots, 125–26
Railroad Retirement Act, 88
railroads, xvii, 21–22, 34–36, 38–39, 57–58, 60–61, 64–65, 76, 121, 176; subsidies, 34, 36, 98. *See also* transcontinental railroad
ranching. *See* agriculture
Rancho Viejo v. Norton, 170, 202–3
Reagan administration, 163, 177, 223
Reagan, Ronald, 177, 189, 223, 242
Reconstruction, 33–34, 76
Reconstruction Act of 1867, 33–34
Recovering America's Wildlife Act (RAWA), 232, 236–38
recreation, outdoor, 24–25, 66, 122
reforestation, 105–106, 227
regulations, xxii, 23, 39, 57–58, 68, 76, 142, 173–74, 176, 191, 212–16, 221, 228. *See also* deregulation; Endangered Species Act of 1973, regulations; land use regulation; United States Forest Service, Cooperation in Wildlife Management Regulation (2005), Planning Rule (2012), Regulation G-20-A, Regulation W-2
The Rehnquist Court, xviii, 134, 150, 162–82, 188–89, 195
Rehnquist, William, 134, 141, 146, 162–64, 174–77, 180, 188
religious freedom, xxiii, 4, 133–34
Reno v. Condon, 175–176, 202–3
Revenue Act of 1894, 72n53
Revolutionary War. *See* American Revolutionary War
Rice v. Santa Fe Elevator Corp., 63, 115–18, 159–60n92, 161n109, 164–66, 180, 182, 189–93, 195,

201–3, 209. *See also* preemption, presumption against
Riis, Jacob, 66
rivers, 21–22, 24–26
roads. *See* highways
robber barons, 38–39, 48, 57–58, 63–64, 76, 87, 138
The Roberts Court, xviii, 181, 188–95
Roberts, John G., Jr., 188, 193–94
Roberts, Owen, 88–89
Rockefeller, John D., 58, 65
Roe v. Wade, 164
Roman Empire, 25
Roman law, 25, 38; Institutes of Justinian, 24, 31n35, 38
Roosevelt, Franklin Delano, xxi, 61, 66, 87–89, 91, 93, 223, 242. *See also* New Deal
Roosevelt, Theodore, 46–47, 49, 52, 68, 76, 83, 96–99, 107, 108n3
Round River, 101
rubber, 22, 27, 58
Ruhl, J. B., 142–43
Russia. *See* Soviet Union.
Rutledge, John, 15

Salic Law, 38
sanitation, 65–66, 97, 230n25
Savage v. Jones, 60–62, 68
savings clauses, 205, 217
Sax, Joseph, 39
Scalia, Antonin, 142–43, 165–66, 177, 192
science, 25, 34–35, 40, 51, 67, 96–99, 107, 125–27, 143, 171, 188. *See also* biologists; ecology
Scottsboro Boys, 92
search and seizure, 82–84
securities, 64, 190
Securities Act of 1933, 62
Securities and Exchange Commission, 80
Securities Exchange Act, 62
Seminole Tribe of Fla. v. Florida, 177, 202–3

seventeenth century, xxiii, 58
sewage, 66–67, 103
Sherlock v. Alling, 146
Sherman Antitrust Act of 1890, xviii, 48, 64–65, 69, 113–14n46, 230n25
Shiras, George, III, 55n18
Shively v. Bowlby et al., 41–42n18
Sierra Club, 126
Silent Spring, 125, 127, 130n18
Simpson, George Gaylord, 131n28
Sinclair, Upton, 67–68
slavery, 23, 33
slums, 66, 97
Smith v. Maryland, 26
social justice movement, 125
Social Security Act of 1935, 62, 90, 105, 116
social upheaval, 57–59, 66, 68, 91, 125, 127–29
social vices, 66, 76, 97
Solid Waste Agency of Northern Cook Cty. v. U.S. Army Corp. of Engineers, 173
Souter, David, 167, 177
South Carolina State Highway Department v. Barnwell Brothers, Inc., 90
South Dakota v. Dole, 175
Southern Railway v. Reid, 60–62, 68
Southern United States, 35, 66
Soviet Union, 120
Spirit of the Laws, 18
Sporting Arms and Ammunition Manufacturers' Institute, 101
state fish and wildlife agencies, 111n40, 137, 212–16; funding, 103–6, 112n43, 214, 232–38; directors, 106, 140, 213–14
state lands, 172
State Wildlife Action Plans, 111–12n42, 236; species of greatest conservation need, 236–37
state wildlife authority. *See* wildlife, state authority over
State Wildlife Grants, 112n43, 236

steam power, 7, 22, 27, 58
Stebbins, George Ledyard, Jr., 131n28
Stevens, John Paul, 177, 192
Stevens, Ted, 139, 212
stocks, 58, 80, 87–88, 104
The Stone Court, 115–18
Stone, Harlan, 90, 115–16
Strahan v. Coxe, 173
suburbs, 121, 222
Sutherland, George, 82, 88–89, 100
Swan Land and Cattle Company, 35
Swan View Coalition v. Turner, Inc., 172

The Taft Court, 80–82, 88, 100, 115–16
Taft, William Howard, 80, 82, 84
Takahashi v. Fish and Game Commission, 120, 122–23, 125, 128, 136, 144, 148
The Taney Court, 21–24, 39, 90–91, 106, 227
Taney, Roger B., 21–23, 26–28
Tangier Sound Waterman's Association v. Douglas, 148–49, 202–3
Tarbell, Ida, 65
taxes, 17, 34; estate, 67, 73n66, 114n54, 231n33; excise, 78, 105, 236; income, 34, 67, 73n66, 76, 90, 114n54, 231n33; progressive, 34, 73n66
technology, 40, 97, 176, 188, 190, 241
Telecommunication Act of 1996, 91
telecommunications, 91, 176, 190
telegraph, 22, 27, 34–35
temperance movement, 75–76, 83
Tennessee Valley Authority v. Hill, 133, 140–44, 151–52, 170, 194, 203
Thomas, Clarence, 177, 197n39
Thorpe v. Rutland and Burlington R.R., 23
timber, 35, 43n22, 136, 140
tobacco, 73n66, 78
Toomer v. Witsell, 120, 123–25, 128, 136, 144–46, 148, 202–3
tort law, 189, 192, 230n20

toxic chemicals, 67, 125
trade, 18, 26, 44, 48, 97, 139, 171
transcontinental railroad, 22, 34
transportation, 23, 91, 97, 101, 176. *See also* highways; railroads
treaties, 4, 7, 15, 17, 48–49, 138, 147, 172, 206
Treaty of Paris (1783), 4, 12n14
Triangle Shirtwaist Factory fire, 72n53
Tribal Wildlife Grants, 236
Tripartite Agreement, 55n21
Truman administration, 120
Trump administration, 189
Trump, Donald J., 192
trusts, 51; trustbusting, 57, 63–65, 69, 138
Tunney, John, 212
Turner, Frederick Jackson, 50
twentieth century, xxiii, 39, 51, 66, 97, 107, 126–27, 138–39, 192, 217
twenty-first century, 15, 51, 96

unemployment, 87–88, 91, 93, 222; compensation, 241
United Nations, 120
United States Attorney General, 78, 223
United States Census Bureau, 50
United States Coast Guard, 79, 82–83
United States Congress, 14, 17, 23, 34, 52, 61–65, 67–68, 80–82, 91–92, 104–6, 116–17, 127, 134, 137–40, 166, 171, 178, 189, 194, 207–8, 215, 223–24, 227, 233, 236–38, 242. *See also* congressional intent
United States Constitution, xxi–xxii, 1, 4–9, 14–15, 21, 23, 26, 37, 51–52, 91, 175, 194, 200, 203, 242; amendments, 4; Article I, 18, 179–80; Article II, 18; Article III, 14, 16, 18; Bill of Rights, 1, 4, 9, 120, 125; Commerce Clause, xxii, 23, 26–27, 37–38, 49, 51–52, 59–63, 65, 87, 90–91, 93, 100–101, 115–18, 124, 127, 135, 138–39, 144–46, 148–49, 151, 165–70, 172–76, 178–82, 199–203,

205, 226, 230n25; Contract Clause, 60; dormant Commerce Clause, 61–62; Double Jeopardy Clause, 82; Due Process Clause, Fifth Amendment, 172; Due Process Clause, Fourteenth Amendment, xxiii, 60; Eighteenth Amendment, 68, 73–74n67, 75–77, 79–83, 90; Eleventh Amendment, 15; enumerated powers, xvii–xviii, xxi–xxii, 1, 5–6, 8–9, 16, 19, 23–24, 27, 51–52, 80, 88, 116–17, 27, 134, 166, 173–74, 180, 191, 199–200, 204–5; Equal Protection Clause, 122–23, 128, 135, 172; Fifteenth Amendment, 33, 90; Fifth Amendment, 83, 158–59n82, 172; First Amendment, 92; Fourteenth Amendment, xxiii, 33, 122–23, 125, 128; Fourth Amendment, 82–84; incorporation, 120, 125; judicial review, 14–16, 18–19, 116, 222, 228; Necessary and Proper Clause, 174–75, 200; Nineteenth Amendment, 67, 76; Privileges and Immunities Clause, 17, 123–24, 128, 134–37, 145, 149, 172; Privileges or Immunities Clause, 92; Property Clause, 54n16, 92, 100, 127, 134–35, 138, 148, 199–200, 203–8; reserved powers, xxi–xxii, 1, 5–6, 9, 17, 23, 91, 151, 162; separation of powers, 14–15, 18–19, 179, 222, 228; Seventeenth Amendment, 67, 90; Sixteenth Amendment, 67–68, 73n66, 76, 90; Supremacy Clause, xxii, 1, 6–7, 16–17, 34, 61–62, 65, 81, 119n17, 134, 138–39, 150–151, 165, 190, 200–201, 208; Taxing and Spending Clause, 138, 174–75, 200, 226; Tenth Amendment, 5–6, 9, 23, 27, 37, 48, 65, 91–93, 124, 128, 138, 147, 162, 165, 174–75, 177, 180, 182, 184n27, 200, 207–8; Thirteenth Amendment, 23, 33; Treaty Clause, 49, 52, 138, 200, 205–6; Twenty-First Amendment, 76

United States Courts of Appeals, 17, 92, 148–50, 193–94, 199–200, 203–5

United States Declaration of Independence, 4

United States Department of Agriculture, 36, 56n28, 104, 221–22; Division of Economic Ornithology and Mammalogy, 221–22; Division of Entomology, 221–22

United States Department of Health and Human Services, 222

United States Department of Homeland Security, 78

United States Department of Housing and Urban Development, 222

United States Department of the Interior, 56n28, 104, 147, 214–15, 221–22; Bureau of Mines, 67

United States Department of Justice, 64, 69, 77–79, 222

United States Department of Labor, 67, 222

United States Department of the Navy, 221

United States Department of State, 221

United States Department of the Treasury, 34, 73–74n67, 75–78, 105, 221–22; Alcohol and Tobacco Tax and Trade Bureau, 78

United States Department of War, 221

United States District Courts, 136, 147, 194

United States Fish and Wildlife Service, 42n22, 55n21, 56n28, 103–5, 137, 141, 173, 193, 212–18, 221–23, 226, 232–34, 238n8; Wildlife and Sport Fish Restoration Chief, 227–28

United States Forest Service, 56n28, 92, 173, 193–94; Cooperation in Wildlife Management Regulation (2005), 205–6; Organic Act (1897), 205–6; Planning Rule (2012), 205–6;

Regulation G-20-A, 92, 95n29; Regulation W-2, 95n29
United States military, 22
United States population, 24, 35, 38, 57, 66, 99, 233
United States Post Office, 221
United States Public Health Service, 67
United States Secretary of Agriculture, 92, 100, 103
United States Secretary of Commerce, 88, 103
United States Secretary of the Interior, 172, 235
United States Secretary of State, 16
United States Supreme Court: court packing, 87–88; original jurisdiction, 16; size of, 23, 87–88
United States Treasury. *See* United States Department of the Treasury
United States v. Bramble, 173
United States v. Darby, 91–92, 167
United States v. E.C. Knight & Co., 65
United States v. Glenn-Colusa Irrigation District, 172, 209n5
United States v. Guthrie, 172
United States v. Helsley, 148
United States v. Lanza, 82
United States v. Lopez, 162, 166–69, 174, 177, 182, 192–93, 202–4
United States v. Lundquist, 173
United States v. Morrison, 162, 166–69, 174, 182, 192–93, 202–4
United States v. Romano, 172
universities, 51–52, 104, 107. *See also* land-grant colleges and universities
urbanization, xvii, 44, 66, 97, 103, 222
Utah Native Plant Society v. U.S. Fish and Wildlife Service, 202–3

Van Buren, Martin, 23
Vanderbilt, Cornelius, 58
Van Devanter, Willis, 88–89
Vietnam War, 125, 128–29
The Vinson Court, 125
Vinson, Fred M., 122–23

Violence Against Women Act, 166
vocational rehabilitation, 105, 227
Volstead Act. *See* National Prohibition Act of 1919
von Humboldt, Alexander, 98, 101
Voting Rights Act of 1965, xviii, 230n20

Wallace, Henry C., 100
Wallop-Breaux Federal Aid in Sport Fish Restoration Act, 111
War of 1812, 16
Ware v. Hylton, 15
The Warren Court, xviii, 120, 125, 127–29, 132n39, 134, 164
Warren, Earl, 127, 134, 164
Washington, Bushrod, 17–18
Washington Conference (1973), 103
Washington, George, 7, 14
The Washington Post, 139
Washington State Department of Fisheries v. FERC, 171
waterfowl-production areas, 149–50
Watergate, 140
Water Pollution Control Act. *See* Clean Water Act of 1972.
water quality. *See* pollution
Watt, James, 185n50, 223
Weber, Wendi, 217
Weeks-McLean Act of 1913, 48
welfare, 66, 222
Western Governors' Conference, 217
Western United States, 34–37, 88, 122, 217
Western Watersheds Project, 126
westward expansion, 21, 23–24, 27, 34–37, 221–22
Weyerhaeuser v. U.S. Fish and Wildlife Service, 188, 193–94
Whaling Convention Act, 206
White, Byron, 136, 164, 177
The White Court, 88
White, Edward Douglass, Jr., 37–38, 49, 61, 80
White-Slave Traffic Act of 1910, 72n53

Whitney, Eli, 22
Wickard v. Filburn, 167
WildEarth Guardians, 126
Wilderness Act of 1964, 205–6, 217
Wilderness Society, 126
Wild Free-Roaming Horse and Burros Act of 1971, 134, 207
wild horses and burros, 206
wildlife: as food source, xxi, 2, 7, 17, 37, 44, 49–50, 52, 100, 124, 137, 145–46; federal funding, 104–6, 232–38; game, 99, 101–3, 113n45, 146; nongame, 103, 112n43; state authority over, xxi–xxiii, 1–2, 26, 33, 37–38, 40, 43n22, 44, 49, 51, 92, 98, 120, 122–23, 125, 128, 133, 135–37, 138–39, 143, 145–46, 148–49, 152, 172, 194, 199–209, 214–16, 218, 227
wildlife biology, 99–100, 107, 126
wildlife conservation, 96–97, 236; funding, 102–3, 111–113n42, 113n45, 232–38
wildlife management, 102, 107, 138–39, 148, 242; cooperative, 96; on public lands, 134, 174, 203–8; professional, 102; scientific, 36, 99, 102, 104, 107
Wildlife Management Authority: The State Agencies' Perspective, 214

Wildlife Management Institute, 102–3, 217
wildlife restoration, 102, 105
wildlife sanctuaries, 49, 51, 99–100, 107
The Wildlife Society, 102, 212, 216, 233, 243
Wilkinson, J. Harvie, III, 199–200
Willms, David, 217
Winthrop, John, 8–9
Woman's Christian Temperance Union, 66, 76
women's suffrage, 67, 76
working class, 48, 58, 68, 80, 115
World's Columbian Exposition of 1893 (World's Fair), 50
World War I, 50, 61, 73n66, 75
World War II, 120–22, 125–26, 222
Wyeth v. Levine, 192
Wyoming, 173, 208, 235–36
Wyoming Statehood Act, 197–98n46
Wyoming v. United States, 174, 202–3, 207–8

Yaffee, Steven, 140
Yellowstone National Park, 43n22, 46, 53n7
Young, Ernest A., 60–62, 92, 116, 177, 180–81, 191, 199

Zimmerman, Joseph, 90–91, 106, 227

About the Author

Lowell E. Baier's intellectual curiosity during his fifty-eight-year career has taken him from practicing attorney to entrepreneur, tireless advocate for natural resources and wildlife conservation, and legal and environmental historian and author. Baier continues contemporaneously to practice law, specializing in wildlife conservation and natural resource policy, legislation, and regulation, and writes extensively on these subjects.

Baier's lifelong passion for protecting the country's natural resources and wildlife conservation began during his childhood while being raised on a farm in northern Indiana and while spending time on his grandfather's homestead ranch in Montana. Those childhood experiences led Baier in his adult life to begin scientifically observing and documenting wildlife and its habitats on extensive treks and expeditions in the mountains and wilderness regions across the North American continent, the Russian Pamirs and Caucasus, and Mongolia's Gobi Desert and Altai Mountains, providing him with firsthand observations of wildlife and human interactions across the globe.

Author photo by Len Spoden.

Baier received his BA in economics and political science from Valparaiso University in 1961 and completed his JD in 1964 at Indiana University's

School of Law. During 2018–2020, he began a PhD program at the University of St. Andrews in Scotland; this book was partially a product of his doctoral dissertation work. Baier holds an honorary LLD degree awarded in 2010, a LHD awarded in 2015, and a PhD awarded in 2019. After graduation he began practicing law in Washington, D.C., a city he'd grown to love when in 1956 his congressional representative, Charles A. Halleck (R-2nd IN), called him to be a Page in the US House of Representatives after becoming an Eagle Scout.

A recognized advisor to elected officials and educators on environmental and conservation issues, Baier took the lead in drafting President George H. W. Bush's wildlife conservation agenda in 1989, and has been an advisor and counselor to all successive presidential administrations. Between 1992 and 2010, Baier was heavily involved in the creation of PhD programs at five separate universities dedicated to postgraduate studies in natural resources and wildlife-conservation management. From 2004 to 2007, he led a national campaign to raise $6.5 million to purchase for the federal government the last and largest remaining piece of privately held land (24,550 acres), which had initially been Theodore Roosevelt's historic Elkhorn Ranch in North Dakota, established in 1884, adjacent the Theodore Roosevelt National Park, also once part of the ranch, thus virtually expanding the national park by one-third its size. The Elkhorn is popularly called the "Cradle of Conservation" and the "Walden Pond of the American West," since there, between 1884 and 1887, Theodore Roosevelt conceived the cornerstones of the American conservation movement as we know it today.

Throughout his career, Baier has tirelessly served on numerous boards and commissions for both local and federal governments, associations, and foundations. Presently he serves on the Executive Committee of the Theodore Roosevelt Association and the President's Council of the National Wildlife Federation, is President Emeritus of the Boone and Crockett Club, was Vice Chair of the National Conservation Leadership Institute, is one of twelve members of the Conservation Leadership Council sponsored by the Environmental Defense Fund, and is a member of the Roosevelt Conservation Roundtable. He is a member of both the Explorers Club and the Cosmos Club.

Baier has been recognized many times for his extraordinary public service at the local level and for his conservation work nationally. In 1986 he was named Citizen of the Year in Rockville, Maryland. In 2008 the National Fish and Wildlife Foundation named him Conservationist of the Year. In 2010 *Outdoor Life* magazine selected Baier as Conservationist of the Year, and the Association of Fish and Wildlife Agencies similarly recognized him in 2013. In 2016 the National Wildlife Federation awarded him their highest honor, the Jay N. "Ding" Darling Conservation Award for a lifetime of conservation service. In 2018 he was one of four judges chosen to select the 2019 Duck Stamp image by the Department of Interior's US Fish and Wildlife Service. The Indiana University Maurer School of Law presented him with its Distinguished Service Award in 2007; in 2014 he was inducted into its Academy of Law Alumni Fellows, the highest honor the law school can bestow on an alumnus; and in 2015 he was awarded the degree of Doctor of Humane Letters. Thereafter the law school building at Indiana University was named Baier Hall in his honor, also in 2015. In 2021 he was awarded the university's Bicentennial Medal by the president. Baier had become an Eagle Scout at age fourteen and received the Distinguished Eagle Scout Award at age seventy-six from the National Boy Scouts of America.

Baier will release a sequel to this book in late 2022, titled *The Codex of the Endangered Species Act, Volume I: The First 50 Years*, memorializing the detailed history of the Endangered Species Act to celebrate its fiftieth anniversary in 2023. The sequel, *The Codex of the Endangered Species Act, Volume II: The Next 50 Years*, will be released in 2023, which will be coedited with Dr. John Organ.